Visual J++

How to Order:

For information on quantity discounts contact the publisher: Prima Publishing, P.O. Box 1260BK, Rocklin, CA 95677-1260; (916) 632-4400. On your letterhead include information concerning the intended use of the books and the number of books you wish to purchase. For individual orders, turn to the back of this book for more information.

Visual J++

Charles A. Wood

PRIMA PUBLISHING

Publisher
Don Roche

Associate Publisher
Ray Robinson

Senior Acquisitions Editor
Alan Harris

Senior Editor
Tad Ringo

Project Editor
Theresa Mathias

Copy Editor
Ruth Slates

Technical Reviewer
Sundar Rajan

Indexer
Sharon Hilgenberg

P ™

is a registered trademark of Prima Publishing, a division of Prima Communications, Inc.

Prima Publishing® is a registered trademark of Prima Communications, Inc.

Prima Publishing, Rocklin, California 95677.

ISBN: 0-7615-0814-7
Library of Congress Catalog Card Number: 96-70098
Printed in the United States of America

96 97 98 99 DD 10 9 8 7 6 5 4 3 2 1

Dedication

I would like to dedicate this book to my wife, Lyn, who somehow always finds the strength to put up with me when I'm writing.

Acknowledgments

I would like to thank all the people that helped on the book. The book production would have been impossible without the help of Theresa Mathias, Alan Harris, Julie Barton, Don Roche, Tad Ringo, Ruth Slates, and Tom Barich. Working with Prima Publishing has been great.

I would also like to thank my family, who all seemed to understand how writing a book can keep a person quite busy.

Contents at a Glance

Table of Contents

Chapter 3 The Visual J++ Environment 53

Chapter 4 The Visual J++ Tools 77

Introduction

Java is a new language that is taking the Internet community and the corporate world by storm. Never has a language gathered so much acceptance in such a short period of time. Finally, Microsoft is entering the Java community in full force with its new Visual J++ compiler. Just as C++ is considered to be a step above normal C, Visual J++ has features that aren't standard in Java but will greatly enhance the power of the language.

Features of Visual J++

The Visual J++ environment contains the following features:

- A full implementation of the Java language
- A visual Java development environment
- A host of tools, including viewers and debuggers
- ActiveX (OCX) support
- Additional class libraries that allow for database access

These features, along with a tutorial of the Java and Visual J++ language will be discussed throughout this book.

Visual J++ versus Java?

The question many of you will be asking is if Microsoft is trying to replace Java. The answer is absolutely not! Visual J++ fully embraces the Java language. Microsoft is merely making the language more powerful with a developer environment, compiler, and ActiveX integration. The compiler can compile over a million lines of code per minute!

The Visual J++ environment is based on the popular Developer Studio integrated development environment (IDE) that is used by Visual C++ and other Microsoft products. Although the environment is Windows-based, the Java classes that are compiled can run on any Java environment.

Sun (the makers of Java) has a license from Microsoft to distribute ActiveX integration in other Web browsers and Java development tool vendors. There are even plans to place ActiveX controls on other environments, such as Macintoshes and UNIX operating systems.

In short, Microsoft has improved on the original Java implementation with Visual J++. However, just like Visual C++ did not replace C++, Visual J++ is not intended to replace Java. Visual J++ is intended to give you, the developer, the best way possible to code your Java applications and applets.

> **NOTE:**
> The Visual J++ compiler is *not* the same thing as the JIT (Just In Time) Java compiler found in many tools, such as Netscape and Internet Explorer. A JIT compiler is part of the Java Virtual Machine, and compiles the Java code as it is received (usually from a Web site). JIT compilers can significantly speed up the performance of your Java applets.

What This Book Does for You

This book is your first training guide and reference to the Visual J++ environment. Because this book was developed using a beta, some features may be only briefly described. The purpose of this book is to teach you how to write Java programs in Visual J++, to give you a complete understanding of Visual J++, and to let you take full advantage of the capabilities of Visual J++. The development community is starved for information about Microsoft's plans for Java development. This book will teach the Visual J++ environment and serve as an excellent training and reference guide.

Hopefully, you have some development experience in a language before reading this book. It isn't necessary, but having experience may make Visual J++ a lot easier to learn and use. This book is designed so that no experience with Java or C++ is assumed. If we've done our job, by the time you're finished with this book, you'll be able to dive into Visual J++ development with no problems.

Conventions Used in This Book

The following conventions are used in this book:

> **NOTES**
> give you more information about a topic, such as background information. Notes are intended to give you additional information which will help you while you try the techniques discussed in this book.

TIPS

are short helpful hints that you can use while you develop your Visual J++ application.

CAUTIONS

are warnings about common mistakes you may make while developing. Cautions are designed to warn you of common mistakes before you make them. Cautions may save you the time and trouble of determining why a compile failed or why a program doesn't run properly.

What are questions?

Questions are common question that you may have while reading or developing. Although not cautions, there are common questions that arise while learning Visual J++ techniques.

Chapter 1

Introducing Visual J++

This chapter is designed to give you a basic overview of some of Visual J++'s features as well as an introduction to the rest of the book. If you've already been working with Visual J++, much of this book will be review. If you're new to Visual J++, this chapter will be very useful when it comes to introducing terms that occur throughout the rest of the book.

At the end of this chapter, you should be able to do the following:

- Identify some major components of the Visual J++ language.

- Identify the major components of the Visual J++ environment.

- Understand the difference between an application and an applet.

- Understand what's needed to write, compile, and test a program.

Visual J++ Startup: Introduction to InfoViewer

When you first open the Visual J++ environment, you'll see an environment almost identical to the Visual C++ environment. This is the Developer's Studio, and it is one of the better development environments on the market today. When the Developer's Studio first opens, you'll see the InfoViewer (see Figure 1.1). Using the InfoViewer is a *fantastic* way to view online help. All of the Java language specifications, as well as all of the Microsoft additions, are documented and easily accessible.

Fig. 1.1
When you first enter the Visual J++ environment, you'll encounter the InfoViewer.

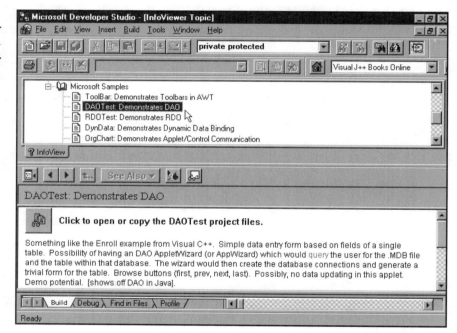

The InfoViewer is in tree view format and is separated into categories (for example, Java API, Volume 1: Core Packages; Java API, Volume 2: Window Toolkit and Applets; and so on). These categories are broken into subcategories (for example, java.lang, java.io, and so on), which in turn are broken even further down (for example, Class Boolean, Class Character, and so on). When you get used to it, searching through the InfoViewer is easy and helpful. Chapter 3 discusses the InfoViewer in more detail.

Your First Visual J++ Programs

The Visual J++ language is covered extensively in this book. In this chapter, you will write two simple Visual J++ programs: one as a stand alone application and one as a World Wide Web applet. Well, let's get on with writing some simple Java programs, and I'll explain it as we go.

HelloFrame: A Stand Alone Application

NOTE:
Most programs in production today are stand alone applications. However, most Java programs are written as applets for a Web server. There really is no need to avoid Java as a serious application development tool, especially because Visual J++ has caused Java development to mature from several disjointed products loosely working together in a (mostly) text-based environment to a tightly integrated graphical development tool that develops graphical programs.

In fact, most of the Java community agrees that Java will soon become a major player in personal and corporate application development. Java has borrowed a lot from C++, but has left many of the more annoying aspects of C++ behind, such as pointers (which are non-existent in Java) and memory management.

To begin writing your first Visual J++ program, choose File, New (see Figure 1.2). The New dialog box appears (see Figure 1.3). Because all Java programs (even those written in Visual J++) must be stored as text, choose Text File.

Now you can start typing your Visual J++ program. Listing 1.1 shows the HelloFrame code as it appears in Figure 1.4. The HelloFrame program will be referred to throughout the rest of the chapter.

Fig. 1.2
Choose File, New
to create a text
file to enter a
Visual J++ program.

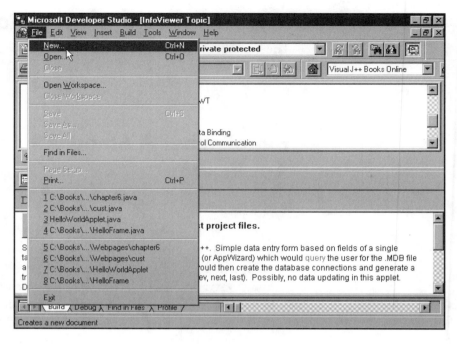

Fig. 1.3
When starting a new
Visual J++ program,
choose Text File to
start entering a Visual
J++ program.

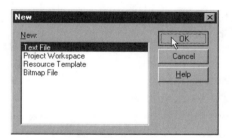

Listing 1.1
HelloFrame.java

```java
import java.awt.*;
import java.applet.*;

public class HelloFrame extends Frame {
    public static void main (String args[]) {
        Frame f = new HelloFrame();
        f.setTitle("Hello World Frame");
        f.resize(300,200);
        f.show();
    }
    public void paint(Graphics g) {
        g.drawString("Hello world!", 50, 25);
    }
}
```

Fig. 1.4
It is not difficult to
start coding in Java
using the Visual J++
environment.

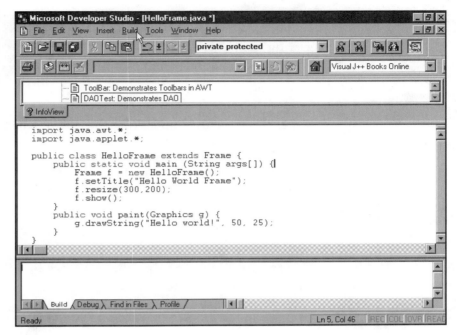

The import Statement

Java's import statement is used in the first two lines in my program:

```
import java.awt.*;
import java.applet.*;
```

The import command is often confused with the #include meta command in C++. However, they really have little in common. Java does not support header files (also known as included files, copybooks, and so on). The import statement allows a type of shorthand in your Java program. Instead of typing java.awt.Image, with an import command of import java.awt.*, you can simply type Image and the Visual J++ compiler will know what you're talking about. The import statement is more of a redirection than a code-copier. In fact, what you import doesn't even have to exist, and you'll receive no error unless you assume it's there. The import command is discussed in more detail in Chapter 2.

Classes in Visual J++

Visual J++ does not allow global methods or variables. In fact, no variables (called *attributes*) or functions (called *methods*) are allowed to exist outside a class. A *class* is an object-oriented construct that groups attributes and methods together. In the sample program, HelloFrame is a class that encapsulates all attributes and methods by declaring itself a class:

```
public class HelloFrame extends Frame {
```

The `public` keyword indicates that this class is accessible to all. The `extends Frame` clause implies that the HelloFrame class is a type of (or inherited from) Frame. A *Frame* is a type of window, and the Frame class itself is part of the Abstract Window Toolkit (AWT) defined by Java. Frames are child windows of the browser or Java viewer that you're running. Frames easily give your program a graphical appearance.

> **CAUTION:**
> There can be only one public class per file. If you want to use another public class, you must open a new file to do so.

The `public` and `class` keywords will be discussed further in Chapter 2. The `extends` keyword will be discussed in Chapters 5 and 6.

Methods in Visual J++

Methods in Visual J++ are the functions that are executed when a Visual J++ program runs. The HelloFrame class contains two methods. The `main` method is executed every time a stand alone Visual J++ program (called an *application*) runs:

```
public static void main (String args[ ]) {
    Frame f = new HelloFrame();
    f.setTitle("Hello World Frame");
    f.resize(300,200);
    f.show();
}
```

In this method, `main` takes command line arguments and stores them in a String array called `args`. Then a new frame is created, the title and size are set, and the frame is shown.

> **NOTE:**
> Case is very important in Java and Visual J++. A String (with a capital S) is a class that's included with Java to handle all string manipulation. When referring to constructs, such as a String array, always use an initial capital letter.

The paint method, shown in the following code, is called from the Frame ancestor when the Frame window first gets painted. The paint method is called whenever a graphical component, like a frame, is drawn on a monitor. Here, you take the graphical representation of a text string and place it on the graphical part of the Frame. You don't have to understand all of this yet (some of the detailed explanation of the paint( ) method is in Chapter 9 and the Java language reference is in Chapter 11).

```
public void paint(Graphics g) {
    g.drawString("Hello world!", 50, 25);
}
```

Compiling Your Visual J++ Program

Now, to compile your new Visual J++ program, choose <u>B</u>uild, <u>C</u>ompile (see Figure 1.5). If you have any mistakes, the compiler will catch them. Make sure you fix them before continuing.

Visual J++ tells you that the program you just typed requires a workspace, and asks if you want to build one (see Figure 1.6). Project workspaces in Visual J++ are a common-sense approach to the traditional packages in Java. Projects allow you to group several Java files together to develop one program. In this way, projects could replace the Java package structure in the near future.

When you click Yes, Visual J++ will try to save your program (see Figure 1.7). *You must save your program with the same name as the class!* Older Java development systems closely tie the name of the Java file with the name of the class. However, this restriction is not necessary and hopefully will be removed once competition starts forcing the Java language to evolve. Anyway, save your program as HelloFrame.java.

Fig. 1.5
Choose Build,
Compile to compile a
Visual J++ program.

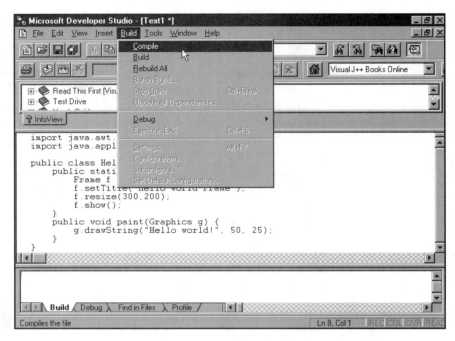

Fig. 1.6
All programs require a
project workspace to
compile.

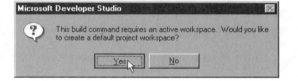

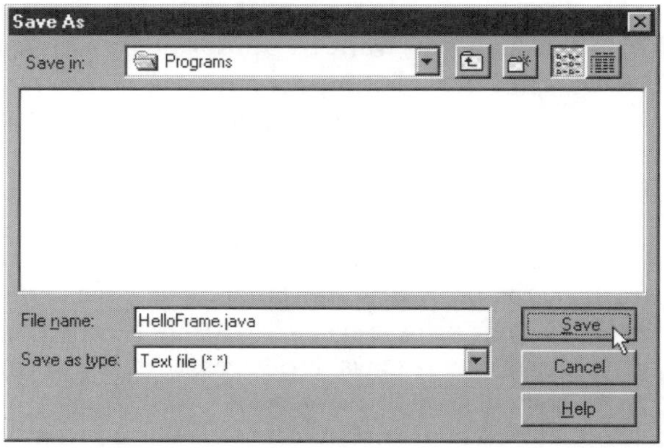

Fig. 1.7
Visual J++ forces you
to save your work
before a compile.

CAUTION:
I saved my program as HELLOFRAME.JAVA and then tried to compile. I got a message similar to the following:

```
C:\Visual J++\HELLOFRAME.JAVA(4,8) : error J0136: Public
➡class 'HelloFrame' should not be defined in 'C:\Visual
➡J++\HELLOFRAME.JAVA'
```

What's the deal?

Java requires that the java file being compiled have the exact same name as the only public class defined within the java file. This includes case. HELLOFRAME.JAVA is *not* the same as HelloFrame.java. You must save your program with the same name *including case* as your public class name with a *lowercase* java extension. This is a restriction from the original Java compiler. Hopefully Microsoft will take it out soon.

NOTE:
If you start a compile, Visual J++ will automatically save your Java program without asking. Figure 1.7 is for the first compile only just so you will name your Java file. (Clicking Cancel in the Save As dialog box shown in Figure 1.7 will allow you to not save your work, but also will halt the compile.)

NOTE:
I never save my current work in the development tool directories. That way, if I want to change Java compilers or upgrade someday, I won't write over or erase all my current work. Key file backups are also easier with a separate directory for programs.

Setting the Class Path

All classes found in the Java compiler are also included in Visual J++. However, you must make sure your tool can find your classes, or you'll get an error similar to the one shown in Figure 1.8.

Fig. 1.8
If Visual J++ can't find the Java classes, ambiguous errors can result.

Unfortunately, you can't set a project workspace's settings until you create the project workspace (which you just did). Choose Build, Settings (see Figure 1.9).

Fig. 1.9
To set your settings, choose Build, Settings.

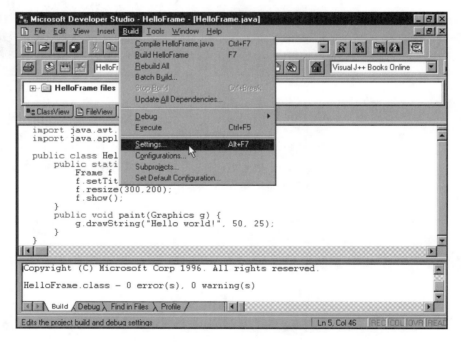

The Project Settings dialog box opens (see Figure 1.10). Type in your class path directory in the Class Path Directories text box. If you installed into the default directories, the class path should be C:\Windows\Java\CLASSES. Then click OK. Now recompile and you should receive no errors (see Figure 1.11).

Fig. 1.10
Your class path must be set correctly in the Project Settings dialog box for your code to work properly.

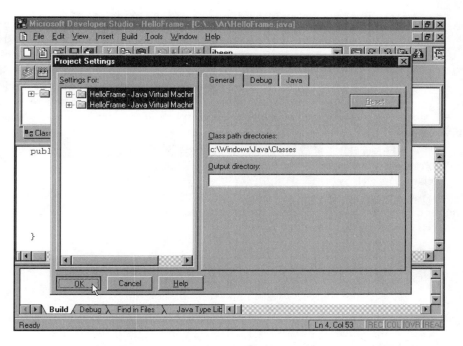

Fig. 1.11
Visual J++ will tell you how many errors occurred on a compile.

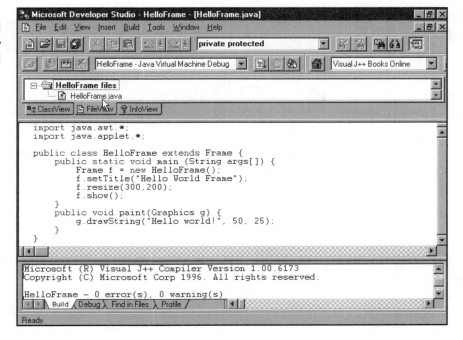

Notice in Figure 1.11 that there are now ClassView and FileView tabs next to the InfoView tab. These tabs enable you to see what files are in your Visual J++ project, what classes have been defined in those files, and what attributes and methods are in each class. (Figure 1.12 shows the ClassView tab.) Furthermore, double-clicking a file, class, or method will open the file (if it isn't open already) and immediately take you to the class, method, or attribute you clicked.

Fig. 1.12
You can get a list of classes as well as attributes and methods within those classes using the ClassView tab.

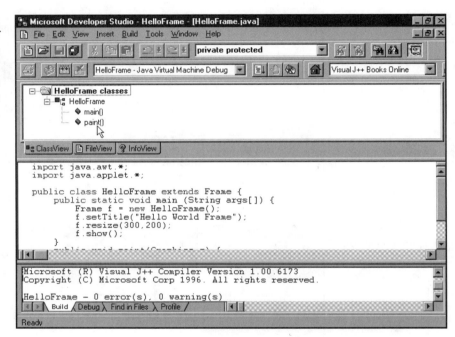

Running Your Visual J++ Program

When you're finished compiling, you can run your Visual J++ program by choosing Build, Execute (see Figure 1.13).

If this is the first time you've run your program, the Information for Running Class dialog box will appear (see Figure 1.14). Type in the name of the class you just compiled. Now choose a stand alone interpreter to run your program if your program is a stand alone program (which HelloFrame is), or choose a Browser if your program is a Web applet.

Fig. 1.13
Choosing Build,
Execute will let you
run your Visual J++
program.

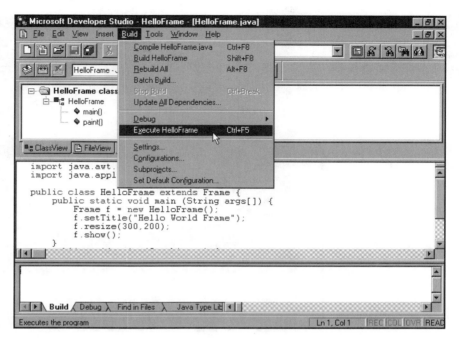

Fig. 1.14
The Information for
Running Class dialog
box lets you define
your Visual J++ class
name; you also define
whether your Visual
J++ class is a stand
alone application or a
Web applet.

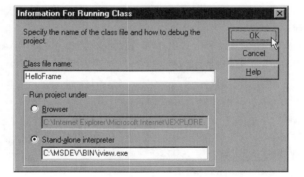

NOTE:
JView is a stand alone Java interpreter that comes with
Visual J++. Although JView does not have the best inter-
face, it certainly can interpret a Visual J++ program.
(Maybe the interface will be enhanced in future versions.)

Your Java interpreter then runs your Visual J++ application. Notice
that the Hello World! frame pops up, as shown in Figure 1.15. (Yes,
it's another trite "Hello World!" program.)

Fig. 1.15
The familiar Hello World! program as a stand alone Visual J++ application.

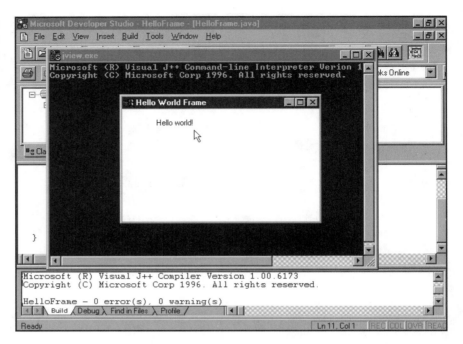

NOTE:
You may notice that the Hello World! frame does not close, even when you click the cancel box or double-click the control box. The only way to close a Visual J++ frame is either programatically or by closing the viewer that's running it.

When you try to close the JView viewer, you'll get an error message telling you that it may not be safe to close down this viewer (see Figure 1.16). Although you should be careful that your Visual J++ program is not writing to a disk at the time, go ahead and cancel the program.

The reason for this message is that JView is a DOS program. (Of course, you all can see why the JView program needs to be enhanced.) There's no way for a DOS program to end gracefully except by exiting while in a Windows environment. In Chapter 10, you'll see how events can be used to end a program gracefully, and how to enable the exit box.

Fig. 1.16
You'll get an error message if you try to close JView. Make sure you're not writing to disk or in the middle of a program execution, and then ignore the error message.

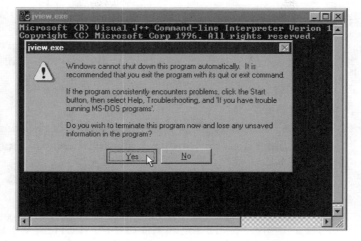

When you're done, choose File, Close Workspace to close the HelloFrame project (see Figure 1.17). You will be asked if you want to close all project windows; answer yes.

Fig. 1.17
Choosing File, Close Workspace will ask you to save and terminate the current project.

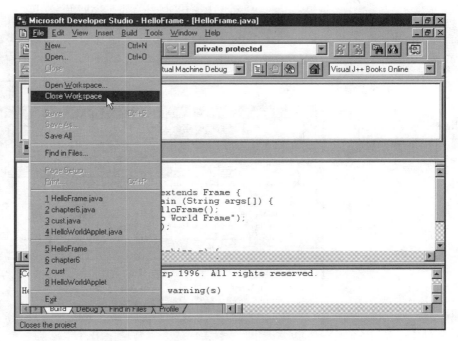

You've just completed your first stand alone Visual J++ application. To recap, Visual J++ has developed projects that every program needs to belong to before compiling. You develop a program in the Developer's Studio, but you run it using a Java application viewer like JView.

Developing a Web Applet

You're not done yet with this chapter. You still have to develop an applet. *Applets* are (usually) tiny programs that run on the World Wide Web.

> **NOTE:**
> **The reason Web programs are tiny is that large programs would take too long to download over a modem to be usable.**

You're not quite done with Hello World programs yet, either. Listing 1.2 and Figure 1.18 shows the text for the HelloWorldApplet.

Listing 1.2
HelloWorldApplet.java

```java
import java.awt.*;
import java.applet.*;

public class HelloWorldApplet extends Applet {
    public void paint(Graphics g) {
        g.drawString("Hello world!", 50, 25);
    }
}
```

Fig. 1.18
The HelloWorldApplet can run on a Web page on the Internet.

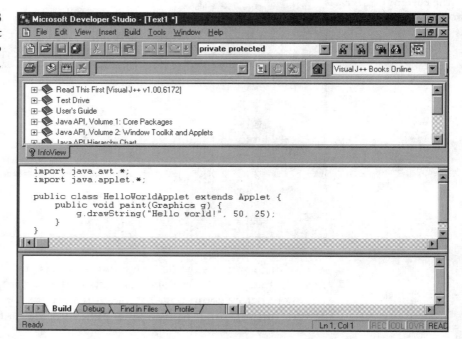

Understanding Applets

You can see by the code in Figure 1.18 that the HelloWorldApplet class extends Applet instead of Frame:

```
public class HelloWorldApplet extends Applet {
```

Applet is a special class that sets up your program to run on a Web browser. Even the window setup and resizing isn't necessary. The `paint` method is called by the Applet class when the applet first starts running. Then you can paint your `Hello World` string onto your Web page using the same techniques you did with your Frame program.

Although there's a little more to running applets, there's not much. Applets are easily developed with Java and Visual J++. This is why Java became such a hit so quickly. Advanced applets techniques, like Threads, is covered in detail in Chapter 9.

Running Your Applet

Now follow the same steps as you did with the HelloFrame package to compile and execute the program. Because this is an applet instead of an application, you'll need to use a Web browser to run your program. I specified Microsoft's Internet Explorer (3.0 or greater), as shown in Figure 1.19, but Netscape (2.0 or greater) and HotJava will work as well.

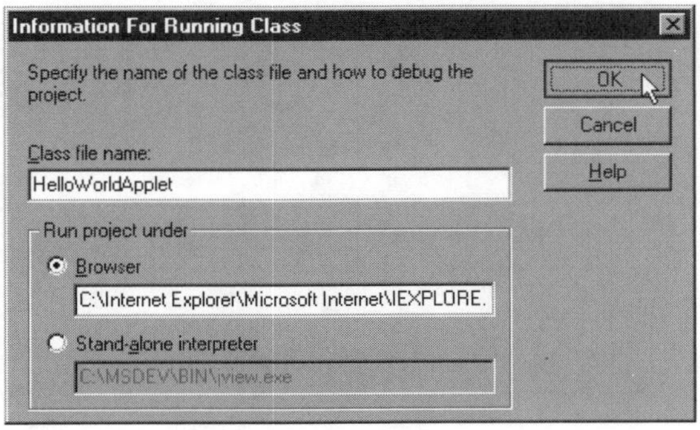

Fig. 1.19
You need to use a browser to run an applet.

NOTE:
After being a little bit cruel (with good reason) to JView, I feel I have to take the other side with Internet Explorer. Internet Explorer 3.0 is a fantastic product. It combines a good interface with strong performance. Netscape also works well, but I find Internet Explorer 3.0 to be a little better suited to my needs in terms of usability.

Also, Internet Explorer 3.0 is *fast*. Both Netscape and Internet Explorer have made huge performance gains with the additions of JIT (Just in Time) compilers that give Java applications a tremendous boost in speed.

Internet Explorer 3.0 will be available on your Visual J++ CD. It is also available on the Internet for download *for free*, not as shareware. Check out **www.microsoft.com** and follow the bouncing ball to download your own copy.

You can see in Figure 1.20 that Internet Explorer 3.0 does a fine job of running the HelloWorld applet.

Fig. 1.20
Web browsers, like Internet Explorer 3.0, can run your Visual J++ programs.

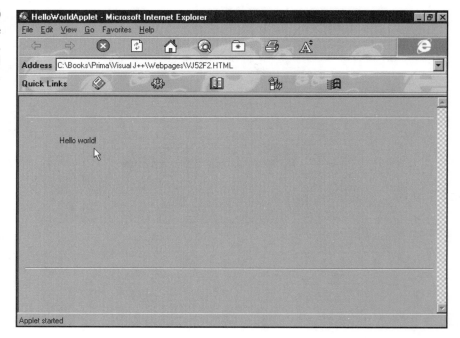

NOTE:
Unlike other Java compilers, like Cafe from Symantec, Visual J++ will generate an HTML file for you if one is not included in your project. This is great because it lets you test your applets easily without any additional work.

Project Workspaces

Project workspaces contain all the information about a program that you need for compiling and execution. Usually, you'll create a workspace on the first compile and then use the workspace for retrieving a project, rather than opening the Java program without a workspace. This will help you because you'll only need to define your environment once. You can then pull up the same environment for later work without having to reset everything (such as how to executed the system, what files are contained in the project, and so on). To open a project workspace, choose File, Open Workspace (see Figure 1.21).

Fig. 1.21
To open an existing project workspace, choose File, Open Workspace.

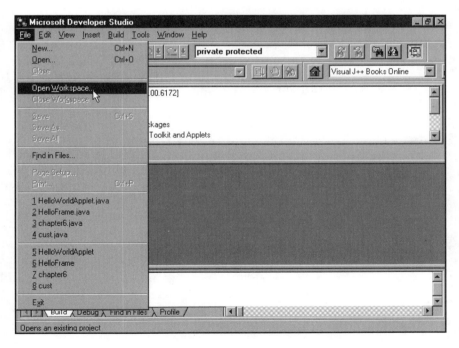

Figure 1.22 shows that you now have two workspace files (with MDB extensions). These workspaces are the projects you just created in the HelloFrame and HelloWorldApplet programs. Instead of opening the raw Java programs, you should always open the project workspaces. All the class library information, executable type information, and list of files that belong to a project are listed in the project workspace.

Fig. 1.22
Here you see the two
project workspaces
you created in this
chapter.

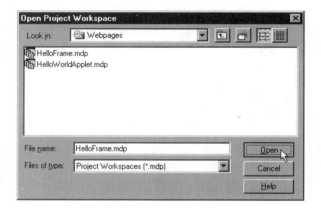

Conclusion

So far, you've written a stand alone Windows program and a Web applet using Visual J++. Hopefully, you now have a bit of a feel for the Visual J++ environment.

The Visual J++ language is covered in more depth in Chapters 2, 5, 6, 7, 9, 10, 11, and 12. The Visual J++ environment is covered in Chapters 3, 4, and 8. Also included later is documentation about available methods and classes included with the Visual J++ system. The appendixes will cover the HTML scripting language used to write Web pages (Visual J++ creates a HTML file for you when running your applet), reserved words in Java, and the Unicode standard. (The Unicode standard is similar in concept to the ASCII standard, but while ASCII is limited to the western world, Unicode is more global in nature.) Finally, Chapter 11 deals with ActiveX and the COM standard, which is a Visual J++ enhancement to the Java language that allows programs to run ActiveX controls.

Chapter 2

The Visual J++ Language

Using the Visual J++ language is a simple and efficient way to program for Web pages, intranet systems, and stand alone programs. As a language, it's easier to learn and use the Visual J++ language than it is to learn C or C++. In addition, Visual J++ is smaller and more efficient than many of the Windows development tools on the market today.

This chapter will cover the basics of the Visual J++ language. In this chapter, you will learn the following:

- ◑ How to use comments and the commenting features in Visual J++

- ◑ Instructions on using variables in Visual J++

- ◑ Logical, string formatting, and arithmetic operators, such as +, = =, and '\n'

- ◑ Decision structures, such as if and switch

- ◑ Looping structures using the for, do, while, continue, and break statements

Using Comments

Comments are important to every language. Good programmers place comments on any *potentially* ambiguous line of code. Others can use these comments to debug any cryptic code; you can even use them if you have to return to your function after any length of time.

Comments in Visual J++ are similar to comments in C++, and are easy to implement. There are three types of comments: single line comments, multiple line comments, and documentation comments.

Single Line Comments

You use the double slash (//) to comment a single line or part of a line. Here are some examples of single line comments:

```
//This is a full line comment.  No other logic is allowed on
➡this line.

l = a + p;    // All living things (l) consist of animals (a)
➡and plants(p)
```

As you can see, // was used to add a line of comments; // was also used to define cryptic variables that are used in a program.

Multiple Line Comments

You'll often want to write a paragraph of comments and you won't want to mess with a // at the beginning of each line. To do this, Visual J++ allows multiple line comments (also called multi-line comments) enclosed within /* and */, such as the following:

```
/*
Program Author:    Chuck Wood
Program Title:     JavaStuff.java
Program History:    9/1/1996 - Wrote Program - Chuck Wood
    10/2/96 - Fixed all the bugs per bug report #1234 - JP
*/
```

As you can see, multiple line comments are great for programmers who want to document exactly what's been done to a program. By using /* and */, multiple line comments are easier to type and read than a large series of single line comments.

Documentation Comments

Java has introduced a special type of comment called a *documentation* or *doc* comment. These comments begin with /** and end with */. Documentation comments are used using the Visual J++doc tool, which is discussed in Appendix D.

You use documentation comments to comment the purpose and/or functionality of the current Java applet or program. The following is an example:

```
/**
JavaStuff is a program that does everything the user wants.
This program is consists of several components.

To solve all the worlds problems, click the Solve button.
To know anything about everything, click the Know button.
To discover the meaning of life, click the Meaning button.
To find personal fulfillment, click the Fulfill button.
When you are ready to quit, click the Bahamas button
    and head to the airport.
*/
```

Although the preceding program may be a little difficult to write, the documentation is easy. The documentation describes the purpose of the function and what the user needs to do to operate the program. Visual J++ can then convert the notes into actual user documentation, in HTML/Web page format when you compile your code. This HTML documentation can then be linked to your page, or can be invoked with Visual J++ by pressing the F1 key. (The *keydown* event is discussed in Chapter 9, "Event Programming in Visual J++.")

The innovative use of documentation comments allows you to type in comments that can be seen by the end user as you develop a program. Comments and code modification are streamlined and much easier to implement.

Understanding Variables in Visual J++

Variables in any language store information as it is being processed. Variables are how a program "remembers" facts and data to process later in the program. Visual J++ has implemented a very complex data type structure similar (but expanded) to that of C++.

> **NOTE:**
> Unlike C++, Visual J++ does not allow memory management. Therefore, pointers are not allowed in Visual J++. This is actually a blessing to those who have spent many days tracking down a memory allocation error in a C or C++ program.
>
> Java has developed other data types in the form of classes that more than compensate for the lack of pointers, making Visual J++ development and maintenance much easier than C and C++ development and maintenance. To see a list of these, open your InfoViewer to java.lang. You'll then see all the classes included with Visual J++ and Java.

Using Data Types

Visual J++ contains an extensive list of data types, which are defined in Table 2.1.

Table 2.1
Visual J++ Data Types

Data Type	Default	Size*	Description
boolean	false	1 bit**	boolean **can be true or false.**
char	null	2 bytes	char **defines a Unicode character. For details, see Appendix C, "Unicode."**
byte	null	1 byte	byte **defines an ASCII character.**
short	0	2 bytes	short **is a signed integer ranging from −32,768 to 32767.**
int	0	4 bytes	int **is a signed integer ranging from −2,147,483,648 to 2,147,483,647.**
long	0	8 bytes	long **is an extremely long signed integer ranging from −9,223,372,036,854,775,808 to 9,223,372,036,854,775,807.**

Data Type	Default	Size*	Description
float	0.0	4 bytes	float is a floating point (also called decimal) number that ranges from +/−1.40239846E-45 (.00000...014 with 44 zeros between the decimal point and the 1) and +/−3.40282347E+38 (3400...0 with 37 zeros at the end). Although numbers can get rather large or small with a float, there are only at most nine significant digits in a float. When numbers get very large or very small, some rounding or truncating will occur.
double	0.0	8 bytes	double is a float that ranges from +/−4.94065645841246544E-324 (.000...494 with 323 zeros between the decimal and the 4) to +/− 1.79769313486231570E+308 (17900...000 with 308 zeros at the end). As with float, the numbers in a double can get very large, but there are only at most eight significant digits in a double. Very large or very small numbers will be rounded or truncated.
String	null***	Varies	String is a class data type. A class data type is not a true data type, but rather a pre-written class that is included with Visual J++. You must include an import java.lang.* statement to use a String declaration. String is used to manipulate strings in a Visual J++ program. Because it is a class data type, it is capitalized. Classes are covered more explicitly in Chapter 5, "Using Classes and Packages in Visual J++."

*1 byte equals 8 bits.

**Visual J++ actually dedicates up to an entire byte to a boolean variable but still only allows true and false values.

***null is a special keyword in Visual J++. It is discussed in Chapter 5, "Using Classes and Packages in Visual J++."

To declare a variable, you use the following format:

```
datatype variable1 {= default}{, variable2 {= default2}}... ;
```

For example, if you want to declare *counter* as an integer, you would use the following Java statement:

```
int counter;
```

To initialize counter to 1 when you declare it, you would use the following Java statement:

```
int counter = 1;
```

Finally, to initialize counter to 1 and to declare a second integer, you could use the comma operator and write the following code:

```
int counter = 1, counter2;
```

As you can see, data types in Visual J++ are larger and more varied than allowed by many C and C++ compilers. These data types alone may force some projects, such as engineering, actuarial, mathematical, or scientific projects, to be written in Visual J++ rather than other languages.

Visual J++ also uses *class* data types. These are data types that are based on a predefined class. Classes are covered in detail in Part II, "Object Oriented Development with Visual J++."

Using Arrays

Arrays are blocks of memory where similar variables are stored. An array is coded with brackets to indicate the number of variables in an array. To allocate 15 integers, you could code the following Visual J++ statement:

```
int numbers[ ] = new int[15];
```

The best way to explain arrays is with an example. For example, if you want to keep track of starting basketball players on a team, you could establish the following array:

```
String starting_players[ ] = new String[5];
```

You could also define an array without explicitly numbering the array. For example, you could code the preceding starting players as follows:

```
String starting_players[ ] = {"Larry", "Mo",
    "Curly", "Shep", "Chuck"};
```

The starting_players would then be stored in memory, as shown in Figure 2.1.

Fig. 2.1
Arrays store information in contiguous blocks of memory.

Starting Players

0	1	2	3	4
Larry	Mo	Curly	Shep	Chuck

Referencing Array Elements

You can reference arrays by using bracketed numbers as references. For example, if starting_players[2] was "Curly" then the following line:

```
g.drawString(starting_players[2] +
    " scored 6 points", 1, 15);
```

would output Curly scored 5 points to the current window.

> **WARNING:**
> Unlike other languages, numbers now range from numbers[0] **to** numbers[14]. **Fifteen numbers have been allocated, but they start from 0, not 1.**

> **NOTE:**
> **To determine the number of elements in an array, you can use the length attribute of an array. For example, the lines of Visual J++ code:**
>
> ```
> String starting_players[ ] = {"Larry", "Mo", "Curly",
>     "Shep", "Chuck"};
> ...
> int array_size = starting_players.length;
> ```
>
> **would assign** 5 **to the** array_size **variable.**

Understanding Multi-Dimensional Arrays

Multi-dimensional arrays allow you to store a "block" of information in memory as opposed to just a "row" of information that is stored by a single dimensional array. Assume the `starting_players` mentioned previously played in 15 games. You can add an additional array containing the points scored per game:

```
String starting_players[ ] = {"Larry", "Mo", "Curly",
    "Shep", "Chuck"};
int points_scored[ ] [ ] = new int [5] [6];
```

The preceding code would store in memory the names of the five starting_players, and then would declare and initialize a 5 × 6 array, as shown in Figure 2.2.

Fig. 2.2
While single-dimensional arrays are stored in "rows" of memory, multi-dimensional arrays are stored in "blocks" of memory.

Starting Players

0	1	2	3	4
Larry	Mo	Curly	Shep	Chuck

Points Scored

0	0	0	0	0	0
1	0	0	0	0	0
2	0	0	0	0	0
3	0	0	0	0	0
4	0	0	0	0	0
5	0	0	0	0	0

Accessing a multi-dimensional array is similar to accessing a single-dimensional array. The following code:

```
String starting_players[ ] = {"Larry", "Mo", "Curly",
    "Shep", "Chuck"};
int points_scored[ ] [ ] = new int [5] [6];
...
// Curly scored 6 points in the fourth game.
points_scored[2][3] = 6;
...
```

```
g.drawString(starting_players[2]
    + " scored " + points_scored[2][3]
    + " points in game four.", 1, 30);
```

would output `Curly scored 6 points in game four.` to the current window.

Using Operators

Operators manipulate or identify variables. Some operators are fairly straight forward, like the equal sign (=) or the plus sign (+), while others in Visual J++ aren't that clear except to C and C++ programmers.

There are five types of operators in Visual J++:

- Arithmetic operators, which include String operators

- Logical operators

- Bit operators

- Combination operators

- Miscellaneous operators

Arithmetic Operators

Arithmetic operators come in two categories: binary and unary. Unary operators interact with only one variable while binary operators interact with two or more variables at a time. Table 2.2 lists the binary arithmetic operators, and Table 2.3 lists the unary arithmetic operators.

Table 2.2
Binary Arithmetic Operators

Operator	Example	Description
*	a * b	* is used for multiplication. a * b would return the product of a multiplied by b.
/	a / b	/ is used for division. a / b would return the quotient of a divided by b.
%	a % b	% is the modulus operator (also called the remainder operator). a % b returns the remainder when a is divided by b.

continues

Table 2.2
continued

Operator	Example	Description
+	a + b	+ is used for addition as well as string concatenation. If a and b are numbers, a + b would return the sum of a and b. If a and b where strings, a + b would return the concatenation of the two strings.
–	a – b	– is used for subtraction. a – b would return the difference between a and b.
=	a = b	= is used for assignment. a = b copies the value of b into a.

Table 2.3
Unary Arithmetic
Operators

Operator	Example	Description
+	+a	+ serves as a unary plus. A unary plus really has no effect on an equation, but can be used for emphasis. For example, instead of typing a * b, you could type +a * b and retrieve the same result.
–	–a	– serves as a unary minus. A unary minus takes the opposite sign of a variable before an operation. –a * b would return the same result as $(-1) * (a * b)$.

+ +	++a
	a++
		+ + is used to increment a variable. When + + is placed before a variable, that variable is incremented before the rest of the operation occurs. When + + is placed after a variable, that variable is incremented after the operation occurs. For example,
		`c = ++a * b;`
		would be the equivalent of
		`a = a + 1;`
		`c = a * b;`
		On the other hand,
		`c = a++ * b;`
		would be the equivalent of
		`c = a * b;`
		`a = a + 1;`

– –	– –a
	a– –
		– – is used to decrement a variable. When – – is placed before a variable, that variable is decremented before the rest of the operation occurs. When – – is placed after a variable, that variable is incremented after the operation occurs. For example,
		`c = --a * b;`
		would be the equivalent of
		`a = a - 1;`
		`c = a * b;`

Operator	Example	Description

		On the other hand,
		`c = a-- * b;`
		would be the equivalent of
		`c = a * b;`
		`a = a - 1;`

(data type) **ing** a	`(String) a` a	**A data type in parentheses is called a cast-** **operator because it casts a variable to a new type for an operation.** `(String) a` **returns** **casted as a string.**

Logical Operators

Logical operators (also known as *boolean operators*) are operators that are used to evaluate whether a statement is true or false. Table 2.4 lists the logical operators.

Table 2.4
Logical Operators

Operator	Example	Description
==	`if (a == b)…`	**== is the logical equals operator. == tests whether two expressions have the same value. If == is used on a class, it tests whether the two classes refer to the same object.**
!=	`if (a != b)…`	**!= is the logical not equals operator. != returns true if two expressions contain different values. If != is used on a class, it tests whether the two classes refer to different objects.**
!	`if (!bool_var)`	**! is the logical not operator. ! tests a boolean expression. If the boolean expression is true `!boolean` returns false. Otherwise, it returns true.**
<	`if (a < b) {…`	**< is the less than operator. It tests whether one value is less than another.**
>	`if (a > b) {…`	**> is the greater than operator. It tests whether one value is greater than another.**

continues

Operator	Example	Description
<=	if (a <= b) {…	<= is the less than or equal operator. It tests whether one value is less than or equal to another.
>=	if (a >= b) {…	>= is the greater than operator. It tests whether one value is greater than or equal to another.
&&	if (bool1 && bool2)…	&& is the logical conditional AND operator. It evaluates two boolean expressions until one evaluates to false. It then returns true if all boolean expressions are true, and returns false if any were false.
||	if (bool1 || bool2)…	|| is the logical conditional OR operator. It evaluates two boolean expressions until one evaluates to true. It then returns true if any boolean expressions are true, and returns false if all were false.
&	if (bool1 & bool2)…	& is the logical AND operator. It evaluates two boolean expressions entirely. It then returns true if all boolean expressions are true, and returns false if any were false. Usually, & is inefficient because all expressions are evaluated before a true or false is returned. && should usually be used instead unless there is a need for all expressions to be processed.
| ^	if (bool1 | bool2) {… if (bool1 ^ bool2) {…	| and ^ are logical OR operators. They evaluate two boolean expressions entirely. They then return true if any boolean expressions are true and false if all were false. Usually, | and ^ are inefficient because all expressions are evaluated before a true or false is returned. || should usually be used instead unless there is a need for all expressions to be processed.

Operator	Example	Description
?:	`a = (bool ? if_true` `➡: if_false);`	**? and : are known as the conditional operator. The conditional operator is used to test a boolean expression and then return one value if the boolean expression is true or another value if the boolean expression is false. Although an** `if...else...` **statement could achieve the same effect, ? and : can be used for simple assignments and are a great space saver in a program. It may also be marginally more efficient than an** `if...else...` **statement.**

NOTE:
Visual J++ has defined two constants to help evaluate boolean expressions: `true` **and** `false`**. For example, the following statement:**

```
if (!boolean_variable) {...
```

is equivalent to

```
if (boolean_variable == false) {...
```

Depending on your particular development environment, using `true` **and** `false` **is often used to make code more readable by other developers.** `true` **and** `false` **can also be used to set a boolean variable to a particular value.**

Bit Operators

Bit operators, also called bitwise operators, are similar to logical operators, except that they work on bits (values 1 and 0) rather than boolean expressions (true and false). Using bits can be effective if computer space is at a premium, because one byte is equivalent to eight bits. In practice, bit operators aren't used much except in some graphical routines that are beyond the scope of this book. However, Java programs often use them to handle keyboard events (see

Chapter 9 for more information about events). Table 2.5 lists the bit operators used in Visual J++.

Table 2.5
Bit Operators

Operator	Example	Description
~	~a	The bitwise complement (~) is used to reverse the sign on a bit. Results: a ~a 1 0 0 1
&	a & b	The bitwise AND (&) performs an AND operation on two variables. This sets the result to 1 if both variables are 1, otherwise it sets the result to 0. Results: a b a & b 0 0 0 0 1 0 1 0 0 1 1 1
^	a ^ b	The bitwise XOR (exclusive OR) operator (^) returns true if one and only one of the two variables tested are true, but if both variables are true. Otherwise, a false value is returned. Results: a b a ^ b 0 0 0 0 1 1 1 0 1 1 1 0
|	a | b	The bitwise OR operator (also known as the inclusive OR operator) returns a true if either of the two variables tested are true. Otherwise, a false value is returned. Results: a b a | b 0 0 0 0 1 1 1 0 1 1 1 1
<<	a << b	<< is the left shift operator. << left-shifts all bits in one variable. In this example, thebits in a are left-shifted b times. The leftmost bits are discarded, and the rightmost bits are set to 0. Each shift has the effect of multiplying an integer by 2.

Operator	Example	Description
>>	a >> b	**>> is the right shift with sign preserve operator. >> right-shifts all bits in a variable. In this example, the bits in** a **are right-shifted left** b **times. The rightmost bit is discarded, and the leftmost bit is set to preserve the sign of the original value. Each shift has the effect of dividing an integer by 2.**
>>>	a >>> b	**>>> is the right shift operator. >>> shifts all bits to the right, just like the >> operator, except the sign is not preserved. The rightmost bit is discarded, and the leftmost bit is set to zero. Sometimes, each shift has the effect of dividing an integer by 2, but the results vary depending on the original sign bit.**

Bitwise operations are pretty complicated. For example, say you had four keyboard situations. You want to make a number that indicates whether an Alt, Ctrl, Shift, or Windows key was pressed. You could assign each of them a number raised to the power of 2, like so:

Key	Value
Shift	$1 = 2^0$
Ctrl	$2 = 2^1$
Windows	$4 = 2^2$
Alt	$8 = 2^3$

You could then add the numbers together into an indicator variable to indicate which key was used. For example, if you press Shift and Ctrl at the same time, the value of the indicator variable would be 3 (Shift (1) + Ctrl (2) = 3).

Now, say you want to test whether Shift was pressed. You *could* test the indicator for each value of Shift as follows:

```
if (indicator == 1 || indicator == 3 ||
    indicator == 5 || indicator == 7 ||
    indicator == 9 || indicator == 11 ||
    indicator == 13 || indicator = 15) {
    //Perform SHIFT logic here
}
```

However, the preceding if statement is very cumbersome. Instead, you could perform the following test:

```
if ((indicator & SHIFT) != 0) {
    //Perform SHIFT logic here
}
```

Say indicator is equal to 11. That would be equivalent to pressing Shift+Ctrl+Alt. The ANDing of indicator would appear as follows:

Expression	Value	Binary
indicator	11	1011
SHIFT	1	0001
SHIFT & indicator	1	0001

If, on the other hand, indicator was set to 14, the table would then appear as follows:

Expression	Value	Binary
indicator	14	1110
SHIFT	1	0001
SHIFT & indicator	0	0000

As you can see, ANDing indicator and SHIFT turned a complicated test into a relatively simple and efficient one. However, bitwise operations are often hard for developers to follow, so keep that in mind before trying to shave a couple of nanoseconds off your execution time.

Combination Operators

Visual J++, like C and C++, allows the use of combination operators. These are operators that perform some operation on themselves. For example, instead of typing the following code:

```
a = a + b;
```

you could type the following:

```
a += b;
```

Combination operators are a shorthand method to reduce equation size and complexity of your Java code. Table 2.6 lists the combination operators.

Table 2.6
Combination Operators

Operator	Example	Equivalent Expression
*=	a *= b	a = a * b
/=	a /= b	a = a / b
%=	a %= b	a = a % b
+=	a += b	a = a + b
-=	a -= b	a = a - b
&=	a &= b	a = a & b
^=	a ^= b	a = a ^ b
|=	a |= b	a = a | b
>>=	a >>= b	a = a >> b
<<=	a <<= b	a = a << b
>>>=	a >>>= b	a = a >>> b

Miscellaneous Operators

Some operators don't fit neatly into any specific category. Table 2.7 describes these operators.

Table 2.7
Miscellaneous Operators

Operator	Example	Description
[ ]	new int[5]	The array operator ([ ]) is used to declare and reference arrays, as discussed earlier in this chapter in the "Referencing Array Elements" section.
.	import java.awt.*	The period operator (.) indicates that a variable is a member of a class. Classes are further discussed in Chapter 5.
,	int a, b;	The comma operator (,) allows the multiple listing of variables in a declaration or multiple statements into a single statement.
instanceof	if (var instanceof ➡Class) {...	The instanceof variable returns a true or false depending on whether a variable is a instance of a class. This instanceof operator is often used with inheritance and is covered in more detail in Chapter 6.

Order of Operations

Visual J++, like other programs, executes mathematical equations based on an order of operations. Assume you had three variables: a, b, and c. Set a = 2, b = 3, and c = 4. The equation:

```
a + b * c;    // 2 + 3 * 4
```

would return 14. Some of you may have thought that it would return 20 because 2 + 3 is 5, and 5 * 4 is 20. However, in Java (as well as most other languages), multiplication occurs before addition, so actually the equation would be interpreted as 3 * 4 is 12 and 12 + 2 is 14.

The idea of placing certain operations before other operations is called *order of operations*. Table 2.8 shows the order of operations in Java.

Table 2.8
Order of operations

Step	Operations in this step
1	( ) [ ] .
2	++ -- ! ~ instanceof + (unary) – (unary)
3	* / %
4	+ (binary) – (binary)
5	<< >> >>>
6	& (bitwise)
7	^ (bitwise)
8	| (bitwise)
9	?:
10	< > <= >= == !=
11	& (logical)
12	^ (logical)
13	| (logical)
14	&&
15	||
16	= *= /= %= += –= <<= >>= >>>= &= ^= |=
17	,

Using Character Literals

Often, you'll want to put a special character inside a string, like a carriage return/line feed or a quote. *Character literals* allow you to accomplish this. Java's character literals, also called escape characters, character escapes, or string formatting characters, are almost identical to those used in C and C++. Table 2.9 lists Java's character literals.

Table 2.9
Character Literals

Character Literal	Symbol
Continuation	\
New Line (NL or CR/LF)	\n
Horizontal Tab (HT)	\t
Backspace (BS)	\b
Carriage Return (CR)	\r
Form Feed (FF)	\f
Backslash (\)	\\
Single Quote (')	\'
Double Quote (")	\"
Octal Bit Pattern(O###)	\###
Hexadecimal Bit Pattern (0x##)	\x##
Unicode Character(0x####)	\u####

Say you want to format a string that looked like this:

```
When Abe said, "Four score and seven years ago," he meant 87
➥years.
```

To format this quote, you would use the following string:

```
String my_quote = "When Abe said, " +
 "\"Four score and seven years ago,\" he meant 87 years.";
```

In many languages, it's difficult to put a quote inside a quoted string, but using character literals in Java makes it easy.

Understanding Decision Structures (*if* and *switch*)

Decision structures allow your program to branch around areas in code based on the values of certain expressions. There are two decision structures in Java: if and switch.

if

The if statement in Java has the following format:

```
if (condition1) {
    // Condition 1 code here
}
else if (condition2) {
    // Condition 2 code here if condition 1 is false
}
else {
    // Default code here if condition 1 and condition 2 are
➥false
}
```

In the preceding if structure, condition1 is evaluated. If condition1 is true, then the condition1 code is executed; if not, then condition2 is evaluated. If condition2 is true, then the condition2 code is executed. If neither condition1 or condition2 is true, then the default code is evaluated. The following is an example of an if statement:

```
String age_group;
int age;
...
if (age == 0) {
    age_group = "Newborn";
}
else if (age <= 6) {
    age_group = "Tot";
}
else if (age < 13) {
    age_group = "Grade schooler";
}
else if (age <= 18) {
    age_group = "Teenager";
}
else {
    age_group = "Adult";
}
```

switch

switch is Java's case statement. Rather than using a complicated if statement when evaluating a single expression, a switch statement can be more efficient and make code development a maintenance a little easier to understand. The switch statement in Java has the following format:

```
switch (expression) {
    case constant1 :
// case1 logic here
// Break ends the switch.
// Otherwise, you execute all remaining logic
        break;
case constant2 :
// case 2 logic here with no break
    case constant3 :
// case 2 and case 3 logic here, since case 2 has no break
        break
    default :
// Logic goes here if no other case was executed.
}
```

Switch is great for testing one expression for several number of values. For example, to evaluate a status code with possible values of I (inactive), A (active), or O (obsolete), you could code the following switch statement:

```
switch (status) {
    case 'I' :
status_string = "Inactive";
        break;
    case 'A' :
        status_string = "Active";
        break;
    case 'O' :
        status_string = "Obsolete";
        break;
    default :
```

```
        status_string = "Bad status value";
}
```

Notice that the `default` keyword is often used for error reporting.

Although you typically wouldn't use a `switch` for this, you could duplicate the age testing done in the previous `if` section with the following `switch` statement:

```
int switch_age;
String switch_age_group;
...
switch (switch_age) {
    case 0 :
switch_age_group = "Newborn";
        break;
    case 1 :
    case 2 :
    case 3 :
    case 4 :
    case 5 :
    case 6 :
        switch_age_group = "Tot";
        break;
    case 7 :
    case 8 :
    case 9 :
    case 10 :
    case 11:
    case 12 :
        switch_age_group = "Grade schooler";
        break;
    case 13 :
    case 14 :
    case 15 :
    case 16 :
    case 17 :
    case 18 :
        switch_age_group = "Teenager";
```

```
        break;
    default :
        switch_age_group = "Adult";
}
```

NOTE:
Although the preceding `switch` statement would work, it's quite cumbersome to the comparable `if` statement. `switch` works best when you're evaluating an expression against individual constants rather than ranges of constants.

Using Looping Structures (*while, do, for, continue,* and *break*)

Looping structures allow you to execute the same code several times until a given condition is met. Visual J++ has three looping statements: `while`, `do while`, and `for`. There are also `break` and `continue` commands that allows you to exit a loop before the loop is done executing.

while and *do*

The `while` statement is similar in structure to an `if` statement. It's format is as follows:

```
while (condition) {
    // Code that loops until a condition is met.
}
```

Using the preceding statement, you could write the following code to display the first 10 powers of 2:

```
import java.awt.Graphics;
import java.lang.*;
...
//While POWERS OF 2 test
    int power = 0;    // Declare power integer
double hold_number;    // Number for holding pow result
    String power_string = "";    // String holds powers of 2
```

```
        // While statements executes when power < 10
        while (power <= 10) {
            // place 2 to the power inside hold_number
            hold_number = Math.pow(2.0, (double) power++);
            // Build power_string from results
            power_string +=
                String.valueOf(hold_number)  + "    ";
}           // End loop
// Display the power_string
            g.drawString(
                "The powers of 2: " + power_string, 1, 75);
```

> **NOTE:**
> **Math is a class inside the java.lang package. The Math class contains many useful math functions, one of which is the** pow **function, used above to raise 2 to a given power.**

The do...while construct is similar to the while statement, except when the testing occurs. The while statement tests before the loop starts (see Figure 2.3). If the condition is false, the loop will not execute at all.

Fig. 2.3
The while statement tests a condition before the loop executes.

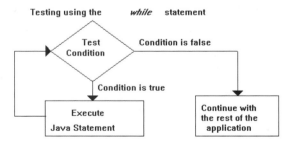

The do statement format is as follows:

```
do {
    // Code that loops until a condition is met.
} while (condition);
```

It executes a loop at least once and then tests the condition. Using the same POWERS OF 2 program with a do...while loop would look like this:

```
import java.awt.Graphics;
import java.lang.*;
...
//do ... while POWERS OF 2 test
int power = 0;      // Declare power integer
double hold_number;      // Number for holding pow result
    String power_string = "";     // String to build powers of 2
    do {
// place 2 to the power inside hold_number
        hold_number = Math.pow(2.0, (double) power++);
        // Build power_string from results
        power_string += String.valueOf(hold_number) +"     ";
} while (power <= 10);
    g.drawString("The powers of 2: " + power_string, 1, 90);
```

The testing for the do loop follows the flowchart shown in Figure 2.4.

Fig. 2.4
The do...while state-ment tests a condition after the loop executes.

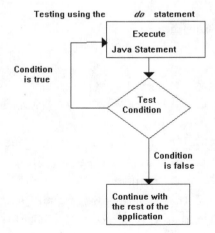

for

The for loop is a special kind of loop in Java. The for statement has the following format:

```
for (initialization; condition; iteration) {
    // Code that loops until the condition is met.
}
```

The `for` statement has the following components:

- **Initialization.** The initialization segment of the `for` statement occurs before the `for` loop begins. This allows you to initialize any variables (separated by a comma), declare any variables of the same type (separated by a comma), or call any functions before the loop starts processing.

- **Condition.** The condition segment of the `for` statement allows you to test a value during each iteration of the loop. `for` testing is identical to `while` testing in that the condition is tested before the loop begins. If the condition is not met, then the loop never executes.

- **Iteration.** The iteration segment of the `for` statement allows you to execute one or several Java commands (separated by a comma) during each iteration of the `for` loop.

Writing a functionally equivalent POWERS OF 2 `for` loop that was used with the `while` and `do...while` program segments previously would look like this:

```
import java.awt.Graphics;
import java.lang.*;
...
//for loop POWERS OF 2 test
    String for_power_string = "";     // String to build powers
of 2
//declare and initialize for_power, test it, and increment it
    for (int for_power = 0; for_power <= 10; for_power++) {
        double for_hold_number;
        // place 2 to the power inside hold_number
        for_hold_number = Math.pow(2.0, (double) for_power);
        // Build power_string from results
        for_power_string += String.valueOf(for_hold_number)
+ "    ";
    }
        g.drawString("The powers of 2: " + for_power_string, 1,
105);
```

break

The break statement exits you out of the current innermost loop. Consider the following POWERS OF 2 program segment:

```
import java.awt.Graphics;
import java.lang.*;

...
//POWERS OF 2 test with a break
    int power = 0;      // Declare power integer
double hold_number;     // Number for holding pow result
    // String to build powers of 2
    String power_string = "";
    while (true) {      // while(true) causes an infinite loop
        // While statements executes when power < 10
        if (power > 10) {
            // Break out of loop if power is greater than 10
            break;
        }
// place 2 to the power inside hold_number
        hold_number = Math.pow(2.0, (double) power++);
        // Build power_string from results
        power_string += String.valueOf(hold_number) + "   ";
}       // End loop
    g.drawString("The powers of 2: " + power_string, 1, 120);
```

Instead of testing for power each time in the while statement, an infinite loop was coded by using while (true). Then power was tested to see if it was greater than 10, and a break was issued if that was true to exit to the statement immediately following the loop.

continue

Continue allows you to skip the rest of the lines in a loop, but not exit the loop. Say you only want to take the even number of powers in the POWERS OF 2 program segment. Consider the following code:

```
import java.awt.Graphics;
import java.lang.*;

...
```

```
//Even POWERS OF 2 test with a continue
    String even_power_string = "";     // String to build powers
➥of 2
//declare and initialize even_power, test it, and increment it
   for (int even_power = 0; even_power <= 10; even_power++){
        // Test if power is being raised to an odd power
        if (even_power % 2 == 1) {
continue; // Continue to the next number if it is.
        }
double even_hold_number;
        // place 2 to the power inside hold_number
        even_hold_number=Math.pow(2.0, (double) even_power);
        // Build power_string from results
        even_power_string +=
                String.valueOf(even_hold_number)  + "    ";
    }
    g.drawString(
      "The even powers of 2: " + even_power_string, 1, 135);
```

Above, `continue` was used to re-loop without executing the rest of the loop if an `even_power` was odd.

Labels with *break* and *continue*

Sometimes, you'll want to `continue` or `break` out of an outer loop rather than an inner loop. For example, say you want to multiply all odd numbers together between 1 and 5. The following nested loops can accomplish this:

```
import java.awt.Graphics;
import java.lang.*;
...
// Labeled break and labeled continue
int outer_loop_counter = 0;
String results = "";

outer_loop:  while (true) {     // outer infinite loop
int inner_loop_counter = 0;
```

```
            outer_loop_counter++;
inner_loop:     while(true) {      // inner infinite loop
            // See if outer loop is done
            if (outer_loop_counter > 5) {
                // Break out of outer loop if it is.
                break outer_loop;
            }
            // Test if outer counter is even
            if (outer_loop_counter % 2 == 0) {
                // Continue outer loop if it is.
                continue outer_loop;
            }
            // See if inner loop is done
            if (++inner_loop_counter > 5) {
                // Break out of inner loop if it is.
                break inner_loop;
            }
            // Test if inner counter is even
            if (inner_loop_counter % 2 == 0) {
// Continue inner loop if it is.
                continue inner_loop;
            }
            results +=
                String.valueOf(outer_loop_counter) + " * " +
                String.valueOf(inner_loop_counter) + " = " +
                String.valueOf(inner_loop_counter
                        * outer_loop_counter) + "   ";
        }     // End of the inner loop
    }     // End of the outer loop
    g.drawString(results, 1, 150);
```

As you can see in the preceding code, multi-level breaks occur inside
the deepest loop level. Multi-level continues also occur. Although
there currently is no goto command inside Visual J++, break and
continue can help branch around in a program.

WARNING:
You should review your program design if you need to use a break or continue. These commands can save a lot of headache, but they're often indicative of a poorly designed program. For example, the previous code written with multi-level breaks and continues could have been written as follows:

```
import java.awt.Graphics;
import java.lang.*;
...
// Multiply all odd numbers below 6
//           without break or continue
String result_string = "";

for (int outer_loop_ctr = 1;
            outer_loop_ctr <= 5;
            outer_loop_ctr += 2) {
    for (int inner_loop_ctr = 1;
            inner_loop_ctr <= 5;
            inner_loop_ctr += 2) {
result_string +=
            String.valueOf(outer_loop_ctr) + " * " +
            String.valueOf(inner_loop_ctr) + " = " +
            String.valueOf(inner_loop_ctr * outer_loop_ctr)
            + "   ";
    }     // End of the inner loop
}    // End of the outer loop
g.drawString(result_string, 1, 165);
```

CAUTION:
Notice that the preceding code has no break or continue, it is much shorter, and it's easier to understand, write, and maintain.

Conclusion

This chapter discussed the basic Visual J++ programming language. Some simple concepts were covered, such as data types and operators, and some more complex topics were discussed, such as loops and when to use or not use `break` and `continue`. However, there's still much to learn about programming in Visual J++. Check out Chapter 5, "Using Classes and Packages in Visual J++," and Chapter 9, "Event Programming in Visual J++," for a more complete understanding of Visual J++ programming.

Chapter 3

The Visual J++ Environment

The Developer Studio (called Studio for short) is one of the more advanced system development tools available. The same environment is used currently with Visual C++ with huge success. You'll find that the studio environment has a lot of different ways to accomplish the same task. This redundancy was placed inside Studio so that different developers could accomplish the same task in the ways that work best for them.

This chapter is designed to walk you through the Visual J++ environment. In this chapter, you'll learn:

- How to customize your toolbars

- The standard Developer Studio functions

- All about managing projects with the Developer Studio

- All about managing resources, such as bitmaps and buttons, with the Developer Studio

- How to navagate through the InfoViewer

Customizing Your Toolbars

Before you learn what buttons perform what functions, you should first know how to add buttons to toolbars and how to view other toolbars on your system. To customize your toolbar, you need to right-click on the toolbar. Then, a popup menu appears as seen in Figure 3.1.

Fig. 3.1
You can choose which toolbars to display, or choose to customize your toolbars by right-

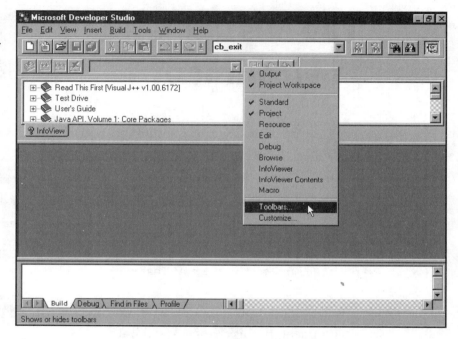

Choose Toolbars from the popup menu (or choose View, Toolbars from the menu) to open the Toolbars dialog box (see Figure 3.2). Here, you can choose which toolbars to show, or even build your own.

Fig. 3.2
The Toolbars dialog box gives you a nice interface to choose which toolbars should be shown, and to set options about your toolbar buttons.

Here, you can reset your toolbars to the way the Microsoft intended (if you went a little crazy with customization). You can choose to show or disable ToolTips, and you can disable showing the shortcut key combination that can perform the same task.

CAUTION:
I really wouldn't disable ToolTips. There pretty useful, especially with the scores of buttons included in the multiple toolbars inside the Developer Studio.

ToolTips are a yellow box that appears if you keep your mouse over a button for a second or two. They're really helpful when you're in a new environment. Figure 3.3 shows the ToolTips for the New button.

Fig. 3.3
Tooltips show the name of the button and the shortcut key that duplicates the button.

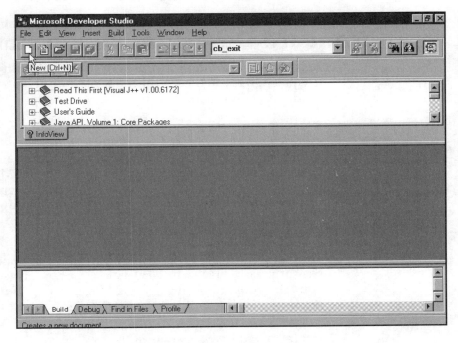

You can customize your toolbar by clicking the Customize button in the Toolbars dialog box (refer to Figure 3.2) or by clicking Customize on the popup menu shown in Figure 3.1. The Customize dialog box appears (see Figure 3.4). From here, you can choose to add buttons to your toolbars or to take buttons off your toolbars by dragging the appropriate buttons around. In Figure 3.4, I'm adding the New button to the Standard toolbar.

Fig. 3.4
Use the Customize
dialog box to add or
remove buttons from
your toolbars.

Standard Developer Studio Functions

This chapter may duplicate some of the functionality you saw in Chapter 1, but you'll get a fuller, more complete discussion of the Studio functions here.

File Functions

Visual J++ provides an easy and very comprehensive way to create, open, and save files in an integrated environment. Much of this is intuitive to most Windows users, but this chapter gives you a chance to review the buttons associated with the file functions.

Creating New Files

To create a new file, click the New button. You can also choose File, New or press Ctrl+N. The New dialog box appears (see Figure 3.5). You can choose to open a new text file, a Project Workspace, a new resource template, or a bitmap (BMP) file.

Fig. 3.5
The New dialog box is
handy for allowing
you to open new files.

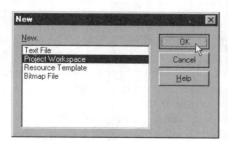

NOTE:
Text files are used for Java programs. However, I would open a Project file first, and then add a Java program to it. This will allow you to set project settings before the first compile rather than compiling to build a default Project Workspace (as was done in Chapter 1) and then setting the project options before compiling again.

You could get around the New dialog box for adding a text (Java) file by clicking the New Source File button.

Opening Existing Files

To open an existing file, click the Open button, or choose <u>F</u>ile, Open. The Open dialog box appears (see Figure 3.6). As you can see by the list of allowable file types, the Developer Studio allows you to work on several types of files.

Fig. 3.6
The Open dialog box allows you to bring an existing file into the Studio.

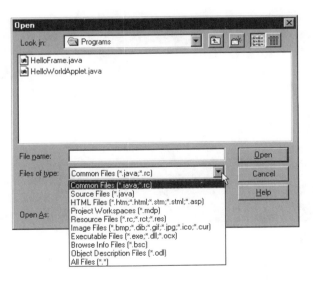

Choose <u>F</u>ile, Open <u>W</u>orkspace, as shown in Figure 3.7, to open the Open Project Workspace dialog box. You can view a list of available Project Workspaces and choose one to bring into the Studio environment (see Figure 3.8).

Fig. 3.7
To open an existing
Project Workspace,
choose File, Open
Workspace.

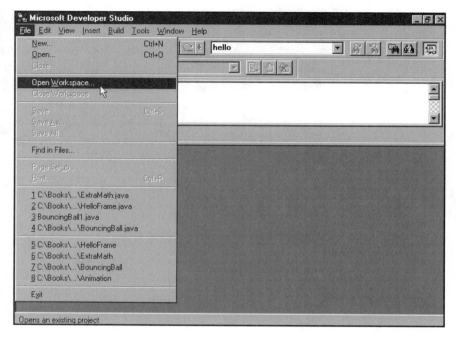

Fig. 3.8
You can use the Open
Project Workspace
dialog box to open an
existing Project
Workspace.

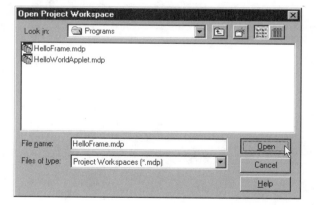

Saving Files

After making changes in your Java file, compiling (building) your
code will automatically save it. However, if you want to save it yourself, click the Save button. The status of your save will then be
shown in the status area at the bottom of the Studio environment,
as shown in Figure 3.9. To save all changed documents, click the
Save All button.

Fig. 3.9
You can see save results in the status area in the Studio environment.

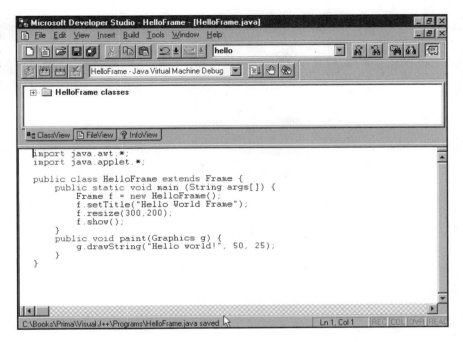

Often, you'll want to take a Visual J++ program and save it as another program file. To do this, choose File, Save As (see Figure 3.10). The Save As dialog box appears (see Figure 3.11). The Save As dialog box shows a list of matching files in the current directory, and allows you to save over an existing file or to create a new file.

NOTE:
You also open the Save As dialog box when you try to save a new file that has not yet been named.

Printing Files

You can print your Java files by clicking the Print button, or by choose File, Print. The Print dialog box appears, as shown in Figure 3.12. Choose the printer you want to print to. If you have text selected, you can also choose to print just a selection rather than a whole file.

TIP:
Printing selections is a great way to print a single method from a multi-method Visual J++ class.

Fig. 3.10
To save your program with a different name, choose File, Save As.

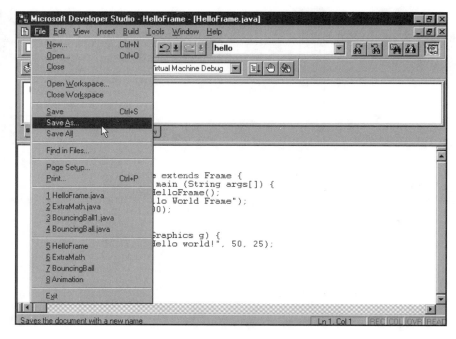

Fig. 3.11
The Save As dialog box allows you to create a new file or save over an existing file.

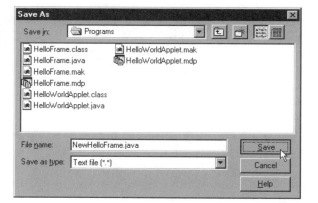

Fig. 3.12
The Print dialog box allows you to choose or setup your printer, and to choose whether to print

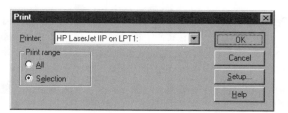

Edit Functions

Again, much of this may be review for several of you, but it also may be a chance to review buttons that are matched up to functions in the Studio environment. The edit functions are divided into the following four categories and discussed in the following sections.

- Selected text functions

- Undo and redo functions

- Find and replace functions

- Bookmarks

Select Text Functions

Many of the edit functions are available only on text that you select. There are many ways to select text:

- You can drag your mouse over the area you want to select.

- You can choose Edit, Select All to select all the text in a document.

- You can hold down the Shift key while using the arrow keys. This selects any text between the original cursor position and the new cursor position.

- You can click an area with your mouse, hold the Shift key down, and then click a different area. All of the text between the two areas will be selected.

The following buttons are available for editing:

 Cuts any selected text (deleting the text from the file) and places the text on the Clipboard. Pressing Ctrl+X or choosing Edit, Cut also cuts selected text to the Clipboard.

 Copies any selected text (leaving the text on the file) and places the text on the Clipboard. Pressing Ctrl+C or choosing Edit, Copy also copies selected text to the Clipboard.

 Pastes any text from the Clipboard to the current cursor location in the Studio. Pressing Ctrl+V or choosing Edit, Paste also pastes text from the Clipboard to your current Studio document.

Undo and Redo Functions

The Developer's Studio supports multi-level undos. To undo the last action you performed, click the Undo button; press Ctrl+Z; or choose Edit, Undo. To see what functions have been done, click the down arrow on the drop-down cursor. From the drop-down Undo window, you can choose which actions to undo (see Figure 3.13).

Fig. 3.13
The drop-down Undo button allows you to undo multiple actions.

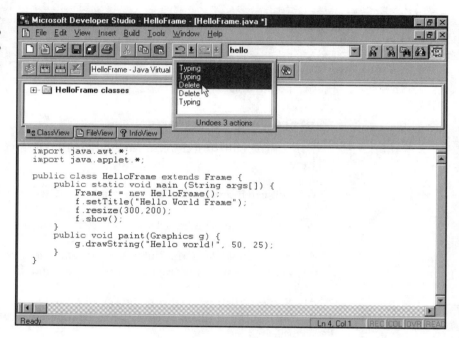

The Redo button redoes actions that were undone. Clicking the Redo button (or pressing Ctrl+Y or choosing Edit, Redo) will redo one action. You can also redo several undone actions using the drop-down Redo window the same way you used the drop-down Undo window.

Find and Replace Functions

Visual J++ supports the standard find and replace functions. Click the Find button (or press Ctrl-F or choose Edit, Find) opens the Find dialog box (see Figure 3.14). Here you can specify the usual find criteria, such as case, whole word, or whether to search up or down.

Click the Find Next button (or press F3) and the Find Previous button (or press Shift+F3) to search forward and backward for the same text found previously.

Fig. 3.14
The Find dialog box allows you to find text in your Visual J++ application.

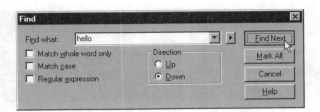

 You can search all the files in a directory for a string if you click the Find in Files button (or choose File, Find in Files). This handy tool allows you to search in multiple files for the occurance of a string. Clicking the Find in Files button opens the Find in Files dialog box, as shown in Figure 3.15.

Fig. 3.15
You can use the Find in Files dialog box to search the contents of multiple files.

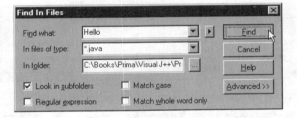

By entering the search string, folder, and file type in your search criteria, you can search the contents of a file. The output of the search goes into the Visual J++ output window (see Figure 3.16).

You can also search and replace text in a file by choosing Edit, Replace (see Figure 3.17). The Replace dialog box appears (see Figure 3.18). Here you specify the search and replace string as well as the search criteria and whether you want the whole file searched or just a selection.

Bookmarks

 Bookmarks allow you to mark a line of text in your environement for review later. To toggle a bookmark off and on, click the Toggle Bookmark button. This places a round blue rectangle by the line of code you want marked, as shown in Figure 3.19.

   You can go to the previous bookmark or the next bookmark by clicking the Previous Bookmark button or the Next Bookmark button, respectively. The Clear All Bookmarks button lets you clear all existing bookmarks.

Fig. 3.16
You can view all Find in Files output in the output window.

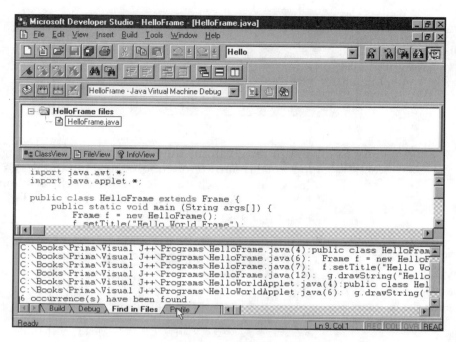

Fig. 3.17
Choosing Edit, Replace will allow you to replace a string of text with another.

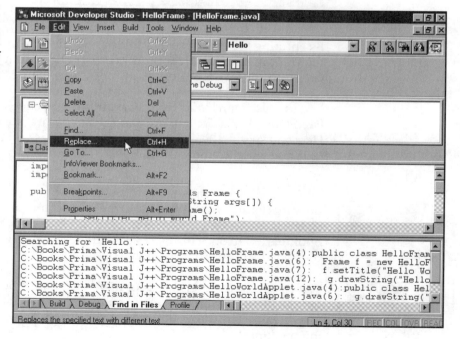

Fig. 3.18
The Replace dialog
box allows you to
specify criteria for a
search and replace.

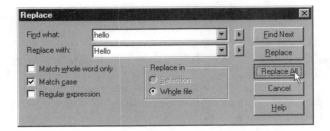

Fig. 3.19
A bookmark on a line
is an easy way to mark
a line for later review.

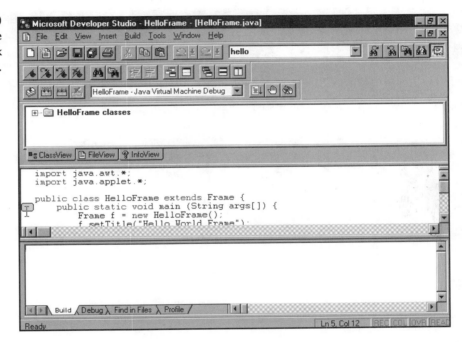

> **NOTE:**
> Although they didn't fit neatly into any category, the
> Indent and Unindent buttons are very useful for format-
> ting when moving code around or adding `if`, `switch`, **or**
> `loop` **statements to a block of code.**

Project Functions

You've already seen how to open a project. Now you will see how
some functions can interact with projects.

Project Settings

As mentioned in Chapter 1, you need to set your class library for each project. To do this, choose Build, Settings, as shown in Figure 3.20, or press Alt+F7. The Project Settings dialog box appears (see Figure 3.21). *Make sure you entered a class directory.* Visual J++ will not compile a Java program without a class directory, and you will receive an ambiguous error message.

Fig. 3.20
To configure your project settings, choose Build, Settings.

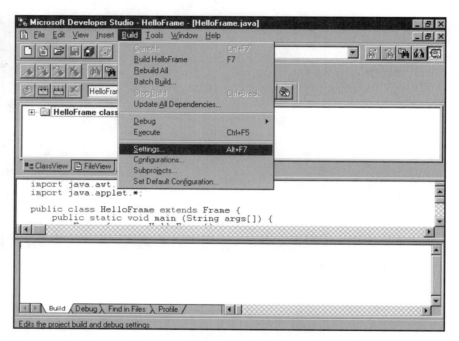

Click the Debug tab in the Project Settings dialog box to specify the name of your class and whether you want to run your Visual J++ project as a stand alone Java application or as a Java applet in a browser (see Figure 3.22). If you don't specify a class name, you will be prompted for one when you execute your project.

Compiling Your Project

There are several ways to compile a Visual J++ project:

 This button compiles a source file. You can also press Ctrl+F7 to compile.

This button builds a project, which means it recompiles all files in a project that haven't been compiled yet. This includes all source files that have changed since the last compile. You can also press F7 to build a project.

 This button rebuilds a project, which means it recompiles all source files inside a project.

Fig. 3.21
Setting the class library is necessary to compile a Visual J++ project.

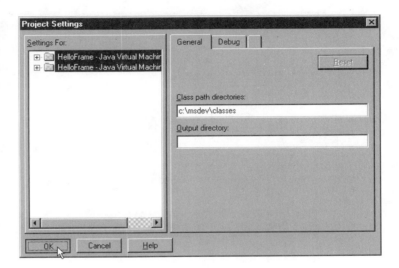

Fig. 3.22
Set your project class to be run, your type of class, and the interpreter or browser needed to run your program.

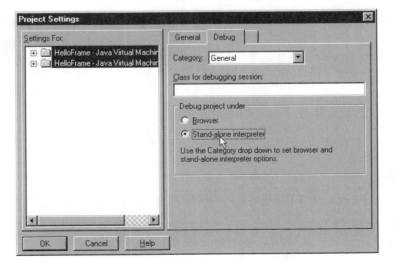

When a compile is finished, the results of the compile are placed in the output window, as shown in Figure 3.23.

Fig. 3.23
The output window holds the results of a compile.

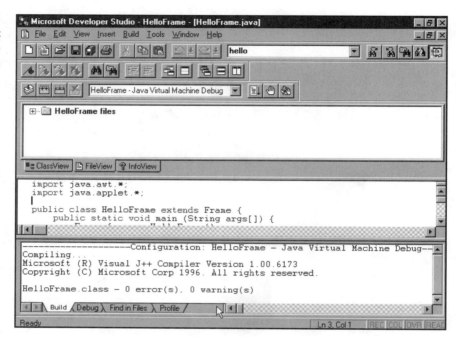

Executing Your Project

To execute your program, choose Build, Execute or press Ctrl+F5. This will build your project if it hasn't been built and then execute your project using either the Java application viewer (JView) that comes with Visual J++ or your Web browser (probably Internet Explorer 3.x), depending if your program is an applet or an application.

If you are compiling for the first time and have not set your program up in the Settings window, the Information For Running Class dialog box will open (see Figure 3.24). Choose if your program is a Web applet or an application, and what the class name is.

The Project Workspace Window

You've already seen the Project Workspace in Chapter 1. The project workspace has three components: ClassViewer, FileViewer, and InfoViewer.

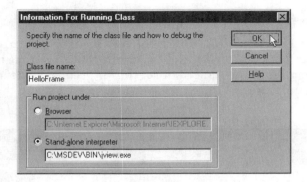

ClassViewer

You can expand the ClassViewer to view all the methods and attributes of a class. You can right-click various entries in the ClassViewer to open a similar popup menu to the one shown in Figure 3.25. You can double-clicking a class or attribute to be immediately brought to that class or attribute. The ClassViewer makes large project management a lot easier than traditional Java methodologies.

Fig. 3.25
The ClassViewer
allows you to
view classes in your
project as well as
perform some
class operations.

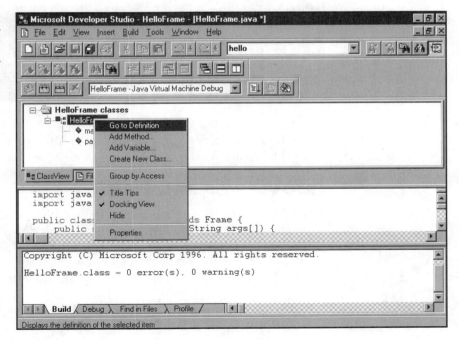

FileViewer

The FileViewer lets you list the files (usually Java program listings) in your project. You can right-click the root to change the class path settings, build the project, or set this project as the default project (see Figure 3.26).

Fig. 3.26
Right-click the root of the FileViewer to perform build and setting operations on the project.

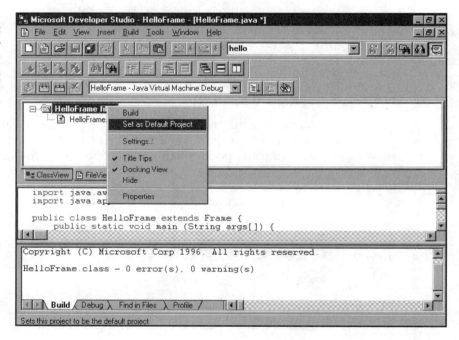

If you right-click a file, you can issue compile statements directly from the Project Workspace Window (see Figure 3.27).

InfoViewer and Help

By clicking the InfoView tab on the Project Workspace window you open the InfoViewer. The InfoViewer is a "drill down" tree structure. When you hit a bottom node and display it, the InfoViewer window displays with the topic you chose. Follow these steps to display help for the Boolean.FALSE attribute (as shown in Figure 3.28):

1. Double-click Java API Volume 1: Core Packages to open the first volume of the Java API.

2. Double-click java.lang to expose the java.lang package.

Fig. 3.27
The FileViewer allows
you to compile
directly from
the Project
Workspace window.

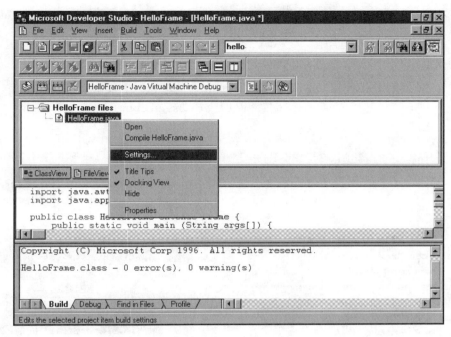

Fig. 3.28
Using the InfoViewer,
it's easy to
look up topics+.

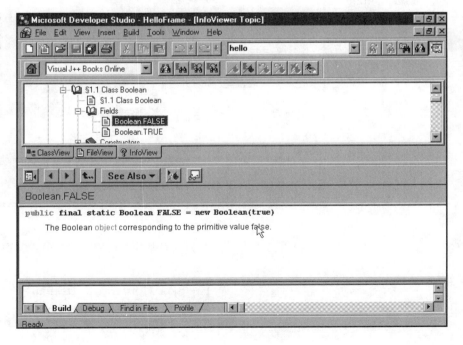

3. Double-click the Boolean class to expose class documentation, fields, and methods.

4. Double-click Fields to see the attributes inside the Boolean class.

5. Double-click Boolean.FALSE to display information about the Boolean.FALSE class attribute.

To look up a word in the InfoViewer without trying to find it in a list, simply place the cursor on the word (or select it) and click the Search button. The proper topic will be displayed. In Figure 3.29, I highlighted resize and clicked the Search button. This caused a list of resize topics to display in help, and then in the InfoViewer.

Fig. 3.29
You can display help for a command by clicking the command and then clicking the Search button, as was done here with the *resize* method.

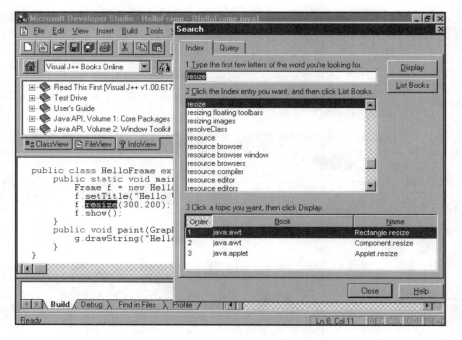

Some of the buttons you can use while displaying an InfoViewer topic are as follows:

The Sync Contents button aligns the InfoView tab in the Project Workspace window with the current topic being displayed. This is useful if you did not double-click to your current topic.

The Previous in Contents button shows the previous InfoViewer topic before the current InfoViewer topic.

 The Next in Contents button shows the next InfoViewer topic after the current InfoViewer topic.

 The Go Back button displays the previous InfoViewer topic. You can also press Ctrl+B to go back to a previous InfoViewer topic.

 You can also set bookmarks in your InfoViewer topic, just like you can in your Java program. When an InfoViewer topic is displayed, you can click the Add Bookmark button. This will display the Add Bookmark dialog box, as shown in Figure 3.30. The Add Bookmark dialog box allows you to add a bookmark to the current InfoViewer topic.

Fig. 3.30
You can use the Add Bookmark dialog box to add an InfoViewer bookmark to the current InfoViewrer topic.

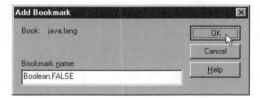

 Click the Help Bookmark List button to open the InfoViewer Bookmarks dialog box, as shown in Figure 3.31. Here, you can list, add, or delete InfoViewer Bookmarks.

Fig. 3.31
The InfoViewer Bookmarks dialog box lets you list, add, and delete InfoViewer Bookmarks.

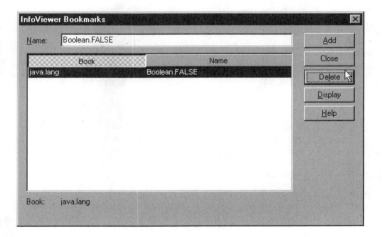

Finally, the InfoViewer also lets you annotate your help. You can do this by clicking the Add/Edit Annotation button. A line appears at the bottom of the InfoViewer topic. Type any additional notes you want to remember about the topic in question. These annotations can be displayed every time an InfoViewer topic is displayed. In Figure 3.32, an annotation was made to Boolean.FALSE.

Fig. 3.32
I'm adding a note to
Boolean.FALSE.

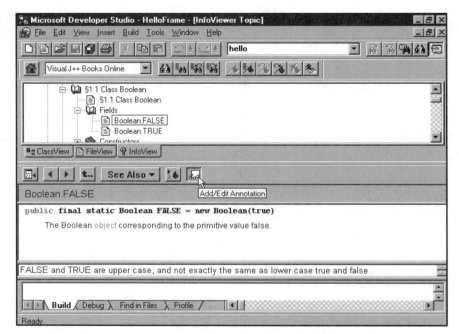

Macros

You can record a series of keys and mouse clicks by recording a macro. You start a macro by clicking the Record button. You then record a series of keystrokes and mouse clicks until you click the Stop button. In Figure 3.33, I clicked the Record button, typed a single string, and clicked the Stop button.

In Figure 3.34, I clicked the Play button several times. Notice that the string repeated. This is because the macro now plays back the recorded keystrokes, and retypes the string.

Fig. 3.33
I recorded a simple macro.

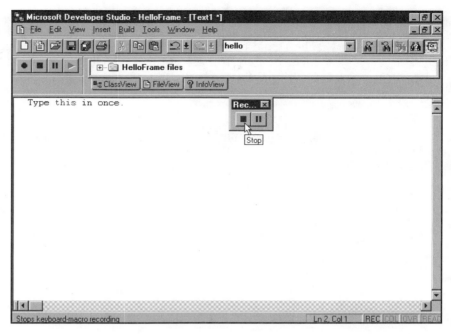

Fig. 3.34
A macro allows the repetion of keystrokes and mouse clicks.

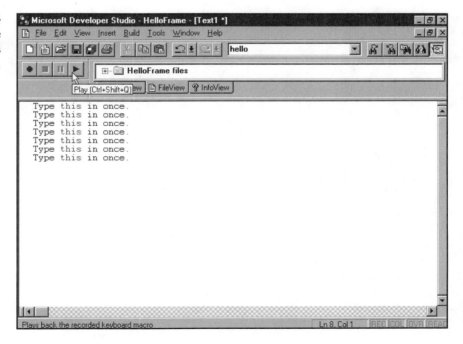

Conclusion

The Visual J++ environment is a robust and fully featured environment that rivals most of the established compilers. Indeed, the Developer Studio is the same environment used in Visual C++, Microsoft Visual Test, and other Microsoft language products.

This chapter taught you how to use the Studio environment. The next chapter will introduce you to some of the tools included with Visual J++, and Chapter 8 shows you how to use the debugger.

Chapter 4

The Visual J++ Tools

This chapter is designed to introduce you to some of the tools that are included with Visual J++. Although far from a complete instruction in some cases (such as with Internet Explorer), this chapter will get you up and running on the tools included with Visual J++. At the end of this chapter, you should know:

- ☻ How to use the Visual J++ Command Line Compiler (JVC).

- ☻ How to use the Visual J++ Java application viewer (JView).

- ☻ What Internet Explorer 3.0 can do for you.

- ☻ How to use the OLE Object Viewer (OLE2VW32).

- ☻ How to use the Applet Wizard to create your own complex applets.

The Visual J++ Command Line Compiler

The JVC is the Visual J++ command line compiler. Instead of using the Visual J++ environment, you can use JVC to compile your code. It's syntax is:

```
JVC [options] <Visual J++ program>
```

The Visual J++ program must be included unless the /? option is used. The following is a list of valid options for Visual J++.

Option	Description
/?	Displays help for JVC.
/cp <classpath>	Sets the class path for compilation.
/cp:p <path>	Prepends the system path to the class path for compilation.
/cp:o	Prints the class path.
/cp:o-	Does not print the class path.
/d <directory>	Sets the directory for the compile class file. (The default is the current directory.)
/g	Generates full debug information (g:l, g:d).
/g-	Does not generate debug (default).
/g:l	Generates line number debug information.
/g:l-	Does not generate line number debug information (default).
/g:t	Generates debug tables.
/g:t-	Does not generate debug tables (default).
/nowarn	Turns warnings off. (The default is to display warnings.)
/nowrite	Compiles but does not generate class files. (The default is to generate a class file.)
/O	Performs full optimization (O:I, O:J).
/O-	Does not perform optimization (default).
/O:I	Optimizes by inlining.
/O:I-	Does not optimize by inlining (default).
/O:J	Optimizes bytecode jumps.
/O:J-	Does not optimize bytecode jumps (default).

Option	Description
/verbose	**Prints messages about the compilation progress. (The default is to not print compilation messages.)**
/w{0-4}	**Sets the warning level. (The default warning level is** /w2**.)**
/x	**Disables extensions.**
/x-	**Enables extensions (default).**

The JVC really shouldn't be used in place of the Visual J++ environment, but it's a nice tool for generating batch compiles if needed. Figure 4.1 shows a compile done with JVC.

Fig. 4.1
Although not used often, the JVC is great for Visual J++ batch compiles.

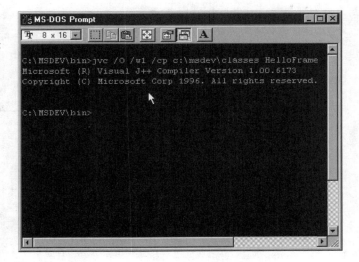

The Visual J++ Applicaiton Viewer

JView is the tool included with Visual J++ to run Java applications that can run without a Web browser, such as Netscape and Internet Explorer. These applications need some type of Java virtual machine environment to run. JView is included with Visual J++ to run Java applications. Although you usually access JView from inside the Visual J++ environment, you can also access it as a stand alone program using the following syntax:

```
JView [options] <classname> [arguments]
```

TIP:
If an argument contains spaces, place it in quotes.

The classname is the name of the Java class you want to run. The classname is always needed unless /? is specified. Arguments are arguments that the Java class needs to run (if any). You can use the following options:

Option	Description
/?	Displays help for JView.
/a	Runs <classname> as an applet.
/cp <classpath>	Sets the class path for compilation.
/cp:p <path>	Prepends the system path to the class path for compilation.
/cp:a <path>	Appends the system path to the class path for compilation.

NOTE:
When using JView, The default is to run the class as an application if it contains a main method and run it as an applet if not, unless /a is specified. However, if you're running an applet, use Internet Explorer (or, if you prefer, Netscape). JView simply isn't as nice as Internet Explorer.

As a command line program, JView typically won't be used with Visual J++ applications, and probably never should be used with Applets unless debugging is necessary. However, you could use JView if you received a Java application class without the Java source code and wanted to view it immediately. Figure 4.2 shows how the HelloFrame program, developed in Chapter 1, is running under the JView.

Fig. 4.2
You can use JView as a
stand alone product
to run Java application
classes.

> **NOTE:**
> *How do you close the HelloFrame window?* Unlike usual win-
> dow programs, you must code for window destruction in
> your Visual J++ programs to make them go away.
> However, this really hasn't been covered yet, so you can't
> close the HelloFrame window. To close it, you must end
> the JView program or the DOS session where the JView
> program is contained. You'll end up receiving the warning
> shown in Figure 4.3, but click Yes to end anyway.

Fig. 4.3
Sometimes you'll need
to get out of JView to
end a Java program.
If you do, you'll
receive this message.

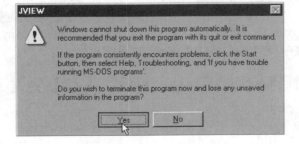

Internet Explorer 3.0

When running an Applet, you should probably use Internet Explorer
3.0. Internet Explorer 3.0 has a Java Virtual Machine that is centered
around Visual J++. You won't find a faster Web browser, or one that's
easier to use. It also has the following benefits:

It's free—not just shareware.

It's very much Visual J++-aware, and includes ActiveX support.

It's a fully featured Web browser.

Figure 4.4 shows Internet Explorer 3.0 running the HelloWorldApplet.

Fig. 4.4
You can use Internet Explorer 3.0 to run local HTML files.

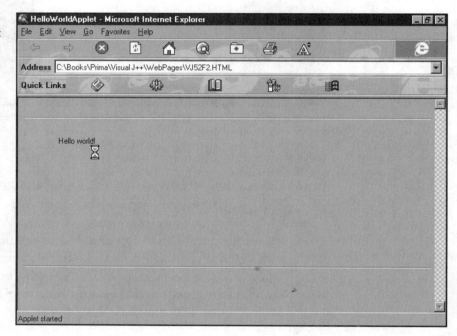

Of course, Internet Explorer makes an excellent Internet Web browser. In Figure 4.5, you can see how the Visual J++ Web site looks on Internet Explorer 3.0 beta. (The Web site, by the way, is **http://www.microsoft.com/visualj/**.

OLE Object View and ActiveX

The OLE Object Viewer allows you to take any registered OLE/ActiveX server and view the functions that are callable within the ActiveX server. Although this is actually a stand alone Windows program (OLE2VW32), you can also get to it by choosing Tools, OLE Object View (see Figure 4.6).

Fig. 4.5
Internet Explorer 3.0
is also an excellent
Web browser.

Fig. 4.6
You can access the
OLE Object Viewer
from the Visual J++
Studio environment by
choosing Tools, OLE
Object View.

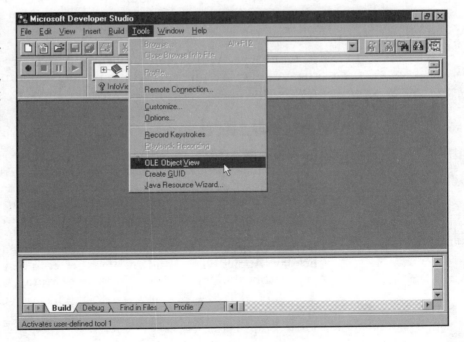

In Figure 4.7, you can see the OLE 2 Object View window. Here, you see a list of available OLE and ActiveX aware programs. I clicked the Microsoft DAO (Data Access Objects) that are included with Visual J++.

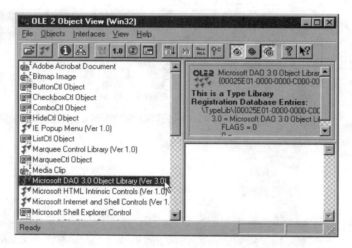

Next, you see a list of TypeInfos (function groups) as well as functions available within each group (such as CreateDatabase), as shown in Figure 4.8. You also see a function prototype that can help you make calls to the OLE/ActiveX control.

The OLE Object Viewer is an excellent and necessary tool for ActiveX programming. With it, you can often debug applications that make ActiveX calls.

Applet Wizard

The Applet Wizard is available inside the Visual J++ environment. With it, you can create complicated applets in a fraction of the time it would take to develop them from scratch. To run the Applet Wizard, you must create a new project. Click the New icon to open the New dialog box, and choose Project Workspace (see Figure 4.9).

The New Project Workspace dialog box appears (see Figure 4.10). Click Java Applet Wizard and give your project a name (such as AppWiz shown in Figure 4.10). Then click Create.

Fig. 4.8
You now see the functions and function prototypes available through ActiveX.

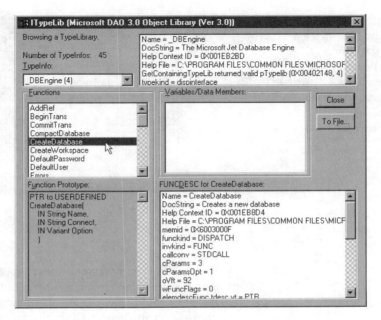

Fig. 4.9
You must create a new project workspace to use the Applet Wizard in Visual J++.

Click here to open the dialog box

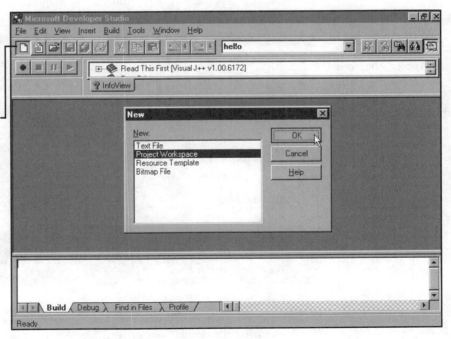

Fig. 4.10
By choosing Java Applet Wizard in the New Project Workspace dialog box, you can start the Applet building process.

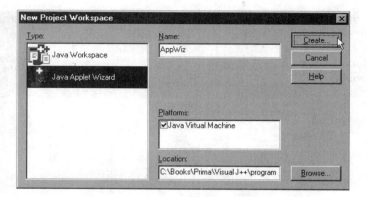

You are now in a five-step process that allows you to build an Applet using the Applet Wizard:

1. Indicate if you want this class to function as an applet, or as both a stand alone application and an applet, as shown in Figure 4.11. Also indicate if Visual J++ should leave comments (in which you can place work or explain what's being generated) in the generated Java code. Usually (especially at first), you should leave comments in.

Fig. 4.11
The first step of the Applet Wizard is to determine if you want your applet to function as an application, and if you want comments.

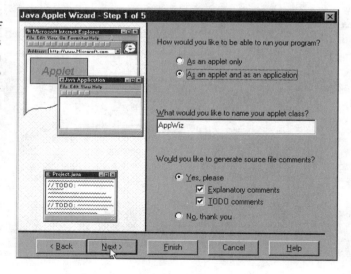

2. Determine whether Visual J++ should generate an HTML file for you, and what the dimensions of your Java Applet should be within the HTML document (see Figure 4.12). Usually, you want an HTML file generated for you. You can make your dimensions larger to span more of the Web page.

Fig. 4.12
The second step of
the Applet Wizard is
to determine the
width and height of
the document in the
Web page.

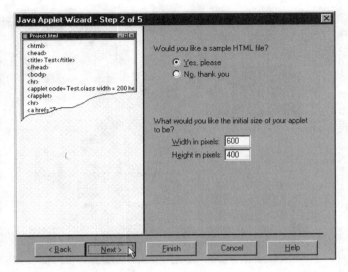

3. Now you need to answer the questions shown in Figure 4.13, which are described below:

- *Do you want your application multi-threaded?* Usually you do, because this enables your application to function a little smoother and also allows multiple Java methods to run at the same time, if needed.

- *Would you like bitmap animation support?* Bitmap animation is one of the most complicated processes in Java, but Visual J++ makes it easy by automatically coding animation and including some sample pictures for you to replace with your own. If you don't require bitmap animation in your application, though, click no.

- *What events would you like prototyped?* You can code for these events if they occur.

NOTE:
If a lot of these concepts are foreign to you, don't worry. They will be covered later in this book.

4. Supply any parameters to your applet, as shown in Figure 4.14. (Often, you won't have any.)

Fig. 4.13
The third step of the Applet wizard deals with multi-threaded support, animation, and event coding in your Applet.

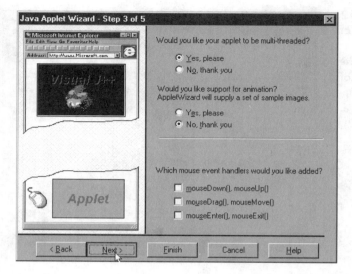

Fig. 4.14
Step four of the Applet Wizard is to provide parameters.

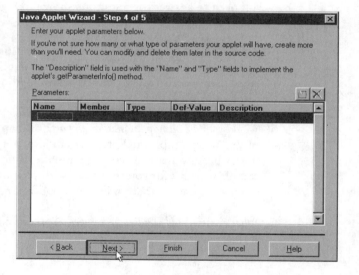

5. Enter comment information that can be retrieved by a `getAppInfo` Java statement. In Figure 4.15, I used the default `Name`, `Author`, and `Created By` clauses already provided by the Applet Wizard.

When you're finished, the Applet Wizard will display the New Project Information window (see Figure 4.16). You can review the choices you made throughout the Applet Wizard before actually generating an Applet.

Fig. 4.15
The last step of the Applet Wizard is to enter comment information about your application.

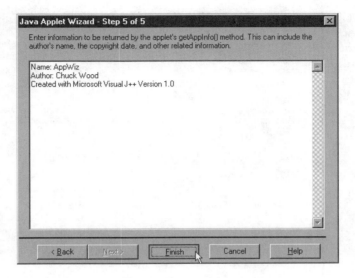

Fig. 4.16
Use the New Project Information window to review information you entered in the Applet Wizard.

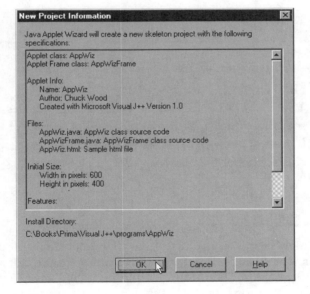

Visual J++ then generates an applet for you, as shown in Figure 4.17. You then must go through all the TODO statements and the code that's specific to your application.

The Applet Wizard is a great way to generate reasonably complicated code in an extremely short amount of time. Visual J++ has really come through with such a tool.

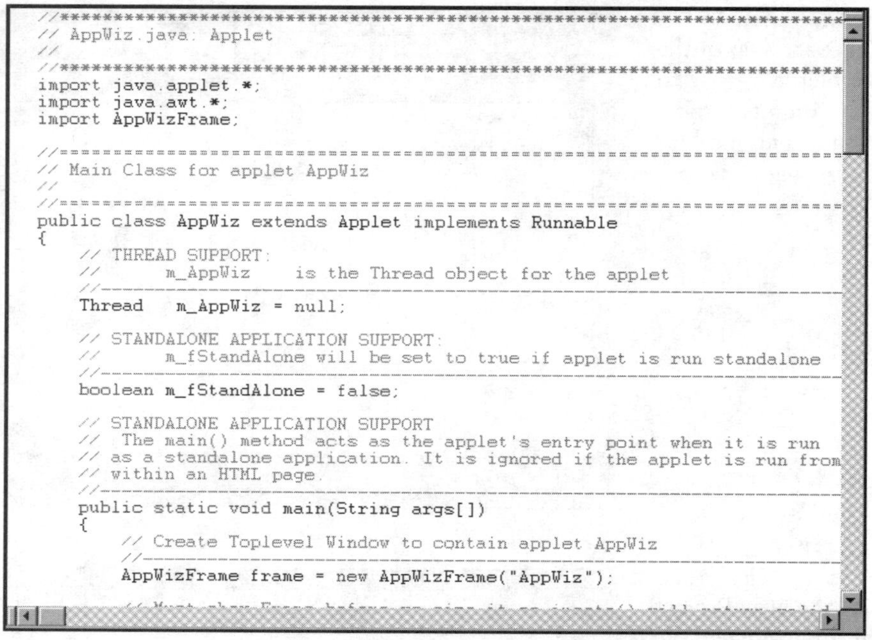

Fig. 4.17
Code is then generated for you in the Applet Wizard.

```
//****************************************************************
// AppWiz.java: Applet
//
//****************************************************************
import java.applet.*;
import java.awt.*;
import AppWizFrame;

//================================================================
// Main Class for applet AppWiz
//================================================================
public class AppWiz extends Applet implements Runnable
{
    // THREAD SUPPORT:
    //      m_AppWiz     is the Thread object for the applet
    //------------------------------------------------------------
    Thread    m_AppWiz = null;

    // STANDALONE APPLICATION SUPPORT:
    //      m_fStandAlone will be set to true if applet is run standalone
    //------------------------------------------------------------
    boolean m_fStandAlone = false;

    // STANDALONE APPLICATION SUPPORT
    //  The main() method acts as the applet's entry point when it is run
    //  as a standalone application. It is ignored if the applet is run from
    //  within an HTML page.
    //------------------------------------------------------------
    public static void main(String args[])
    {
        // Create Toplevel Window to contain applet AppWiz
        //--------------------------------------------------------
        AppWizFrame frame = new AppWizFrame("AppWiz");
```

NOTE:
There is also a Resource Wizard that allows you to add menus, dialogs, and so on to your Visual J++ Applet. However, resources and the Resource Wizard are beyond the scope of this book.

Conclusion

Visual J++ has a host of tools available to the developer. JVC and JView are used internally, but still can be useful outside the Visual J++ environment. The Internet Explorer 3.0 is a wonderful tool that allows you to test your Visual J++ applets as well as easily surf the Web. The OLE Object viewer is a necessary tool for ActiveX development and, especially, for ActiveX debugging. Finally, the Applet Wizard is a great tool to generate complicated applets in a short amount of time.

To get a better handle on some of the topics discussed in this chapter, you may want to check out Chapters 9, 10, and 11.

Chapter 5

Using Classes and Packages in Visual J++

Programming in Visual J++ is impossible without a proper understanding of classes. Classes are the heart of object-oriented programming, and Visual J++ requires you to encapsulate every method (function) and attribute (variable) in a class. This chapter discusses classes, packages and projects, and modifiers used in Visual J++ and Java.

Understanding Classes

Classes are data and functions grouped together into a single entity. Classes often represent "real world" entities. The data in a class is the attributes and states that make up the entity. Tied to the class, then, are the class functions (or methods) that manipulate the class data. Figure 5.1 visually depicts a class structure.

Fig. 5.1
Data and functionality are tied together in a a class structure.

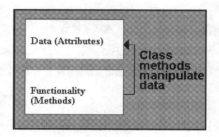

In Visual J++, for example, if you want a program to take surveys over the Internet, you need a Survey class that would have the following type of structure:

```
public class Survey {

// Attributes (A.K.A. variables) of Survey
    String surveyQuestion = "How do you like my book on" +
            " a scale of 1 to 10?";
    String mailToID = "jmanager@provider.net";


// Methods (A.K.A. functions) of Survey
    public void SurveyQuestion( ) {
        String survey_results = new String ("");
        // ... Entry code here
        EMailResults( survey_results );
    }

    public void EMailResults( String survey_results ) {
        // ... Mail the results of the survey here
    }
}
```

The preceding class is a shell for a survey system written in Visual J++. The survey questions are taken in during the init method. The attributes surveyQuestion and mailToID are then declared and assigned values. init ( ) initializes the Survey template and then calls the EMailResults ( ) method that will mail the results of the survey. (Note that EMailResults and init are not filled in yet. The functionality will be added later in the book.)

Of course, there are still huge holes in the survey system. Chapter 13, "Writing a Survey Application," discusses a true survey system.

Instantiating a Class

As soon as you define a class, you can use that class as a data type. Consider the following code:

```
public class SurveySystem {
    public static void init( ) {
        Survey s = new Survey ( );
        String address = s.mailToID;
    }
}
```

Notice that in the init ( ) method, s has been declared as a attribute of type Survey. This is called *instantiation*. Instantiation is when you make an "instance" of a class by declaring it as a data type. Java allows most classes to be instantiated using the same technique used when declaring data types like integers.

Using Attributes

Attributes are the data inside the class. They're often called columns, fields, or variables. To understand attributes in Visual J++, you need to understand how attributes are declared, how they're accessed outside of the class, how scope relates to attributes, and how attributes are initialized.

Attribute Declaration

Although attributes can be declared anywhere in your class definition, attributes are usually declared before any methods in your class. This is so other developers can look at all the data elements of your class easily.

Notice in the `SurveySystem` class declared previously, the `address` variable was assigned to `s.mailToID`:

```
Survey s = new Survey ( );
        String address = s.mailToID;
```

In this code, `s` is declared as an instance of `Survey`, and then `address` is assigned the `mailToID` string found in the `s` instance of the `Survey` class. The period (.) here is called the "period operator." It signifies that the attribute on the right side of the operator is found in a class on the left side of the operator.

Using Null

All data types are initialized to some value. However, all classes are initialized to null. *Null* is a value that is not zero and is not an empty string. Rather, a null value indicates that a class has not been assigned yet.

Null classes cannot be accessed. You get a `NullPointerException` exception error. (Errors are covered in more detail in Chapter 6, "Error Handling in Visual J++.") You must first initialize a class before accessing any of its attributes.

Final Attributes

The `final` keyword is used with attributes to declare constants. For example, consider the following declaration:

```
public class Class1 {
    final int number = 7;
    //...rest of functions and methods
}
```

The `number` attribute is not set to 7, and then `number` can't be changed throughout the rest of the program. Furthermore, `number` is not allowed to be changed by other classes, either. If possible, the Visual J++ compiler will convert `final` attributes and attributes to constant values.

Calling Methods

Methods are the functions that act on data. In an object-oriented language like Visual J++, you should define the data elements for your class and only then define what functions should alter or retrieve those data elements.

A method declaration indicates the first line of a method. The syntax of a method declaration is as follows:

```
modifiers returnType methodName (arguments) {
    // Method code goes here
}
```

The following table describes each component of a method:

Component	Description
modifiers	*Modifiers* **affect the method in some way. Some modifiers, like** `public`**, deal with the scope of the method.** (*Scope* **determines which other functions can call the method.) Some modifiers are covered later in this chapter, and some that deal with inheritance and polymorphism are covered in the next chapter.**
returnType	**The** *return type* **is the data type or class that is returned to the calling method. For example, if you had the following method:**
	public class ChucksMathMethods {
	public `double` **square (float a) {**
	double answer = a * a;
	return answer;
	}
	}
	The `double` **in the function declaration tells Visual J++ that the** `square` **method returns a double.**
methodName	**The** *method name* **is simply what the method is called. In the previous example, the method name is** `square`**.**
arguments	*Arguments* **are passed to the method from the calling program. In the previous example,** `a` **is a float variable that is passed to** `square`**.**

To call the previous function from within the same class, you could simply type something like the following code:

```
double twoSquared = square(2.0);
```

If you want to call this function from another class, type something like the following code:

```
double twoSquared = ChucksMathMethods.square(2.0);
```

Notice that you can call a method from another class by using the period operator, just as you would access an attribute that's outside a class.

Using *this*

C and C++ use the `this` keyword to refer to a current instance of a class. Calling a keyword "this" is very confusing and hard to teach, yet Java still adopted it. `this` is a keyword in Java that refers to the current instance of the class, just like in C and C++. Often, when a method needs to pass itself to another method, `this` is used to refer to itself. For example, if you were instantiating one class that required that the current class be passed to it, you could code the following:

```
Class1 {
     fillMeIn(class2 secondClass) { ... }
}
Class2 {
    doClass1( ) {
        Class1 c1;
        c1.fillMeIn(this);
    }
}
```

As you can see by the preceding example, `Class1` has a function called `fillMeIn` which requires an argument of type `Class2`. `Class2` on the other hand has a method that has an instance of `Class1` in it. Here, `Class2` uses the `this` keyword to pass itself to `Class1`. Although this is quite confusing, `this` is a useful (if ambiguous) keyword, and you'll be seeing more of it in this book and in future Visual J++ development.

Using Packages in Visual J++

Sometimes, you'll have a group of classes that act together. You can group related classes together into a package. A *package* is simply a group of classes that often interact with each other.

Understanding Java Packages

Visual J++ is a superset of the Java language. As such, it contains all the Java packages. These packages include java.lang, java.awt, java.io, java.net, java.util, java.applet, java.awt.peer, and java.awt.image. Each package contains one or more classes (see Figure 5.2). You have already used several classes in the java.lang package, including Math and String.

Fig. 5.2
This is a small segment of the classes inside the Java language (java.lang) package.

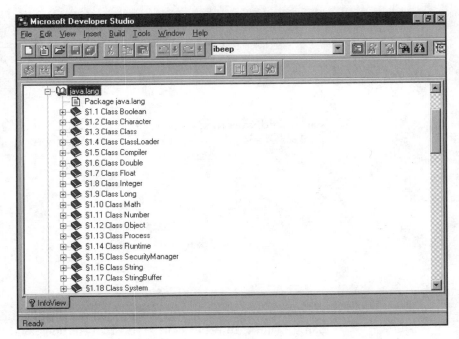

Importing Classes and Packages

The import command is used to reduce the amount of package and class referencing you need to do in a program. Both classes and packages can be imported. The format for the import command is as follows:

import *class*

or

import *package.**

If you want to import the Graphics class of the java.awt package, you could issue the following import statement:

import java.awt.graphics;

If, on the other hand, you want to import the entire java.awt package, your import statement would look like this:

```
import java.awt.*;
```

Without import, your code could get cumbersome. For example, in the following code:

```
public class HelloWorld {
    public void paint(java.awt.Graphics g) {
        g.drawString("Hello world!", 50, 25);
    }
}
```

you would have to specify java.awt before each class in the java.awt package. Using import, you could reference your classes (like Graphics) as follows:

```
import java.awt.*;
public class HelloWorld {
    public void paint(Graphics g) {
        g.drawString("Hello world!", 50, 25);
    }
}
```

Notice that the Graphics class needed to be fully qualified when not using import. In other words, you had to type java.awt.Graphics every time you wanted to use the Graphics class inside the java.awt package. When you use import, you don't need to fully qualify your classes. This can make development somewhat faster and easier to maintain.

> **WARNING:**
> If you're importing one or more packages that contain classes with the same names, you may need to fully qualify the class name. The Visual J++ classes don't contain any duplicate function names, but your own packages or third-party packages might.

NOTE:
C and C++ programmers often confuse `import` with the `#include` meta-command. In truth, they are quite different. `#include` actually makes a copy of the included file into your source code at compile time. `import`, on the other hand, simply allows you shortcuts to referencing. You could write an entire Java program without using `import`. The only drawback would be that you would have to type in longer class names. On the other hand, you'd be hard-pressed to write a C or C++ program without using `#include` because C and C++ don't let you reference any areas outside of the immediate source code without at least a function prototype.

Using Projects

Today, most sophisticated development environments use project or make files. *Projects* are unique to Visual J++, and are required for every compile in Visual J++. When you begin a compile, Visual J++ tells you that a project workspace has not been defined, and asks you if you want to define a project workspace (see Figure 5.3).

Fig. 5.3
You must define a project before compiling in Visual J++.

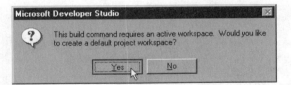

When you define a project, you can see the project displayed in the Project Workspace window (see Figure 5.4).

You can either dock the Project Workspace window at the top, bottom, left, or right of your main window, or you can float it, as shown in Figure 5.5. When you right-click a classes entry, a shortcut menu appears that allows you to change the properties of the Project Workspace window or add a class.

If you right-click a class inside a project, a shortcut menu appears that allows you to go to the definition of a class, add a method or attribute to a class, group class definitions by access, add a class, or change the Project Workspace properties (see Figure 5.6).

Fig. 5.4
The Project
Workspace window
allows you to view
classes and files found
inside your project.

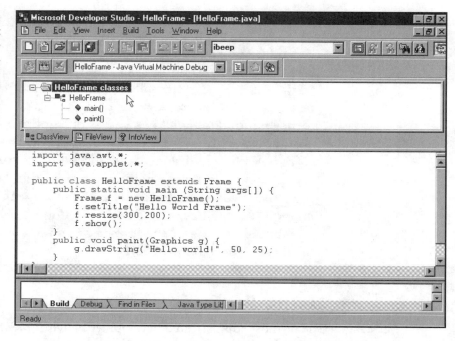

Fig. 5.5
Right-clicking the
class name in the
Project Workspace
window pops up a
shortcut menu that
allows you to add a
class or change the
settings of the
Project Workspace.

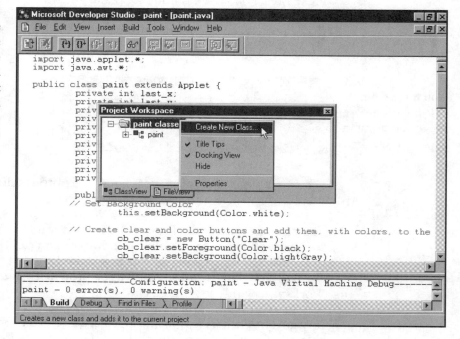

Fig. 5.6
In addition to adding
a class and Project
Workspace settings,
right clicking a
class allows you
to add methods
or attributes,
and to group
methods by access.

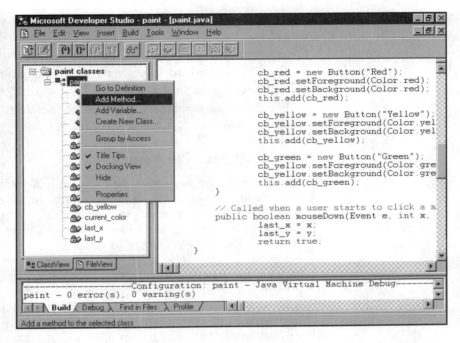

Choose Add Method from the shortcut menu. The Add Method dialog box appears (see Figure 5.7). In the Add Method dialog box, you
are prompted for information needed to define your class. (Modifiers
are discussed at the end of this chapter and in the next chapter.)

Fig. 5.7
The Add Method
dialog box prompts
you for information
needed to create your
modifier declaration.

NOTE:
Of course, you don't *have* to use the Add Method dialog box to add a method to your class. Some (myself included) find it faster to type the declaration in the Source window rather than use a dialog box to paint the declaration.

Projects versus Packages

Using the `package` statement at the beginning of your Visual J++ module allows you to group classes in that module together with classes in other modules. You must then put these modules in a separate directory or to be accessed by the Visual J++ compiler. The entire Java library, which is included with Visual J++, is grouped into packages.

Packages are somewhat hard to work with. First, all class members must be in a single directory. Second, each of those class definitions must contain a `package` statement to indicate that they're part of a package instead of a stand-alone class. Contrast this with projects, where you simply add the Java program or Java class to the project listing. Microsoft did a very good thing by adding project support.

You could argue that packages should be avoided. The only advantage that packages give you is that:

- Packages allow you to group related classes together. This is accomplished more easily and intuitively by using projects.

- Packages allow one class to share another class's variables when the default scope or the `private protected` scope is used. However, allowing another class of the same package to change your system's attributes violates encapsulation

Class Paths

When you first declare a project, you may get the following errors:

```
C:\Books\Prima\Visual Java\Webpages\HelloFrame.java(4,28) : error
➥J0049: Undefined name 'Object'

C:\Books\Prima\Visual Java\Webpages\HelloFrame.java(4,28) : error
➥J0044: Cannot find definition for class 'Object'
```

NOTE:
Object **in these error messages refers to java.lang. All classes in Java are inherited from the Object class inside java.lang. Inheritance will be covered in Chapter 6.**

If you inherit a class other than Object**, then this error will report that error instead. For example, if you were coding a Web applet, the undefined name would be** Applet **instead of** Object **in both error messages.**

If you get an undefined Object error, it probably means that you don't have the correct class path set in your project settings. A *class path* is the path to the Java and Visual J++ classes. To change the settings for your project, choose <u>B</u>uild, <u>S</u>ettings (see Figure 5.8).

Fig. 5.8
You change your project settings by choosing <u>B</u>uild, <u>S</u>ettings.

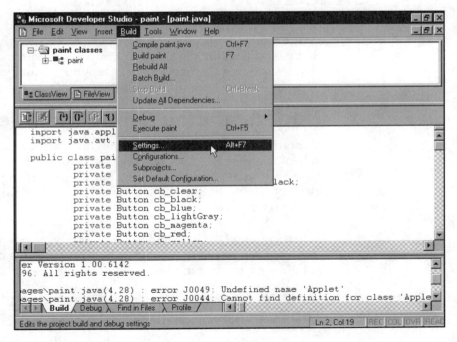

The Project Settings dialog box appears. In the <u>C</u>lass Path Directories text box, enter the path for the Visual J++ class library (see Figure 5.9). (You probably have it set to C:\WINDOWS\JAVA\CLASSES or C:\MSDEV\CLASSES depending on which beta or production version you installed, and which directory you have chosen to install to.)

Fig. 5.9
You set your class
path in the Project
Settings dialog box.

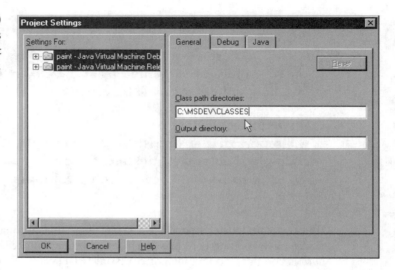

Understanding Modifiers

Modifiers are keywords placed before a class, method, or attribute declaration that change the behavior of that class, method, or attribute. Some modifiers are discussed here; others are discussed in Chapter 4, "Understanding Object Oriented Design in Visual Java," and in Chapter 7, "Understanding Threads."

Understanding Scope Modifiers

Scope refers to how a attribute or method can be accessed from outside of it's method, class, or package. Scope is often called "visibility." If you say an attribute or method has scope to a method or that an attribute or method is visible to another method, you mean that it can be referenced from that method.

Visual J++ and Java let you declare several types of scope by using *scope modifiers* to tell the compiler how much access other methods should have to class methods and attributes. Some scopes are covered here and others are discussed in the next chapter.

Public Scope

Declaring a class, attribute, or method *public* means that the methods of any other class can access the public class, attribute, or method. Most classes are public and can be used anywhere. The following is an example of public declarations:

```
public class HelloWorldApplet extends Applet {
    public int x=50, y=25;
    public void paint(Graphics g) {
        g.drawString("Hello world!", x, y);
    }
}
```

In this code, the class `HelloWorldApplet`, the integers x and y, and the method `paint( )` are all declared `public`.

> **WARNING:**
> While teaching a class, a student asked me why you wouldn't want all of your classes, attributes, and methods public. That way you could access them from anywhere. Indeed, many languages, like COBOL and BASIC are based on global access for every variable and method. (Methods in COBOL and BASIC are called paragraphs and subroutines.)
>
> The problem you have with all public variables (and the reason why COBOL and BASIC are dying or being remade into languages like Visual Basic) is that if you use too much public scope, you violate a principal called *encapsulation*. Encapsulation means that all the functionality and data are grouped together (in a class) *and* that the data is never modified except through the class function.
>
> Team development is facilitated by encapsulation because you can assign modules of the system to different developers. Those developers will need to know very little about the other modules of the system. Maintenance is also *greatly* enhanced, because tracking data bugs is more centralized, and therefore easier to do.
>
> Chapter 4 discusses encapsulation at length.

Private Scope

Private scope means that an attribute or method can only be accessed within it's own class. (Classes can't be private.) This means that if a method is declared private, only other methods in it's own class are allowed to call it. No method outside the class is allowed to execute the method. If an attribute is declared private, that means it can only be accessed by methods inside the same class as the attribute.

NOTE:
Private access to variables is strongly encouraged. Your control of bugs and error tracking is greatly enhanced if a variable is not accessed by any other method that uses your class. Furthermore, you can more tightly control what gets in and out of a class if you encapsulate your class.

Methods should be declared private if no other program should be allowed to call them. Declaring a method private often reduces the amount of error checking needed on that method. For example, if I declare a private method, than I can be pretty sure what goes into it. On the other hand, if I declare a public method, I need to do a lot of error checking to make sure that any arguments passed to my method are valid.

Default Scope

The *default* scope is used when no other scope modifier is declared. If no other scope is declared, then a class, attribute, or method is visible throughout the entire class and package, but nowhere else.

NOTE:
Although projects are typically better suited for grouping classes together than Java packages, packages can be used to declare "friend" classes that have access to each other's variables.

However, the default scope modifier is usually a bad idea because it violates class encapsulation. Often, the default modifier is used in a package-less system as a double for a private declaration.

Understanding the Static Modifier

You use the *static* modifier to allow the use of methods and attributes without the need to instantiate the class. The static keyword is often used to save space if only one version of the data is needed at any given time, and to share variables between different instantiations of the same class.

Although classes are not allowed to be declared static, you can in effect make a static class by declaring all the attributes and methods inside a class to be static. (This is done in java.lang.Math.)

Static Attributes and Instantiation

You can use the static keyword when declaring class attributes. Static attributes are different than "normal" class attributes in the following ways:

- ◑ Every attribute that uses the static keyword is automatically instantiated once and only once. Every instance of a class shares the same static attributes. This means that every time any instance of a class changes that attribute, it is changed for all classes.

- ◑ Every static attribute is available to any class without instantiating the class.

- ◑ Although they don't need to be, static attributes (being as close as Visual J++ gets to global attributes) should be initialized with a new command when declared if they're classes.

To illustrate this point about static attributes, say you want to assign an integer from Class1 to Class2. The following code can accomplish this without using static attributes:

```
public class Class2 {
    public static void main (String argv[ ]) {
        int num = new integer( );
        Class1 FirstClass = new Class1( );
        num = FirstClass.number;
        //...rest of method
    }
}
class Class1 {
    int number;
    //...rest of code
}
```

> **NOTE:**
> Although the preceding code will compile, it won't really run because there's no logic in the methods. The code is used to illustrate the use of modifiers.

When using another class's attributes, as in Class 2, you must first declare an instance of that class. Notice the `FirstClass` is declared as a `Class1` type. Now, see a similar example when using class attributes:

```
public class ClassTwo {
    public static void main (String argv[ ]) {
        int num;
        num = ClassOne.number;
        //...rest of method
    }
}
class ClassOne {
    static int number;
    //...rest of functions and methods
}
```

Now, you don't need to instantiate `Class1` at all when using `Class1` attributes. The attribute is already instantiated in the `Class1` declarations. Remember, however, that you don't always want to use static attributes. Say you had a `Class3` declaration that also used the `Class1.number` attribute:

```
public class Class3 {
    public static void main (String argv[ ]) {
        int newNumber = new integer( );
        newNumber = 7;
        Class1.number = newNumber;
        //...rest of method
    }
}
```

I have now set `Class1.number` to 7 *for all classes*! This means that, without knowing it, if `Class3` were invoked, the `Class2` num attribute in the main function would be reset to 7. Therefore, `Class3` has affected

Class2 functionality without an explicit call to Class2. This may be desirable, but if you want each instance of a class to be independent of other instances, you cannot use a static attribute, and you must instantiate each class before using it.

Although final attributes don't need to be declared static, it makes sense and it's also often done by the Visual J++ compiler implicitly. If the number is the same constant throughout each class, then static attributes will share the same area in memory. Furthermore, other classes can access the constant value without having to instantiate your class.

Static Methods

Static methods are methods that can be accessed from other classes without the need to instantiate the class. Static methods are great to use because you don't need the overhead of instantiating a class to call them, but there are a couple restrictions:

- Static methods can only use static attributes and local variables. All non-static attributes have not been instantiated, and therefore cannot be accessed by a method that may or may not have been instantiated.

- Static methods cannot call other non-static class methods. Again, because the class may or may not have been instantiated, a static method must not call non-static methods.

- Because it isn't instantiated, a static method cannot use the this keyword. Because this refers to the current instantiation of a class, and your method may not have been instantiated, it may not use the this keyword.

Static methods may be invoked through an instance of the containing class as follows:

```
class1 {
    static myfunc( ) { ... }
}
...
class2 {
    class1 c1
    c1.myfunc( )
}
```

You could also not instantiate a static class method and use the entire qualified function name to call a static function:

```
class1 {
    static myfunc( ) { ... }
}
...
class2 {
    class1.myfunc( )
}
```

Notice that I didn't need to instantiate class1 to call a static method within class1.

> **WARNING:**
> Don't use static methods too frivolously. Often, function *can* be executed without instantiation, so the developer makes them static. Later, stronger links are added to the function that require them to be part of an instance. This change would require heavy maintenance involving the instantiation of a class every time the function is used.
>
> Rather, you should ask if a function *should* be executed without a class being declared. This is often the case when a class is simply a collection of stand-alone functions (such as java.lang.Math, where all the methods are stand-alone math functions).

Understanding the Native Modifier

The *native modifier* is used on methods only when the method you're declaring is actually written in an outside language, such as C++, and currently exists on the Java server machine. The native keyword allows you to declare a function written in another language as a modifier for a method.

The native modifier is beyond the scope of this book, because the native functions will probably not be written in Java.

Conclusion

In this chapter, you learned about Visual J++ classes, packages and projects, and modifiers. However, the discussion of classes is far from over. Chapter 4, "Understanding Object Oriented Design in Visual J++," discusses the role of classes in object-oriented development. There, you'll learn some new modifiers and some additional syntax for declaring and using classes.

Chapter 6

Understanding Object-Oriented Design in Visual J++

As you have seen, every Visual J++ method must be contained inside a class. Furthermore, there are no global variables: every variable must be a class attribute or part of a method (which also must be part of a class). Classes can be considered the logical representation of objects, and the basis for object-oriented development. In fact, Visual J++ is an object-oriented language and *must* be written using object-oriented development.

Object-oriented development has reached buzz-word status. *Object-oriented development* deals with trying to translate real world objects (such as employee, paycheck, item, invoice, customer, and so on) into objects (or classes in Visual J++). Often, in advertisements and magazine articles, companies try to equate object-oriented development with good products. In truth, it takes a lot of analysis and design to develop a *well written* object-oriented system—usually more so than traditional structured and functional designs.

Object-oriented analysis (OOA) and object-oriented design (OOD) are somewhat beyond the scope of this book. However, a new advanced Visual J++ book from Prima publishing and myself (Chuck Wood) will be arriving at your bookstores soon. In the meantime, if you really need to write a complex Visual J++ system, be sure you invest some time on learning object-oriented design techniques. As mentioned, you can't help but deliver an object-oriented program or system with Visual J++. However, you should try to make it a *good* object-oriented program or system.

This chapter deals with some basic object-oriented constructs in Visual J++:

- Encapsulation, constructors, and scope

- Inheritance, multiple inheritance with interfaces, abstract classes, and final classes

- Polymorphism, method overloading and overriding, and attribute overriding

- Instances and the `instanceof` operator

- Object-oriented modifiers (abstract, final, protected, and private protected)

Encapsulation

Encapsulation deals with isolating classes from other classes. The idea behind encapsulation is that your class's attributes should not be accessible from other classes. If one class (classA) needs to modify the attributes of another class (classB), then classA should call a method within classB to modify the variables. That way, classB will be in control of its variables at all times. If you need to track down a problem with a class, setting the right breakpoint becomes easy rather than tedious.

There are two methods that object-oriented languages use to enforce encapsulation: scope and class constructors.

Scope

Scope is when you limit the access to a class attribute, method, or method variable. When designing a class, you should take care to not allow access to any attribute outside your class unless that attribute is constant (final) or unless your class doesn't care if the variable changes (such as an error code).

Say classA contains attribute1 that is used within method2. Classes classB, classC, and classD need to retrieve and modify this attribute. Figure 6.1 shows the non-encapsulated way to do this.

Fig. 6.1
Often, other classes need to view and modify attributes in a class.

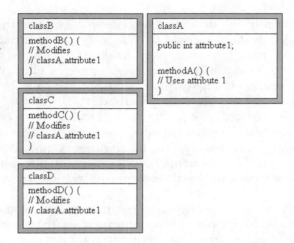

Now say that methodA detects a problem with attribute1. The developer of classA has no idea what other developer and what other class has referenced his attribute. Furthermore, if the attribute has a common name (such as type, x, and so on), then searching for all the places it was modified would be very cumbersome.

Now say that methodA was more encapsulated, attribute1 was private instead of public, and two methods were written to set and retrieve attribute1, as shown in Figure 6.2.

Fig. 6.2
A more encapsulated way to change an attribute is to allow public methods do the work.

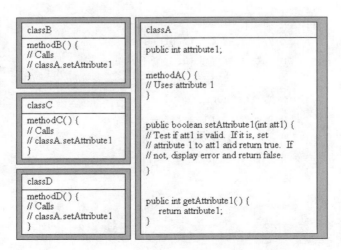

Now some of you might point out that this seems like more work up front, and you *may* be right. Instead of simply accessing an attribute, you had to write two methods which do the setting and retrieving for you.

If some checking or processing is desired *every time* that an attribute changes, then one method to change the attribute may actually be easier to write than to expect every developer to perform the same checks over and over again. However, even if it seems a little more cumbersome, encapsulating your attributes is worthwhile. Not only are you able to make sure the calling method sets the attribute properly, you're also able to notify the calling method with a return code or a displayed message that the value passed to it was invalid. This could make both debugging and development much easier as time goes on. (See what I mean about object-oriented development often requiring more thought than traditional development methodologies?)

Runtime errors are also easier to catch, because you only modify attributes in one place. You can trace the attribute modification from that one place rather than trying to track down which class modified your work. In short, although it requires some code and a little more thought, encapsulation will actually save you time in the long run, and maybe even in the short run.

Class Constructors

Constructors are methods with the same name as their classes. Constructors allow the developer to initialize a class when it is first declared (or constructed). For example, say you had a Customer class. You want to be able to assign a first name and last name right away in the constructor, so you write code similar to the following:

```
public class Customer {
    private String first_name;
    private String last_name;

// Here's the constructor
    Customer (String fname, String lname) {
        first_name = fname;
        last_name = lname;
    }
}
```

Now, to construct a Customer class, you simply need to code the constructor similar to the following:

```
Customer cust = new Customer("Chuck", "Wood");
```

Now, you can't ever declare a customer without also giving a first and last name. (The section "Overloading Methods," later in this chapter will discuss how to have multiple constructors for the same class.)

Constructors have the following format:

```
public ClassName (arg1, arg2,...) { ...
```

Constructors are methods that have the following properties:

- Constructors are always named the same as the class, just like C++.

- Constructors are not allowed to return a value, so no return data type (even void) is allowed to be declared. This is unique among methods. Every other method must declare a return data type, or void if no data type is returned.

- Constructors are usually declared public so that a class can be instantiated by other classes. An exception would be a class with two constructors; one public and one private, the private being used by a static main function for instantiation. (If this is a little ambiguous to you, read on. This chapter delves into some of these topics in the "Using Abstract Classes and Methods" section.

CAUTION:
Constructors cannot be declared native, abstract, static, synchronized, or final. Also, constructors usually are not declared private because then constructors could not be used outside their own class.

Inheritance

Inheritance is the cornerstone of object-oriented development. When one class (classA) is inherited from another class (classB), classA is a child, descendent, type, or subclass of classB. Examples are easiest to use here. Say you have two types of customers: corporate and personal. The methods and attributes in the classes would probably look something like what is shown in Figure 6.3.

Fig. 6.3
PersonalCustomer
and
CorporateCustomer
are inherited from
Customer.

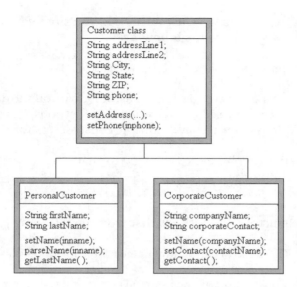

As you can see by the chart in Figure 6.3, all Customers would share certain attributes, but PersonalCustomer and CorporateCustomer have different attributes.

The way to implement inheritance in Visual J++ is by using the `extends` keyword. If PersonalCustomer `extends` Customer, then PersonalCustomer is inherited from Customer. Listing 6.1 shows the Visual J++ code to handle this situation. Lines of code using the `extends` keyword are in boldface type.

> **NOTE:**
> Listing 6.1 contains code that will be discussed throughout the rest of this chapter, so if you see some code that seems ambiguous, all will be explained as you continue reading.
>
> Also, remember that there is only one public class allowed per Java file. (This is a Java leftover restriction that I hope Microsoft does away with eventually! With the use of projects rather than packages, it simply isn't needed anymore.) As a result, be sure to split up the listing into separate files when building your project.

```
public abstract class Customer {
    protected String addressLine1;
    protected String addressLine2;
    protected String city;
    protected String state;
    protected String ZIP;
    protected String phone;
    protected double sales;

    public Customer ( ) {
        addressLine1 = "";
        addressLine2 = "";
        city = "";
        state = "";
        ZIP = "";
        phone = "";
        sales = 0;
    }
    public void setAddress(String line1, String line2,
        String city, String state, String ZIP) {
// 2 address line setAddress code goes here
    }
    public void setAddress(String line, String city,
        String state, String ZIP) {
        // single address line setAddress code goes here
    }
    public String getAddress( ) {
        // Returns the four line address
        return addressLine1 + "\n"
            + addressLine2 + "\n"
            + city + " " + state + " " + ZIP;

    }
    public final void setPhone(String phone) {
        // setphone code goes here
    }
// The abstract modifier says that this method
// to be executed by subclasses.
    public abstract void setName(String name);
}

public final class PersonalCustomer extends Customer {
    private String firstName;
    private String lastName;
    private float sales;
```

continues

Listing 6.1
Continued

```
public PersonalCustomer ( ) {
    super();
    firstName = "";
    lastName = "";
    sales = 0;
}
public void setName(String name) {
    // call parseName to set firstName and lastName
}
public void parseName(String name) {
    // set firstName and lastName from a passed name
}
public String getAddress( ) {
    // Returns a three line address
    return addressLine1 + "\n"
            + city + " " + state + " " + ZIP;
}
public String getLastName( ) {
    return lastName;
}
}

public final class CorporateCustomer extends Customer {
    private String companyName;
    private String corporateContact;

    public CorporateCustomer ( ) {
        super();
        companyName = "";
        corporateContact = "";
        sales = 0;
    }
    public void setName(String name) {
        // sets companyName
    }
    public void setContact(String name) {
        // sets the corporateContact from a passed name
    }
    public String getContact( ) {
        return corporateContact;
    }
}
```

Now the CorporateCustomer objects and the PersonalCustomer objects can both access the setAddress and setPhone methods without having to instantiate a separate Customer. This is seen by the following code:

```
public void mymethod ( ) {
    PersonalCustomer me = new PersonalCustomer( );
    me.setName("Chuck Wood");
    me.setAddress("123 4th St.", "",
      "Anywhere", "US", "00000-0000");
    me.setPhone("(800) 555-1212");    // Call for information
}
```

As you can see, the me instance of the PersonalCustomer class has access to the setName, setAddress, and setPhone methods—two of which (setAddress and setPhone) are defined in the Customer superclass and one (setName) which is defined in the PersonalCustomer subclass.

Used properly, inheritance can cut *a lot* of time and size from a big project. Rather than cutting and pasting code and having to make the same modification several times, inheritance lets you streamline your code by keeping common code centralized.

> **NOTE:**
> *All* classes are inherited for the java.lang.Object class unless another class is explicitly specified. Therefore,
>
> ```
> public abstract class Customer {
> ```
>
> **and**
>
> ```
> public abstract class Customer extends java.lang.Object{
> ```
>
> **do exactly the same thing.** Object **contains the following methods:** equals, getclass, hashCode, notify, notifyAll, toString, wait, clone, **and** finalize. **These methods are described in the alphabetical method listing in Chapter 13. You can also look up their functions in the Infoviewer in the Visual J++ environment, as shown in Figure 6.4.**
>
> **Because all classes have** Object **for an ancestor, it's good to know what methods are available as well as what methods (like** equals **and** toString**) need to be overridden to still function properly.**

Fig. 6.4
You can use the
Infoviewer to describe
what methods are in
the Object class.

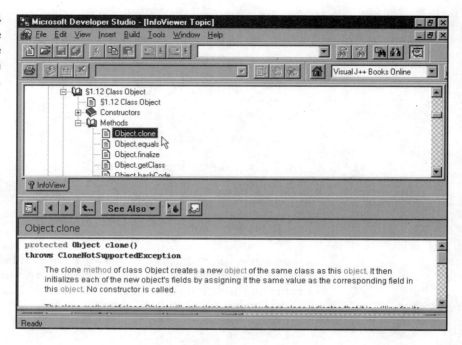

protected and *private protected* Modifiers

Some of you may have noticed the `private protected` modifier on the Strings in the Customer class in Listing 6.1. An attribute or method can be declared protected or private protected:

⚬ The `private protected` modifier allows you to access an attribute or method from with the same class (such as private). In addition, you can access a private protected attribute or method from within a subclass. For example, the PersonalCustomer class can access the `city` attribute in the Customer class without a problem.

⚬ The `protected` modifier allows you to access methods and classes from within the same class and from within subclasses (just as the private protected modifier does). The protected modifier allows any other class in the same package to also access your attribute.

The `protected` modifier let your subclasses control some of their inherited attributes and methods without going through the parent function.

final Classes

If a class is declared final, as the PersonalCustomer and CorporateCustomer classes are in Listing 6.1, then you are not allowed to inherit that class. This lets the developer control whether he wants any subclasses on his class.

Usually, final classes are declared that way if there is a strong reason not to override the constructor. If the constructor of a class plays an important role in setting a class up for use, then inheriting the class will automatically change the constructor to a new method. This new method may or may not call the superclass's constructor.

Using Abstract Classes and Methods

In Listing 6.1, notice the `abstract` keyword on the `class` declaration:

```
public abstract class Customer {
```

and on the `setName` method of the Customer class:

```
public void abstract setName(String name) {
```

An `abstract` method tells any function calling this method to look for the same method inside a subclass. `Abstract` methods can only exist within Abstract classes. An Abstract class means that the class can't be instantiated, but can only be inherited (extended). In this case, while the following statement:

```
PersonalCustomer me = new PersonalCustomer( );
```

is a valid statement, the following statement:

```
Customer me2 = new Customer( );
```

will generate an error. This is because you tried to make an instance of a Customer class, and the Customer class is abstract. Therefore, no instance can be made of the Customer class. However, the PersonalCustomer class is not abstract. Therefore, you can instantiate the PersonalCustomer class.

Consider the following code:

```
public void addCustomer ( String name, String type) {
    Customer me;
    if (type.equals("Corporate")) {
```

```
        me = new CorporateCustomer();
    }
    else if (type.equals("Personal")) {
        me = new PersonalCustomer();
    }
    else
        return;
    me.setName(name);
}
```

Notice that me is considered a Customer, but can also be instantiated to a subclass of Customer. Depending on the type passed, me is instantiated to either a PersonalCustomer instance or a CorporateCustomer instance. Then, the addname function is called. The addname function needed to be declared abstract for this to compile (otherwise, there's no way to know that every subclass of Customer has a setName method). However, once me is instantiated to the proper class, the proper addname function will run.

Instances, Casting, and the *instanceof* Operator

Often, you'll need to know if a variable is an instance of a class. For this, Visual J++ uses the instanceof operator. The instanceof operator checks to see wheter a object is an instance of a class or is an instance of a subclass. For example, say you made some changes to the addCustomer method:

```
public String addAnotherCustomer (String name,String type) {
    Customer me;
    if (type.equals("Corporate")) {
        me = new CorporateCustomer();
    }
    else if (type.equals("Personal")) {
        me = new PersonalCustomer();
    }
    else
        return null;
    me.setName(name);
    if (me instanceof CorporateCustomer)
        return "CC";
```

```
    else
        return "PC";
}
```

You then returned the type of class you instantiated based on information from the `instanceof` operator.

The `instanceof` operator is very useful for array processing when using subclasses. For example, an array of Customers needs to be processed, and their last name or corporate contact needs to be returned based on the type of customer they are. The following code could do this:

```
String person;
Customer custArray[];
// Previous code in method
for (int loop = 0; loop < custArray.length; loop++) {
    if (custArray[loop] instanceof PersonalCustomer) {
        PersonalCustomer PCHolder = (
            PersonalCustomer) custArray[loop];
        person =  PCHolder.getLastName( )
    }
    else if (custArray[loop] instanceof CorporateCustomer) {
        CorporateCustomer CCHolder =
                (CorporateCustomer) custArray[loop];
        person =  CCHolder.getContact( )
    }
    // ... Continue loop
}
//Continue method
```

Notice how you use the `instanceof` operator to determine the type of Customer. Then you define a temporary holder variable, and *cast* the customer array element to the specific class. The line of code:

```
PersonalCustomer PCHolder =
    (PersonalCustomer) custArray[loop];
```

casts a `custArray` element (of the Customer class) to a more specific PersonalCustomer instance. Then a specific method to PersonalCustomer (`getLastName`) can be used to retrieve the last name of the customer.

Superclasses are often casted into subclasses to make them more specific and able to use more functionality than contained in their superclass.

Polymorphism

Polymorphism is the ability of a subclass to change the behavior of the inherited methods based on both the needs of the class and the parameters that are passed. Polymorphism is achieved in Visual J++ through overriding attributes and methods, and by overloading methods.

Overriding Attributes and Methods

Notice in the Customer class in Listing 6.1, the getAddress routine is listed to return a four line address:

```
public String getAddress( ) {
    // Returns the four line address
    return addressLine1 + "\n"
            + addressLine2 + "\n"
            + city + " " + state + " " + ZIP;
}
```

However, a very similar function is in the PersonalCustomer class to return a three line address:

```
public String getAddress( ) {
    // Returns a three line address
    return addressLine1 + "\n"
            + city + " " + state + " " + ZIP;
}
```

Because both classes have the same name, return the same data type (String), and have the same arguments, the getAddress method in the PersonalCustomer class overrides the getAddress method in the Customer class. If you're using a PersonalCustomer class, a getAddress method call will only return a three line address. However, if you are using a CorporateCustomer (which does *not* override the getAddress method), then a four line address will be returned.

Similarly, the line in the PersonalCustomer class:

```
private protected float sales;
```

overrides the `sales` in the Customer class:

```
private protected double sales;
```

Class attributes are overriden by name. This is usually only done to change a data type, to change the scope or protection, or to change the value of a constant in a subclass.

The *super* Keyword

The `super` keyword is used to access a parent class.

- In the first line of a constructor, the `super( )` function can be called to call the superclass's constructor from a subclass constructor. Note that this can be done *only as the first line in a constructor*. Anywhere else will result in an error. A call to the parent constructor is done anyway unless you make a call to an overload constructor from within another constructor.

- You can reference a subclass's ancestor using the `super` keyword with dot notation:

```
super.x = 1
super.setX(1)
```

The `super` keyword is a neat way to set variables or call methods in an ancestor class that have been overridden by your subclass.

> **NOTE:**
> Some developers argue that too much use of the `super` keyword is indicative of poor object-oriented design. If you override your class attibutes or variables and then constantly have to reference the ancestors, perhaps the subclass really shouldn't override the parent class.

Overloading Methods

In Java, methods are called *not only* by their name, but also by their return type and parameters. In the Customer class in Listing 6.1, there are two methods called `setAddress`:

```
public void setAddress(String line1, String line2,
             String city, String state, String ZIP) {
    // 2 address line setAddress code goes here
}
public void setAddress(String line, String city,
             String state, String ZIP) {
    // single address line setAddress code goes here
}
```

However, one is used for a four line address with two street address lines and one is used for a three line address with a single street address line. If you call `setAddress` with five strings, the four line address `setAddress` method is called. If you call `setAddress` with four strings, the three line address `setAddress` method is called.

Method overloading is a very powerful and useful tool. Often, method overloading can be used to allow defaults to simplify method calls in classes that normally take many arguments. Also, method overloading can be used to handle different datatypes with a similar method call. For example, several `display (argument)` methods could be written to display floats, Dates, Strings, or other data types. Then, when a developer wants to display something, the proper display method will automatically be called depending on the data type.

Final Methods

Do you remember that final classes are classes that can't be inheritied? Final methods are similar. The final method in the Customer class, `setPhone`, cannot be overriden:

```
public final void setPhone(String phone) {
    // setphone code goes here
}
```

Usually, methods are declared final if the parent class is trying to protect its own variables. In the case of `setPhone`, assumably that phone number argument that is passed to the `setPhone` method goes through some edits before being stored as the Customer phone attribute. Because Customer can't be sure that it's child classes will be as meticulous when accepting phone numbers, the Customer class does not allow any descendent classes.

Using Interfaces

Say your boss asks you to write a Visual J++ Intranet Web applet that displays the corporate names of the top 10 customers in terms of sales. Your boss then hints that similar display requests will be coming soon and because he's been properly hyped about the power of Visual J++ and object-oriented development, he expects the other requests to take *a lot* less time. Right away, you make a list of things to do in Visual J+:

⊙ Make a SortArray abstract class, in case he makes you do similar stuff later.

⊙ Inherit the SortArray into your display applet.

Right there, you stop. You know that all Web applets are inherited from java.applet.Applet. Because Java doesn't support multiple inheritance, how are you going to implement this. (It looks like a lot of caffiene-induced long nights ahead, right? Not necessarily!) Figure 6.5 shows what you really want.

Fig. 6.5
Multiple inheritance is not allowed in Visual J++, but you can get around this restriction with interfaces.

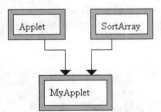

In fact, there are a lot of cases where you want to borrow the functionality of one class while at the same time using the functionality of another class. Because MyApplet already is inherited from Applet, I can't also inherit from SortArray. Java's and Visual J++'s answer to multiple inheritance situations is *interfaces*. Interfaces are a lot like abstract classes, and are defined by the word "interface" rather than "class." Interfaces are "empty" abstract modules that you fill in with your subclass when they're inherited. You still have to write a class that sorts objects, but then you write an interface between the two classes.

Before you begin, there are some things you should know about interfaces:

- All interfaces are abstract and can't be instantiated. Even if you don't use the `abstract` modifier on the class name, an interface, by definition, is still abstract.

- Interfaces are not allowed to have non-static class attributes. Interfaces are designed to hold functionality only, and not to replace classes. However, you are allowed to have static class attributes inside an interface.

- Unlike inheritance with the `extends` keyword, you can use multiple interfaces with a single class using the following syntax:

```
public class ClassName extends ParentClass
      implements Interface1, Interface2, ... {
```

- Interfaces can be inherited from each other and can implement other interfaces just like classes using the following syntax:

```
public interface Interface1 extends Interface2
      implements Interface3, Interface4 ... {
```

- Interfaces must be public and cannot be final because they are, by nature, abstract.

- Interface methods can't be declared native, static, synchronized, or final. Also, interface methods are all abstract and *cannot contain any lines of code!* All code for the interface must be written in the implementing class.

NOTE:
It was all fine until that last bullet point! Why write an interface that can't contain any code? If you need to code for every single interface method on each implementation, why bother implementing an interface at all?

That's a very good question, and a question that most Java books seem to dodge. The answer is that you *only* want to define abstract methods inside an interface. Then you can use the interface name as a data type in another class's method(s). Figure 6.6 shows that one class implements the interface and defines all the abstract functions. Then another class (the class you wanted to inherit from, but couldn't because it would involve multiple inheritance) uses the interface as a data type for an argument in one or several methods.

If you don't have a similar structure, then you aren't using interfaces correctly. Don't think of an interface as a parent class. Instead, think of an interface as a gateway between two classes so that the functionality of one class can be implemented by another class. Remember that an interface is implemented by one class, and used as a method argument in another class.

Keeping this in mind, the reason you use interfaces is so one class can implement methods from another class. Usually, you'll end up with small interfaces (with very few methods) acting as a bridge between two classes.

Fig. 6.6
Interfaces are implemented by one class and used as a method argument's data type in another class.

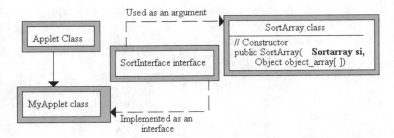

Listing 6.2 shows the code of an interface, and the rest of this chapter discusses it. (Bold code marks the declaration of each interface or class for readability.)

Listing 6.2
Object Bubble Sort

```
public interface SortInterface {
    public abstract boolean isGreaterThan (
            Object obj1, Object obj2);
}
public class SortArray {
    public SortArray(SortInterface si,
            Object object_array [ ]) {
// Go through the array several times
```

continues

Listing 6.2
Continued

```
            for (int loop1 = 0;
                 loop1 < object_array.length;
                 loop1++) {
              for (int loop2 = 0;
                   loop2 < object_array.length - loop1 -
➥1;
                   loop2++) {
// Swap array elements if they aren't in the right order
                if (si.isGreaterThan(object_array[loop2],
                               object_array[loop2 +
➥1])) {
                  Object holder;
                  holder = object_array[loop2];
                  object_array[loop2] =
                               object_array[loop2 +
➥1];
                  object_array[loop2 + 1] = holder;
                }
              }
            }
        }
    }
public class MyApplet extends java.applet.Applet
                                    implements
➥SortInterface {
    CorporateCustomer best_custs[];

    public void addCusts() {
       // calls in a loop to addObject[(Object) customer]
➥to
       // fill the array
    }
    public void displayCusts() {
        SortArray sa = new SortArray(
                 this, (Object[ ]) best_custs);
        // code to display customers 0 through 9 on the web
➥page
    }
// Since we want high sales on top, in this case,
// "greater than" means having lower sales.  The low sales
//  will be at the bottom of the array and the high sales
// will be in the first array elements.
    public boolean isGreaterThan (Object cust1,
                              Object cust2) {
        CorporateCustomer c1 = (CorporateCustomer) cust1;
        CorporateCustomer c2 = (CorporateCustomer) cust2;
```

```
        if (c1.sales < c2.sales) {
            return true;
        }
        return false;
    }
}
```

> **CAUTION:**
> Remember, you must separate all public interfaces and public classes into separate Java files; otherwise, your code will not compile correctly. They are combined here for readability.

As you can see by the first line of code in Listing 6.2, interfaces are declared interfaces using the `interface` keyword rather than the `class` keyword:

```
public interface SortInterface {
```

Rather than being extended, interfaces are implemented, as shown by the `MyApplet` declaration found in Listing 6.2:

```
public class MyApplet
    extends java.applet.Applet implements SortInterface {
```

Now look at the constructor for the SortArray class:

```
public SortArray(SortInterface si, Object object_array [ ]){
```

Notice that the SortArray requires you to pass it a `SortInterface` class. This is so the SortArray class can call the `isGreaterThan` method that it needs for testing:

```
if (si.isGreaterThan(
    object_array[loop2], object_array[loop2 + 1])) {
```

Now it's up to the class that implements the SortInterface class to determine the criteria for sorting objects. In this case, it's sorted on sales descending (so the highest sales are at the low end of the array, and the lowest sales are at the high end of the array):

```
// Since we want high sales on top, in this case,
// "greater than" means having lower sales.  The low sales
// will be at the bottom of the array and the high sales
// will be in the first array elements.
    public boolean isGreaterThan (
                    Object cust1, Object cust2) {
        CorporateCustomer c1 = (CorporateCustomer) cust1;
        CorporateCustomer c2 = (CorporateCustomer) cust2;
        if (c1.sales < c2.sales) {
            return true;
        }
        return false;
    }
```

Finally, you call the SortArray method that takes a SortInterface data type as an argument (in this case, it's the SortArray constructor). Of course, you still need to decide how to display this on the Web page.

```
public void displayCusts() {
    SortArray sa = new SortArray(
                    this, (Object[ ]) best_custs);
    // code to display customers 0 through 9 on the web page
}
```

You simply had to override one method, just as you would have had to do with multiple inheritance, and the sort routine will work with the class. Now if the boss wants a different sort order displayed every day, you can accomodate him and still (hopefully) get some sleep.

> **NOTE:**
> Some may view interfaces as a watered-down implementation of multiple inheritance. This is true, but with all the problems that multiple inheritance brings other languages, perhaps a limited form of multiple inheritance is called for.

Conclusion

This chapter covers some important aspects of object-oriented development in Visual J++. The importance of encapsualtion is stressed by using scope and constructors. Inheritance using both the `extends` keyword (for class to class inheritance) and the `implements` keyword (for interface inheritance) were also discussed.

Interfaces were discussed at length. Although it's a little hard to grasp their use, once you do your programs can become even more modular, building off each other with each new system developed.

Remember that a good grasp of object-oriented design is still needed. There will be a chapter devoted to object-oriented design in and advanced Visual J++ book by myself (Chuck Wood) and Prima Publishing due out sometime this year.

Chapter 7

Error Handling in Visual J++

Java has a unique method of error trapping. With Java, you can trap any errors you want using a construct known as a `try`, `catch`, `finally` block. You can also trigger an error using a `throw` statement. Finally, in addition to the system errors that can occur or are already defined for you, you can define your own errors that function just like the system errors.

Understanding Visual J++ Errors and Exceptions

Visual J++ and Java share the same error structure. As shown in Figure 7.1, Visual J++ contains two classes of errors. Errors descended from an Error class are called *Errors* (with a capitol E). Errors usually indicate a serious problem, like you're out of memory or the Java virtual machine is not responding. *Exceptions*, on the other hand, are usually situational and probably due to a programming situation rather than a system problem. Examples of Exceptions include end of file errors, divide by zero, and so on.

Figure 7.1
The Visuall J++ error structure has two categories of errors: Error and Exception.

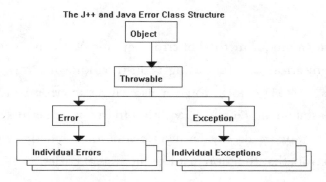

All Errors and Exceptions are descended from a Throwable class. The Throwable class allows the user to use a class to both trigger and catch. You will learn more about the Throwable class in the section "Creating Your Own Errors and Exceptions and the throw statement" later in this chapter.

Using Error Handling Statements

Java's error handling statements allow you to effectively trap and trigger errors. The try, catch, finally block allows you to trap errors that may occur while the throw statement lets you trigger an error.

The *try, catch, finally* Block

Exceptions and sometimes Errors often need to be trapped for processing Say you had the following code:

```
public static double myPower (double a, double b) {
    double answer = Math.pow(a, b);
    return answer;
}
```

Now you know that the method sometimes throws an
ArithmeticException, and you want to catch it, and perhaps give an
error message that is understood by the user. ArithmeticException
is a predefined Visual J++ Exceptions. (Tables 7.1 and 7.2 list Errors
and Exceptions.) You could use a try, catch, finally block to
catch any error that may have occurred. The following code could
accomplish this:

```
public static double myPower (double a, double b) {
    try {
        double answer = Math.pow(a, b);
        return answer;
    }
    catch (ArithmeticException e) {
        errorMessage(Double.toString(a) + " raised to the "
                + Double.toString(b)+ "!!!  " +
                "ArithmeticException occurs."
                + e.getMessage());
        return 0.0;
    }
    finally {
        errorMessage(Double.toString(a) + " raised to the "
                + Double.toString(b)
                + "!!!  An unknown error has occurred.  "
                + e.getMessage());
        return 0.0;
    }
}
```

Now, looking at the preceding code, instead of just executing a
method, first try a method. If an error occurs that you expected, you
can use the catch keyword to catch the error. The finally keyword is
used to catch any errors not anticipated.

> **TIP:**
> It's assumed that your `errorMessage` method is a method you wrote to display errors, whether that would be on an applet, at the bottom of the window, or whatever. Error message routines are necessary for any system and every frame. I would suggest using the showStatus Applet function to show a line of text at the bottom of the browser window, and perhaps a popup window for serious errors. More on graphical programming will be covered in Chapter 10, "Graphics, Graphical User Interfaces, and Animation."

Creating Your Own Errors and Exceptions, and the *throw* Statement

Unfortunately, you can't catch all the errors you want to. For example, if you take a negative number to a negative power, Visual J++ could give you a NaN as an answer. (In the Double and Float classes, NaN means that the number is Not a Number.) You may need to create your own statements to handle this. Consider the following code:

```
class myException extends Exception {
    public myException () {
        super ();    // Run the parent constructor.
    }
    public myException (String s) {
        super (s);    // Run the parent constructor.
    }
}


public static double myPower (double a, double b)
                       throws myException {
    try {
        double answer = Math.pow(a, b);
        // Test for Not a Number
        if (Double.isNaN(answer)) {
```

```
            throw new myException(
    "Can't take a fractional power of a negative number");
}

        return answer;

    }
    catch (ArithmeticException e) {
        System.out.println(Double.toString(a)
            + " raised to the " + Double.toString(b)+ "!!!   "
            + e.getMessage());
        return 0.0;
    }
    catch (myException e) {
        System.out.println(Double.toString(a)
            + " raised to the " + Double.toString(b)
            + "!!!  An invalid number was returned."
            + e.getMessage());
        return 0.0;
    }
    finally {
        errorMessage(Double.toString(a) + " raised to the "
            + Double.toString(b)
            + "!!!  An unknown error has occurred.   "
            + e.getMessage());
        return 0.0;

    }

}
```

The first class inherits from the Exception class. In this class, you are just defining a new exception for use in a system.

In the myPower method declaration in the preceding code, the throws keyword is used. The throws keyword indicates that an error is thrown during the execution of this function. Then, in the middle of the code, you use the throw keyword to trigger myException. Then a catch keyword is used to execute code if myException is thrown.

Although it may seem like a bit of work, exception handling in Java is easy to understand and maintain. It's also much more versatile than error and exception handling in other languages.

> **CAUTION:**
> If a method throws an error, the error *must* be caught every time the method is called by another method, or a syntax error will result. Often, you will see lines of code like the following:
>
> ```
> try { fis = new FileInputStream(selectedFile); }
> catch (FileNotFoundException e) { }
> catch (IOException e) { }
> ```
>
> Although the code will work, basically you have disabled and ignored any errors that result from opening a FileInputStream. (File I/O is covered in Chapter 12, "Input and Output with Files and Databases.")
>
> Ignoring errors is sometimes expedient, while testing for every thown error is often not necessary. However, by ignoring errors that occur, you may make debugging and run time error trapping a lot more difficult.

Visual J++ Errors

Java and Visual J++ define several Errors for you. Table 7.1 lists these Errors.

Table 7.1
Visual J++ Errors

Error	Package	Description
AbstractMethodError	java.lang	An attempt was made to call an abstract method or a method within an abstract class. Only methods inherited from abstract methods can be called.
AWTError	java.awt	A serious error has occurred when using the AWT package.
ClassCircularityError	java.lang	An ancestor class is trying to inherit one of it's descendent classes. This is not allowed.

Error	Package	Description
ClassFormatError	java.lang	**An invalid file format for a class has been detected.**
Error	java.lang	Error **is the parent class for all other error objects.**
IllegalAccessError	java.lang	**An attempt was made to use a class, variable, or method which is not available to the calling class.**
IncompatibleClass ➡ChangeError	java.lang	IncompatibleClass ➡ChangeError **is the parent class for all inter-class operational errors.**
InstantiationError	java.lang	**You tried to instantiate an abstract class or an interface. You can only instantiate classes that are inherited from abstract classes.**
InternalError	java.lang	**An internal error has occurred in the Java virtual machine.**
LinkageError	java.lang	LinkageError **is the parent for several other errors that involve multi-class operations. Linkage errors occur when a one class (Class1) has a dependency on another class (Class2), but Class2 was changed after Class1 was compiled.**
NoClassDefFoundError	java.lang	**A class definition could not be found.**
NoSuchFieldError	java.lang	**A specified field could not be found.**
NoSuchMethodError	java.lang	**A specified method could not be found.**
OutOfMemoryError	java.lang	**The Java Virtual Machine that you're running has run out of memory.**
StackOverflowError	java.lang	**The memory stack is full. You are calling programs too deep, or using too large (or too many) variables in your path of execution.**

continues

Error	Package	Description
ThreadDeath	java.lang	An instance of ThreadDeath is thrown in the victim thread when thread.stop() is called. This is not a subclass of Exception but rather a subclass of Error because too many people already catch Exception. Instances of this class should be caught explicitly only if you're interested in cleaning up when being asynchronously terminated. If ThreadDeath is caught, it is important to rethrow the object so that the Thread will actually die. The top-level error handler will not print out a message if ThreadDeath falls through.
UnknownError	java.lang	An unknown (but serious!) error has occured in the execution of your program.
UnsatisfiedLinkError	java.lang	Visual J++ has loaded another class, but cannot reconcile all the links to that other class.
VerifyError	java.lang	A class has not passed the byte-code verification tests.
VirtualMachineError	java.lang	VirtualMachineError is the parent class to several serious environment errors. It indicates that some serious resource problem exists on the host Java machine.

Table 7.1 Continued

Visual J++ Exceptions

Several Exceptions are also predefined. Table 7.2 shows a list and description of the predefined exceptions that can be thrown.

Table 7.2
Visual J++ Exceptions

Exception	Package	Description
ArithmeticException	java.lang	An arithmetic error, such as dividing by zero, has occurred.
ArrayIndexOutOfBounds ➥Exception	java.lang	An array index is less than 1 or is greater than the array size defined in the declaration.
ArrayStoreException	java.lang	The wrong data type or class is being stored in an array.
AWTException	java.awt	Some exception has occurred in the AWT package.
ClassCastException	java.lang	An invalid cast from one data type to another has occurred.
ClassNotFoundException	java.lang	A class that was called could not be found and/ or loaded successfully.
CloneNotSupported ➥Exception	java.lang	An attempt has been made to clone an object that is not clonable.
EmptyStackException	java.util	The stack is empty and has no data.
EOFException	java.io	End of file has been reached during an input command.
Exception	java.lang	Exception is the parent (or grandparent) class that all Throwable exceptions descend from.
FileNotFoundException	java.io	A file was not found during an open command.
IllegalAccessException	java.lang	A particular method could not be found inside a class.
IllegalArgumentException	java.lang	Arguments from a calling method do not matched the called method.
IllegalMonitorState ➥Exception	java.lang	An illegal monitor state has been detected.

continues

Table 7.2
Continued

Exception	Package	Description
`IllegalThreadState` `➥Exception`	`java.lang`	**A thread is not in the proper state for the requested operation.**
`IndexOutOfBoundsException`	`java.lang`	**Parent class for** `ArrayIndexOutOf-` `BoundsException` **and** `StringIndexOutOf-` `BoundsException`. **Indicates that an array or string has exceeded its maximum length.**
`InstantiationException`	`java.lang`	**An attempt was made to instantiate either an abstract class or an interface.**
`InterruptedException`	`java.lang`	**Indicates that some other thread has interrupted this thread.**
`InterruptedIOException`	`java.io`	**An I/O operation has been interrupted.** `bytesTransferred` **is a class variable used to indicate how many bytes were transferred.**
`IOException`	`java.io`	**Parent class to all java.io exceptions. Indicates that an I/O error has occurred.**
`MalformedURLException`	`java.net`	**An URL that has been passed to a method is corrupt or unintelligible.**
`NegativeArraySizeException`	`java.lang`	**An attempt was made to create an array with a negative size.**
`NoSuchElementException`	`java.util`	**Signals that an enumeration is empty.**
`NoSuchMethodException`	`java.lang`	**A specified method could not be found.**
`NullPointerException`	`java.lang`	**An attempt was made to access a Class (such as, call a class method or access a class attribute) that has not been instantiated (and therefore is equal to null).**

Exception	Package	Description
NumberFormatException	java.lang	An invalid number format has occurred. This often happens when using the `tostring( )` method.
ProtocolException	java.net	A connect gets an `EPROTO` return. This exception is specifically caught in class Socke.
RuntimeException	java.lang	Parent class to many exceptions. This error occurs during the runtime of a program inside a Java virtual machine.
SecurityException	java.lang	An operation attempted by a Visual J++ program is not allowed due to security reasons.
SocketException	java.net	An error has occurred while attempting to use a socket (like winsock).
StringIndexOutOfBounds ➡Exception	java.lang	An attempt was made to access a string that is greater than its length.
UnknownHostException	java.net	The address of the host specified by a network client could not be resolved.
UnknownServiceException	java.net	An attempt was made to use a service that is not supported by the network.
UTFDataFormatException	java.io	A malformed UTF-8 string has been read in a input stream.

NOTE:
An ancestor class to all exceptions and errors is the Throwable class. Although not an error or exception in itself, Throwable can be thrown by another class, often to indicate that some error should be thrown. For example, the `empty finalize` method of the Object class throws throwable.

Exceptions and Errors thrown by Classes

Sometimes when you receive an exception, it would be useful to see what could have caused that exception. Some exceptions and errors, like AbstractMethodError, are the result of improper use of the Visual J++ language. Others are specifically thrown by functions inside classes. Table 7.3 lists errors and exceptions and the Java and Visual J++ functions that throw those errors and exceptions.

Table 7.3
Errors and Exceptions thrown by Methods

Error or Exception	Function that Throws the Error or Exception
ArithmeticException	Math.log
ArithmeticException	Math.pow
ArithmeticException	Math.sqrt
ArrayIndexOutOfBoundsException	Container.getComponent
ArrayIndexOutOfBoundsException	System.arraycopy
ArrayIndexOutOfBoundsException	Vector.elementAt
ArrayIndexOutOfBoundsException	Vector.insertElementAt
ArrayIndexOutOfBoundsException	Vector.removeElementAt
ArrayIndexOutOfBoundsException	Vector.setElementAt
ArrayStoreException	System.arraycopy
AWTError	Toolkit.getDefaultToolkit
ClassFormatError	ClassLoader.DefineClass
ClassNotFoundException	Class.forName
ClassNotFoundException	ClassLoader.findSystemClass
ClassNotFoundException	ClassLoader.loadClass
CloneNotSupportedException	Object.Clone
EmptyStackException	Stack.peek
EmptyStackException	Stack.pop
EOFException	DataInput.readBoolean
EOFException	DataInput.readByte
EOFException	DataInput.readChar
EOFException	DataInput.readDouble
EOFException	DataInput.readFloat
EOFException	DataInput.readFully
EOFException	DataInput.readInt

Error or Exception	Function that Throws the Error or Exception
EOFException	DataInput.readLong
EOFException	DataInput.readShort
EOFException	DataInput.readUnsignedByte
EOFException	DataInput.readUnsignedShort
EOFException	DataInput.skipBytes
EOFException	DataInputStream.readFully
Error	URL.setURLStreamHandler ➥Factory
Error	URLConnection.setContent ➥HandlerFactory
FileNotFoundException	FileInputStream.FileInput ➥Stream
IllegalAccessException	Class.newInstance
IllegalArgumentException	Choice.select
IllegalArgumentException	GridLayout.GridLayout
IllegalArgumentException	Hashtable.Hashtable
IllegalArgumentException	Label.setAlignment
IllegalArgumentException	Scrollbar.Scrollbar
IllegalArgumentException	Thread.setPriority
IllegalMonitorStateException	Object.notify
IllegalMonitorStateException	Object.notifyAll
IllegalMonitorStateException	Object.wait
IllegalThreadStateException	Process.exitValue
IllegalThreadStateException	Thread.countStackFrames
IllegalThreadStateException	Thread.setDaemon
IllegalThreadStateException	Thread.start
IllegalThreadStateException	Thread.destroy
InterruptedException	MediaTracker.waitForAll
InterruptedException	MediaTracker.waitForID
InterruptedException	Object.wait
InterruptedException	PixelGrabber.grabPixels
InterruptedException	Process.waitFor
InterruptedException	Thread.join

continues

Table 7.3
Continued

Error or Exception	Function that Throws the Error or Exception
InterruptedException	Thread.sleep
IOException	BufferedInputStream.➥available
IOException	BufferedInputStream.read
IOException	BufferedInputStream.reset
IOException	BufferedInputStream.skip
IOException	BufferedInputStream.flush
IOException	BufferedInputStream.write
IOException	ByteArrayOutputStream.➥writeTo
IOException	ContentHandler.getContent
IOException	DataInput.readBoolean
IOException	DataInput.readByte
IOException	DataInput.readChar
IOException	DataInput.readDouble
IOException	DataInput.readFloat
IOException	DataInput.readFully
IOException	DataInput.readInt
IOException	DataInput.readLine
IOException	DataInput.readLong
IOException	DataInput.readShort
IOException	DataInput.readUTF
IOException	DataInput.readUnsignedByte
IOException	DataInput.readUnsignedShort
IOException	DataInput.skipBytes
IOException	DataInputStream.read
IOException	DataInputStream.readBoolean
IOException	DataInputStream.readByte
IOException	DataInputStream.readChar
IOException	DataInputStream.readDouble
IOException	DataInputStream.readFloat
IOException	DataInputStream.readFully
IOException	DataInputStream.readInt

Error or Exception	Function that Throws the Error or Exception
IOException	DataInputStream.readLine
IOException	DataInputStream.readLong
IOException	DataInputStream.readShort
IOException	DataInputStream.readUTF
IOException	DataInputStream.➥readUnsignedByte
IOException	DataInputStream.➥readUnsignedShort
IOException	DataInputStream.skipBytes
IOException	DataOutput.write
IOException	DataOutput.writeBoolean
IOException	DataOutput.writeByte
IOException	DataOutput.writeBytes
IOException	DataOutput.writeChar
IOException	DataOutput.writeChars
IOException	DataOutput.writeDouble
IOException	DataOutput.writeFloat
IOException	DataOutput.writeInt
IOException	DataOutput.writeLong
IOException	DataOutput.writeShort
IOException	DataOutput.writeUTF
IOException	DataOutputStream.flush
IOException	DataOutputStream.write
IOException	DataOutputStream.➥writeBoolean
IOException	DataOutputStream.writeByte
IOException	DataOutputStream.writeBytes
IOException	DataOutputStream.writeChar
IOException	DataOutputStream.writeChars
IOException	DataOutputStream.➥writeDouble
IOException	DataOutputStream.writeFloat
IOException	DataOutputStream.writeInt

continues

Table 7.3
Continued

Error or Exception	Function that Throws the Error or Exception
IOException	DataOutputStream.writeLong
IOException	DataOutputStream.writeShort
IOException	DataOutputStream.writeUTF
IOException	DatagramSocket.receive
IOException	DatagramSocket.send
IOException	FileInputStream.available
IOException	FileInputStream.close
IOException	FileInputStream.finalize
IOException	FileInputStream.getFD
IOException	FileInputStream.read
IOException	FileInputStream.skip
IOException	FileOutputStream. ➥FileOutputStream
IOException	FileOutputStream.close
IOException	FileOutputStream.finalize
IOException	FileOutputStream.getFD
IOException	FileOutputStream.write
IOException	FilterInputStream.available
IOException	FilterInputStream.close
IOException	FilterInputStream.read
IOException	FilterInputStream.reset
IOException	FilterInputStream.skip
IOException	FilterOutputStream.close
IOException	FilterOutputStream.flush
IOException	FilterOutputStream.write
IOException	OutputStream.close
IOException	OutputStream.flush
IOException	OutputStream.write
IOException	InputStream.available
IOException	InputStream.close
IOException	InputStream.read
IOException	InputStream.reset
IOException	InputStream.skip

Error or Exception	Function that Throws the Error or Exception
IOException	LineNumberInputStream.➥available
IOException	LineNumberInputStream.read
IOException	LineNumberInputStream.reset
IOException	LineNumberInputStream.skip
IOException	PipedInputStream.➥PipedInputStream
IOException	PipedInputStream.close
IOException	PipedInputStream.connect
IOException	PipedInputStream.read
IOException	PipedOutputStream.➥PipedOutputStream
IOException	PipedOutputStream.close
IOException	PipedOutputStream.connect
IOException	PipedOutputStream.write
IOException	PrintStream.write
IOException	Properties.load
IOException	PushbackInputStream.➥available
IOException	PushbackInputStream.read
IOException	PushbackInputStream.unread
IOException	RandomAccessFile.➥RandomAccessFile
IOException	RandomAccessFile.close
IOException	RandomAccessFile.getFD
IOException	RandomAccessFile.➥getFilePointer
IOException	RandomAccessFile.length
IOException	RandomAccessFile.read
IOException	RandomAccessFile.➥readBoolean
IOException	RandomAccessFile.readByte
IOException	RandomAccessFile.readChar
IOException	RandomAccessFile.readDouble

continues

Table 7.3
Continued

Error or Exception	Function that Throws the Error or Exception
IOException	RandomAccessFile.readFloat
IOException	RandomAccessFile.readFully
IOException	RandomAccessFile.readInt
IOException	RandomAccessFile.readLine
IOException	RandomAccessFile.readLong
IOException	RandomAccessFile.readShort
IOException	RandomAccessFile.readUTF
IOException	RandomAccessFile.➡readUnsignedByte
IOException	RandomAccessFile.seek
IOException	RandomAccessFile.skipBytes
IOException	RandomAccessFile.write
IOException	RandomAccessFile.➡writeBoolean
IOException	RandomAccessFile.writeByte
IOException	RandomAccessFile.writeBytes
IOException	RandomAccessFile.writeChar
IOException	RandomAccessFile.writeChars
IOException	RandomAccessFile.➡writeDouble
IOException	RandomAccessFile.writeFloat
IOException	RandomAccessFile.writeInt
IOException	RandomAccessFile.writeLong
IOException	RandomAccessFile.writeShort
IOException	RandomAccessFile.writeUTF
IOException	Runtime.exec
IOException	SequenceInputStream.close
IOException	SequenceInputStream.read
IOException	ServerSocket.ServerSocket
IOException	ServerSocket.accept
IOException	ServerSocket.close
IOException	ServerSocket.➡setSocketFactory
IOException	Socket.Socket

Error or Exception	Function that Throws the Error or Exception
IOException	Socket.close
IOException	Socket.getInputStream
IOException	Socket.getOutputStream
IOException	Socket.setSocketImplFactory
IOException	SocketImpl.accept
IOException	SocketImpl.available
IOException	SocketImpl.bind
IOException	SocketImpl.close
IOException	SocketImpl.connect
IOException	SocketImpl.create
IOException	SocketImpl.getInputStream
IOException	SocketImpl.getOutputStream
IOException	SocketImpl.listen
IOException	SocketImpl.nextToken
IOException	URL.getContent
IOException	URL.openConnection
IOException	URL.openStream
IOException	URLConnection.connect
IOException	URLConnection.getContent
IOException	URLConnection.➥getInputStream
IOException	URLConnection.➥getOutputStream
IOException	URLConnection.guess➥ContentTypeFromStream
IOException	URLStreamHandler.➥openConnection
MalformedURLException	URL.URL
NoClassDefFoundError	ClassLoader.findSystemClass
NoSuchElementException	Enumeration.nextElement
NoSuchElementException	StringTokenizer.nextElement
NoSuchElementException	StringTokenizer.nextToken
NoSuchElementException	Vector.firstElement

continues

Table 7.3
Continued

Error or Exception	Function that Throws the Error or Exception
NoSuchElementException	Vector.lastElement
NullPointerException	Choice.addItem
NullPointerException	Dictionary.put
NullPointerException	File.File
NullPointerException	Hashtable.contains
NullPointerException	Hashtable.put
NullPointerException	ThreadGroup.ThreadGroup
NumberFormatException	Double.Double
NumberFormatException	Double.valueOf
NumberFormatException	Float.Float
NumberFormatException	Float.valueOf
NumberFormatException	Integer.Integer
NumberFormatException	Integer.parseInt
NumberFormatException	Integer.valueOf
NumberFormatException	Long.Long
NumberFormatException	Long.parseInt
NumberFormatException	Long.valueOf
OutOfMemoryError	Object.clone
SecurityException	SecurityManager.➥SecurityManager
SecurityException	SecurityManager.checkAccept
SecurityException	SecurityManager.checkAccess
SecurityException	SecurityManager.➥checkConnect
SecurityException	SecurityManager.➥checkCreateClassLoader
SecurityException	SecurityManager.checkDelete
SecurityException	SecurityManager.checkExec
SecurityException	SecurityManager.checkExit
SecurityException	SecurityManager.checkLine
SecurityException	SecurityManager.checkListen
SecurityException	SecurityManager.➥✳heckPropertiesAccess

Error or Exception	Function that Throws the Error or Exception
SecurityException	SecurityManager.➥checkPropertyAccess
SecurityException	SecurityManager.checkRead
SecurityException	SecurityManager.checkWrite
SecurityException	System.setSecurityManager
SecurityException	Thread.checkAccess
SecurityException	ThreadGroup.checkAccess
SocketException	DatagramSocket.➥DatagramSocket
SocketException	ServerSocket.➥setSocketFactory
SocketException	Socket.setSocketImplFactory
StringIndexOutOfBoundsException	String.String
StringIndexOutOfBoundsException	String.charAt
StringIndexOutOfBoundsException	String.substring
StringIndexOutOfBoundsException	StringBuffer.charAt
StringIndexOutOfBoundsException	StringBuffer.getChars
StringIndexOutOfBoundsException	StringBuffer.insert
StringIndexOutOfBoundsException	StringBuffer.setCharAt
StringIndexOutOfBoundsException	StringBuffer.setLength
Throwable	Object.finalize
UnknownHostException	InetAddress.getAllByName
UnknownHostException	InetAddress.getByName
UnknownHostException	InetAddress.getLocalHost
UnknownHostException	Socket.Socket
UnknownServiceException	URLConnection.getContent
UnknownServiceException	URLConnection.➥getInputStream
UnknownServiceException	URLConnection.➥getOutputStream
UnsatisfiedLinkError	Runtime.load
UnsatisfiedLinkError	Runtime.loadLibrary
UnsatisfiedLinkError	System.load
UnsatisfiedLinkError	System.loadLibrary

Conclusion

This chapter lists the Java errors that are included with the Java language. In addition to standard Java errors, there is also a com.ms.com.ComException exception added by Microsoft to Visual J++ for error handling with ActiveX. Check out Chapter 11, "The ActiveX and COM Specifications," for more information.

Error handling in Java is robust. You are able to trap any error, create your own errors, and trigger any existing error or exception. Although it takes a little bit of coding, Java really makes error handling intuitive and maintainable.

Chapter **8**

Debugging

Debugging, which is a reasonably sophisticated task in Java, is made simple in Visual J++. With a completely visual integrated debugger built into the Visual J++ compiler, Java development has never been easier.

In this chapter, you'll be introduced to the debugger. In the debugger, you'll debug a Visual J++ program, called ExtraMath, which performs a `log10` function. (Because Java and Visual J++ don't come with a `log10` function, you may want to keep ahold of this. It really does work, or it will by the time you're finished debugging.)

> **NOTE:**
> Java's `java.lang.Math` class contains a natural log function. Most of us, however, are used to working with base-10 logarithms, if we work with logarithm's at all. (On your calculator, natural log is the `ln` function while base-10 logs use the `log` button.)
>
> Java does not contain a base-10 logarithm function, so I thought writing one can show you how to debug, but may also be useful to some of you in your day-to-day work environment.

When you complete this chapter, you should know the following:

- ❂ How to view current variables in scope.

- ❂ What watches are and how to set them.

- ❂ What breakpoints are and how to set them.

- ❂ How to step through a program in the debugger.

The *log10* Method

The class you are about to debug, ExtraMath, comes with only one function, log10. The code is reasonably easy and reasonably buggy, but compiles cleanly:

```
import java.awt.*;

public class ExtraMath extends Frame {
    int x;
    public static void main (String args[]) {
        ExtraMath em = new ExtraMath();
        em.setTitle("Log Rolling");
        em.resize(300,200);
        em.show();
        em.start();
    }
    public void start () {
        printAnswer (1000);
        printAnswer (100);
        printAnswer (50);
        printAnswer (-1);
    }
    public void printAnswer (double a) {
        int answer = (int) Logs.log10(x);
        String output = "The log (base 10) of "
                                + String.valueOf(a)
                                + " is "
                                + Integer.toString(answer);
```

```java
MessageBox mb = new MessageBox(this, output);
        mb.resize(400,400);
        mb.show();
    }
}
class Logs {
    public static double log10(double x)
                throws ArithmeticException {
        double myAnswer = Math.log((double)x)
                                        / Math.log(10);

        return myAnswer;

    }

}
class MessageBox extends Dialog{
    private Panel southPanel;
    private Button cb_OK;
    private Label lb_message;
    public MessageBox(Frame parent, String output) {
        this(parent, output, "Message for you");
    }
    public MessageBox(Frame parent,
                            String output, String title) {
        super(parent, title, true);
        //Add an exit button and a grid panel.
        Panel mySouthPanel = new Panel();
        lb_message = new Label(output);
        southPanel.setBackground(Color.lightGray);
        southPanel.setLayout(new FlowLayout());
        southPanel.add(cb_OK = new Button("OK"));
        add("South", southPanel);
        add("North", lb_message);
    }
    public boolean handleEvent (Event event) {
        //Was the exit button pushed?
        if (event.target == cb_OK) {
            dispose();
            java.lang.System.exit(0);
        }
```

```
else {
    // Otherwise, let the superclass handle it
    return super.handleEvent(event);
}
return true;
    }
}
```

Let's briefly discuss the three classes in ExtraMath.java:

- ⊙ The `ExtraMath` class is the user interface. It contains the code that the user sees, and automatically takes the base-10 log of 1000, 100, 50, and –1.

- ⊙ The `Logs` class contains only the `log10` method. The `log10` method returns the base 10 logarithm of a number.

- ⊙ The `MessageBox` class displays a message and awaits your reply.

It compiles, so it should work, right? `<rofl>` (This is an *emoticon*. It appears in e-mail, News groups, and such on the Internet, and it means "Roll On Floor, Laughing." It's what you should be doing after reading the first question in this paragraph.) Well, let's go through the debugger to find out what's wrong.

Entering the Debugger

When you run the previous program, nothing shows up, and you immediately get a `NullPointerException`. You must debug the program. You can start one of several ways:

- ⊙ You could choose Build, Debug, Go, as shown in Figure 8.1, to start your program. Your program won't stop until it finishes or it encounters a breakpoint. You can achieve the same effect by pressing F5 or by clicking the Go button.

> **NOTE:**
> The Restart button will start the program and the debugging process from the beginning of the program, and therefore can be used to start a program in the debugger. This button can also be handy if you need to restart after finding some errors, but are not yet ready to leave the debugger.

Fig. 8.1
You can enter the debugger any number of ways, including through the menu.

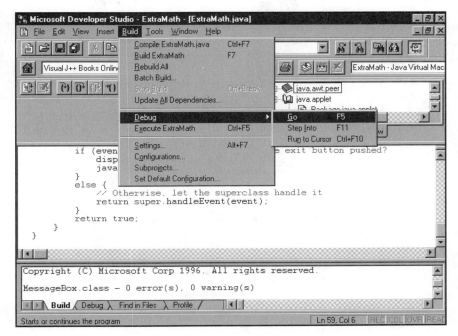

○ You could choose <u>B</u>uild, <u>D</u>ebug, Step <u>I</u>nto. This will step you into the next deepest method, or, in this case, into the `main` method, which is the first method of this system. The same effect can be achieved by pressing F11 or by clicking the Step Into button.

○ You could choose <u>B</u>uild, <u>D</u>ebug, Ru<u>n</u> to Cursor to execute until the current line of code (where the cursor sits) is reached. You can achieve the same effect by pressing Ctrl+F10 or by clicking the Run to Cursor button.

The Debugger

Now you're in the debugger. As you can see in Figure 8.2, your Visual J++ environment has changed somewhat.

Your Visual J++ program is still running in a window. Below it are two sub-windows. On the lower-left side of the window is the Variables window. This shows all variables in scope. Notice that there is a tree view for all classes and structures. (For example, the ExtraMath class has one attribute: x. Because x has not been initialized, it is set to a random value.)

Fig. 8.2
The debugger environ-
ment is similar to the
Visual J++ develope-
ment environment.

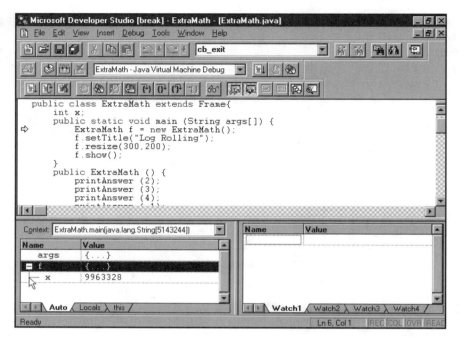

Watches

On the right side is the Watch window. A watch is a variable that
you constantly monitor during debugging. It's usually good to take
such variables out of the variable list, especially if the variable list is
pretty long.

In Figure 8.3, you can see how watches look. In the first column,
I clicked the watch row and typed **f.x**. In the second row, I dragged
x over from the variables list instead of typing it. (Notice how the formatting is a little different when you drag a variable as opposed to
when you type it.)

You can also enter variables into the list by highlighting a variable
and then either pressing Shift+F9, clicking the QuickWatch button,
or clicking Debug, QuickWatch, as shown in Figure 8.4. Notice how
the menu has changed. The Debug menu item is great for reviewing
your choices during debugging.

When you choose a QuickWatch, the QuickWatch dialog box opens
(see Figure 8.5). Here, the variable name you had highlighted or had
your cursor on is in the Expression text box.

Fig. 8.3
You can type or drag variables from the variable list into the watch list.

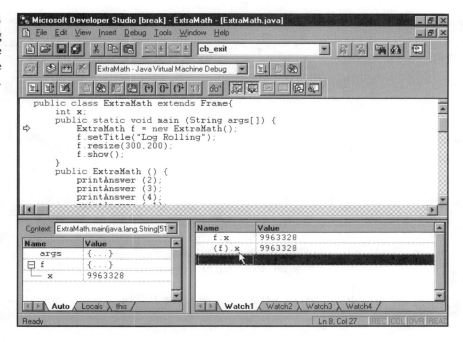

Fig. 8.4
QuickWatches are an easy way to enter a variable from source to the watch list.

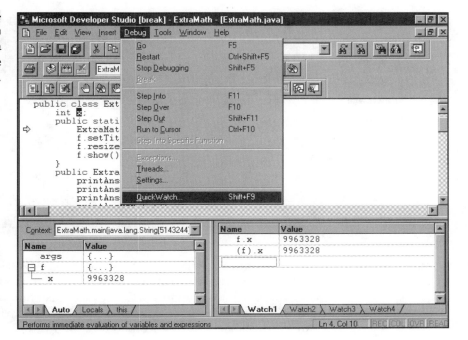

Fig. 8.5
You can review variables and change values inside the QuickView dialog box.

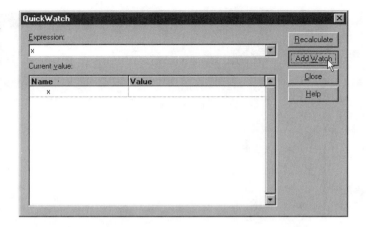

In the QuickWatch dialog box, you can retype the name, recalculate what you've typed, and re-enter a value. In Figure 8.6, I changed the name to f.x (so the debugger could find the variable) and then changed the value in f.x to 100 by double-clicking the Value and entering the new value. From here, you can also add the variable to your watch by clicking the Add Watch button.

Fig. 8.6
You can change variables in the debugger if you want different test cases without new data.

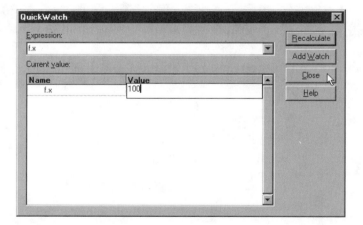

When you return to the debugger from the QuickWatch dialog box, you'll notice that any f.x value is recalculated, as shown in Figure 8.7. What you *won't* see in Figure 8.7 (because this book uses grayscale figures) is that the new values are in red. This tells you that it was changed in the debugger, and therefore might not by valid. This is really handy if you go too crazy with the debugger. You'll often be able to realize that some of your program's problems stem from changing the variables too much.

Fig. 8.7
Changing a value changes all displays of that value to red.

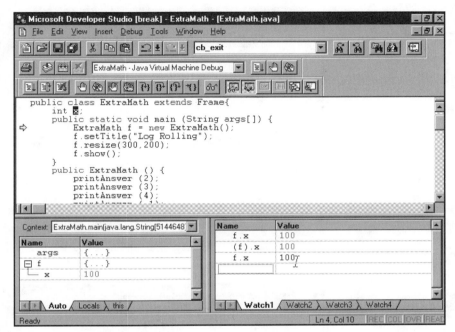

Stepping through Your Program

Using the Step Into button, you can continue stepping through other methods in your class while debugging, as shown in Figure 8.8.

Because ExtraMath extends Frame, you can even step into the Frame constructor (see Figure 8.9). Although this may be helpful, usually you step into the Java classes by accident. Click the Step Out button, press Shift+F11, or choose <u>D</u>ebug, Step O<u>u</u>t. This will execute the current function outside the debugger until you're back in the calling module.

Fig. 8.8
Using the Step
Through button, you
can execute a function
without stepping into
it, and break at the
following line.

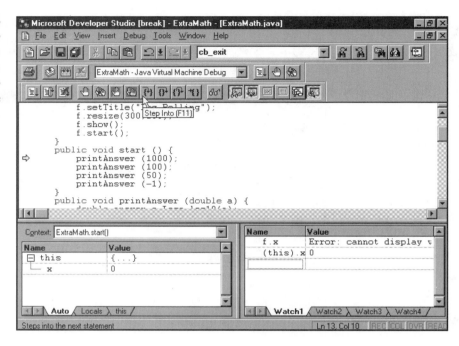

Fig. 8.9
You can even step into
the Java and
Microsoft class
libraries using the
Visual J++ debugger.

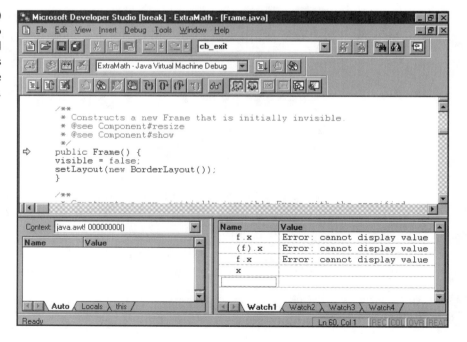

When you finally step through your program, you'll find that the
error is in the MessageBox call in the printAnswer method:

```
public void printAnswer (double a) {
    int answer = (int) Logs.log10(x);
    String output = "The log (base 10) of "
                                    + String.valueOf(a)
                                    + " is "
                                    + Integer.toString(answer);
    MessageBox mb = new MessageBox(this, output);
    mb.resize(400,400);
    mb.show();
}
```

Now you can set a breakpoint there to find out what's happening.

Breakpoints

Sometimes tracing all the way through a program can take a lot of time. Breakpoints were designed to let the developer signify which line of code he or she wanted to stop on. With the cursor on line 20 (which is where it locked up while stepping through the code), you could choose Edit, Breakpoints or press Alt+F9 (see Figure 8.10) to toggle a breakpoint on and off line 20.

Fig. 8.10
You can use the menu to set up breakpoint for debugging in your Visual J++ program.

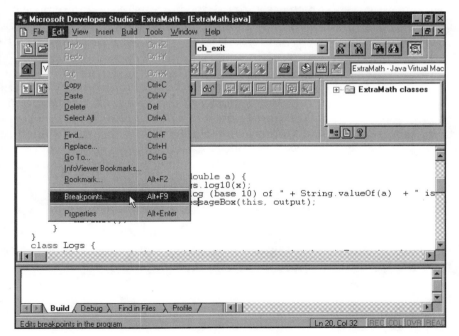

The Breakpoints dialog box opens. You can use the Breakpoints dialog box to specify exact lines to break on. By clicking the arrow next to the Break At text box, the current line of code will appear (see Figure 8.11). You can also use the Breakpoints dialog box to remove certain breakpoints.

Fig. 8.11
You can display the current line of code in the Breakpoints dialog box.

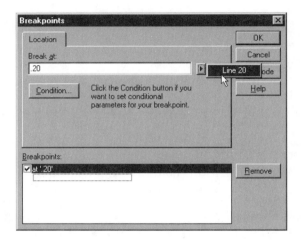

Although the Breakpoints dialog box has it's uses, it's usually much easier to use the buttons to set and remove breakpoints. The Insert/Remove Breakpoint button can toggle a breakpoint off and on a line. A line with a breakpoint set has a red dot to the far left, as shown in Figure 8.12.

You can also enable and disable breakpoints. Sometimes you have several breakpoints set, and you don't want to go through all your classes and reset them, but you also don't want them to function as you're running your program. To keep a breakpoint but disable it, click the Enable/Disable Breakpoint button. A disabled breakpoint on a line of code is a hollow red circle, as shown in Figure 8.13.

NOTE:
You can remove all breakpoints or disable all breakpoints by clicking the Remove All Breakpoints button or the Disable All Breakpoints button.

Fig. 8.12
Breakpoints are indicated by a red dot.

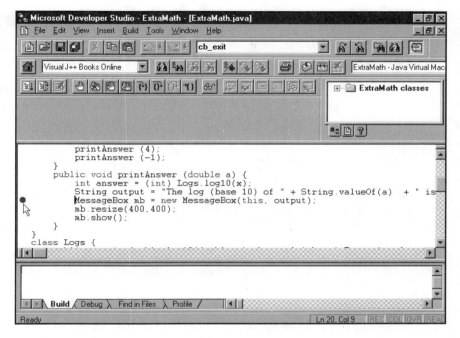

Fig. 8.13
A disabled breakpoint is indicated by a hollow red circle.

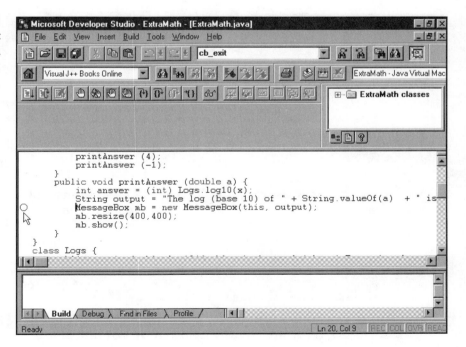

The Stack and the Disassembler

Two features of the debugger which are pretty advanced are the Stack and the Disassembler. The Stack shows a list of what methods were called and what line they were called from. This can come in handy when trying to trace a Visual J++ program. To view the stack, click the Call Stack button. You should then see something similar to Figure 8.14.

Fig. 8.14
The stack provides a history of what methods were called and from where.

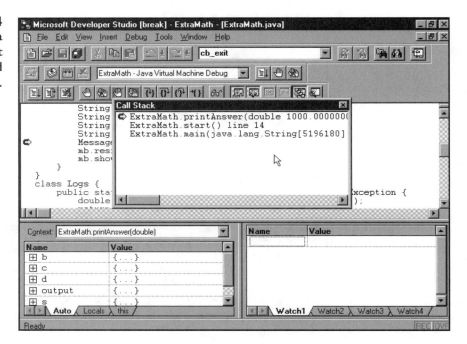

The disassembler is only for the very advanced. By clicking the Dissassembly button, a disassembled listing of your Java program appears(see Figure 8.15). If you know the assembly language and an assembly dump would help you debug your program, then by all means use it. However, it has limited use for most people, and most people should employ more conventional (not to mention easier and quicker) means of debugging.

Finishing Up Debugging

In the printAnswer method, you'll notice in Figure 8.16 that I took the log of x rather than a. Also, I truncated my log10 results to an integer, which surely was a bad thing to do.

Fig. 8.15
Dissassembling your
Visual J++ program
is only for the
most advanced of
developers.

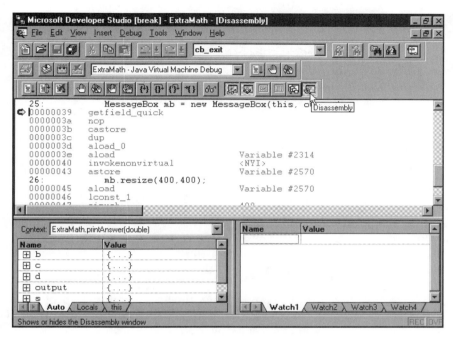

Fig. 8.16
Debugging code can
shed some light
on variables and
program flow.

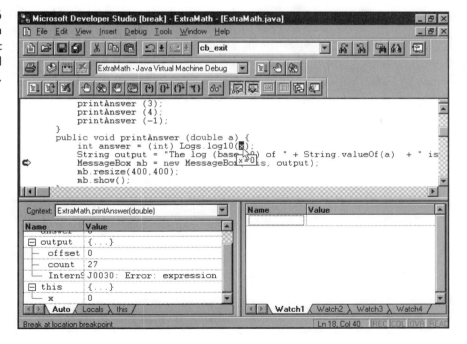

By debugging my `printAnswer` module with a better module, I may be able to make this ExtraMath class work after all. The following code is the corrected function:

```
public void printAnswer (double a) {
    double answer = Logs.log10(a);
    String output = "The log (base 10) of "
                            + Double.toString(a)
                            + " is " + Double.toString(answer);
    MessageBox mb = new MessageBox(this, output);
    mb.resize(400,400);
    mb.show();
}
```

Conclusion

In this chapter, you saw how a compiled program will often bomb with results that can be impossible to track down. Using a debugger, you can track down bugs that occur in both variable values and program flow.

For more information on Visual J++, see Chapter 3, "The Visual J++ Environment." There are also ways to debug at runtime outside of the debugger by displaying a status line in your frame. This is covered in Chapter 10, "Graphics, Graphical User Interfaces, and Animation."

Chapter 9

Event Programming in Visual J++

Event-driven programming is fastly replacing traditional programming with modern developers. Event programming involves reacting to events rather than controlling flow. Event-driven design tends to lead to easier to use, more versatile programs.

In this chapter, you will see how to capture keyboard and mouse events. By the end of this chapter, you should be able to identify:

- The keyboard events you can capture

- The mouse events you can capture

- What special keys are and how to handle them

- How to handle right mouse clicks and right mouse drags

Understanding Events

Traditional programming used to involve a single entry point. These programs don't yield control back to the operating system (or in Java's and Visual J++'s case, the virtual machine) until the programs are completely finished. Event-driven programs, on the other hand, have a different entry point for every event, and they yield control back to the operating system or virtual machine as often as possible. Figure 9.1 graphically shows this.

Fig. 9.1
Event-driven programs leave a lot more control to the operating system and have a lot of entry and exit points.

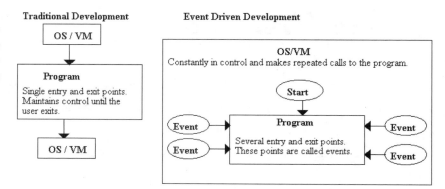

Events are how Windows programs respond to user interaction. Java supports two types of events: mouse events and keyboard events. Listing 9.1 (with each method declaration bolded for readability) is used in this event discussion.

Listing 9.1
Events.java

```java
import java.applet.*;
import java.awt.*;

public class events extends Applet {
// Keyboard Events
    public boolean keyDown(Event event, int key) {
        String before = "";
        String after = "";
        switch(event.id) {
            case Event.KEY_PRESS :      // "Regular" Key
                before = "";
                after = regular_key(event);
                break;
            case Event.KEY_ACTION :     // Function Key
```

```
                    before = "Function ";
                    after = function_key(key);
                    break;
            }
        showStatus(special_keys(event)+before
                        +"Key Down: "+after);
        return true;
    }
    private String regular_key (Event event) {
        int this_key = 0;
        String return_value = "ASCII code: " +
                String.valueOf(event.key) + " - ";
        // Adjust for the control key
        if (event.controlDown()
                                && event.key < ' ') {
            this_key = event.key + 64;
        }
        else {
            this_key = event.key;
        }
        switch (this_key) {
            case ' ' :
                return_value = return_value + "Space";
                break;
            case '\n' :
                return_value = return_value + "Return";
                break;
            case '\t' :
                return_value = return_value + "Tab";
                break;
            case '\010' :
                return_value = return_value + "Backspace";
                break;
            case '\033' :
                return_value = return_value + "Escape";
                break;
            case '\177' :
                return_value = return_value + "Delete";
                break;
            default :
                char return_char[] = {(char) this_key, 0};
                return_value = return_value
                        +
String.copyValueOf(return_char);
break;
```

continues

Listing 9.1
Continued

```
      }
     return return_value;
   }
private String function_key(int key) {
   switch (key) {
      case Event.HOME :
           return "Home";
      case Event.UP :
           return "Up";
      case Event.PGUP :
           return "PgUp";
      case Event.LEFT :
           return "Left";
      case Event.RIGHT :
           return "Right";
      case Event.END :
           return "End";
      case Event.DOWN :
           return "Down";
      case Event.PGDN :
           return "PgDn";
      case Event.F1 :
           return "F1";
      case Event.F2 :
           return "F2";
      case Event.F3 :
           return "F3";
      case Event.F4 :
           return "F4";
      case Event.F5 :
           return "F5";
      case Event.F6 :
           return "F6";
      case Event.F7 :
           return "F7";
      case Event.F8 :
           return "F8";
      case Event.F9 :
           return "F9";
      case Event.F10 :
           return "F10";
      case Event.F11 :
           return "F11";
      case Event.F12 :
           return "F12";
      default:
```

```
                       return "Unknown Function Key";
            }
    }
    private String special_keys(Event event) {
        String return_value = "";
        if (event.shiftDown()) {
            return_value = return_value + "Shift+";
        }
        if (event.controlDown()) {
            return_value = return_value + "Ctrl+";
        }
        if ((event.modifiers != 0) &&
            ((event.modifiers & event.ALT_MASK) != 0)){
            return_value = return_value + "Alt+";
        }
        if (event.metaDown()) {
            return_value = return_value + "Windows+";
        }
        return return_value;
    }
// Mouse Events
    public boolean mouseDown(Event event, int x, int y) {
        String special_k = special_keys(event);
        int metaPosition = special_k.indexOf("Meta+");
        if (metaPosition == -1) {
            showStatus(special_k
                + "Left Mouse Down: (" + x + "," + y
➥+ ")");
        }
        else {
            special_k = stripMeta(special_k, metaPosition);
            showStatus(special_k
                + "Right Mouse Down: (" + x + "," + y
➥+ ")");
        }
        return true;
    }
    public boolean mouseDrag(Event event, int x, int y) {
        String special_k = special_keys(event);
        int metaPosition = special_k.indexOf("Meta+");
        if (metaPosition == -1) {
            showStatus(special_k
                + "Left Mouse Drag: (" + x + "," + y
➥+ ")");
        }
```

continues

Listing 9.1
Continued

```
        else {
            special_k = stripMeta(special_k, metaPosition);
            showStatus(special_k
                + "Right Mouse Drag: (" + x + "," + y +
➥")");
        }
        return true;
    }
    public String stripMeta(String special_k,
                                            int
➥metaPosition) {
        String beforeMeta = "";
        String afterMeta = "";
        if (metaPosition > 0) {
            beforeMeta = special_k.substring(0,
                                    metaPosition);
        }
        if (special_k.length( ) > metaPosition + 5) {
            afterMeta = special_k.substring(
                        metaPosition + 6,
➥special_k.length());
        }
        return beforeMeta + afterMeta;
    }
    public boolean mouseUp(Event event, int x, int y) {
        showStatus(special_keys(event) +
            "Mouse Up: (" + x + "," + y + ")");
        return true;
    }
    public boolean mouseEnter(Event event, int x, int y) {
        showStatus(special_keys(event) + "Mouse Enter");
        return true;
    }
    public boolean mouseExit(Event event, int x, int y) {
        showStatus(special_keys(event) + "Mouse Exit");
        return true;
    }
}
```

Keyboard Events

When you press a key on the keyboard, the keyDown event is called from the parent Component class or subclass. (Applet and Frame are both subclasses of Component.) Using the keyDown event and the static constants KEY_PRESS and KEY_ACTION in the Event class, you can test the event ID to see if a regular (non-function) or function key was pressed. A special `keys` function is called to test whether Shift, Alt, Ctrl, or Meta keys were pressed at the same time:

```
public boolean keyDown(Event event, int key) {
    String before = "";
    String after = "";
    switch(event.id) {
        case Event.KEY_PRESS :      // "Regular" Key
            before = "";
            after = regular_key(event);
            break;
        case Event.KEY_ACTION :     // Function Key
            before = "Function ";
            after = function_key(key);
            break;
    }
    showStatus(special_keys(event) + before
                    +"Key Down: " + after);
    return true;
}
```

> **NOTE:**
> The `showStatus` **method is a Java method that shows a String at the bottom of your browser window. You can use the** `showStatus` **method for debugging, error messages, or standard messages without forcing the user to click OK to continue the program.**

Regular Keys

Regular keys include all the keys on the keyboard that return ASCII values. The `regular_key` method is called in the `keyDown` event if the event ID tested in the `keyDown` event is `Event.KEY_PRESS`, which is a static constant contained in the Event class. Before you're too far into the function, you must first see if the Ctrl key is being pressed with a regular key. By pressing the Ctrl key with another ASCII key, you change the ASCII value. The first `if` block in the `regular_key` method (shown in Listing 9.1) handles this:

```
if (event.controlDown() && event.key < ' ') {
    this_key = event.key + 64;
}
else {
    this_key = event.key;
}
```

> **NOTE:**
> **The Ctrl key is also tested for in the** special_keys
> **method, so your program doesn't need to remember that**
> **you've changed the ASCII value.**

Now you must test the this_key varible you first tested for special characters. I test for space, Return ('\n'), Tab ('\t'), Backspace ('\010'), Esc ('\033'), and Delete ('\177'). If none of these were pressed, I return the string containing the actual character pressed. Figure 9.2 shows the result of a regular key (such as the Delete key) being pressed.

Fig. 9.2
The keys you press (in this case, the Delete key) are echoed at the bottom of the applet viewer when using the showStatus method.

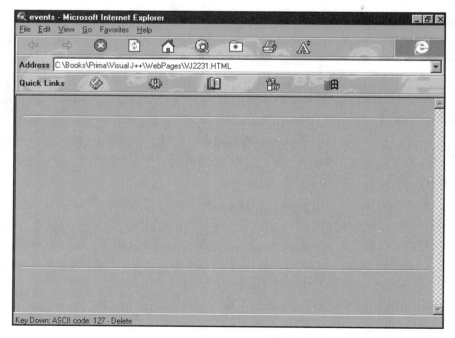

Special Keys

Special keys are Shift, Alt, Ctrl, and Meta. Using Event methods, you can test for special keys using the shiftDown, controlDown, and metaDown methods:

> **NOTE:**
> There is no real equivalent of a "meta" key on most Windows machines, however, several UNIX boxes have them. Because Java and Visual J++ code works on *all* Java virtual machines, meta keys can be tested for even though there's no real equivalent in the Windows/DOS world.
>
> The meta key is also triggered as pressed for a right mouse click and a right mouse drag.

```
private String special_keys(Event event) {
    String return_value = "";
    if (event.shiftDown()) {
        return_value = return_value + "Shift+";
    }
    if (event.controlDown()) {
        return_value = return_value + "Ctrl+";
    }
    if ((event.modifiers != 0) &&
        ((event.modifiers & event.ALT_MASK) != 0)) {
        return_value = return_value + "Alt+";
    }
    if (event.metaDown()) {
        return_value = return_value + "Windows+";
    }
    return return_value;
}
```

The Alt key has no method for testing. However, there is a static Event constant called ALT_MASK. When ALT_MASK is logically ANDed with the Event modifiers attribute, if a non-zero value is returned, then the Alt key is being pressed (see Figure 9.3).

Fig. 9.3
The ALT_MASK Event constant ANDed with the modifiers Event attribute yields a non-zero value if the Alt key is currently pressed.

	Meta	Alt	Ctrl	Shift
modifiers	0	1	1	1
ALT_MASK	0	1	0	0
AND value	0	1	0	0

Figure 9.3 shows that a bitwise AND between ALT_MASK and modifiers yields a non-zero value.

> **NOTE:**
> The reason that the Alt key is not considered that important is because the Alt key is often to go to the menu *outside* of the Java program. Often, if you hit the Alt key, your events are no longer considered as being part of your Visual J++ program.

The special_keys method returns "Shift+", "Alt+", "Ctrl+", or "Meta+", or any combination of the four based on what special keys are being hit when an event occurs. For exmaple, a Shift+Ctrl+A will appear at the bottom of the Applet (see Figure 9.4).

Fig. 9.4
Modifier keys can be displayed using the String returned by the special_keys method. Here Shft and Ctrl are pressed at the same time as the letter A.

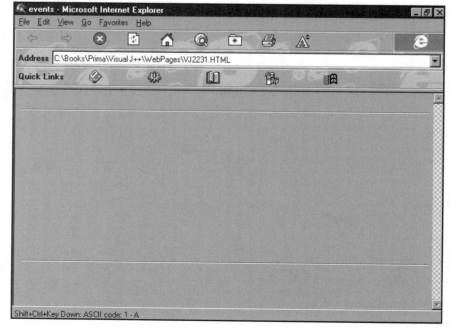

Function Keys

Function keys are tested using the `Event.key` attribute. The key can be tested for several Event class constants, including `HOME`, `UP`, `PGUP`, `PGDN`, `LEFT`, `RIGHT`, and `END` as well as F1 through F12. This is shown by the `function_key` class in Listing 9.1:

```
private String function_key(int key) {
    switch (key) {
        case Event.HOME
///...
```

The `function_key` method is called in the `keyDown` event if the event ID tested in the `keyDown` event is equal to the `Event.KEY_ACTION` constant, which is a static constant contained in the Event class. When you press a function key (sush as F1), the results can be seen at the bottom of the Applet (see Figure 9.5).

Fig. 9.5
When you press a function key, such as F1, the events applet traps the F1 and displays that F1 was pressed.

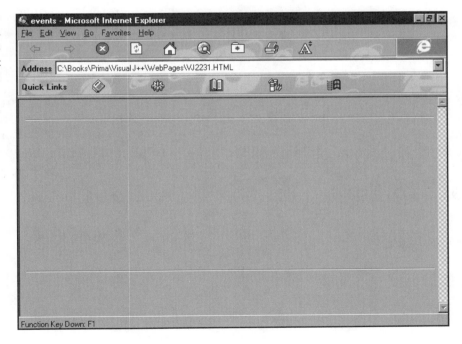

Mouse Events

The following tables list the available mouse events that are called from the parent Component class.

Event Name	Description
mouseDown	The left or right mouse button was pressed. (Right button clicks are indicated by a Meta key modifier.)
mouseDrag	The left or right mouse button was dragged, which means that a button was held down while the mouse moved. (Right button drags are indicated by a Meta key modifier.)
mouseUp	The left or right mouse button was released. (There is no indicator to tell whether the left or right mouse button was released.)
mouseEnter	The mouse pointer has entered the applet area. If the mouse pointer is outside the applet area, then no mouse movements are recorded.
mouseExit	The mouse pointer has left the applet area.

TIP:
Any mouse clicks or drags that occur *outside* the applet area are not considered applet events. The mouse pointer must be in the applet are to trigger a mouse event.

Notice in Listing 9.1 that all these events are coded for. They all have an Event, x, and y parameter passed to them. However, in the mouseDown and mouseDrag events, either the left or mouse button is clicked and dragged. The right mouse button is indicated with a Meta modifier special key. The mouseDown method from Listing 9.1 is shown below:

```
public boolean mouseDown(Event event, int x, int y) {
    String special_k = special_keys(event);
    int metaPosition = special_k.indexOf("Meta+");
    if (metaPosition == -1) {
        showStatus(special_k + "Left Mouse Down: ("
                        + x + "," + y + ")");
    }
    else {
        special_k = stripMeta(special_k, metaPosition);
        showStatus(special_k + "Right Mouse Down: ("
                        + x + "," + y + ")");
```

```
    }

    return true;
}
```

Although there are different ways to test for the Meta key, the code in the `mouseDown` and `mouseDrag` events tests for Meta by seeing if the String returned by the special_keys method contains a "Meta+" substring. If it does, a special function was written to strip the "Meta+" from the special_keys String. Then a `showStatus` call is issued with the remaining modifiers (such as Shift, Alt, and Ctrl), and the x and y positions of the mouse pointer. Figure 9.6 shows what happens when the right mouse button is clicked while the Shift key is being pressed. (Notice the "Meta+" substring is stripped out.)

Fig. 9.6
Right-clicking while holding the Shift key down produces the proper message at the bottom of the browser.

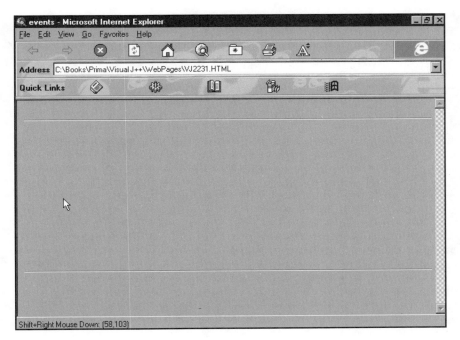

Conclusion

Traditional programming without events forced the user to trap for every user action. This made programming user interfaces extremely difficult. The user interfaces that resulted from traditional programming were often difficult to use and non-standard.

Graphical operating systems like Windows changed this by adding event processing. This takes much of the development for flow of control development away and allows the developer to code for events. In Chapter 10, "Graphics, Graphical User Interfaces, and Animation," you'll see even more events as they are applied to graphical user interfaces.

Chapter 10

Graphics, Graphical User Interfaces, and Animation

Graphics are at the heart of Windows and World Wide Web programming. In fact, some of the text-based functions, like `System.out.println`, aren't covered in depth because of the limited usefulness text-based functions have in a graphical environment.

In this chapter, you will learn the following:

- How to use components, such as command buttons and radio buttons

- How to do simple animation

- How to design and implement a user interface

- How to use Panels and layouts to help you manage your graphical environment

- More on events in a graphical environment.

Graphics with Java's Abstract Windows Toolkit

At the heart of graphics is Java's Abstract Windows Toolkit (AWY). The AWT contains classes (that contain methods) that allow the Java user to *easily* and *quickly* utilize graphics in a program. Say you want to write a routine that allows you to draw lines or freeform in a variety of colors. The user interface could look like Figure 10.1.

Fig. 10.1
Our requirements are that we have two sets of radio buttons, two buttons for clearing and exiting, and a area for the user to paint on.

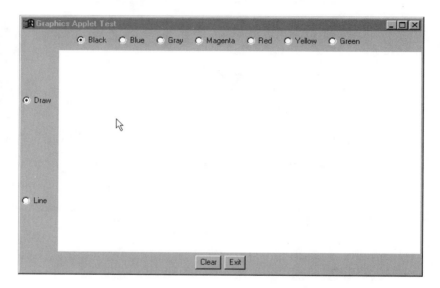

The code to generate this is in Listing 10.1.

Listing 10.1
graphicsApplet.java

```java
import java.awt.*;
import java.applet.*;
public class graphicsApplet extends Applet {
    public void init() {
        Frame f = new graphics();
        f.setTitle("Graphics Applet Test");
        f.resize(600,400);
        f.show();
    }
}
class graphics extends Frame {
    int last_x;
    int last_y;
```

```java
    private Color current_color = Color.black;
    private boolean isLineDrawn = false;
    private Checkbox rb_black;
    private Checkbox rb_blue;
    private Checkbox rb_lightGray;
    private Checkbox rb_magenta;
    private Checkbox rb_red;
    private Checkbox rb_yellow;
    private Checkbox rb_green;
    private Checkbox rb_draw;
    private Checkbox rb_line;
    private Button cb_clear;
    private Button cb_exit;
    public graphics () {
        //Define Panels and the layouts they use
        Panel myNorthPanel = new Panel();
        Panel myWestPanel = new Panel();
        Panel mySouthPanel = new Panel();
        myNorthPanel.setBackground(Color.lightGray);
        mySouthPanel.setBackground(Color.lightGray);
        myWestPanel.setBackground(Color.lightGray);
        myNorthPanel.setLayout(new FlowLayout());
        myWestPanel.setLayout(new GridLayout(2, 1));
        mySouthPanel.setLayout(new FlowLayout());

        // Create the clear and exit command buttons.
        mySouthPanel.add(cb_clear = new Button("Clear"));
        mySouthPanel.add(cb_exit = new Button("Exit"));

        // Define CheckboxGroups
        CheckboxGroup cbgNorth = new CheckboxGroup();
        CheckboxGroup cbgWest = new CheckboxGroup();
        myNorthPanel.add(rb_black = new Checkbox(
                        "Black", cbgNorth, true));
myNorthPanel.add(rb_blue = new Checkbox(
                        "Blue", cbgNorth, false));
        myNorthPanel.add(rb_lightGray = new Checkbox(
                        "Gray", cbgNorth, false));
        myNorthPanel.add(rb_magenta = new Checkbox(
                        "Magenta", cbgNorth, false));
        myNorthPanel.add(rb_red = new Checkbox(
                        "Red", cbgNorth, false));
        myNorthPanel.add(rb_yellow = new Checkbox(
                        "Yellow", cbgNorth, false));
        myNorthPanel.add(rb_green = new Checkbox(
```

continues

Listing 10.1
Continued

```
                                          "Green", cbgNorth, false));
        cbgWest = new CheckboxGroup();
        myWestPanel.add(rb_draw = new Checkbox(
                               "Draw", cbgWest, true));
        myWestPanel.add(rb_line = new Checkbox(
                               "Line", cbgWest, false));
        // Add the panels to the frame
        add("North", myNorthPanel);
        add("West", myWestPanel);
        add("South", mySouthPanel);
    }
    public void clear(Graphics g) {
        Rectangle r = bounds();
        g.setColor(Color.white);
        g.fillRect(r.x, r.y, r.width, r.height);
    }
    public void paint(Graphics g) {
        clear(g);
    }
    public static void main (String args[]) {
        Frame f = new graphics();
        f.setTitle("Radio Button Test");
        f.resize(600,400);
        f.show();
    }
    // Called when a user starts to click a mouse
    public boolean mouseDown(Event e, int x, int y) {
        if (isLineDrawn && last_x != 0) {
            draw(last_x, last_y, x, y);
            last_x = 0;
            last_y = 0;
        }
        else {
            last_x = x;
            last_y = y;
        }
        return true;
    }
    // Called when a user starts to click and drag a mouse
    public boolean mouseDrag(Event e, int x, int y) {
        if (isLineDrawn == false) {
            draw(last_x, last_y, x, y);
            last_x = x;
            last_y = y;
        }
        return true;
    }
```

```
public void draw(int last_x, int last_y, int x, int y)
{
        Graphics g = getGraphics();
        g.setColor(current_color);
        g.drawLine(last_x, last_y, x, y);
}
// Called when a user draws a line or draws with a
➥drag.
// Called when a user clicks a button or chooses a
➥color
public boolean handleEvent (Event event) {
    // If the clear button was clicked, handle it.
    if (event.target == cb_clear) {
        last_x = 0;
        last_y = 0;
        clear(getGraphics());
    }
    else if (event.target == cb_exit) {
        dispose();
        java.lang.System.exit(0);
    }
    else if (event.target == rb_line) {
        isLineDrawn = true;
        last_x = 0;
        last_y = 0;
    }
    else if (event.target == rb_draw) {
        isLineDrawn = false;
    }
    else if (event.target == rb_black) {
        current_color = Color.black;
    }
    else if (event.target == rb_blue) {
        current_color = Color.blue;
    }
    else if (event.target == rb_lightGray) {
        current_color = Color.lightGray;
    }
    else if (event.target == rb_magenta) {
        current_color = Color.magenta;
    }
    else if (event.target == rb_red) {
        current_color = Color.red;
    }
    else if (event.target == rb_yellow) {
```

continues

Listing 10.1
Continued

```
                current_color = Color.yellow;
        }
        else if (event.target == rb_green) {
            current_color = Color.green;
        }
        else {
            // Otherwise, let the superclass handle it
            return super.handleEvent(event);
        }
    return true;
    }
}
```

Using the graphicsApplet program, you'll be able to create works of art, as shown in Figure 10.2. (To me, this figure represents the inner struggles of a programmer.)

Fig. 10.2
Pictures (such as my attempt at art) can be drawn using the graphicsApplet program.

Applets and Applications Together

Notice that there are two classes in the graphicsApplet.Java file. The second is the actual program. If you compiled the graphics class, it would run as a stand alone application. However, just by duplicating the main() function inside an applet, you can turn your stand alone application into a Web-ready applet:

```
public class graphicsApplet extends Applet {
    public void init() {
        Frame f = new graphics();
        f.setTitle("Graphics Applet Test");
        f.resize(600,400);
        f.show();
    }
}
```

This is often done so that programs can run alone, but also can run on the Internet if desired.

> **NOTE:**
> How do you override the Graphics class? Notice that the second class is called `graphics`. This is not to be confused with the Graphics class. Names in Visual J++ are case-sensative. (It's probably *not* a good idea to have two classes with the same name but different cases, but I just wanted to illustrate that it could be done.)

Visual J++ Window Controls

Window controls are constructs (like command buttons or check boxes) that allow the user to enter information or make selections in a Windows or graphical program. This excerpt from Listing 10.1 shows how to declare Checkboxes and Buttons:

```
private Checkbox rb_black;
private Checkbox rb_blue;
private Checkbox rb_lightGray;
private Checkbox rb_magenta;
private Checkbox rb_red;
private Checkbox rb_yellow;
private Checkbox rb_green;
private Checkbox rb_draw;
private Checkbox rb_line;
private Button cb_clear;
private Button cb_exit;
```

Visual J++ supports the following controls:

Control	Description
Button	Allows the users to execute some functionality by clicking it.
Canvas	Allows the user to set aside a graphical area on a window or panel. This graphical area allows you to divide your frame into separate graphical areas.
Checkbox	Allows the user to make yes or no decisions by clicking the check box on and off. If Checkbox is added to a CheckBoxGroup, it become a radio button—the user is allowed a multiple choice, mutually exclusive selection.
Choice	Choice is a list bos. It allows the user to open a drop-down list and choose between available values.
Label	A Label is static text.
List	List shows a list of Strings for the user to choose from. It differs from Choice in that Choice is a drop-down list, while List always displays the choices.
Scrollbar	This allows you to put a scrollable (up, down, page up, page down) element on your panel or window. This control often isn't necessary because Visual J++ does a good job of determining when a scrollbar is needed and adding it without any code.
TextArea	This is a multi-line text area.
TextField	This is a single-line text area.

Sophisticated use of controls can make a good user interface.

Panels and Layouts

Instead of using just one graphics area, the graphics area is divided into panels. A *panel* is a window inside a window. By taking a frame and dividing it into panels, you can rearrange your controls on your window. Traditionally, Visual J++ places all controls on the window in a left-to-right, top-to-bottom order. There are three panels defined in the graphics class in Listing 10.1: myNorthPanel, myWestPanel, and mySouthPanel:

```
//Define Panels and the layouts they use
Panel myNorthPanel = new Panel();
Panel myWestPanel = new Panel();
Panel mySouthPanel = new Panel();
myNorthPanel.setBackground(Color.lightGray);
mySouthPanel.setBackground(Color.lightGray);
```

```
myWestPanel.setBackground(Color.lightGray);
myNorthPanel.setLayout(new FlowLayout());
myWestPanel.setLayout(new GridLayout(2, 1));
mySouthPanel.setLayout(new FlowLayout());
```

TIP:
All applets are also considered panels.

First, you create new panels with the new directive. Then, you set the background on the panels to light grey. (This is to contrast with the white background drawing area.) Finally, you assign a layout to each of the panels.

A layout allows you to format your panel in an appropriate manner. For example, FlowLayout is the default layout for a panel. Objects will be centered and placed in a left-to-right, top-to-bottom order. This is good for both the command buttons (Clear and Exit) and the color radio buttons. The GridLayout allows you to setup a grid to load your controls. In myWestPanel, I don't want my two choices going across the screen horizontally; I want them listed vertically, on top of each other. A GridLayout of two rows and one column is used to achieve this.

Adding Controls to Panels

The add method is used to add controls to the panels. Notice the syntax I used to make the code a little more manageable. The following line of code:

```
mySouthPanel.add(cb_clear = new Button("Clear"));
```

is equivalent to the following two lines of code:

```
cb_clear = new Button("Clear");
mySouthPanel.add(cb_clear);
```

Although it may take some getting use to, assigning and adding buttons with one line of code is easier to read and maintain then using two lines of code. This is because each line deals with the addition of a new control rather than using mutliple lines for the same task.

CheckboxGroups turn Checkboxes into radio buttons. By placing Checkboxes in a CheckboxGroup, you turn all the check boxes from on/off switches to a series of multiple choice questions. The following code is from Listing 10.1, and is used to add controls to the panels:

```
// Create the clear and exit command buttons.
mySouthPanel.add(cb_clear = new Button("Clear"));
mySouthPanel.add(cb_exit = new Button("Exit"));
// Define CheckboxGroups
CheckboxGroup cbgNorth = new CheckboxGroup();
CheckboxGroup cbgWest = new CheckboxGroup();
myNorthPanel.add(rb_black = new Checkbox(
                    "Black", cbgNorth, true));
myNorthPanel.add(rb_blue = new Checkbox(
                    "Blue", cbgNorth, false));
myNorthPanel.add(rb_lightGray = new Checkbox(
                    "Gray", cbgNorth, false));
myNorthPanel.add(rb_magenta = new Checkbox(
                    "Magenta", cbgNorth, false));
myNorthPanel.add(rb_red = new Checkbox(
                    "Red", cbgNorth, false));
myNorthPanel.add(rb_yellow = new Checkbox(
                    "Yellow", cbgNorth, false));
myNorthPanel.add(rb_green = new Checkbox(
                    "Green", cbgNorth, false));
cbgWest = new CheckboxGroup();
myWestPanel.add(rb_draw = new Checkbox(
                    "Draw", cbgWest, true));
myWestPanel.add(rb_line = new Checkbox(
                    "Line", cbgWest, false));
```

Adding Panels to the Frame

Now you must add all the panels you created to your frame. The following extract from Listing 10.1 shows that you can add myNorthPanel, myWestPanel, and mySouthPanel to the "North", "West", and "South" areas on the graphics frame:

```
// Add the panels to the frame
add("North", myNorthPanel);
add("West", myWestPanel);
add("South", mySouthPanel);
```

Clearing the Drawing Area

When you press clear or when you first open your graphics frame, you'll want to clear an appropriate area and make it white. This must be done *after* the Graphics have been set up for the frame. (In other words, if you tried to clear an area in the constructor, you would end up with a NullPointerException error.)

The best place to handle graphics for the first time is by overriding the paint method. By the time the Frame ancestor calls the paint method, the Graphics for the Frame has already been set up:

```
public void clear(Graphics g) {
    Rectangle r = bounds();
    g.setColor(Color.white);
    g.fillRect(r.x, r.y, r.width, r.height);
}
public void paint(Graphics g) {
    clear(g);
}
// ...Some other Listing 10.1 code goes here.
//  Then you test for a click on cb_clear...
    if (event.target == cb_clear) {
        last_x = 0;
        last_y = 0;
        clear(getGraphics());
        }
```

In the clear method, you get the rectangle which is the bounds for the draw area after the panels have been in place. Then, you set the color to white and fill the rectangle with a white color. The paint method calls the clear method. Also, the clear method is called when the user clicks the cb_clear button.

Drawing Graphics

The mouseDown and mouseDrag events are called by the ancestor Component class when a user clicks or drags a mouse. First, you must test whether you're supposed to draw a line. If not, just draw no matter if they click or drag. In this case, the "line" you draw with draw(last_x, last_y, x, y); will draw a line between two points that are touching each other, giving the effect of freeform drawing. If you're supposed to draw a line, then the user must click one area on the Frame and then other, thereby drawing a line between the two.

The draw function was written to set the current color and draw. This is shown in the mouseDown and mouseDrag events in Listing 10.1:

```
// Called when a user starts to click a mouse
public boolean mouseDown(Event e, int x, int y) {
    if (isLineDrawn && last_x != 0) {
        draw(last_x, last_y, x, y);
        last_x = 0;
        last_y = 0;
    }
    else {
        last_x = x;
        last_y = y;
    }
    return true;
}
// Called when a user starts to click and drag a mouse
public boolean mouseDrag(Event e, int x, int y) {
    if (isLineDrawn == false) {
        draw(last_x, last_y, x, y);
        last_x = x;
        last_y = y;
    }
    return true;
}
public void draw(int last_x, int last_y, int x, int y) {
    Graphics g = getGraphics();
    g.setColor(current_color);
    g.drawLine(last_x, last_y, x, y);
}
```

Event Handling Revisited

When discussing events previously, you learned how keyboard and mouse events could be caught. Now, you need to use events to tell you which button or check box was clicked.

Every time an event occurs, the handleEvent method is called. (Because you override the handleEvent method, the Component ancestor will call the handleEvent method.) In the handleEvent method, you test the `Event.target`. The `Event.target` attribute defines the target of the event. (If you click `cb_clear`, then `cb_clear` is the `Event.target`, and so on.) In Listing 10.1 (and in the following code), you test `event.target` to see if `cb_clear`, `cb_exit`, one of the colors, or `Draw/Line` was clicked:

NOTE:
Why do you sometimes capitalize Event. target and othertimes you don't?

My editors had the same question. When I'm talking about the Event.target attribute, I'm talking about the target attribute of the Event class. When I'm talking about testing event.target in Listing 10.1, I'm talking about testing the target attribute of the event *instance* of the Event class, which isn't capitalized.

```
public boolean handleEvent (Event event) {
    // If the clear button was clicked, handle it.
    if (event.target == cb_clear) {
        last_x = 0;
        last_y = 0;
        clear(getGraphics());
    }
    else if (event.target == cb_exit) {
        dispose();
        java.lang.System.exit(0);
    }
    else if (event.target == rb_line) {
        isLineDrawn = true;
        last_x = 0;
        last_y = 0;
    }
    else if (event.target == rb_draw) {
        isLineDrawn = false;
    }
    else if (event.target == rb_black) {
```

```
            current_color = Color.black;
        }
        else if (event.target == rb_blue) {
            current_color = Color.blue;
        }
        else if (event.target == rb_lightGray) {
            current_color = Color.lightGray;
        }
        else if (event.target == rb_magenta) {
            current_color = Color.magenta;
        }
        else if (event.target == rb_red) {
            current_color = Color.red;
        }
        else if (event.target == rb_yellow) {
            current_color = Color.yellow;
        }
        else if (event.target == rb_green) {
            current_color = Color.green;
        }
        else {
            // Otherwise, let the superclass handle it
            return super.handleEvent(event);
        }
        return true;
    }
```

> **CAUTION:**
> Notice how the `super.handleEvent` **method is called if the event isn't one of those you're testing for. This is necessary to allow events that aren't part of your class to continue processing.**

Using the `handleEvent` method, you can trap for control events much like you trapped for mouse and keyboard events earlier.

> **NOTE:**
> **Instead of using the** `handleEvent` **method, you could also use the** `action` **method. The** `action` **method is identical to the** `handleEvent` **method except that it also returns the object that the event was performed on. If, due to some advanced object-oriented reason, you don't know the object that the event was performed on, you could call** `action` **insead of** `handleEvent`**.**

Animation

Animation is easy in Java. However, *good* animation involves some trickiness. Listing 10.2 is a simple program that produces a red ball that bounces around a frame. (Very useful in real world applications, right? Still, it could make for a fun Web page.) The program is discussed following the listing, and then you get a chance to make enhancements to it.

Listing 10.2
BoucingBall.java

```java
import java.awt.*;

public class BouncingBall extends Frame {
    private int ballX;  // Used for the center of the circle
    private int ballY;  // Used for the center of the circle
    private int maxX;    // Used to determine when to bounce
    private int maxY;    // Used to determine when to bounce
//ballDiameter is used to determine ball size
//        as well as the MIN and MAX
    private int ballDiameter = 100;
    private int incrementX = 1;
    private int incrementY = 1;
    private Button cb_exit;    //Used for the exit button
// Used to show the status of the ball
    private Label lb_status;
    public static void main (String args[]) {
        BouncingBall bb = new BouncingBall();
        bb.setTitle("Bouncing Ball Test");
        bb.resize(600,400);
        bb.show();
        bb.start();
    }
    public BouncingBall () {
```

continues

Listing 10.2
Continued

```
//Initialize Variables
        ballX = (ballDiameter / 2) + 1;
        ballY = (ballDiameter / 2) + 1;
        maxX = 600 - ballDiameter;
        maxY = 350 - ballDiameter;
//Add an exit button and a grid panel.
        Panel mySouthPanel = new Panel();
        mySouthPanel.setBackground(Color.lightGray);
        mySouthPanel.setLayout(new GridLayout(1, 2));
        mySouthPanel.add(lb_status = new Label(""));
        mySouthPanel.add(cb_exit = new Button("Exit"));
        add("South", mySouthPanel);
    }
    public void start() {
        //Now animate
        Graphics g = getGraphics();
        while (true) {
            g.setColor(Color.white);
            g.fillOval(ballX, ballY,
                        ballDiameter, ballDiameter);
            ballX += incrementX;
             // Boooiiinng (Bounce)
            if (ballX > maxX || ballX < 1) {
                //Change horizontal direction
                incrementX *= -1;
                ballX += (2 * incrementX);
            }
            ballY += incrementY;
             // Boooiiinng (Bounce)
            if (ballY > maxY || ballY < 1) {
                incrementY *= -1;     //Chg vertial
➥direction
                ballY += (2 * incrementY);
            }
            showStatus("Ball at (" + String.valueOf(ballX)
                + "," + String.valueOf(ballY) + ")");
            g.setColor(Color.red);
            g.fillOval(ballX, ballY,
                        ballDiameter, ballDiameter);
// I don't care if my sleep is interrupted
            try {Thread.sleep(10); }
            catch (InterruptedException e) { }
        }
    }
    public void showStatus(String s) {
        lb_status.setText(s);
    }
```

```
public boolean handleEvent (Event event) {
    //Was the exit button pushed?
    if (event.target == cb_exit) {
        dispose();
        java.lang.System.exit(0);
    }
    else {
        // Otherwise, let the superclass handle it
        return super.handleEvent(event);
    }
    return true;
}
}
```

Figure 10.3 shows how the bouncing ball program will look.

Fig. 10.3
The bouncing ball program shows a red ball bouncing with the position of the ball in a status bar at the bottom of the window.

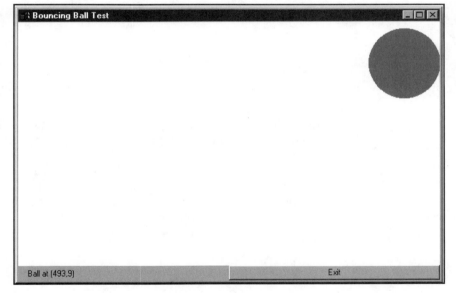

Missing Frame Methods *start* and *showStatus*

Two functions in Applet that are pretty useful are the showStatus method, which simply displays a line of text at the bottom of the window, and the start method, which is called after the applet is constructed and painted.

Unfortunately, such methods are not available inside Frame. The reason for this is that a Frame doesn't have a status area to display status messages, whereas most browsers do. Also, Frames are controlled through a main method; therefore, they don't need functions that are automatically called, such as the start and init methods.

However, because I like these methods so much, I usually end up duplicating them on a frame. The start method is the easiest to duplicate. Simply name a method start:

```
public void start() {
```

and then call it at the end of your main method, after the Frame has been constructed and shown:

```
public static void main (String args[]) {
    BouncingBall bb = new BouncingBall();
    bb.setTitle("Bouncing Ball Test");
    bb.resize(600,400);
    bb.show();
    bb.start();
}
```

By doing this, you can mimic the Applet start method. (It also makes conversion from a Frame to an Applet easier.)

Mimicing the showStatus method is a little more difficult. The (x,y) coordinates of the bouncing ball need to be displayed while the ball is bouncing, and this is easily done with a status string. Because frames don't have a status area like applets do, you must create one. I usually end up doing this through a GridLayout or a GridBagLayout and a Label:

```
mySouthPanel.setLayout(new GridLayout(1, 2));
mySouthPanel.add(lb_status = new Label(""));
```

Then, the showStatus method becomes a simple matter of setting the label to a given text:

```
public void showStatus(String s) {
    lb_status.setText(s);
}
```

The Guts of the Bouncing Ball Program

There are no more new topics to be covered in the BouncingBall program. All of the logic behind the bouncing ball is in the start method:

```
public void start() {
    //Now animate
    Graphics g = getGraphics();
    while (true) {
        g.setColor(Color.white);
        g.fillOval(ballX, ballY,
                        ballDiameter, ballDiameter);
        ballX += incrementX;
        if (ballX > maxX || ballX < 1) {
            // Boooiiinng (Bounce)
            incrementX *= -1;   //Change horizontal direction
            ballX += (2 * incrementX);
        }
        ballY += incrementY;
            // Boooiiinng (Bounce)
        if (ballY > maxY || ballY < 1) {
            incrementY *= -1;      //Change vertical direction
            ballY += (2 * incrementY);
        }
        showStatus("Ball at (" + String.valueOf(ballX) + ","
            + String.valueOf(ballY) + ")");
        g.setColor(Color.red);
        g.fillOval(ballX, ballY,
                        ballDiameter, ballDiameter);
// I don't care if my sleep is interrupted
        try {Thread.sleep(10); }
        catch (InterruptedException e) { }
    }
}
```

The start method does the following:

- It draws a white oval and fills it with a white color to clear any previous circles.

- The start method then calculates the new ball position by incrementing (or decrementing) the current x and y coordinates by 1. If the ball goes beyond the minimum or maximum frame area, the ball "bounces." This is accomplished by changing the increment sign, so that, if needed, a ball going left will go right (and vice versa) and a ball going up will go down (and vice versa).

- The ball is repainted red at the new position.

- The sleep function from the Thread class is then called to sleep for 10 milliseconds., and the whole process starts again. The sleep function in this case performs three functions. First, it slows the ball movement down. Second, it lets the red ball stay longer than the 'white ball,' which can't be seen on the screen and is used to blank out the previous ball. Finally, the Thread sleep function allows other events (like clicking the exit button) to occur while still in the loop. (The Thread class will be covered later in this chapter in the following section.)

Again, this is not too difficult, because this code is an extension of ideas previously discussed in this book.

System Resources and Threads

Some of you may notice how much of a system hog this program is. With an infinite loop defined and a ball being drawn and erased constantly in the infinite loop, this system can become a resource nightmare. To implement a cleaner version of the program, you need to use threads.

Threads allow several routines to run concurrently. If you had methods A, B, and C that could run independently of each other, traditional programs would still force you to run A, then B, and then C. Java and Visual J++ are multi-threaded. This means that you can allow methods A, B, and C to run concurrently, and hopefully finish in a lot less time, as seen in Figure 10.4.

Fig. 10.4
Threads allow several
methods to run
concurrently.

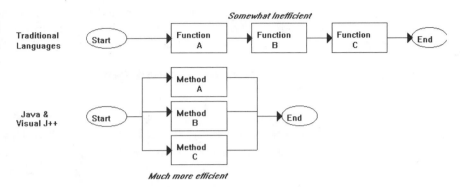

NOTE:
If you only use one processor in your computer, like most
of us, can you only work on one procedure at a time? It's
true that a processor can only perform one task at a
time. However, the processor often waits for other components to finish their tasks before it can continue. For
example, if a Pentium is doing floating point arithmetic,
it funnels that request to a built-in math copressor and
waits for a result.

With multi-threading, your program can take advantage
of a processor's waiting time to run through other functionality. The end result is a much faster program. Also,
on Pentium-type chips whose architecture encourages
multi-threaded environments, percentage increases in
speed can be really high.

To implement threads, you can extend the Thread class. The following class declaration:

```java
public class MyThread extends Thread {
    public void methodA { ... }
    public void methodB { ... }
    public void methodC { ... }
}
```

will declare a new Thread class called `MyThread` with methods `methodA`, `methodB`, and `methodC`. All methods in the `MyThread` class will be forced to run concurrently with all other methods.

The *synchronous* Modifier

> **NOTE:**
> Threads are great if it's OK to run all methods concurrently, but what if you want some of your methods to run concurrently, but others to run independently? The synchronous modifier may be able to help.

The `synchronous` modifier added to a modifier *will not* force a method to run independently of all other methods, but *will* not allow any modification of the containing instance of the class until it is finished running. (However, static variables can still change.) For example, consider the following changes to the MyThread class:

```
public class MyThread extends Thread {
    public void methodA ( ) { ... }
    public synchronous void methodB ( ) { ... }
    public void methodC ( ) { ... }
    // Overrides the Thread run method.
    public void run( ) { ... }
}
```

Once `methodB` has started, any changes to the current instance of the `MyThread` class are not allowed except from `methodB` until `methodB` finishes. (`methodA` and `methodC` *can still run*, but can't change the contents of the `MyThread` class `methodB` is finished.) The synchronous modifier is handy to keep certain methods waiting until other methods are finished running.

Thread Methods

There are several Thread methods you should know about. The most important method is the `run` method. The `run` method contains the body of Java code that the thread runs. Without overriding the `run` method, you have no thread.

The `wait` method causes a thread to wait until notified, while the `notify` and `notifyAll` methods are called within a synchronized method to notify any waiting methods to start again. The `notify` method notifies all waiting methods within it's containing class, while `notifyAll` notifies all waiting methods from any class.

The `suspend` method causes a thread to immediately halt, while the `resume` method starts up all the classes that have been suspended. These are similar to the `wait` and `notify` methods, but are defined within the Thread class rather than the Object class.

Finally, `sleep` allows your program to wait for a given number of milliseconds. You already used the `sleep` method in the BouncingBall class:

```
// I don't care if my sleep is interrupted
try {Thread.sleep(10); }
catch (InterruptedException e) { }
```

Notice that you had to use a `try...catch` block when using the `sleep` method. This is in the Java specifications, and the Visual J++ compiler forces you to at least acknowledge that you don't care if an `InterruptedException` is thrown from within the `sleep` method.

The Runnable Interface

But you can't inherit a Thread. Your class already inherits an Applet or a Frame. Do you need to create a new class for your stuff?

No. Implement the Runnable interface.

Often, your classes will already be inherited from another Class. You *could* go to a lot of trouble and create another class that inherits Thread, then instantiate that class in your object. However, that's usually not needed. You often use a Thread just so you don't monopolize a machine. This can also be achieved with the Runnable interface.

The Runnable interface is implemented by the Thread class. The Runnable interface provides a means of using Threads without actually extending the Thread class. This is done by creating an instance of a thread and passing itself as the target.

> **NOTE:**
> You should *always* implement a Runnable interface rather than extend a Thread if all you're going to override is the `run` method. It's more efficient.

To implement a Runnable interface, you need to perform five steps:

1. Add `implements Runnable` to your class declaration.

    ```
    public class MyClass extends Frame implements Runnable {...
    ```

2. Add a Thread attribute to your class.

    ```
    Thread myThread;
    ```

3. Move all of your `start` method code to a `run` method, which you need to create to use a Runnable interface.

    ```
    public void run() {
    // All your thread code goes in here.
    }
    ```

4. In your `start` method, instantiate your Thread and pass yourself as a parameter. Testing for null first forces the `myThread` varaible to be uninstantiated.

    ```
    public void start() {
        if (myThread == null) {
            myThread = new Thread(this);
            myThread.start();
        }
    }
    ```

5. Code a `stop` event. The `stop` event will override the `Applet` event, and can also be called from your program if you're using a Frame instead of an Applet:

    ```
    public void stop() {
        if (myThread != null) {
            myThread.stop();
    ```

```
                    myThread = null;
            }
        }
```

BouncingBall Modifications

Threads are a lot easier to understand with a real world example, so I'll show you with modifications to the BouncingBall program. I made the changes bold, and italicized the class and method names for readability:

```
import java.awt.*;
public class BouncingBall extends Frame implements Runnable{
    Thread myThread;
    private int ballX;      // Used for the center of circle
    private int ballY;      // Used for the center of circle
    private int maxX;       // Used to determine when to bounce
    private int maxY;       // Used to determine when to bounce
//ballDiameter is used to determine ball size
//      as well as the MIN and MAX
    private int ballDiameter = 100;
    private int incrementX = 1;
    private int incrementY = 1;
    private Button cb_exit;     //Used for the exit button
    // Used to show the status of the ball
    private Label lb_status;
    public static void main (String args[]) {
        BouncingBall bb = new BouncingBall();
        bb.setTitle("Bouncing Ball Test");
        bb.resize(600,400);
        bb.show();
        bb.start();
    }
    public BouncingBall () {
//Initialize Variables
        ballX = (ballDiameter / 2) + 1;
        ballY = (ballDiameter / 2) + 1;
        maxX = 600 - ballDiameter;
        maxY = 350 - ballDiameter;
```

```
//Add an exit button and a grid panel.
        Panel mySouthPanel = new Panel();
        mySouthPanel.setBackground(Color.lightGray);
        mySouthPanel.setLayout(new GridLayout(1, 2));
        mySouthPanel.add(lb_status = new Label(""));
        mySouthPanel.add(cb_exit = new Button("Exit"));
        add("South", mySouthPanel);
    }
    public void start() {
        if (myThread == null) {
            myThread = new Thread(this);
            myThread.start();
        }
    }
    public void stop() {
        if (myThread != null) {
            myThread.stop();
            myThread = null;
        }
    }
    public void run() {
        //Now animate
        Graphics g = getGraphics();
        while (true) {
            g.setColor(Color.white);
            g.fillOval(ballX, ballY,
                            ballDiameter, ballDiameter);
            ballX += incrementX;
            // Boooiiinng (Bounce)
            if (ballX > maxX || ballX < 1) {
                incrementX *= -1; //Chg horizontal direction
                ballX += (2 * incrementX);
            }
            ballY += incrementY;
            // Boooiiinng (Bounce)
            if (ballY > maxY || ballY < 1) {
                incrementY *= -1; //Chg vertical direction
```

```
                    ballY += (2 * incrementY);
                }
                showStatus("Ball at (" + String.valueOf(ballX)
                    + "," + String.valueOf(ballY) + ")");
                g.setColor(Color.red);
                g.fillOval(ballX, ballY,
                            ballDiameter, ballDiameter);
                try {Thread.sleep(10); }
                catch (InterruptedException e) { }
            }
        }
        public void showStatus(String s) {
            lb_status.setText(s);
        }
        public boolean handleEvent (Event event) {
            //Was the exit button pushed?
            if (event.target == cb_exit) {
                stop();
                dispose();
                java.lang.System.exit(0);
            }
            else {
                // Otherwise, let the superclass handle it
                return super.handleEvent(event);
            }
            return true;
        }
    }
}
```

As you can see by the bolded text, I implemented the changes suggested in the previous section almost word for word. Also, not many changes were necessary to turn my `start` method into a multi-threaded `run` method.

Resolving Flickering

When you run the program in the preceding section, you'll notice a lot of flickering when the ball is repainted. This can be very annoying to the viewer of the program. The reason the ball flickers is because the ball is blanked out with a white ball and then repainted red.

Flickering results from repainting what you don't need to repaint. Because you're only moving one pixel at a time, it would suffice to just wipe out the outer circle of pixels. This could be accomplished by changing the `fillOval` call in the `run` method:

```
g.setColor(Color.white);
g.fillOval(ballX, ballY, ballDiameter, ballDiameter);
```

to a `drawOval` call, which only draws the outer oval:

```
g.setColor(Color.white);
g.drawOval(ballX, ballY, ballDiameter, ballDiameter);
```

Because the `drawOval` method draws an outline of an oval, you would only be clearing out the outside edge of pixels using the `drawOval` method.

> **NOTE:**
> Although this method works *logically*, some graphical setups *physically* leave holes in their circles where the filled in circle may leak through, and the white clearing would have to be done a different, more complicated way. However, the point is still made that you should endeavor to redraw only what you have to, and not redraw the picture every time a little portion of it changes.

Using Bitmaps in Animation.

Often, you'll want to use actual bitmaps (usually JPG or GIF files) for animation rather than drawing pictures yourself. This is accomplished most easily using the Applet wizard to build a graphical Web page. This section discusses the Java code needed to perform this task. Assume you had four bitmap pictures of clocks, as seen in Figure 10.5. These bitmaps are CLOCK1.GIF, CLOCK2.GIF, CLOCK3.GIF, and CLOCK4.GIF on your CD.

Fig. 10.5
Four bitmaps of
clocks used for
animation

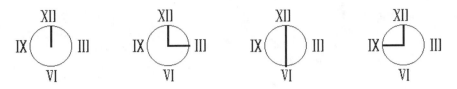

Listing 10.3 shows the code needed to display these four bitmaps sequentially to achieve an animation effect.

Listing 10.3
clock.java

```
import java.applet.*;
import java.awt.*;
public class Clock extends Applet implements Runnable {
    private Image m_Images[];   // Image array for animation
    private int m_nCurrImage;   // Current Image to display
    private int m_nImgWidth  = 0;  //Width of Image
    private int m_nImgHeight = 0;  // Height of Image
// Boolean set to true when all the images have loaded
    private boolean  m_fAllLoaded = false;
    private final int NUM_IMAGES = 4;  // Number of Images
    public void init() {
        resize(320, 240);
        //Run thread, which calls the run method
        Thread clockThread = new Thread(this);
        clockThread.start();
    }
    public void run() {     // Called for Thread support.
        m_nCurrImage   = 0;
        String imageName;
// Array to store images
        m_Images   = new Image[NUM_IMAGES];
        Graphics g = getGraphics();
        showStatus("Loading images...");
        for (int i = 1; i <= NUM_IMAGES; i++) {
            imageName = "CLOCK" + i + ".gif";  //
Image file
            m_Images[i-1] = getImage(
                    getDocumentBase(), imageName);
            // Get width and height of one image. Assume
            // all images are same width and height
            if (m_nImgWidth == 0) {
                try    {
                    while ((m_nImgWidth =
                            m_Images[i-1].getWidth(null))
< 0)
```

continues

Listing 10.3
Continued

```
                               Thread.sleep(1);
                    while ((m_nImgHeight =
                         m_Images[i-1].getHeight(null))
➥< 0)
                         Thread.sleep(1);
                  }
                  catch (InterruptedException e) { }
            }
            // Force image to fully load
            g.drawImage(m_Images[i-1], -1000, -1000,
➥this);
         }
         // Wait until images are fully loaded
         while (!m_fAllLoaded) {
             try { Thread.sleep(10); }
             catch (InterruptedException e) { }
         }
         showStatus("Done loading images.");
         while (true) {
             try { // Draw next image in animation
                 displayImage(g);
                 m_nCurrImage++;
                 if (m_nCurrImage == NUM_IMAGES)
                     m_nCurrImage = 0;
                 Thread.sleep(500);
             }
             catch (InterruptedException e) {stop();}
         }
     }
     private void displayImage(Graphics g) {
         if (!m_fAllLoaded)
             return;
         g.drawImage(m_Images[m_nCurrImage],
                 (size().width - m_nImgWidth)   / 2,
                 (size().height - m_nImgHeight) / 2, null);
     }
     public void paint(Graphics g) {
         if (m_fAllLoaded) {
             Rectangle r = g.getClipRect();
             g.clearRect(r.x, r.y, r.width, r.height);
             displayImage(g);
         }
     }
```

```
    public boolean imageUpdate(Image img, int flags,
                               int x, int y, int w,
int h) {
        // Nothing to do if images are all loaded
        if (m_fAllLoaded)
            return false;
        // Want all bits to be available before painting
        if ((flags & ALLBITS) == 0)
            return true;
        // All bits are available, so increment loaded
count
        // of fully loaded images, starting animation if
all
        // images are loaded
        if (++m_nCurrImage == NUM_IMAGES) {
            m_nCurrImage = 0;
            m_fAllLoaded = true;
        }
        return false;
    }
    public void stop() {
        if (m_Clock != null) {
            m_Clock.stop();
            m_Clock = null;
        }
    }
}
```

In Listing 10.3, you use a three step process to display bitmaps:

1. First, you load the images into an Image class array. The Image class is used to store images loaded from a GIF or JPG file.

2. After loading the images into an array, you loop through the images continuously, clearing out the previous Image before displaying a new Image array element.

3. If the Web browser is stopped, the thread is stopped and does not continue unless the Web browser is started once more.

All this is done using threads for better user interaction. Figure 10.6 shows how Clock.java looks while running.

Fig. 10.6
Clock.java displays
an animated clock
while running.

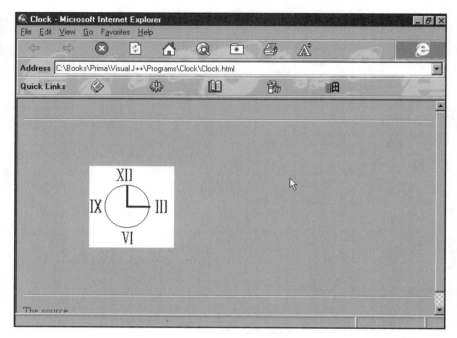

The Applet Wizard, Revisited

The previous code was originally written using the Applet Wizard, then revised to make the code shorter and friendlier. To review a little of Chapter 4, you first click File, New to open the New dialog box, as shown in Figure 10.7. From here, choose Project Workspace and click OK.

The New Project Workspace dialog box then appears, as shown in Figure 10.8. To start the Applet Wizard, you must choose Java Applet Wizard, enter the name of your Java class (Clock) and click Create.

Then, in Step 1 of 5 in the Java Applet Wizard, choose Applet only and click Next, as shown in Figure 10.9.

Continue using the defaults in the Java Applet Wizard as you did in Chapter 4 until you reach Step 3 of 5. Here, choose multi-threaded and support for animation, as shown in Figure 10.10.

Using the Applet Wizard, you pretty much only need to change the number of pictures where you define the class attributes:

```
private final int NUM_IMAGES = 4;   // Number of Images
```

and the path name where the pictures reside in the run method:

```
imageName = "CLOCK" + i + ".gif";   // Image file
```

Fig. 10.7
Choose Project
Workspace in the New
dialog box to begin
using the Applet
Wizard.

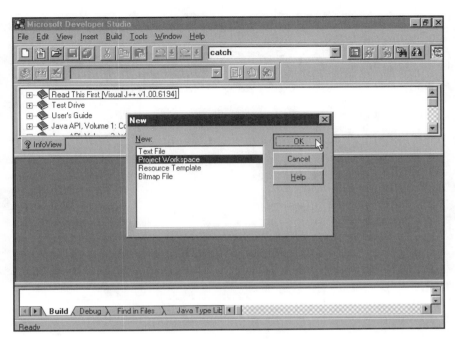

Fig. 10.8
The New Project
Workspace dialog box
allows you to choose
the Applet Wizard to
create an applet
automatically.

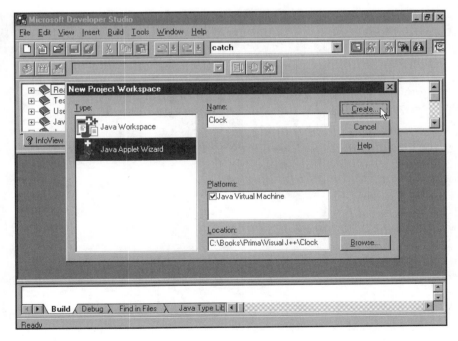

Fig. 10.9
The Java Applet
Wizard - Step 1 of 5
allows you to choose
your applet name and
how you want your
program to run.

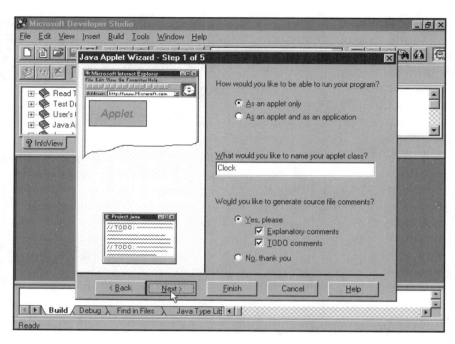

Fig. 10.10
For effective bitmap
animation using
the Applet wizard,
click yes to
multi-threaded and
animation support.

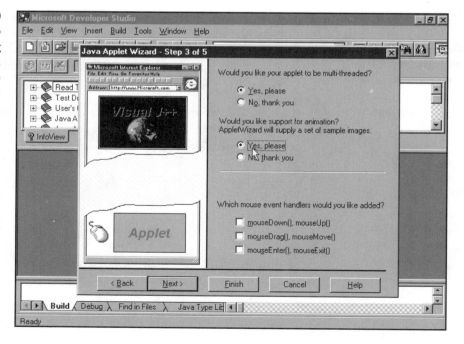

> **NOTE:**
> I changed the name of the Applet Wizard's `strImage` variable to `imageName`. Although this is personal preference only, I thought that `imageName` is easier to understand than `strImage`.

With these two changes, I changed the number of images from 18 (default with the Applet wizard) and from IMAGES\IMG00xx.GIF to CLOCKx.GIF (where x is the number of the picture). Of course, as mentioned previously, I made other changes to make my code a little more user friendly and a little shorter, but the above two changes are all that's really needed to display a series of customized bitmaps when you use the Applet Wizard. It may be a good idea to generate your own code using the Applet Wizard to compare to Listing 10.3.

Understanding Java Code for Bitmap Animation.

This section will describe the `init`, `run`, `paint`, `displayImage`, and `imageUpdate` methods as they are used for animation in Listing 10.3.

The *init* Method

The `init` method is called by the Applet parent class whenever the applet starts. In Listing 10.3, the `init` method declares a new Thread and starts it. This will automatically call the run method.

```
public void init() {
    resize(320, 240);
    //Run thread, which calls the run method
    Thread clockThread = new Thread(this);
    clockThread.start();
}
```

NOTE:

The Applet Wizard used `init`, `start`, and `stop` methods to stop animation when the browser window was no longer active, and restart it when it became active once more. The `start` and `stop` methods are called by the Applet parent class when an applet starts or stops. This is usually a better way to do *any* animation *except* a clock. (Even then, you can inquire the time on the system clock whenever your window becomes active once more.) This code can be seen as follows:

```java
public class Clock extends Applet implements Runnable {
    Thread m_Clock = null;
// ... Rest of Class Attributes are declared here.
    public void init() {
        resize(320, 240);
    }
    public void start() {
        if (m_Clock == null) {
            m_Clock = new Thread(this);
            m_Clock.start();
        }
    }
    public void stop() {
        if (m_Clock != null) {
            m_Clock.stop();
            m_Clock = null;
        }
    }
// ... Rest of class methods goes here
}
```

Only animating when needed can save on system resources. However, in this case I kept the animation going to make the code easier to understand and to contrast continuous animation with the way the Applet Wizard generates code.

The *run* Method

The run method is the most complicated method in the Clock program. The run method is called when the Thread class in the init is intantiated. Here, you show a status message saying that the images are loading. First, an array is initialized to hold the images you receive from the hard drive:

```
m_Images   = new Image[NUM_IMAGES];
```

Then, the four images are loaded. (NUM_IMAGES is set to four.) The names of the images are CLOCK1.GIF, CLOCK2.GIF, CLOCK3.GIF, and CLOCK4.GIF. While they are loading, the for loop used to load the images waits until the width and height of the images can be determined. A Thread.sleep function is called to facilitate any user action, like a mouse click. Finally, each image is drawn as it is loaded to force the image to fully load before continuing:

```
for (int i = 1; i <= NUM_IMAGES; i++) {
    imageName = "CLOCK" + i + ".gif";  // Image file
    m_Images[i-1] = getImage(
            getDocumentBase(), imageName);
    // Get width and height of one image. Assume
    // all images are same width and height
    try    {
        while ((m_nImgWidth =
            m_Images[i-1].getWidth(null)) < 0)
            Thread.sleep(1);
        while ((m_nImgHeight =
            m_Images[i-1].getHeight(null)) < 0)
            Thread.sleep(1);
    }
    catch (InterruptedException e) { }
    // Force image to fully load
    g.drawImage(m_Images[i-1], -1000, -1000, this);
}
```

Because functions called by a thread can run simultaneously, the run method then loops until the m_fAllLoaded boolean flag is set.

```
// Wait until images are fully loaded
while (!m_fAllLoaded) {
    try { Thread.sleep(10); }
    catch (InterruptedException e) { }
}
```

Finally, loop is executed, which cycles through the images and calls the displayImage method each time. After displaying the image, this loop then sleeps for half of a second (500 milliseconds). If interrupted, the stop Applet method is called.

```
while (true) {
    try { // Draw next image in animation
        displayImage(g);
        m_nCurrImage++;
        if (m_nCurrImage == NUM_IMAGES)
            m_nCurrImage = 0;
        Thread.sleep(500);
    }
    catch (InterruptedException e) {stop();}
}
}
```

The *paint* Method

The paint method is called every time a component (like an applet) makes any graphical calls. In this case, if all the images are loaded, paint will determine the size of the current graphical area by using the getClipRect method. Then it will clear only that part of the window. Finally, a new image will be displayed using the current graphics area.

```
public void paint(Graphics g) {
    if (m_fAllLoaded) {
        Rectangle r = g.getClipRect();
        g.clearRect(r.x, r.y, r.width, r.height);
        displayImage(g);
    }
}
```

The *displayImage* Method

All the `displayImage` method does is display an image in the center of the window. This is done with the Graphics.drawImage method:

```
private void displayImage(Graphics g) {
    g.drawImage(m_Images[m_nCurrImage],
            (size().width - m_nImgWidth)   / 2,
            (size().height - m_nImgHeight) / 2, null);
}
```

The *imageUpdate* Method

The `imageUpdate()` method is called repeatedly by the AWT while images are being painted. The flags parameter can be bitwise ANDed with any of the ImageObserver attributes, like ALLBITS, to give information about the status of images that are currently being painted. When the last image is done being loaded, the boolean `m_fAllLoaded` flag is set to true. The `m_fAllLoaded` flag is used throughout the Clock program to make sure that all images are loaded before other processing can continue.

```
public boolean imageUpdate(Image img, int flags,
                            int x, int y, int w, int h) {
    // Nothing to do if images are all loaded
    if (m_fAllLoaded)
        return false;
    // Want all bits to be available before painting
    if ((flags & ALLBITS) == 0)
        return true;
    // All bits are available, so increment loaded count
    // of fully loaded images, starting animation if all
    // images are loaded
    if (++m_nCurrImage == NUM_IMAGES) {
        m_nCurrImage = 0;
        m_fAllLoaded = true;
    }
    return false;
}
```

Fonts

You can change the font of any Graphics or Component class or subclass. Listing 10.4 shows HelloWorldApplet.java introduced in Chapter 1. However, it has been rewritten to change the font of "Hello World!" to Arial, 24 point. (Changed lines, other than the name of the class, are in bold.)

Listing 10.4
Hellofont.java

```
import java.awt.*;
import java.applet.*;

public class HelloFont extends Applet {
        private Font arialFont;

        public void init() {
                arialFont = new Font("Helvetica", Font.ITALIC +
➥Font.BOLD, 24);
        }


        public void paint(Graphics g) {
            g.setFont(arialFont);
            g.drawString("Hello World!", 1, 75);
        }
}
```

Notice that, even though Arial font was specified in the previous paragraph, it looks like Helvetica font is used instead. This is because Java's Helvetica font maps to Arial font. The following table shows the fonts specified by the Java standard.

Windows Font	Corresponding Java Font
Arial	Helvetica (default)
Courier New	Courier
MS Sans Serif	Dialog or DialogInput
Times New Roman	TimesRoman
WingDings	ZapfDingbats

If you use the Java fonts in your programs, all Java virtual machines are required to support the above six fonts. If you try to use a font that is not specified by the Java standard, some programs will not be able to use your font. This may cause your text to display in a some other font or to not display at all.

Conclusion

The graphical capabilities of Java are astounding. They allow you to write fairly complex programs (like the graphicsApplet program) with a fraction of the work involved if you were to write the same program in other languages.

Although Java has some advanced text-based display capabilities, most agree that text-based applications are not going to be around much longer—except perhaps in some vertical markets or in some archaic corporate legacy systems. Look for an advanced book (due out by the end of the year) coming from me (Chuck Wood) and Prima Publishing to cover even more graphics and animation.

Chapter 11

The ActiveX and COM Specifications

Microsoft added their developer's studio to Visual J++ to aid in Java development. However, with the actual J++, they only made one enhancement over the original Java specifications. Microsoft has added ActiveX controls to the Java language.

In this chapter, you will learn:

- ☉ How ActiveX and COM relate to each other

- ☉ Exactly how COM software is implemented

- ☉ How to call ActiveX programs within Visual J++

- ☉ How to use the Java Type Library Wizard to help you with your ActiveX calls.

How ActiveX and COM relate

ActiveX controls are a good and necessary component to a strongly interenet-influenced language like Java. ActiveX controls used to be known as OLE (Object Linking and Embedding) Automation, since using ActiveX, one program could be "automated" with another. However, the term OLE Automation is now obsolete and replaced with ActiveX.

ActiveX is a major part of COM controls (Common Object Modules). COM allows a developer to write components, and these components will then be able to be pieced together to form a new or part of a new system. Although developed independently, Visual J++ (and Java) and the COM specification seem made for each other. Because of Visual J++'s automatic garbage collection as well as the use of multiple interfaces makes Visual J++ a natural candidate for COM implementation.

Using COM to Expose Methods

The most apparent benefit of COM with Visual J++ is that applets will expose all public methods so you can call them from programming languages like C++, or scripting languages like VBScript.

Also, Visual J++ applications and applets can access other applications that have COM (or OLE) components. For instance, since Excel and PowerPoint both use OLE, Visual J++ programs will be able to display and manipulate Excel and PowerPoint files. Also, the DAO (Database Access Objects) use COM for database access.

Finally, you'll be able to write ActiveX controls with Visual J++. These ActiveX controls can then be used in other popular development tools like Visual Basic, C++, PowerBuilder, and Borland Delphi.

Cross Platform Development

ActiveX controls are designed to be cross platform. In fact, a company called Metrowerks announced that it will develop a cross-platform ActiveX controls that are compatable with the Macintosh in the Internet Explorer 3.0 for Macintosh. Also, Sun has a free license to ActiveX from Microsoft.

Understanding Component Software

Component software allows you to not only talk to talk to current interfaces, but it also allows you to develop upgraded software that can evolve over time *without the need to update other existing software*! So far, that's a lot like DDE and DLLs, but there are some important differences:

- ◑ Microsoft's DDE interface and (usually) DLLs were not standard and could be implemented in any fashion that an application wanted. Conversely, COM has a set of guidelines that must be used.

- ◑ COM is not language or compiler dependent. In Microsoft's own words, "COM therefore defines a *binary interoperability standard* rather than a language-based interoperability." Often you couldn't call DLLs (except new ActiveX DLLs) from other DLLs using the same language but different compilers without writing and Assembler layer to handle the interface.

- ◑ COM is location independent. You can even distribute ActiveX controls of of Web server or run ActiveX controls on the users own machine, passing it data from your Visual J++ application.

As shown by Figure 11.1, ActiveX and COM are a great way for two (or more) applications to "talk" to each other and assist each other in using building blocks already in place for real good software development.

Fig. 11.1
ActiveX (and therefore COM) objects are methods within applications that are callable from other applications.

The best part of the COM interface is that the applications *talk directly to each other* via memory pointers that are set up internally. The COM layer between the two applications drops as soon as a connection is made. Therefore, very little overhead (except that of two programs running concurrently) is needed.

How COM Works in Visual J++

Any COM object works seamlessly in Visual J++. Visual J++ looks at a COM object as a Java class. This makes implementing COM (ActiveX, OLE, etc.) easier in Java than almost any other language.

Calling COM Modules from Visual J++

You'll be amazed at how easily Visual J++ handles ActiveX integration. Microsoft has included a Beeper ActiveX module (beeper.dll) which you need to copy to your program's current directory. All Beeper does is send a beep to the computer speaker.

Microsoft has included an IBeeper typename inside the beeper.dll ActiveX interface. Inside the IBeeper typename, you can find a Beep() method with no parameters. Using program listing 11.1, you can see how COM and ActiveX are implemented in Visual J++. Try typing in the program and running it right away before continuing, and the bolded lines will be explained later in this section.

Listing 11.1
The HelloBeep ActiveX
program

```
import java.awt.*;
import java.applet.*;
// Import the class files that JavaTLB generates from
➡beeper.dll
import beeper.*;
public class HelloBeep extends Frame {
    //Beeper COM Interface variable
    IBeeper COMBeeper;

    public static void main (String args[]) {
      Frame f = new HelloBeep();
      f.setTitle("Beep 'Hello' to the world");
      f.resize(300,200);
      f.show();
    }
    public HelloBeep() {
      //Initialize your COMBeeper variable.
      COMBeeper = (IBeeper) new Beeper();
    }
    public boolean handleEvent(Event event) {
      if (event.id == Event.WINDOW_DESTROY) {
          dispose();
          java.lang.System.exit(0);
          return true;
      }
      else {
          return super.handleEvent(event);
      }
    }
```

```
    public boolean mouseDown(Event this_event, int x,
➥int y) {
    Graphics g = getGraphics();
    g.drawString("Hello World (Beep)!", x, y);
    // Call Beeper object 'Beep' method to send
    //a beep to the PC speaker.
    COMBeeper.Beep();
    return true;
    }
}
```

When you get your program running, it should display "Hello World (Beep)!" at the mouse pointer every time you click the mouse button as seen in Figure 11.2. Furthermore, a beep should accompany each mouse click.

Fig. 11.2
The HelloBeep program displays a string at every mouse click and beeps each time.

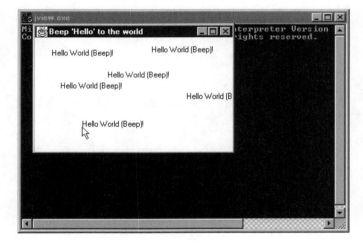

Using the OLE Object Viewer, Revisited

You can view what's inside a registered ActiveX control by using the OLE Object Viewer found inside the Visual J++ environment. To open the Object Viewer, click on Tools, OLE Object Viewer, as seen in Figure 11.3

Next you should see the *Beeper 1.0 Type Library (1.0)* somewhere on your list of ActiveX controls, as seen in Figure 11.4. Double click on it.

Fig. 11.3
To enter the OLE
Object Viewer, click
Tools, OLE Object
Viewer.

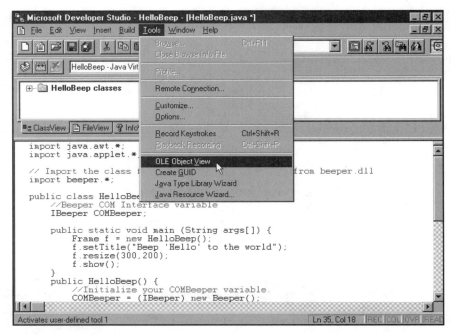

Fig. 11.4
Beeper is listed as an
ActiveX control in the
OLE Object Viewer.

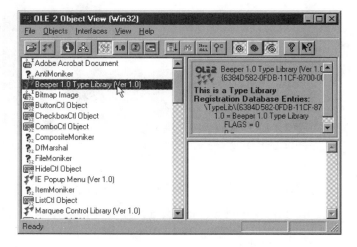

> *I don't see Beeper anywhere. What do I do?*
>
> **The reason you don't see the beeper program is because you haven't successfully built listing 11.1 yet. Try building it if you haven't. Remember to find and copy beeper.dll from the Visual J++ installation to your program's directory.**
>
> **When you get a successful build, Visual J++ automatically registers Beeper as an ActiveX control without you doing anything (again). You'll then be able to view the Beeper ActiveX control through your OLE Object Viewer.**

By double clicking on Beeper, you then see Beeper (0) listed as the TypeInfo. Each TypeInfo translates into a class, if possible, but most TypeInfos that can be used begin with "I" to symbolize that they are a ActiveX interface.

> **NOTE:**
> **Don't confuse ActiveX interfaces with Java interfaces. They are two different things. Java interfaces contain no functionality and are used to tie two classes together. ActiveX interfaces contain functionality and are used by an applicaiton to communicate with another application.**

You can see in Figure 11.5 that there are two TypeInfos listed: Beeper and IBeeper. Since IBeeper is the ActiveX interface, use click on that. IBeeper would by analogous to a class in Java in that it contains both attributes (which are not accessible from Visual J++) and methods to act on those attributes.

You can see in Figure 11.6 that methods are contained within IBeeper. If these methods are meant for public use, they usually contain a DocString in the FUNCDESC area which describes the method. A C++ function prototype is also displayed which will easily convert into Visual J++ to let you know the parameters (if any) that are needed and the return data type.

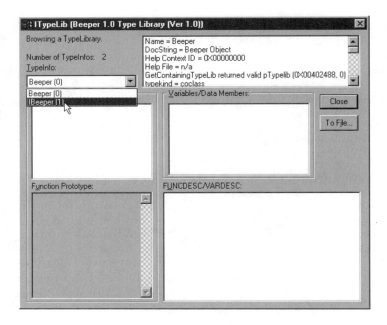

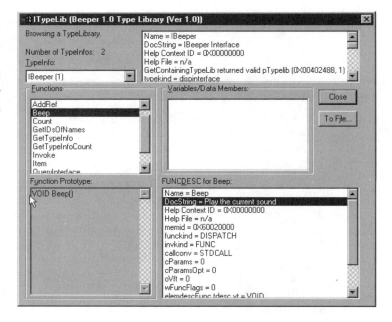

To review what you need to know about ActiveX controls so far:

- ActiveX controls contain TypeInfos, which are a lot like classes in Java. (So much like classes, that Visual J++ treats them as classes.)

- Every TypeInfo contains several methods (a.k.a functions) which can be reviewed both as a function prototype and as a string containing a line of documentation.

- Visual J++ can register ActiveX controls that have not yet been registered when one is used inside a compile.

- The OLE Object viewer can view the TypeInfos and methods of an ActiveX control, making debugging and programming for ActiveX controls even easier than it is already.

The Import Statement with ActiveX

In the program shown in listing 11.1, we use an import command to define a ActiveX program as a class:

```
// Import the class files that JavaTLB
// generates from beeper.dll
import beeper.*;
```

This import statement does two things in Visual J++:

1. Visual J++ looks for a beeper.class or beeper.java program, just like Java.

2. If step 1 fails, it will look for an .OCX, TLB, DLL, or .EXE file that is ActiveX aware. It will then run JavaTLB to internally and automatically convert the ActiveX function calls to class TLB prototypes, which can then be used within your Java program. *All this without any work from the developer!!!* As a Java developer, you would treat an ActiveX control just as you would a Java class.

NOTE:
Not all applications listed in the OLE Object Viewer can be used as classes in Visual J++. Only OLE 2.0 Automation Type Libraries are listed. (Automation type libraries are indicated by what looks like three red pointers pointing to the northeast side of your monitor.) Automation type libraries support ActiveX calls and can be treated like classes inside Visual J++.

Using ActiveX Controls Inside Your Program

As was said earlier, ActiveX TypeInfos are a lot like Java classes, and Visual J++ allows you, the developer, to treat them as classes. Below you see an excerpt from Listing 11.1 where an instance of the IBeeper TypeInfo (COMBeeper) is declared. This is all you need to do to be allowed to use IBeeper methods from your Visual J++ program:

```
//Beeper COM Interface variable
IBeeper COMBeeper;
```

In the constructor, the IBeeper "class" was instantiated with a *new* statement, just as you would have to do with a "normal" class:

```
//Initialize your COMBeeper variable.
COMBeeper = (IBeeper) new Beeper();
```

Finally, in the mouseDown event, an IBeeper method was called to beep your PC Speaker:

```
// Call Beeper object 'Beep' method
// to send a beep to the PC speaker.
COMBeeper.Beep();
```

Notice that this also is how you would code if IBeeper were a class rather than an ActiveX control. Visual J++ does what no other language has yet accomplished. Visual J++ makes ActiveX integration transparent to you, the developer.

Catching Errors in ActiveX Modules—Beeper

There is one problem in Listing 11.1. Every sixth time you click, you don't get a beep. This was an error purposefully introduced into Beeper by Microsoft to allow you to test your error handling capabilities.

Method that uses a COM function can contain a *try...catch* clause that tests for a com.ms.com.ComException. A ComException is an error that occurs during a COM or ActiveX call. Listing 6.2 changes Listing 6.1 somewhat to integrate error trapping as well.

Listing 6.2
New MouseDown
Event for HelloBeep
application

```
public boolean mouseDown(Event this_event, int x, int y) {
    Graphics g = getGraphics();
    g.drawString("Hello World (Beep)!", x, y);
/*
Call Beeper object 'Beep' method to send a beep to the PC
speaker. The
Beep object has been written such that on the sixth call
to Beep(), the
Beep object will return an OLE error code. OLE error codes
get thrown as
ComExceptions.
```

This sample catches the exception, releases the Beeper object by set-ting it to null, creates a new Beeper object, beeps yet another time, and continues:

```
*/
    try {
        COMBeeper.Beep();
    }
    catch(com.ms.com.ComException e) {
        // Release the Beeper object by setting COMBeeper=null
        COMBeeper=null;
        // Create a new Beeper object
        COMBeeper = (IBeeper) new Beeper();
        COMBeeper.Beep();
    }
    return true;
}
```

In the above code, the ComException is caught and handled. You'll also notice that by setting COMBeeper to null, you release the resources for COMBeeper. Otherwise, the resources stay until COMBeeper goes out of scope.

Using the Java Type Library Wizard

Although, with some digging, you can find out the name of the DLL, TLB, OCX, or EXE file that is related to your ActiveX control, you probably want to use the Java Type Library Wizard (JTLW). The JTLW is used to generate the import statement you need in your Visual J++ code to call an ActiveX control. To use the JTLW, click Tools, Java Type Library Wizard as seen in Figure 11.7

Fig. 11.7
Click Tools, Java Type
Library Wizard to use
the JTLW.

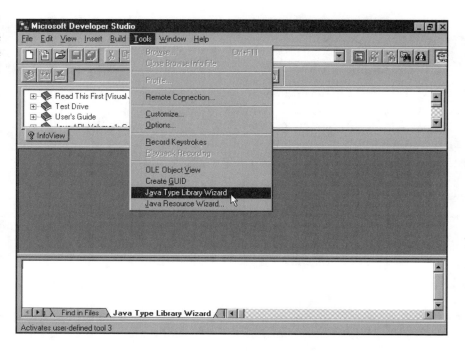

Immediately, the JTLW opens and you should see a list of all available registered ActiveX controls, as seen in figure 11.8. Notice that Beeper is at the top of the list. If you highlight your ActiveX choice, you can see the location of the file that corresponds to the ActiveX control at the bottom of the JTLW window.

Fig. 11.8
The JTLW window lets
you choose which type
libraries you want to
convert to import
statements.

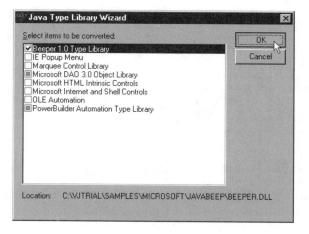

When you check beeper and click OK, as seen in Figure 11.8, the import statement is returned to you in the Java Type Library Wizard tab of the output window, as shown in Figure 11.9.

Fig. 11.9
The import statement that relates to the ActiveX control you chose in the JTLW is displayed in the output window.

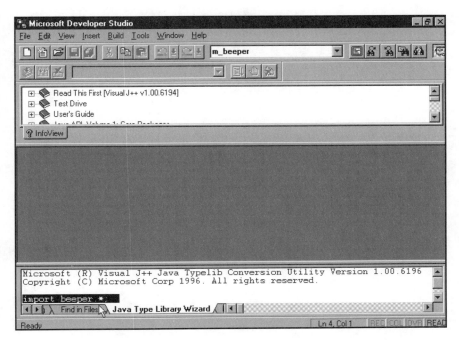

The JTLW is a great way to figure out what import statements are needed without going through the headache of trying to determine which file goes with an ActiveX control.

Calling Visual J++ Modules via ActiveX

All Visual J++ classes (and all Java classes, for that matter) are exposed as ActiveX controls through the Microsoft Java VM, which is the Java Virtual Machine that runs under Internet Explorer 3.0. If you have a Java class running under Internet Explorer 3.0, you can then make ActiveX calls to your Java program through the Java VM running under IE 3.0.

Conclusion

Visual J++ is well suited to ActiveX/COM development. This is because, as all Java classes are COM objects, also all COM objects appear to Visual J++ as Visual J++ classes.

There is *a lot* to ActiveX / COM control development in Visual J++. Look for the advanced book from myself (Chuck Wood) and Prima Publishing coming out later this year for a fuller look at ActiveX development with Visual J++.

Chapter 12

Input and Output with Files and Databases

Traditional Java accomplishes it's disk IO with streams. These streams can be divided into input, output, and random access (I/O) streams. However, while traditional file I/O has it's place, you should really consider implementing database support that is included with Visual J++. Databases tend to offer a greater control of a database, and usually have other means to access your data rather than to write a new program for every data file.

This chapter is dedicated to teaching both the traditional stream I/O and the new database access that has been added to Visual J++. In this chapter, you should learn:

- How to get directory and file information.

- How to use input and output streams in your Visual J++ programs.

- The place and function of random access streams in Visual J++.

- How to use Microsoft's DAO (data access objects).

- About the ODBC (Online Database Connectivity) and it's importance in development.

Getting Directory and File Information

You'll often need to see file information. For example, you'll need to know if a file is a directory, the size of a file, the read-only attribute of a file, when the file was last modified, and so on. The best way to show how to do this is with an example program written in Visual J++.

In this program, called FileFunctions, you will display the current directory and sort entries in the directory by name, size, modification date, or group them by writability based on command buttons on the top of the Frame (see Figure 12.1).

Fig. 12.1
The FileFunctions class will display files and sort on those files.

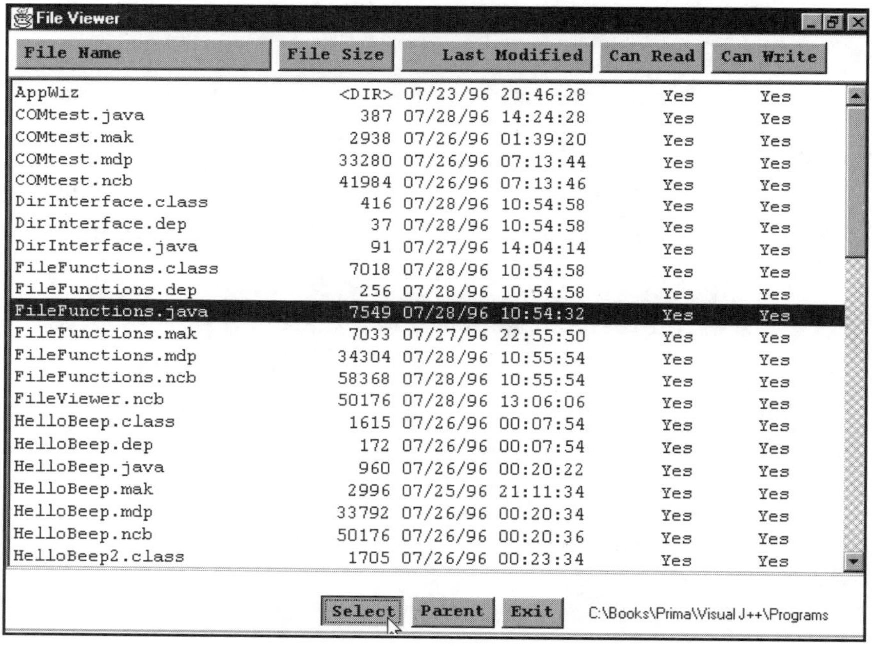

File Name	File Size	Last Modified	Can Read	Can Write
AppWiz	<DIR>	07/23/96 20:46:28	Yes	Yes
COMtest.java	387	07/28/96 14:24:28	Yes	Yes
COMtest.mak	2938	07/26/96 01:39:20	Yes	Yes
COMtest.mdp	33280	07/26/96 07:13:44	Yes	Yes
COMtest.ncb	41984	07/26/96 07:13:46	Yes	Yes
DirInterface.class	416	07/28/96 10:54:58	Yes	Yes
DirInterface.dep	37	07/28/96 10:54:58	Yes	Yes
DirInterface.java	91	07/27/96 14:04:14	Yes	Yes
FileFunctions.class	7018	07/28/96 10:54:58	Yes	Yes
FileFunctions.dep	256	07/28/96 10:54:58	Yes	Yes
FileFunctions.java	7549	07/28/96 10:54:32	Yes	Yes
FileFunctions.mak	7033	07/27/96 22:55:50	Yes	Yes
FileFunctions.mdp	34304	07/28/96 10:55:54	Yes	Yes
FileFunctions.ncb	58368	07/28/96 10:55:54	Yes	Yes
FileViewer.ncb	50176	07/28/96 13:06:06	Yes	Yes
HelloBeep.class	1615	07/26/96 00:07:54	Yes	Yes
HelloBeep.dep	172	07/26/96 00:07:54	Yes	Yes
HelloBeep.java	960	07/26/96 00:20:22	Yes	Yes
HelloBeep.mak	2996	07/25/96 21:11:34	Yes	Yes
HelloBeep.mdp	33792	07/26/96 00:20:34	Yes	Yes
HelloBeep.ncb	50176	07/26/96 00:20:36	Yes	Yes
HelloBeep2.class	1705	07/26/96 00:23:34	Yes	Yes

Select Parent Exit   C:\Books\Prima\Visual J++\Programs

Listing 12.1 shows the FileFunctions class listing. This listing will be discussed throughout this section. The File class is used extensively, because you can define a File without actually using it for input and output.

> **NOTE:**
> The FileFunctions class implements the SortInterface and
> instantiates the SortArray class to sort the file entries.
> The SortInterface class and the SortArray class were dis-
> cussed in Chapter 5.

Listing 12.1
File Functions.java

```java
import java.awt.*;
import java.io.*;
import java.util.*;

public class FileFunctions extends Frame
➥implements SortInterface, DirInterface {
    private File currentDir;
    private int sortOrder = 1;
    // 1 is file name, 2 is length,
    //3 is modified, 4 is can read, 5 is can write.
    private List ls_fileList;
    private Button cb_parent;
    private Button cb_name;
    private Button cb_length;
    private Button cb_modified;
    private Button cb_read;
    private Button cb_write;
    private Button cb_exit;
    private Button cb_select;
    private Label lb_status;
    private Label lb_cwd;
    private DirInterface di;
    private static final int NAME_WIDTH = 25;
    private static final int LENGTH_WIDTH = 10;
    private static final int MOD_WIDTH = 18;
    private static final int CAN_READ_WIDTH = 9;
    private static final int CAN_WRITE_WIDTH = 9;
    public static void main (String args[]) {
        FileFunctions f = new FileFunctions();
        f.setTitle("Directory");
        f.reshape(0,0,640,480);
        f.show();
    }
    private FileFunctions() {
        di = this;
```

continues

Listing 12.1
Continued

```
                        continueConstruction(); //Call rest of
    ➡constructor
            }
        public FileFunctions(DirInterface dir) {
                di = dir;
                continueConstruction(); //Call rest of
    ➡constructor
            }
        private void continueConstruction(){
                Font f = new Font("Courier", Font.PLAIN, 14);
                Font boldF = new Font("Courier", Font.BOLD, 14);
                Panel p_north = new Panel();
                Panel myCenterPanel = new Panel();
                Panel p_south = new Panel();
                p_north.setLayout(new
    ➡FlowLayout(FlowLayout.LEFT));
                p_south.setLayout(new
    ➡FlowLayout(FlowLayout.LEFT));
                myCenterPanel.setLayout(new GridLayout(1,1));
                myCenterPanel.add(ls_fileList = new List());
                p_south.add(lb_status = new Label (pad("",70)));
                p_south.add(cb_select = new Button ("Select"));
                cb_select.setFont(boldF);
                p_south.add(cb_parent = new Button ("Parent"));
                cb_parent.setFont(boldF);
                p_south.add(cb_exit = new Button ("Exit"));
                cb_exit.setFont(boldF);
                p_south.add(lb_cwd = new Label (pad("",70)));
                p_north.add(cb_name = new Button (pad("File
    ➡Name", NAME_WIDTH-3)));
                cb_name.setFont(boldF);
                p_north.add(cb_length = new Button
    ➡(frontPad("File Size", LENGTH_WIDTH-2)));
                cb_length.setFont(boldF);
                p_north.add(cb_modified = new Button
    ➡(frontPad("Last Modified",MOD_WIDTH-2)));
                cb_modified.setFont(boldF);
                p_north.add(cb_read = new Button (frontPad("Can
    ➡Read",CAN_READ_WIDTH-2)));
                cb_read.setFont(boldF);
                p_north.add(cb_write = new Button (frontPad("Can
    ➡Write",CAN_WRITE_WIDTH-2)));
                cb_write.setFont(boldF);
                directoryList(System.getProperty("user.dir"));
```

```
                    //Set the font to a proportional Courier font
                    ls_fileList.setFont(f);
                    // Add the panels to the frame
                    add("North", myNorthPanel);
                    add("South", mySouthPanel);
                    add("Center", myCenterPanel);
              }
         public boolean isGreaterThan(Object obj1, Object
➡obj2){
                    // Default sort is file name
                    String s1 = (String) obj1;
                    String s2 = (String) obj2;
                    // Sort by file length
                    switch (sortOrder) {
                         case 2 :
                              s1 = s1.substring(NAME_WIDTH + 1);
                              if (s1.indexOf("DIR") > 0) {
                                   s1 = " ";
                              }
                              s2 = s2.substring(NAME_WIDTH + 1);
                              if (s2.indexOf("DIR") > 0) {
                                   s2 = " ";
                              }
                              break;
                         case 3 :                         // Sort
➡by modification date
                              s1 = s1.substring(NAME_WIDTH +
➡LENGTH_WIDTH + 1);
                              s1 = s1.substring(6,8) +
➡s1.substring(0,5) + s1.substring(9);
                              s2 = s2.substring(NAME_WIDTH +
➡LENGTH_WIDTH + 1);
                              s2 = s2.substring(6,8) +
➡s2.substring(0,5) + s2.substring(9);
                              break;
                         case 4 :                         // Sort
➡by readability
                              s1 = s1.substring(NAME_WIDTH +
➡LENGTH_WIDTH + MOD_WIDTH + 1);
                              s2 = s2.substring(NAME_WIDTH +
➡LENGTH_WIDTH + MOD_WIDTH + 1);
                              break;
                         case 5 :                         // Sort
➡by writeability
```

continues

Listing 12.1
Continued

```
                         s1 = s1.substring(NAME_WIDTH +
➡LENGTH_WIDTH + MOD_WIDTH + CAN_READ_WIDTH + 1);
                         s2 = s2.substring(NAME_WIDTH +
➡LENGTH_WIDTH + MOD_WIDTH + CAN_READ_WIDTH + 1);
                    break;
            }
            if (s1.compareTo(s2) > 0) {
                return true;
            }
            return false;
        }
        public void directoryList(String currentDirectory){
            lb_cwd.setText(currentDirectory);
            currentDir = new File(currentDirectory);
            loadLists(currentDir.list());
        }
        private void sortFiles() {
            String myArray[] = new String
➡[ls_fileList.countItems()];
            for (int i=0; i < ls_fileList.countItems(); i++)
{
                myArray[i] = ls_fileList.getItem(i);
            }
            SortArray s = new SortArray (this, myArray);
            loadAfterSort(myArray);
        }
        private void loadAfterSort(String fileList[]) {
            ls_fileList.clear();
            for (int i=0; i < fileList.length; i++) {
                ls_fileList.addItem(fileList[i]);
            }
        }
        private void loadLists(String fileNames[]) {
            File iFile;
            ls_fileList.clear();
            for (int i=0; i < fileNames.length; i++) {
                iFile = null;           //Deallocate for
➡garbage collection
                iFile = new File (fileNames[i]);
                Date lastModified = new Date
➡(iFile.lastModified());
                String holder =
➡pad(iFile.getName(),NAME_WIDTH)
                    + frontPad(iFile.isDirectory() ?
                        "<DIR>":
➡String.valueOf(iFile.length()), LENGTH_WIDTH)
```

```
                                    + " " + lastModified.toLocaleString()
➡+ " "
                        + frontPad((iFile.canRead() ? "
➡Yes"  : "  No"),CAN_READ_WIDTH)
                        + frontPad((iFile.canWrite() ? "
➡Yes"  : "  No"),CAN_WRITE_WIDTH)
                            ;
                ls_fileList.addItem(holder);
            }
            sortFiles();
        }
    public boolean handleEvent(Event event) {
            if (event.id == Event.WINDOW_DESTROY ||
➡event.target == cb_exit) {
                dispose();
                java.lang.System.exit(0);
            }
            else if (event.target == cb_name) {
                sortOrder = 1;
                sortFiles();
            }
            else if (event.target == cb_length) {
                sortOrder = 2;
                sortFiles();
            }
            else if (event.target == cb_modified) {
                sortOrder = 3;
                sortFiles();
            }
            else if (event.target == cb_read) {
                sortOrder = 4;
                sortFiles();
            }
            else if (event.target == cb_write) {
                sortOrder = 5;
                sortFiles();
            }
            else if (event.target == cb_parent) {
                String newFile = currentDir.getParent();
                if (newFile == null) {
                    newFile = "C:";
                }
                lb_status.setText(newFile);
                currentDir = null;              //Initiate
➡garbage collection
```

continues

Listing 12.1
Continued

```
                          currentDir = new File(newFile);
                          loadLists(currentDir.list());
                  }
            else if (event.target == cb_select) {
                  String myFileString =
➤ls_fileList.getSelectedItem();
                  if (myFileString == null) {
                          lb_status.setText("Nothing was
➤selected.");
                  }
                  else {
                      myFileString =
➤myFileString.substring(0, NAME_WIDTH);
                      myFileString = myFileString.trim();
                      lb_status.setText(myFileString + "
➤was selected.");
                      File myFile = new File(myFileString);
                      if (myFile.isDirectory()) {
                              currentDir = null;
➤//Initiate garbage collection
                              currentDir = myFile;
                              loadLists(currentDir.list());
                      }
                      else {
                              di.selectFile(myFile);
                      }
                  }
            }
            else {
                  return super.handleEvent(event);
            }
            return true;
      }
      public String pad(String inString, int length) {
            String newString = new String(inString);
            for (int x = inString.length(); x < length;
➤x++) {
                  newString = newString.concat(" ");
            }
            return newString;
      }
      public String frontPad(String inString, int length) {
            String newString = new String("");
            for (int x = inString.length(); x < length;
➤x++) {
                  newString = newString.concat(" ");
```

```
        }
        newString = newString.concat(inString);
        return newString;
    }
    public void selectFile(File f) {
// Needed to implement DirInterface so this program can
➥use a
// Main method to call itself.
    }
}
```

Directory Information

There are several methods that help with directory information.
The first is used in the continueConstruction method. Using the
System.getProperty method found in java.lang, you can inquire on
the current working directory by using the following command:

```
//Get current working directory
String cwd = System.getProperty("user.dir");
```

The isDirectory method can be found in the loadLists directory.
It tests a File to see if it's a directory or not:

```
if (iFile.isDirectory()) {
```

> **NOTE:**
> The preceding two lines of code don't appear in Listing
> 12.1, but the methods do. I simplified the method call to
> make it more readable and understandable.

The list method returns a String array that lists the files in a directory, or a null if the File being tested is not a directory. This can be
seen in the directoryList method, where the list method is called
to return a String array as a parameter to the loadLists method:

```
public void directoryList(String currentDirectory){
    lb_cwd.setText(currentDirectory);
    currentDir = new File(currentDirectory);
    loadLists(currentDir.list());
}
```

Finally, the getParent method will return the name of the path containing the file or directory. When you click the Parent command button in the handleEvent method, the following code executes:

```
else if (event.target == cb_parent) {
    String newFile = currentDir.getParent();
    if (newFile == null) {
        newFile = "C:";
    }
    lb_status.setText(newFile);
    currentDir = null;              //Initiate garbage collection
    currentDir = new File(newFile);
    loadLists(currentDir.list());
}
```

This returns the parent code. If an error occurs, then the parent directory is set to "C:", which is the root directory of the C: drive.

> **NOTE:**
> You set currentDir **to null before assigning it a new value so that the Java virtual machine knows to "garbage collect" the old** currentDir **file information. Garbage collection involves freeing up previously used resources. Java performs its own garbage collection, but sometimes it will "clean up" faster if you do little tricks, such as assigning classes to null before reassigning them.**

File Information

In the loadLists method in Listing 12.1, the files that are found are listed with their name, size, last modification date, and if they are readable and writable from the current Java virtual machine.

```
private void loadLists(String fileNames[]) {
    File iFile;
    ls_fileList.clear();       //Clear the ls_fileList List
➥object
    for (int i=0; i < fileNames.length; i++) {
```

```
            iFile = null;            //Deallocate for garbage
➥collection
            iFile = new File (fileNames[i]);
            Date lastModified = new Date (iFile.lastModified());
            String holder = pad(iFile.getName(),NAME_WIDTH)
                  + frontPad(iFile.isDirectory() ?
                      "<DIR>": String.valueOf(iFile.length()),
➥LENGTH_WIDTH)
                  + " " + lastModified.toLocaleString() + " "
                  + frontPad((iFile.canRead() ? "  Yes"  :
➥"  No"),CAN_READ_WIDTH)
                  + frontPad((iFile.canWrite() ? "  Yes"  :
➥"  No"),CAN_WRITE_WIDTH)
                  ;
            ls_fileList.addItem(holder);       // Adds an item
➥to the ls_fileList List object.
   }
   sortFiles();
}
```

The following file methods are used to retrieve file information:

Method	Description
File(*String name*)	The File constructor creates a file that references a name passed to it. You can then use File methods to obtain information about this File.
File.getName()	The getName **method returns the name of a File.**
File.length()	The length **method returns a long containing the length of a File.**
File.lastModified()	The lastModified **method returns a long date representing the last modification date of a File.**
File.canRead()	The canRead **method returns a true or false indicating if the File can be read from in the Java virtual machine.**
File.canWrite()	The canWrite **method returns a true or false indicating if the File can be written to from theJava virtual machine.**

> **NOTE:**
> The `canRead` **and** `canWrite` **methods don't just return the read-only attribute. They also indicate if a file can be read from inside the Java virtual machine. Often, the only files you have access to inside the Java virtual machine are the files in the same directory as the class you are running.**

The `pad` and `frontPad` methods are methods that were written to pad spaces to a string. That way, by using a proportional font like Courier, you can space your directory listing columns evenly on one string, making processing a little faster and a lot easier than synchronizing multiple lists inside a display.

> **NOTE:**
> **Some of you may see the conditional operators (? and :) used. These are discussed in Chapter 2. You use conditional operators to assign a value based on whether an expression is true or false. For example, the expression**
>
> `iFile.canRead() ? " Yes" : " No"`
>
> **returns a "** `Yes`**" string if** `iFile.canRead()` **returns a true, and "** `No`**" if** `iFile.canRead()` **returns a false.**

Interfaces Revisited

The FileFunctions class in Listing 12.1 makes ample use of interfaces, implementing both `DirInterface` and `SortInterface` Because of the heavy use of "home grown" interfaces, some review is warranted. These interfaces grant the FileFunctions class power that is hard to come by in other traditional languages.

Writing the *DirInterface* Interface

The `DirInterface` allows the FileFunctions class to pass control back to a calling program when selectFile is called. It only contains one method to be coded: selectFile(File f). Because the FileFunctions class is self-instantiating, an empty `selectFile` method is included with the FileFunctions class to allow it to instantiate itself in the `main` method.

The following is the listing for the DirInterface:

```java
import java.io.*;

public interface DirInterface {
    public void selectFile(File f);
}
```

As you can see, there's not much to it. Basically, DirInterface allows you to define your own selectFile function to be called from the FileFunctions class in the handleEvent method:

```java
public class FileFunctions extends Frame implements
➥SortInterface, DirInterface {
    private DirInterface di;
// ... the main logic, then the Constructors ...
    private FileFunctions() {
        di = this;
        continueConstruction();        //Call rest of
➥constructor
    }
    public FileFunctions(DirInterface dir) {
        di = dir;
        continueConstruction();        //Call rest of
➥constructor
    }
// ... More code goes here until the middle of the handleEvent
➥method...
    else if (event.target == cb_select) {
        String myFileString = ls_fileList.getSelectedItem();
        if (myFileString == null) {
            lb_status.setText("Nothing was selected.");
        }
        else {
            myFileString = myFileString.substring(0,
➥NAME_WIDTH);
            myFileString = myFileString.trim();
            lb_status.setText(myFileString + " was
➥selected.");
```

```
                    File myFile = new File(myFileString);
                    di.selectFile(myFile);
            }
        }
// ... The rest of the code goes here ...
        public void selectFile(File f) {
// Needed to implement DirInterface so this program can use a
// main method to call itself.
        }
```

The di attribute is a class that implements DirInterface. Now the FileFunctions class can call the selectFile method of the containing class. Figure 12.2 shows graphically what is occuring. Using the DirInterface, the selectFile method of the Calling class can be called by a FileFunctions instance.

Fig. 12.2
Using the *DirInterface*, the FileFunctions class can call a method in any instantiating class.

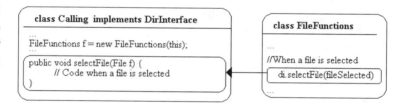

Using the *SortInterface* Interface

Using the same interface concept, you can call the SortInterface interface, as was done in Chapter 5. As you remember, the SortInterface interface is defined as follows:

```
public interface SortInterface {
    public abstract boolean isGreaterThan (Object obj1, Object
➥obj2);
}
```

Then the SortArray class calls the isGreaterThan method of the containing class to help bubble sort objects:

```
public class SortArray {
     public SortArray(SortInterface si, Object object_array [ ])
➡{
// Go through the array several times
          for (int loop1 = 0; loop1 < object_array.length;
➡loop1++) {
                for (int loop2 = 0; loop2 < object_array.length
➡- loop1 - 1; loop2++) {
// Swap array elements if they aren't in the right order
                     if (si.isGreaterThan(object_array[loop2],
➡object_array[loop2 + 1])) {
                          Object holder;
                          holder = object_array[loop2];
                          object_array[loop2] =
➡object_array[loop2 + 1];
                          object_array[loop2 + 1] = holder;
                     }
                }
          }
     }
}
```

Each loop1 iteration of the SortArray loop lets the heaviest array member "sink" to the bottom and lets all other array members "float" to the top.

> **NOTE:**
> There *are* more efficient sorts than the bubble sort. However, the bubble sort is the easiest to understand. If you want, you can replace the SortArray with any sorting algorithm you like, but the preceding algorithm does work, and can be easily coded and maintained.

The most wonderful thing about the SortArray class and the SortInterface object is that you get to define how each object will be sorted in your own isGreaterThan routine. The following isGreaterThan is an excerpt from Listing 12.1, and can be found in the FileFunctions class:

```java
public boolean isGreaterThan(Object obj1, Object obj2){
    String s1 = (String) obj1;         // Default sort is
➥file name
    String s2 = (String) obj2;
    switch (sortOrder) {
        case 2 :                    // Sort by file length
            s1 = s1.substring(NAME_WIDTH + 1);
            if (s1.indexOf("DIR") > 0) {
                s1 = " ";
            }
            s2 = s2.substring(NAME_WIDTH + 1);
            if (s2.indexOf("DIR") > 0) {
                s2 = " ";
            }
            break;
        case 3 :                    // Sort by modification date
            s1 = s1.substring(NAME_WIDTH + LENGTH_WIDTH +
➥1);
            s1 = s1.substring(6,8) + s1.substring(0,5) +
➥s1.substring(9);
            s2 = s2.substring(NAME_WIDTH + LENGTH_WIDTH +
➥1);
            s2 = s2.substring(6,8) + s2.substring(0,5) +
➥s2.substring(9);
            break;
        case 4 :                    // Sort by writeability
            s1 = s1.substring(NAME_WIDTH + LENGTH_WIDTH +
➥MOD_WIDTH + 1);
            s2 = s2.substring(NAME_WIDTH + LENGTH_WIDTH +
➥MOD_WIDTH + 1);
            break;
    }
    if (s1.compareTo(s2) > 0) {
        return true;
    }
    return false;
}
```

Notice that you defined four sorting/grouping algorithms based on what the user wanted to sort on at the time. However, to achieve four different sorts, you *only had to define four different comparison criterias!* This is different than traditional sorts that would have forced you to write four completely different sorting algoritms to sort an array four different ways.

Not only does the SortArray class sort the String array, but it doesn't even know it's a String array while it's performing the sort. It could be any array of Objects, or even different types of Objects. All that's needed is for you, the developer, to define exactly what "is greater than" means when comparing your objects by defining an isGreaterThan method. This is the power of interfaces, where an instance of a class can actually call the containing class's methods to function properly, as shown in Figure 12.3.

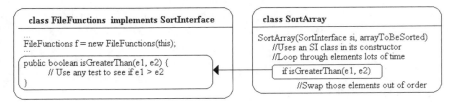

Fig. 12.3
Using the *SortInterface* interface, SortArray can "talk" to FileFunctions.

File Input and Output with Streams

Streams are how Java handles file input and output. There are various types of input, output, and random access streams that you can use inside your Java programs. Listing 12.2 reads in and displays a text file, allows you to make changes, and prints the file or saves it.

Listing 12.2
Title Here

```
import java.awt.*;
import java.io.*;
import java.util.*;

public class StreamFunctions extends Frame implements
➥DirInterface {
    private FileFunctions ff;
    private File selectedFile;
    private Label lb_status;
    private Label lb_fileName;
    private TextArea ta_display;
    private Button cb_print;
    private Button cb_save;
```

continues

Listing 12.2
Continued

```java
private Button cb_exit;
public static void main (String args[]) {
    StreamFunctions sf = new StreamFunctions();
    sf.start();
}
public StreamFunctions () {
    //Build the StreamFunctions frame, but don't
➥show it yet.
    Panel mySouthPanel = new Panel();
    mySouthPanel.setLayout(new
➥FlowLayout(FlowLayout.LEFT));
    mySouthPanel.add(lb_status = new Label
➥(FileFunctions.pad("",70)));
    mySouthPanel.add(cb_print = new Button
➥("Print"));
    mySouthPanel.add(cb_save = new Button ("Save"));
    mySouthPanel.add(cb_exit = new Button ("Exit"));
    mySouthPanel.add(lb_fileName = new Label
➥(FileFunctions.pad("",70)));
    add("South", mySouthPanel);
    ta_display = new TextArea (8,40);
    add("Center", ta_display);
}
public void start() {
    setTitle("File Viewer");
    resize(640,480);
    //Show the FileFunctions frame first
    ff = new FileFunctions(this);
    ff.setTitle("File Viewer");
    ff.resize(640,480);
    ff.show();
}
public void selectFile(File f) {   //Method needed for
➥DirInterface
    selectedFile = f;
    //Load the selected File
    loadFile();
    //Show the StreamFunctions Frame.
    show();
    //Hide the FileFunctions Frame
    ff.hide();
}
public void loadFile() {
    byte buffer[] = new byte [(int)
➥selectedFile.length()];
    FileInputStream fis;
```

```
                    try {
                            fis = new FileInputStream(selectedFile);
                            for(long inCount = 0; inCount
➥< selectedFile.length();) {
                                    inCount += fis.read(buffer, (int)
➥inCount,
                                            (int) (selectedFile.length() -
➥inCount));
                            }
                            String bufferString = new String(buffer,
➥0);
                            ta_display.setText(bufferString);
                            fis.close();
                    }
                    catch (FileNotFoundException e) {
                            lb_status.setText("An
FileNotFoundException occured in the loadFile method.");
                    }
                    catch (IOException e) {
                            lb_status.setText("An IOException occured
➥in the loadFile method.");
                    }
            }
        public boolean handleEvent(Event event) {
                    if (event.id == Event.WINDOW_DESTROY ||
➥event.target == cb_exit) {
                            ff.show();
                            hide();
                    }
                    else if (event.target == cb_print) {
                            try {
                                    FileOutputStream fos = new
➥FileOutputStream("LPT1");
                                    PrintStream ps = new PrintStream(fos,
➥ true);
                                    ps.print(ta_display.getText());
                                    ps.print('\f');      //Now print a
➥form feed
                                    ps.close();
                                    fos.close();
                                    ps = null;
                                    fos = null;
                            }
                            catch (IOException e) {
```

continues

Listing 12.2
Continued

```
                                        lb_status.setText("An IOException
➥occured while printing.");
                    }
                }
                else if (event.target == cb_save) {
                    try {
                        FileOutputStream fos = new
➥FileOutputStream(selectedFile);
                        DataOutputStream dos = new
➥DataOutputStream(fos);
                        dos.writeBytes(ta_display.getText());
                        dos.close();
                        dos = null;
                        fos.close();
                        fos = null;
                    }
                    catch (IOException e) {
                        lb_status.setText("An IOException
➥occured while writing.");
                    }
                }
                else {
                    return super.handleEvent(event);
                }
                return true;
        }
}
```

Notice the flow of control in the StreamFunctions class:

1. The StreamFunctions class actually displays the FileFunctions window first using the start method.

2. When a file is selected in the FileFunctions window, the selectFile method is called in the StreamFunctions class. (All this is done through the DirInterface interface.)

3. The selectFile method hides the FileFunctions Frame and shows the StreamFunctions frame.

4. Figure 12.4 shows the resulting window for the StreamFunctions class.

The code in Listing 12.2 will be referenced throughout this section.

Fig. 12.4
The StreamFunctions
class produces output
that looks like this.

```
File Viewer                                                              _ 8 X
import java.awt.*;
import java.io.*;
import java.util.*;

public class FileFunctions extends Frame implements SortInterface, DirInterface {
        private File currentDir;
        private int sortOrder = 1;  // 1 is file name, 2 is length,
        //3 is modified, 4 is can read, 5 is can write.
        private List ls_fileList;
        private Button cb_parent;
        private Button cb_name;
        private Button cb_length;
        private Button cb_modified;
        private Button cb_read;
        private Button cb_write;
        private Button cb_exit;
        private Button cb_select;
        private Label lb_status;
        private Label lb_cwd;
        private DirInterface di;
        private static final int NAME_WIDTH = 25;
        private static final int LENGTH_WIDTH = 10;
        private static final int MOD_WIDTH = 18;
        private static final int CAN_READ_WIDTH = 9;
        private static final int CAN_WRITE_WIDTH = 9;
        public static void main (String args[]) {
                FileFunctions f = new FileFunctions();
                f.setTitle("Directory");
                f.reshape(0,0,640,480);
                f.show();
        }
```

                        Print   Save   Exit

Input Streams

Input streams are how file input is accomplished in Java. There is one
input stream in Listing 12.2 in the `loadFile` method:

```java
public void loadFile() {
    byte buffer[] = new byte [(int) selectedFile.length()];
    FileInputStream fis;
    try {
        fis = new FileInputStream(selectedFile);
        for(long inCount = 0; inCount <
➡selectedFile.length();) {
            inCount += fis.read(buffer, (int) inCount,
                (int) (selectedFile.length() - inCount));
        }
        String bufferString = new String(buffer, 0);
        ta_display.setText(bufferString);
        fis.close();
```

```
            fis = null;                //Deallocate for garbage
➥collection
    }
    catch (FileNotFoundException e) {
            lb_status.setText("An FileNotFoundException occured in
➥the loadFile method.");
    }
    catch (IOException e) {
            lb_status.setText("An IOException occured in the
➥loadFile method.");
    }
}
```

As you can see, the FileInputStream is defined and then allocated with the File that was passed to the selectFile method. This file is read from until it is complete, and then the FileInputStream is closed and set to null to help garbage collection. The beautiful part about this is the simplicity in which a whole file is read in and converted to a TextArea. Again, you would have trouble making it so easy in other languages.

Types of Input Streams

There are several types of input streams, as shown in Figure 12.5.

Fig. 12.5
All input streams are inherited from the abstract InputStream class.

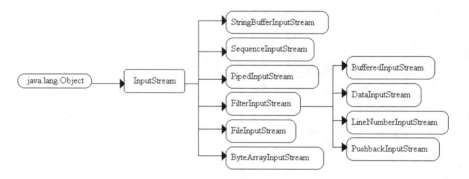

The following is a list of the types of InputStreams:

InputStream **Class**	**Description**
InputStream	InputStream **is the ancestor of all** InputStream **classes. You cannot instantiate an** InputStream **class, but it contains some useful methods, such as** read**, that are present in all** InputStream **descendents.**
StringBufferInputStream	**This is an input stream that treats a String as if it were a file. This is useful for logical files present entirely in a String in memory.**
SequenceInputStream	**This input stream is used to concatenate two or more input streams and treat them as if they were one file. This is handy if you're trying to emulate replication and have to files with identical layouts.**
PipedInputStream	**This input stream reads data from a tempory memory table loaded by a** PipedOutputStream**. This is very useful for writing and retrieving temporary files.**
FilterInputStream	**This class is the parent class for any type of stream that filters a file's data. It should not be instantiated itself.**
FileInputStream	**This input stream provides low level input from a file. Although used in Listing 12.2, you would often want some of the additional functionality found in other** InputStream **classes.**
ByteArrayInputStream	**This class is used to read from a byte array in memory as if reading from a file. This is useful for logical files present entirely in an array in memory.**
BufferedInputStream	**This data stream buffers input data by reading large amounts of storage into a buffer. Using a** BufferedInputStream**, instead of making repeated reads to the slow disk drive, you make repeated reads to a buffered memory area.**
DataInputStream	DataInputStreams **are the most versatile of all input streams. They are able to read all sorts of data types. In addition to bytes and characters,** DataInputStreams **can read boolean, double, floats, integers, longs, shorts, and other formats not found in other input classes. Check out the InfoViewer to see all the methods for reading inside the** DataInputStream **class.**

`InputStream` **Class**	**Description**
`LineNumberInputStream`	**This input stream class keeps track of line numbers as you read a file. The** `getLineNumber` **and** `setLineNumber` **methods can be used to retrieve or reset (respectively) the line numbers in a** `LineNumberInputStream` **class.**
`PushbackInputStream`	**This input stream class allows you to "unread" one byte of data onto the data buffer. This is handy if you need to write a parser to parse a file.**

> **CAUTION:**
> **The reason that a** `BufferedInputStream` **was not used in Listing 12.2 is that a large buffer that probably contains the whole file is read in at one time anyway. In this case, a** `BufferedInputStream` **would "double buffer" all reads, thereby actually decreasing read time.**
>
> **You also should not use a** `BufferedInputStream` **if you intend on reading from different or random sections of a file rather than reading sequentially. Buffering only works well with sequential input.**

Although there are many input stream classes suited to many different needs, Listing 12.2 used a `FileInputStream` for no-frills input. Any other overhead was unnecessary.

Important Input Stream Methods

Some methods you may find useful available to all input streams are as follows:

InputStream Method	**Description**
`read({byte b[]{, int` ➥`offset, int length}})`	**The** `read` **method reads a byte of data or, if a byte array is passed, an array of bytes. An offset length can also be given to read characters into a sub-array. A file is read until the b.length characters are read or an end of file occurs.**

InputStream Method	Description
skip(long n)	The skip method skips a number of bytes. This is helpful for non-sequential reads of a file.
close( )	The close method does not have to be called, but closing a file may speed up the recovery of resources.
mark(int numberOfReads)	The mark function sets a mark on the current position of a file so that a call to the reset method will return the file pointer to the marked position. The numberOfReads argument is the number of times you can read from this file before the mark becomes invalid.
reset	The reset moves the file pointer to the last marked position.
markSuported	The markSupported function returns a true or false indicating whether or not marks are supported in the current Java implementation.

Output Streams

OutputStream classes allow for easy output to a file or printer in Java. In Listing 12.2, both saving back to a file and printing a file are supported.

File Output in Java

The StreamFunctions class allows you to save any changes you made to your selected file. In the handleEvent method, the following section of code is present:

```
else if (event.target == cb_save) {
    try {
        FileOutputStream fos = new
➥FileOutputStream(selectedFile);
        DataOutputStream dos = new DataOutputStream(fos);
        dos.writeBytes(ta_display.getText());
        dos.close();
        dos = null;
        fos.close();
        fos = null;
    }
    catch (IOException e) {
```

```
        lb_status.setText("An IOException occured while
➥writing.");
    }
}
```

The following steps occur in the preceding code:

1. A `FileOutputStream` is defined for the current selected file.

2. A `DataOutputStream` is formed from the new `FileOutputStream`. This is so you can use the `writebytes` command, which is a way to write from a String rather than a byte array.

3. The `selectFile` is rewritten using a huge String and the `DataOutputStream`.

4. The `FileOutputStream` and the `DataOutputStream` are closed and set to null to aid in garbage collecting.

Printer Output in Java

Printer output is also considered an `OutputStream`, but unlike other `OutputStreams`, printer output requires that you first define another `OutputStream` to be used as a constructor argument before a `PrintStream` can be constructed. In the `handleEvent` method, the following section of code is present:

```
else if (event.target == cb_print) {
    try {
        FileOutputStream fos = new FileOutputStream("LPT1");
        PrintStream ps = new PrintStream(fos, true);
        ps.print(ta_display.getText());
        ps.print('\f');        //Now print a form feed
        ps.close();
        fos.close();
        ps = null;
        fos = null;
    }
    catch (IOException e) {
        lb_status.setText("An IOException occured while
➥printing.");
    }
}
```

The following steps to print a file occur in the preceding code:

1. Define a `FileOutputStream` as "LPT1". This is the same stream that is defined to your printer. You can also use "PRN" or "LPT2" if you have a second parallel port.

2. Next, you construct a `PrintStream` using the fos `FileOutputStream` you just defined.

3. Print the String you need to print on the printer.

4. When you're finished, print a form feed (`'\f'`) to eject the last page.

5. Close all `OutputStream` classes and set all `OutputStream` variables to null.

`PrintStreams` aren't really necessary in that any writes to the fos `FileOutputStream` will go to the printer. However, `PrintStreams` come with some useful functions, such as `print` and `println`, that can make printing to a file a little easier.

> **TIP:**
> **See the InfoViewer for all the print methods you can use.**

Types of Output Streams

There are several types of OutputStreams, as shown in Figure 12.6.

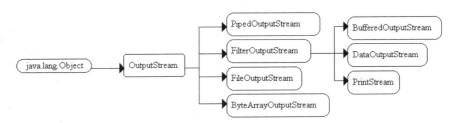

Fig. 12.6
All output streams
are inherited from
the abstract
OutputStream class.

The following is a list of all output streams and how they're used:

OutputStream Class	Description
OutputStream	OutputStream **is the ancestor of all OutputStream classes. You cannot instantiate an OutputStream class, but it contains some useful methods, such as** write, **that are present in all OutputStream descendents.**
PipedOutputStream	**This output stream writes data to a tempory memory table to be read later by a** PipedInputStream. **This is very useful for writing and retrieving temporary files.**
FilterOutputStream	**This class is the parent class for any type of stream that filters a file's output. It should not be instantiated itself.**
FileOutputStream	**This output stream provides low level output from a file. Although used in Listing 12.2, you would often want some of the additional functionality found in other OutputStream classes.**
ByteArrayOutputStream	**This class is used to write to a byte array in memory as if writing to a fil. This is useful for building logical files present entirely in an array in memory.**
BufferedOutputStream	**This data stream buffers output data by writing large amounts of storage into a buffer. Using a** BufferedOutputStream, **instead of making repeated writes to the slow disk drive, you make repeated writes to a buffered memory area.**
DataOutputStream	DataOutputStreams **are the most versatile of all output streams. They are able to read all sorts of different data types. In addition to bytes and characters,** DataOutputStreams **can read boolean, double, floats, integers, longs, shorts, and other formats not found in other output classes. Check out the InfoViewer to see all the methods for reading inside the** DataOutputStream **class.**
PrintStream	**A** PrintStream **is useful because of the print and println methods that accompany a** PrintStream. PrintStreams **are used to write text files or to (of course) print to a printer.**

> **CAUTION:**
> Just like you didn't need to buffer the input when reading, writing data also occurs only once from one big array. Buffering output would probably be a waste of time and may actually run slower due to "double buffering."

Listing 12.2 used a `FileOutputStream` and a `DataOutputStream` to process data for saving, and a `FileOutputStream` and a `PrintStream` to process data for printing. You'll find that the versatility of `OutputStream` classes can make writing to a file a little easier.

Important *OutputStream* Methods

There are three major OutputStream methods you can use:

`OutputStream` **Method**	**Description**
`write([int b / byte b[]`	The `write` method can write a byte to a file, or can write an array or sub array to a file.
`close()`	The `close` method closes the output file, flushes all buffers, and deallocates resources used by a file.
`flush()`	The `flush` method forces any information in a buffer to be written. This is useful when exiting a class.

Unlike the `InputStream` methods, you will often use more specialized `OutputStream` class methods. For example, in Listing 12.2, the `writeBytes` method of the `DataOutputStream` class and the `print` method of the `PrintStream` class were the methods that were used to perform stream output.

Random Access (I/O) Streams

There is a `RandomAccessFile` class that can handle both input and output. You'll find that the methods used in the `RandomAccessFile` class are as versatile as the `DataInputClass` and `DataOutputClass` classes combined.

Often, you'll want to both read and write to a file. However, as in the `StreamFunctions` class, you'll want to do your input, close your file and release any resources, and then later do your output. This would probably not entail using a random access file.

There are no `mark` or `reset` methods in a `RandomAccessFile` object. However, there is one method, `seek(long position)`, which will reposition the read and write pointers in a stream to a different location in a file.

Database I/O with DAO and ODBC

File I/O is necessary for any language, but to develop in today's client-server arena, you previously needed to use CGI or ISAPI calls to load database information into a Web page and then pull that information off using Java.

Microsoft has changed all that with the inclusion of DAO (Data Access Objects) and ODBC support in their Visual J++ product.

DAO are ActiveX objects used for database manipulation, DAO are important since they allow Java developers database access that previously has been denied to them. Although these ActiveX objects are not complete as of this writing, by the time Visual J++ ships, DAO access should be fully documented and implemented.

The importance of relational database access cannot be overemphasized. Relational database development has allowed developers to write sophisticated multi-user systems without worrying about database-centric topics like concurrency and multiple access. These are typically handled by the shop DBA for the entire programming staff!

Microsoft will soon incorporate ODBC support for their Visual J++ product (although they haven't yet done so in their beta product). *ODBC* (Open DataBase Connectivity) is a standard by which most major databases can be accessed. Because most databases have an ODBC interface, ODBC will allow you to access current client/server databases from within your Java program without complicated CGI or ISAPI calls.

The addition of ODBC into Visual J++ turns Java into a full-featured client/server development tool, and paves the way for migration from slower or harder to maintain legacy systems. The importance of including ODBC into your system cannot be overemphasized.

> **NOTE:**
> Other Java compiler vendors are starting to work on a cooperative standard for Java called JDBC, which will allow access to ODBC files. The JDBC standard should be implemented soon in several products. However, Microsoft will *probably* stick to the ODBC standard because they defined the standard and because ODBC will probably run a little faster than JDBC (JDBC will have a layer of processing between Java and ODBC that straight ODBC will not have).
>
> Because ODBC is an open standard, also look for other companies to start offering ODBC support for non-Visual J++ products. In fact, there are some third-party ODBC offerings for Java currently available.

Conclusion

File I/O and directory management are important to any language, and Java makes them relatively easy with an array of predefined file-handling classes. In this chapter, you learned how to do several directory and stream functions that make file manipulation and I/O possible.

With respect to I/O, Microsoft has upped the ante with the addition of database support in Visual J++. The addition of database support is necessary and beneficial to any language. In today's development environment, database support is a must for client/server development, and Java can't be a serious development tool without it. In fact, ActiveX support and Database support are the two main factors that will ensure a strong place for Visual J++ in the Java development market.

If some programs in this chapter were confusing, you may want to review Chapter 10, "Graphics, Graphical User Interfaces, and Animation." Also, since DAO and ODBC will be implemented with an ActiveX module, you may also want to see Chapter 11, "The ActiveX and COM Specifications."

Chapter 13

Java Methods

Visual J++ does a great job with online help. Using the Visual J++ InfoViewer, shown in Figure 13.1, you can look up classes, methods and attributes within those classes, and receive a short description of each function. However, with the use of multiple `import` statements in a big program, methods don't need to be fully qualified. This chapter contains a comprehensive list of all Java methods in alphabetical order, and a description of what they do. You may also find this listing useful to see what methods of the same name are available to different classes.

Figure 13.1
You can use the
InfoViewer in
Visual J++ to view
class and method
information online.

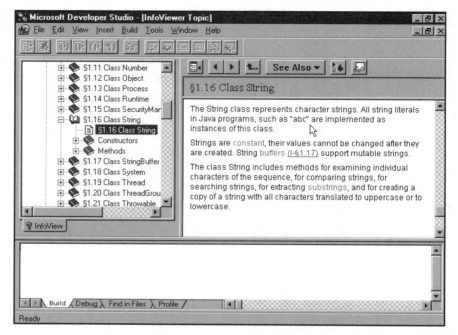

abs—java.lang.Math

```
public static int abs(datatype a)
```

Returns the absolute value of *a*. The datatype can be an integer, long, float, or double.

AbstractMethodError—
java.lang.AbstractMethodError

```
public AbstractMethodError({String detailMessage})
```

An attempt was made to call an abstract method or a method within an abstract class. Only methods inherited from abstract methods can be called. If detailMessage is specified, the detailMessage will be displayed when this throwable is thrown.

accept—java.io.FilenameFilter

```
public abstract boolean accept(File dir, String fileName)
```

Returns true if a file name is in a file directory; otherwise, false is returned.

accept—java.net.ServerSocket

```
public Socket accept()
```

Accepts a connection, and blocks until a connection is made. An IOException is thrown if there is an I/O error while waiting for a connection.

acos—java.lang.Math

```
public static double acos(double a)
```

Returns the arc cosine (inverse cosine) of an angle measured in radians.

> **NOTE:**
> Radians, like degrees, are a way to measure angles. (2*PI) radians is equal to 360 degrees. (Therefore, each radian is equal to about 57.2958 degrees.) Many mathemeticians feel that radians are an easier way to do trigonometry.

action—java.awt.Component

```
public boolean action(Event evt, Object what)
```

This is called if an action occurs in the Component. The evt Event identifies the event that caused this method to execute, and the what Object indentifies the event that's occuring. For more information, see the handleEvent method.

activeCount—java.lang.Thread

```
public static int activeCount()
```

Returns the number of active Threads in this Thread group.

activeCount—java.lang.ThreadGroup

```
public synchronized int activeCount()
```

Returns the number of active Threads in a ThreadGroup.

activeGroupCount—
java.lang.ThreadGroup

```
public synchronized int activeGroupCount()
```

Returns an estimate of the number of active ThreadGroups in this ThreadGroup.

add (layout)—java.awt.Container

```
public synchronized Component add(String name, Component comp)
```

Adds a Component to a Container and to the layout manager of this Container using the name provided as an argument. Also see the remove method, the add(non-layout) method, and the LayoutManager class.

add (MenuItem)—java.awt.Menu

```
public synchronized MenuItem add(MenuItem item)
```

Adds an item to a menu.

add (non-layout)—java.awt.Container

```
public Component add(Component comp {, int pos})
```

Adds a component to a container. The component is added at a given position if the position is specified. If a –1 is specified for the position, the component is inserted at the end of the component list. Also see the remove method and the add(layout) method.

add (String)—java.awt.Menu

```
public void add(String label)
```

Adds an item to a menu with a specified label.

add (union)—java.awt.Rectangle

```
public void add(Rectangle r)
```

Adds a rectangle to a rectangle, resulting in the union of the two rectangles. See the union method for more information.

add—java.awt.MenuBar

```
public synchronized Menu add(Menu m)
```

Adds a menu to a menu bar.

add—java.awt.Rectangle

```
public void add([int newx, int newy / Point xy])
```

Adds a point to a rectangle. This reshapes the rectangle into the smallest rectangle that contains both the rectangle and the point.

addConsumer— java.awt.image.FilteredImageSource

```
public synchronized void addConsumer(ImageConsumer ic)
```

Registers an ImageConsumer with a FilteredImageSource so the ImageConsumer can access an image. Also see the startProduction, removeConsumer, and isConsumer methods.

addConsumer— java.awt.image.ImageProducer

```
public abstract void addConsumer(ImageConsumer ic)
```

Registers an ImageConsumer with an ImageProducer so the ImageConsumer can access an image. Also see the startProduction, removeConsumer, and isConsumer methods.

addConsumer— java.awt.image.MemoryImageSource

```
public synchronized void addConsumer(ImageConsumer ic)
```

Registers an ImageConsumer with an MemoryImageSource so the ImageConsumer can access an image. Also see the startProduction, removeConsumer, and isConsumer methods.

addElement—java.util.Vector

```
public final synchronous void addElement(Object obj)
```

Adds an Object to the end of a Vector.

addHelpMenu— java.awt.peer.MenuBarPeer

```
public abstract void addHelpMenu(Menu helpmenu)
```

Adds a help menu to a menu bar.

addImage—java.awt.MediaTracker

```
public void addImage(Image image,
        int identifier {, int width, int height})
```

Adds an image to the list of images being tracked by a `MediaTracker` object. The `identifier` argument is used to track this image later. The image will eventually be rendered using the `width` and `height` arguments, or at the orginal size if the `width` and `height` arguments are omitted.

addItem—java.awt.Choice

```
public synchronized void addItem(String item)
```

Adds an item to a Choice. `addItem` throws `NullPointerException` if the item to be added is null.

addItem—java.awt.List

```
public synchronized void addItem(String item {, int index})
```

Adds an item to a List in the `index` position. If the `index` is omitted or is –1, then item is added to the end of the list.

addItem—java.awt.peer.ListPeer

```
public abstract void addItem(String item {, int index})
```

Adds an item to a List in the `index` position. If the `index` is omitted or is –1, then item is added to the end of the list.

addItem—java.awt.peer.MenuPeer

```
public abstract void addItem(MenuItem item)
```

Adds an item to a menu.

addLayoutComponent— java.awt.BorderLayout

```
public void addLayoutComponent(String name, Component comp)
```

Adds the specified named component to the layout. `name` is the String name and `comp` is the component to be added.

addLayoutComponent— java.awt.CardLayout

```
public void addLayoutComponent(String name, Component comp)
```

Adds the specified component with the specified name to the layout.

addLayoutComponent— java.awt.FlowLayout

```
public void addLayoutComponent(String name, Component comp)
```

Adds the specified component to the layout. The `name` argument is the name of the component, and the `comp` argument is the component to be added.

addLayoutComponent— java.awt.GridLayout

```
public void addLayoutComponent(String name, Component comp)
```

Adds a component to a layout. The `name` argument is the name of the component.

addLayoutComponent— java.awt.LayoutManager

```
public abstract void addLayoutComponent(
    String name, Component comp)
```

Adds the specified component with the specified name to the layout. `name` is the component name and `comp` is the component to be added.

addMenu—java.awt.peer.MenuBarPeer

```
public abstract void addMenu(Menu m)
```

Adds a menu to a menu bar.

addNotify—java.awt.Button

```
public synchronized void addNotify()
```

Creates a peer of the button. This peer lets you to change the appearance of the button without changing its functionality. addNotify overrides addNotify from the Component class.

addNotify—java.awt.Canvas

```
public synchronized void addNotify()
```

Creates a peer of the canvas. This peer allows you to change the user interface of the canvas without changing its functionality. addNotify in the Canvas class overrides addNotify in the Component class.

addNotify—java.awt.Component

```
public void addNotify()
```

Notifies a component to create a peer. A peer lets you to change the appearance of a component without changing its functionality. For more information, see the getPeer and removeNotify methods.

addNotify—java.awt.Checkbox

```
public synchronized void addNotify()
```

Creates a peer of the Checkbox. The peer allows you to change the appearance of the Checkbox without changing its functionality. addNotify in the Checkbox class overrides addNotify in the Component class.

addNotify— java.awt.CheckboxMenuItem

```
public synchronized void addNotify()
```

Creates a peer of a checkbox menu item. A peer lets you change the appearance of the checkbox menu item without changing its functionality. `addNotify` in the `CheckboxMenuItem` class overrides `addNotify` in the `MenuItem` class.

addNotify—java.awt.Choice

```
public synchronized void addNotify()
```

Creates the Choice's peer. A peer lets you to change the appearance of a Choice without changing its functionality. `addNotify` in the Choice class overrides `addNotify` in the Component class.

addNotify—java.awt.Container

```
public synchronized void addNotify()
```

Notifies a Container and all Components contained in a Container to create a peer. The `addNotify` method in the Container class overrides the `addNotify` method in the Component class. Also check out the `removeNotify` method.

addNotify—java.awt.Dialog

```
public synchronized void addNotify()
```

Creates a Dialog's peer which lets you to change the appearance of the Dialog without changing its functionality. The `addNotify` method in the Dialog class overrides the `addNotify` method in the Window class.

addNotify—java.awt.FileDialog

```
public synchronized void addNotify()
```

Creates the FileDialog's peer. The peer lets you to change the appearance of the FileDialog without changing its functionality. The `addNotify` method in the FileDialog class overrides the `addNotify` method in the FileDialog class.

addNotify—java.awt.Frame

```
public synchronized void addNotify()
```

Creates a Frame's peer. A peer lets you to change the appearance of a Frame without changing its functionality. The `addNotify` method in the Frame class overrides the `addNotify` method in the Window class.

addNotify—**java.awt.Label**

```
public synchronized void addNotify()
```

Creates a peer for a label. A peer lets you to change the appearance of a label without changing its functionality. The addNotify method in the Label class overrides the addNotify method in the Component class.

addNotify—**java.awt.List**

```
public synchronized void addNotify()
```

Creates a peer for a list. A peer lets lets you change a list's appearance without changing its functionality. The addNotify method in the List class overrides the addNotify method in the Component class. Also see the removeNotify method.

addNotify—**java.awt.Menu**

```
public synchronized void addNotify()
```

Creates a peer for a menu. A peer lets you change the appearance of the menu without changing its functionality. The addNotify method in the Menu class overrides the addNotify method in the MenuItem class.

addNotify—**java.awt.MenuBar**

```
public synchronized void addNotify()
```

Creates a peer for a MenuBar. A peer lets you change the appearance of the MenuBar without changing its functionality.

addNotify—**java.awt.MenuItem**

```
public synchronized void addNotify()
```

Creates a MenuItem's peer. A peer lets you change the appearance of a MenuItem without changing its functionality.

addNotify—**java.awt.Panel**

```
public synchronized void addNotify()
```

Creates a Panel's peer. A peer lets you change the appearance of the panel without changing its functionality. The addNotify method in the Panel class overrides the addNotify method in the Container class.

addNotify—java.awt.Scrollbar

```
public synchronized void addNotify()
```

Creates a Scrollbar's peer. A peer lets you change the appearance of a Scrollbar without changing any of its functionality. The addNotify method in the Scrollbar class overrides the addNotify method in the Component class.

addNotify—java.awt.TextArea

```
public synchronized void addNotify()
```

Creates a TextArea's peer. A peer lets you change the appearance of a TextArea without changing any of its functionality. The addNotify method in the TextArea class overrides the addNotify method in the Component class.

addNotify—java.awt.TextField

```
public synchronized void addNotify()
```

Constructs a TextField's peer. A peer lets you change the appearance of a TextField without changing its functionality. The addNotify method in the TextField class overrides the addNotify method in the Component class.

addNotify—java.awt.Window

```
public synchronized void addNotify()
```

Creates a peer for a Window. A peer lets you change the appearance of the Window without changing its functionality. The addNotify method in the Window class overrides the addNotify method in the Container class.

addObserver—java.util.Observable

```
public synchronized void addObserver(Observer o)
```

Adds an observer to the observer list.

addPoint—java.awt.Polygon

```
public void addPoint(int x, int y)
```

Adds another point to a polygon.

addSeparator—java.awt.Menu

```
public void addSeparator()
```

Adds a separator line to a menu at the current position.

addSeparator—java.awt.peer.MenuPeer

```
public abstract void addSeparator()
```

Adds a separator line to a menu at the current position.

after—java.util.Date

```
public boolean after(Date when)
```

Checks whether one date is after another date. True is returned if the current Date comes after the when Date.

allowsMultipleSelections—java.awt.List

```
public boolean allowsMultipleSelections()
```

Returns true if this list allows multiple selections; otherwise, false is returned. Also see the setMultipleSelections method.

and—java.util.BitSet

```
public void and(BitSet set)
```

Logically ANDs the current BitSet object with another BitSet object.

append—java.lang.StringBuffer

```
public synchronized StringBuffer append(datatype value)
```

Appends a value to the end of a StringBuffer. The datatype of the value can be Object, String, character array (char str[]{, offset, int length}), booean, character, integer, long, float, or double.

When appending a character, character array, or String, the append method is public synchronized; otherwise, it's public.

appendText—java.awt.TextArea

```
public void appendText(String str)
```

Appends text to the end of a TextArea. Also see the `insertText`, `getText`, `setText`, and `replaceText` methods.

Applet—java.applet.Applet

```
public  Applet()
```

Constructor for the Applet Class.

appletResize—java.applet.AppletStub

```
public abstract void appletResize(int width, int height)
```

Called when the applet wants to be resized.

ArithmeticException—java.lang.ArithmeticException

```
public ArithmeticException({String detailMessage})
```

An arithmetic error, such as dividing by zero, has occurred. If `detailMessage` is specified, the `detailMessage` will be displayed when this throwable is thrown.

arraycopy—java.lang.System

```
public static void arraycopy(Object src, int src_position,
    Object dst, int dst_position, int length)
```

Copies an array defined by `src`, `src_position`, and `length` to a destination defined by `dst` and `dst_position`. This method does not allocate the new array. An `ArrayIndexOutOfBoundsException` is thrown if the any arguments cause an array to go out of bounds, and an `ArrayStoreException` is thrown if an element in the source could not be stored in the destination due to a type mismatch.

ArrayIndexOutOfBoundsException— java.lang.ArrayIndexOutOfBounds Exception

```
public ArrayIndexOutOfBoundsException({String detailMessage})
```

An array index is less than 1 or is greater than the array size defined in the declaration. If detailMessage is specified, the detailMessage will be displayed when this throwable is thrown.

ArrayStoreException— java.lang.ArrayStoreException

```
ArrayStoreException({String detailMessage})
```

The wrong data type or class is being stored in an array. If detailMessage is specified, the detailMessage will be displayed when this throwable is thrown.

asin—java.lang.Math

```
public static double asin(double a)
```

Returns the arc sine (inverse sine) of an angle measured in radians.

atan2—java.lang.Math

```
public static double atan2(double x, double y)
```

Converts cartesian coordinates (x, y) to polar coordinates (r, theta). The r aspect of a polar coordinate is the size of the line segment between the origin and the coordinate. The theta argument is the r line segment and the x axis.

atan—java.lang.Math

```
public static double atan(double a)
```

Returns the arc tangent (inverse tangent) of an angle measured in radians.

available—java.io.BufferedInputStream

```
public synchronized int available()
```

Returns the total number of bytes that can be read without blocking output to a stream. The available method in the `BufferedInputStream` class overrides the available method in the `FilterInputStream` class.

> **NOTE:**
> The total number of bytes available in the available method is the number of bytes in the buffer summed with the number of bytes in the stream.

available—java.io.ByteArrayInputStream

```
public synchronized int available()
```

Returns the total number of available bytes in a `ByteArrayInputStream` buffer. The available method in the `ByteArrayInputStream` class overrides the available method in the `InputStream` class.

available—java.io.FileInputStream

```
public int available()
```

Returns the total number of bytes that can be read without blocking output to a stream. An `IOException` is thrown if an I/O error occurs. The available method in the `FileInputStream` class overrides the available method in the `InputStream` class.

available—java.io.FilterInputStream

```
public int available()
```

Returns the total number of bytes that can be read without blocking output to a stream. The available method in the `FilterInputStream` class overrides the available method in the `InputStream` class.

available—java.io.InputStream

```
public int available()
```

Returns the total number of bytes that can be read without blocking output to a stream. An IOException is thrown if an I/O error occurs.

available—java.io.LineNumberInputStream

```
public int available()
```

Returns the total number of bytes that can be read without blocking output to a stream. An IOException is thrown if an I/O error occurs. The available method in the LineNumberInputStream class overrides the available method in the FilterInputStream class.

available—java.io.PushbackInputStream

```
public int available()
```

Returns the total number of bytes that can be read without blocking output to a stream. An IOException is thrown if an I/O error occurs. The available method in the PushbackInputStream class overrides the available method in the FilterInputStream class.

available—java.io.StringBufferInputStream

```
public synchronized int available()
```

Returns the total number of bytes that can be read without blocking output to a stream. The available method in the StringBufferInputStream class overrides the available method in the InputStream class.

AWTError—java.awt.AWTError

```
public  AWTError(String msg)
```

Constructs an AWTError with a message as an argument.

AWTException— java.awt.AWTException

```
public   AWTException(String msg)
```

Constructs an AWTException with a message as an argument.

*before—*java.util.Date

```
public boolean before(Date when)
```

Checks whether one date is before another date. True is returned if the current Date comes before the when Date.

*BitSet—*java.util.BitSet

```
public   BitSet({int nbits})
```

Constructs an empty BitSet object. A size of nbits can be specified.

*Boolean—*java.lang.Boolean

```
public   Boolean([boolean value / String s])
```

Constructs a Boolean object initialized with a boolean value or a String.

*booleanValue—*java.lang.Boolean

```
public boolean booleanValue()
```

Returns the value of a Boolean object as a boolean.

*BorderLayout—*java.awt.BorderLayout

```
public   BorderLayout({int hgap, int vgap})
```

Constructs a new BorderLayout. If the horizontal and vertical gaps (hgap and vgap) are specified, this constructor constructs a BorderLayout with the specified gaps.

*bounds—*java.awt.Component

```
public Rectangle bounds()
```

Returns the current bounds of a component. For a related method, see reshape.

brighter—java.awt.Color

```
public Color brighter()
```

Returns a brighter version of a color.

BufferedInputStream— java.io.BufferedInputStream

```
public  BufferedInputStream(InputStream in{, int size})
```

Constructs a new `BufferedInputStream` with the specified buffer size or the default buffer size if the size is omitted.

BufferedOutputStream— java.io.BufferedOutputStream

```
public  BufferedOutputStream(OutputStream out{, int size})
```

Constructs a new `BufferedOutputStream` with the specified buffer size or the default buffer size if the size is omitted.

Button—java.awt.Button

```
public  Button({String label})
```

Constructs a button. If a label is provided, then a label is added to the button upon construction.

ByteArrayInputStream— java.io.ByteArrayInputStream

```
public  ByteArrayInputStream(byte buf[]{, int offset,
    int length})
```

Constructs a `ByteArrayInputStream` from a byte array. If you only want to create a `ByteArrayInputStream` from part of an array, you can use the optional `offset` and `length` arguments.

ByteArrayOutputStream— java.io.ByteArrayOutputStream

```
public  ByteArrayOutputStream({int size})
```

Constructs a new `ByteArrayOutputStream` object. This `ByteArrayOutputStream` will be set to the specified initial size if a specified size is given.

bytesWidth—java.awt.FontMetrics

```
public int bytesWidth(byte data[], int off, int len)
```

Returns the width of the specified array of 8-bit ASCII character bytes in a `FontMetrics` font. This is useful for C and C++ type strings. The `data` argument is the array of bytes to be checked, the `off` argment is the offset to start checking, and the `length` is the number of characters in the character array that you want checked. Also check out the `charWidth`, `charsWidth`, and `stringWidth` methods.

canRead—java.io.File

```
public boolean canRead()
```

Returns true if the file in a `File` object exists and has read access; otherwise, false is returned.

Canvas—java.awt.Canvas

```
public  Canvas()
```

Constructor for the `Canvas` class.

canWrite—java.io.File

```
public boolean canWrite()
```

Returns true if the file in a `File` object exists and has write access; otherwise, false is returned.

capacity—java.lang.StringBuffer

```
public int capacity()
```

Returns how many characters a `StringBuffer` object can hold before reallocation.

capacity—java.util.Vector

```
public final int capacity()
```

Returns the capacity of the vector.

CardLayout—java.awt.CardLayout

```
public  CardLayout({int hgap, int vgap})
```

Creates a new card layout. You can specify gaps on a card if you use a constructor with hgap (horizontal gap) and vgap (vertical gat) defined.

ceil—java.lang.Math

```
public static double ceil(double a)
```

Returns the smallest whole number greater than or equal to a.

Character—java.lang.Character

```
public  Character(char value)
```

Constructs a Character object and initializes it.

charAt—java.lang.String

```
public char charAt(int index)
```

Returns the character at a specified position in the String. A StringIndexOutOfBoundsException is thrown if the position specified is outside less than 0 or greater than the length of the String.

charAt—java.lang.StringBuffer

```
public synchronized char charAt(int position)
```

Returns the character at a specific position from the StringBuffer. An StringIndexOutOfBoundsException exception is thrown if the position is invalid.

charsWidth—java.awt.FontMetrics

```
public int charsWidth(char data[], int off, int len)
```

Returns the width of a specified 16 bit Unicode character array in a `FontMetrics` font. The `data` argument is the array of characters to be checked, the `off` argment is the offset to start checking, and the `length` is the number of characters in the character array that you want checked. Also check out the `charWidth`, `stringWidth`, and `bytesWidth` methods.

charValue—java.lang.Character

```
public char charValue()
```

Returns the character value of a `Character` object.

charWidth—java.awt.FontMetrics

```
public int charWidth([int/char] ch)
```

Returns the width of the specified character in a `FontMetrics` font. The `ch` argument can be an integer or a character. Also see the `stringWidth`, `charsWidth`, and `bytesWidth` methods.

checkAccept— java.lang.SecurityManager

```
public void checkAccept(String host, int port)
```

Throws a `SecurityException` if a socket connection to the specified port on the specified host has not been accepted.

checkAccess— java.lang.SecurityManager

```
public void checkAccess([Thread / ThreadGroup] g)
```

Checks to see if a Thread or ThreadGroup has enough access to modify the `SecurityManager` object. A `SecurityException` is thrown if the Thread does not have enough access.

checkAccess—java.lang.Thread

```
public void checkAccess()
```

Checks whether the current Thread is allowed to modify this ThreadGroup. If not, a SecurityException is thrown.

checkAccess—java.lang.ThreadGroup

```
public final void checkAccess()
```

Checks to see if the current Thread is allowed to modify this ThreadGroup, and throws a SecurityException if it's not.

checkAll—java.awt.MediaTracker

```
public synchronized boolean checkAll({boolean loadall})
```

Checks to see if all images have finished loading. If the loadall argument is true, starts loading any images that are not yet being loaded. If the loadall is false or omitted, no images start loading that haven't yet loaded. If an image load was aborted or encountered an error then that image is considered already loaded. See the isErrorAny, checkID, checkAll, and isErrorID methods for more information.

Checkbox—java.awt.Checkbox

```
public  Checkbox({String label,
    {CheckboxGroup group, boolean state}})
```

Constructs a Checkbox with the specified label (or no label if the label is omitted), specified Checkbox group (or no Checkbox group if the group is omitted), and specified boolean state. (state defaults to false if state is omitted). If the specified CheckboxGroup is not equal to null, then this Checkbox becomes a radio button. If the Checkbox becomes a radio button, only one Checkbox in a CheckboxGroup may be set at a time.

CheckboxGroup— java.awt.CheckboxGroup

```
public  CheckboxGroup()
```

Creates a new CheckboxGroup.

CheckboxMenuItem— java.awt.CheckboxMenuItem

```
public  CheckboxMenuItem(String label)
```

Creates a checkbox menu item with the specified label.

checkConnect— java.lang.SecurityManager

```
public void checkConnect(String host,
    int port{, Object context})
```

Throws a SecurityException violation if a socket is not connected to a specified port. If the context is specified, checks to see if the current execution context is allowed to connect to the indicated host and port, and throws a SecurityException if they are not.

checkCreateClassLoader— java.lang.SecurityManager

```
public void checkCreateClassLoader()
```

Checks to see if the ClassLoader has been created. A SecurityException exception is thrown a ClassLoader has not been created.

checkDelete— java.lang.SecurityManager

```
public void checkDelete(String file)
```

Throws a SecurityException violation if a file cannot be deleted or the file is not found.

checkError—java.io.PrintStream

```
public boolean checkError()
```

Flushes the print stream and returns true if the print stream has ever encountered an error on the output stream.

checkExec—java.lang.SecurityManager

```
public void checkExec(String cmd)
```

Checks to see if a command is executed by trusted code. A SecurityException occurs if the command is not executed by trusted code.

checkExit—java.lang.SecurityManager

```
public void checkExit(int status)
```

Checks to see if the system has exited the virtual Java machine. If the system has exited, a SecurityException is thrown.

checkID—java.awt.MediaTracker

```
public synchronized boolean checkID(
    int identification {, boolean loadall})
```

Checks to see if all images tagged with an identification have finished loading. If the loadall argument is true, starts loading any images with the same identification that are not yet being loaded. If the loadall is false or omitted, no images start loading that haven't yet loaded. If an image load was aborted or encountered an error then that image is considered already loaded. See the isErrorAny, checkAll, and isErrorID methods for more information. True is returned if all images were loaded. False is returned if they haven't been loaded.

checkImage—java.awt.Component

```
public int checkImage(
    Image image, {int width, int height,} ImageObserver observer)
```

Returns the status of an image during construction. Using the same flags as the ImageObserver interface, the return value can be ABORT, ALLBITS, ERROR, FRAMEBITS, HEIGHT, PROPERTIES, SOMEBITS, and WIDTH. For related information, see the prepareImage method or the ImageObserver class. If you only want to check a portion of the image, you must specify length and width.

> **TIP:**
> This `checkImage` **method does not cause an image to begin loading. To load an image, use the** `prepareImage` **method.**

checkImage— java.awt.peer.ComponentPeer

```
public abstract int checkImage(
    Image image, int width, int height, ImageObserver observer)
```

Returns the status of an image during construction. Using the same flags as the `ImageObserver` interface, the return value can be `ABORT`, `ALLBITS`, `ERROR`, `FRAMEBITS`, `HEIGHT`, `PROPERTIES`, `SOMEBITS`, and `WIDTH`. For related information, see the `prepareImage` method or the `ImageObserver` class. If you only want to check a portion of the image, you must specify length and width.

*checkImage—*java.awt.Toolkit

```
public abstract int checkImage(
    Image image, int width, int height, ImageObserver observer)
```

Returns the status of the construction of the indicated method at the indicated width and height for the default screen. See the `ImageObserver` class for more information.

*checkLink—*java.lang.SecurityManager

```
public void checkLink(String lib)
```

Checks to see if a library exists. A `SecurityException` occurs if the library does not exist.

checkListen— java.lang.SecurityManager

```
public void checkListen(int port)
```

Checks a port to see if a server socket is listening to it. A `SecurityException` is thrown if the port is not being listened to.

checkPackageAccess— java.lang.SecurityManager

```
public void checkPackageAccess(String pkg)
```

Checks to see if an applet can access a package.

checkPackageDefinition— java.lang.SecurityManager

```
public void checkPackageDefinition(String pkg)
```

Checks to see if an applet can define classes in a package.

checkPropertiesAccess— java.lang.SecurityManager

```
public void checkPropertiesAccess(
    {String sysprop{, String def}})
```

Checks to see who has access to the System properties. This can be done by an individual system property is a property is specified. If a default value is specified, then the property is set to a default value if there currently is no property setting. A SecurityException error occurs if a security error has occurred.

checkRead—java.lang.SecurityManager

```
public void checkRead(
    [ FileDescriptor fd / String file{, Object context}])
```

Throws a SecurityException violation if an input file, a file with the specified file descriptor, or a current context are not allowed to be read from.

checkSetFactory— java.lang.SecurityManager

```
public void checkSetFactory()
```

Checks to see if an applet can set a object factory that is network-related.

Send Us
YOUR **COMMENTS**

Dear Reader:

Thank you for buying this book. In order to offer you more quality books on the topics *you* would like to see, we need your input. At Prima Publishing, we pride ourselves on timely responsiveness to our readers' needs. If you complete and return this brief questionnaire, *we will listen!*

Name (First) _____ (M.I.) ____ (Last) _____

Company _____ Type of business _____

Address _____ City _____ State ____ ZIP ____

Phone _____ Fax _____ E-mail address: _____

May we contact you for research purposes? ❏ Yes ❏ No

(If you participate in a research project, we will supply you with the Prima computer book of your choice.)

❶ How would you rate this book, overall?

❏ Excellent   ❏ Fair
❏ Very good   ❏ Below average
❏ Good   ❏ Poor

❷ Why did you buy this book?

❏ Price of book   ❏ Content
❏ Author's reputation ❏ Prima's reputation
❏ CD-ROM/disk included with book
❏ Information highlighted on cover
❏ Other (please specify): _____

❸ How did you discover this book?

❏ Found it on bookstore shelf
❏ Saw it in Prima Publishing catalog
❏ Recommended by store personnel
❏ Recommended by friend or colleague
❏ Saw an advertisement in: _____
❏ Read book review in: _____
❏ Saw it on Web site: _____
❏ Other (please specify): _____

❹ Where did you buy this book?

❏ Bookstore (name): _____
❏ Computer store (name): _____
❏ Electronics store (name): _____
❏ Wholesale club (name): _____
❏ Mail order (name): _____
❏ Direct from Prima Publishing
❏ Other (please specify): _____

❺ Which computer periodicals do you read regularly? _____

_____

_____

_____

❻ Would you like to see your name in print?

May we use your name and quote you in future Prima Publishing books or promotional materials?

❏ Yes   ❏ No

❼ Comments & suggestions: _____

_____

_____

8 **I am interested in seeing more computer books on these topics**

❏ Word processing   ❏ Databases/spreadsheets   ❏ Networking   ❏ Programming
❏ Desktop publishing   ❏ Web site development   ❏ Internetworking ❏ Intranetworking

9 **How do you rate your level of computer skills?**   **10** **What is your age?**

❏ Beginner   ❏ Under 18   ❏ 40–49
❏ Intermediate   ❏ 18–29   ❏ 50–59
❏ Advanced   ❏ 30–39   ❏ 60–over

SAVE A STAMP

Visit our Web site at **http://www.primapublishing.com**

and simply fill out one of our online response forms.

Carmel, IN 46032
701 Congressional Blvd., Suite 350
Computer Products Division
PRIMA PUBLISHING

PLEASE
PLACE
STAMP
HERE

checkTopLevelWindow—
java.lang.SecurityManager

```
public boolean checkTopLevelWindow(Object window)
```

Returns false when the toplevelwindow creation is allowed but the window should indicate some sort of visual warning. A true value means the window creation is allowed with no special restrictions. If a window is not allowed to be created, this method will throw a SecurityException.

checkWrite—
java.lang.SecurityManager

```
public void checkWrite([ FileDescriptor fd / String file])
```

Throws a SecurityException violation if an output file or a file with the specified file descriptor are not allowed to be written to.

Choice—java.awt.Choice

```
public  Choice()
```

Constructs a new Choice.

ClassCastException—
java.lang.ClassCastException

```
public ClassCastException({String detailMessage})
```

An invalid cast from one data type to another has occurred. If detailMessage is specified, the detailMessage will be displayed when this throwable is thrown.

ClassCircularityError—
java.lang.ClassCircularityError

```
public ClassCircularityError({String detailMessage})
```

An ancestor class is trying to inherit one of it's descendent classes. This is not allowed. If detailMessage is specified, the detailMessage will be displayed when this throwable is thrown.

classDepth—java.lang.SecurityManager

```
protected int classDepth(String name)
```

Returns the position of the stack frame containing the first occurrence of a class identified by the name parameter.

ClassFormatError— java.lang.ClassFormatError

```
public ClassFormatError({String detailMessage})
```

An invalid file format for a class has been detected. If detailMessage is specified, the detailMessage will be displayed when this throwable is thrown.

ClassLoader—java.lang.ClassLoader

```
protected  ClassLoader()
```

Constructs a new Class loader.

classLoaderDepth— java.lang.SecurityManager

```
protected int classLoaderDepth()
```

Returns the position of the stack frame containing the first occurrence of the current ClassLoader.

ClassNotFoundException— java.lang.ClassNotFoundException

```
public ClassNotFoundException({String detailMessage})
```

A class that was called could not be found and/or loaded successfully. If detailMessage is specified, the detailMessage will be displayed when this throwable is thrown.

clear—java.util.BitSet

```
public void clear(int bit)
```

Clears a bit in a BitSet object.

clear—java.util.Hashtable

```
public synchronized void clear()
```

Clears the hashtable so that it is empty.

clear—java.awt.List

```
public synchronized void clear()
```

Clears a list. Also see the delItem and delItems methods.

clear—java.awt.peer.ListPeer

```
public abstract void clear()
```

Clears a list. Also see the delItem and delItems methods.

clearChanged—java.util.Observable

```
protected synchronous void clearChanged()
```

Clears an observable change.

clearRect—java.awt.Graphics

```
public abstract void clearRect(
    int x, int y, int width, int height)
```

Fills a rectangle (identified by x, y, width, and height) with the background color. Also check out the drawRect and fillRect methods.

clipRect—java.awt.Graphics

```
public abstract void clipRect(
    int x, int y, int width, int height)
```

Forms a clipping area denoted by x, y, width, and height. For more information, see the getClipRect method.

clone—java.util.BitSet

```
public Object clone()
```

Clones the BitSet. The clone method in the BitSet class overrides the clone method in the Object class.

clone—java.awt.GridBagConstraints

```
public Object clone()
```

Creates a clone of a GridBagConstraints object. The clone method in the GridBagConstraints class overrides the clone method in the Object class.

clone—java.util.Hashtable

```
public synchronized Object clone()
```

Creates a clone of the hashtable. The keys and elements themselves are *not* cloned. The clone method in the Hashtable class overrides the clone method in the Object class.

clone—java.awt.image.ImageFilter

```
public Object clone()
```

Clones this ImageFilter. The clone method in the ImageFilter class overrides the clone method in the Object class.

clone—java.awt.Insets

```
public Object clone()
```

Creates a clone of the object. The clone method in the Insets class overrides the clone method in the Object class.

clone—java.lang.Object

```
protected Object clone()
```

Creates and returns a clone of an object. A new instance is allocated and a bitwise clone of the current object is place in the new object. An OutOfMemoryError occurs if there is not enough memory to clone the object, and a CloneNotSupportedException exception is thrown if the Object doesn't support the Cloneable interface.

clone—java.util.Vector

```
public synchronized Object clone()
```

Clones a vector. The elements inside the vector are not cloned. The clone method inside the Vector class overrides the clone method inside the Object class.

CloneNotSupportedException— java.lang.CloneNotSupportedException

```
public CloneNotSupportedException({String detailMessage})
```

An attempt has been made to clone an object that is not clonable. If `detailMessage` is specified, the `detailMessage` will be displayed when this throwable is thrown.

close—java.io.FileInputStream

```
public void close()
```

Closes the input stream and releases all of the `FileInputStream` object's resources. An `IOException` is thrown if there is an I/O error. The `close` method in the FileInputStream class overrides the `close` method in the InputStream class.

close—java.io.FileOutputStream

```
public void close()
```

Closes the output stream and releases all of the `FileOutputStream` object's resources. An `IOException` is thrown if there is an I/O error. The `close` method in the FileOutputStream class overrides the `close` method in the OutputStream class.

close—java.io.FilterInputStream

```
public void close()
```

Closes the input stream and releases all of the `FilterInputStream` object's resources. An `IOException` is thrown if there is an I/O error. The `close` method in the FilterInputStream class overrides the `close` method in the InputStream class.

close—java.io.FilterOutputStream

```
public void close()
```

Closes the output stream and releases all of the `FilterOutputStream` object's resources. An `IOException` is athrown if there is an I/O error. The `close` method in the FilterOutputStream class overrides the `close` method in the OutputStream class.

close—java.io.InputStream

```
public void close()
```

Closes the input stream and releases all of the `InputStream` object's resources. An `IOException` is thrown if there is an I/O error.

close—java.io.OutputStream

```
public void close()
```

Closes the output stream and releases all of the `OutputStream` object's resources. An `IOException` is thrown if there is an I/O error.

close—java.io.PipedInputStream

```
public void close()
```

Closes the input stream and releases all of the `PipedInputStream` object's resources. An `IOException` is thrown if there is an I/O error. The `close` method in the PipedInputStream class overrides the `close` method in the InputStream class.

close—java.io.PipedOutputStream

```
public void close()
```

Closes the output stream and releases all of the `PipedOutputStream` object's resources. An `IOException` is thrown if there is an I/O error. The `close` method in the PipedOutputStream class overrides the `close` method in the OutputStream class.

close—java.io.PrintStream

```
public void close()
```

Closes the print stream and releases all of the `PrintStream` object's resources. An `IOException` is thrown if there is an I/O error. The `close` method in the PrintStream class overrides the `close` method in the FilterOutputStream class.

close—java.io.RandomAccessFile

```
public void close()
```

Closes the RandomAccessFile object and releases all of it's resources. An IOException is thrown if there is an I/O error.

close—java.io.SequenceInputStream

```
public void close()
```

Closes the input stream and releases all of the FilterInputStream object's resources. An IOException is thrown if there is an I/O error. The close method in the SequenceInputStream class overrides the close method in the InputStream class.

close—java.net.ServerSocket

```
public void close()
```

Closes the server socket. An IOException is thrown if there is an I/O error while closing the socket.

close—java.net.Socket

```
public synchronized void close()
```

Closes the socket. An IOException is thrown if an I/O occurs while closing the socket.

Color—java.awt.Color

```
public Color(
    [int rgb]/[int red, int green, int blue]
    /[float red, float green, float blue])
```

Creates a combined rgb value or a color with the specified red, green, and blue values. If the red, green, and blue values are integers, they must be between 0 and 255. If the red, green, and blue values are float, they must be between 0.0 and 1.0. RGB values are integers with the following bit breakdown: the red component is in bits 16–23, the green component is in bits 8–15, and the blue component is in bits 0–7. The actual color used in rendering will depend on finding the best match given the color space available for a given output device. For related methods, see the getRed, getGreen, getBlue, and getRGB methods.

ColorModel— java.awt.image.ColorModel

```
public  ColorModel(int bits)
```

Constructs a `ColorModel`. The bits argument describes the size of a pixel in a `ColorModel`.

command—java.lang.Compiler

```
public static Object command(Object any)
```

Instantiates an object, thereby causing a command to be executed.

commentChar— java.io.StreamTokenizer

```
public void commentChar(int ch)
```

Identifies the character that starts a single line comment.

compareTo—java.lang.String

```
public int compareTo(String anotherString)
```

Compares two strings. If the current string is less than `anotherString`, a 1 is returned. If they are equal, a 0 is returned. If `anotherString` is greater than the current String, a –1 is returned.

compileClass—java.lang.Compiler

```
public static boolean compileClass(Class class)
```

Invokes the compiler to compile a class.

compileClasses—java.lang.Compiler

```
public static boolean compileClasses(String classes)
```

Invokes the compiler to load and compile classes contained within a String.

concat—**java.lang.String**

```
public String concat(String str)
```

Concatenates one string to the current string.

connect—**java.io.PipedInputStream**

```
public void connect(PipedOutputStream pos)
```

Connects a `PipedInputStream` to a `PipedOutputStream`. See the `PipedInputStream` constructor for more details.

connect—**java.io.PipedOutputStream**

```
public void connect(PipedInputStream pis)
```

Connects a `PipedOututStream` to a `PipedInputStream`. See the `PipedOutputStream` constructor for more details.

connect—**java.net.URLConnection**

```
public abstract void connect()
```

Connects a `URLConnection` object after it has been constructed. An `IOException` is thrown if you try to connect a `URLConnection` more than once.

contains—**java.util.Hashtable**

```
public synchronized boolean contains(Object value)
```

Returns true if an `Object` is an element of the `hashtable`. Also see the `containsKey` method for a more efficient way to test for objects. A `NullPointerException` occurs if the `Object` being searched for is null.

contains—**java.util.Vector**

```
public final boolean contains(Object elem)
```

Searches the vector for an `Object` and returns true if it's found; otherwise, false is returned.

containsKey—java.util.Hashtable

```
public synchronized boolean containsKey(Object key)
```

Returns true if the `hashtable` contains an element for a key.

ContentHandler— java.net.ContentHandler

```
public  ContentHandler()
```

Constructs a new `ContentHandler` object.

controlDown—java.awt.Event

```
public boolean controlDown()
```

Checks if the control key is down. Also checks out the `modifiers` attribute and the `shiftDown` and `metaDown` methods.

copyArea—java.awt.Graphics

```
public abstract void copyArea(int x, int y,
    int width, int height, int newx, int newy)
```

Copies an area of the screen (identified by `x`, `y`, `width`, and `height`) to another area identified by `newx` and `newy`. (The width and the height would be the same.)

copyInto—java.util.Vector

```
public final synchronous void copyInto(Object anArray[])
```

Copies elements of a vector into an `Object` array.

copyValueOf—java.lang.String

```
public static String copyValueOf(
    char data[]{, int offset, int count})
```

Creates a new array that is a copy of the `data` argument (with `offset` and `count`, if given). Then returns a String that is equivalent to the specified character array.

cos—java.lang.Math

```
public static double cos(double a)
```

Returns the trigonomectric cosine of an angle measured in radians.

countComponents—java.awt.Container

```
public int countComponents()
```

Returns the number of components in a container. Also see getComponent.

countItems—java.awt.Choice

```
public int countItems()
```

Returns the number of items in a Choice. For a related methods, see the getItem methods and the addItem method.

countItems—java.awt.List

```
public int countItems()
```

Returns the number of items in the list. Also see the getItem method.

countItems—java.awt.Menu

```
public int countItems()
```

Returns the number of items in a menu.

countMenus—java.awt.MenuBar

```
public int countMenus()
```

Returns the number of menus on a MenuBar.

countObservers—java.util.Observable

```
public synchronized int countObservers()
```

Returns the number of observers.

countStackFrames—java.lang.Thread

```
public int countStackFrames()
```

Returns the number of stack frames in this Thread. The Thread must be suspended when this method is called, or an IllegalThreadStateException is thrown.

countTokens—java.util.StringTokenizer

```
public int countTokens()
```

Returns the number of tokens in a StringTokenizer's String.

create—java.awt.Graphics

```
public Graphics create({int x,int y,int width, int height})
```

Returns a copy of a Graphics object. If x, w, width, and height are specified, the create method returns a copy of the Graphics object with the specified parameters. Also see the translate method.

createButton—java.awt.Toolkit

```
protected abstract ButtonPeer createButton(Button target)
```

Returns a Peer interface to a newly created Button.

createCanvas—java.awt.Toolkit

```
protected abstract CanvasPeer createCanvas(Canvas target)
```

Returns a Peer interface to a newly created new Canvas.

createCheckbox—java.awt.Toolkit

```
protected abstract CheckboxPeer createCheckbox(
    Checkbox target)
```

Returns a Peer interface to a newly created new Checkbox.

createCheckboxMenuItem— java.awt.Toolkit

```
protected abstract CheckboxMenuItemPeer
    createCheckboxMenuItem(CheckboxMenuItem target)
```

Returns a Peer interface to a newly created new CheckboxMenuItem.

createChoice—java.awt.Toolkit

```
protected abstract ChoicePeer createChoice(Choice target)
```

Returns a Peer interface to a newly created new Choice.

createContentHandler— java.net.ContentHandlerFactory

```
public abstract ContentHandler createContentHandler(
    String mimetype)
```

Creates a ContentHandler object to read an object from a URLStreamHandler. The mimetype argument is the mime type for which a content handler is desired.

createDialog—java.awt.Toolkit

```
protected abstract DialogPeer createDialog(Dialog target)
```

Returns a Peer interface to a newly created new Dialog.

createFileDialog—java.awt.Toolkit

```
protected abstract FileDialogPeer
        createFileDialog(FileDialog target)
```

Returns a Peer interface to a newly created new FileDialog.

createFrame—java.awt.Toolkit

```
protected abstract FramePeer createFrame(Frame target)
```

Returns a Peer interface to a newly created new Frame.

createImage—java.awt.Component

```
public Image createImage([ImageProducer producer]
      / [int width, int height])
```

Creates an image from an image producer or an off-screen drawable Image.

createImage— java.awt.peer.ComponentPeer

```
public abstract Image createImage([ImageProducer producer]
      / [int width, int height])
```

Creates an image from an image producer or an off-screen drawable Image.

createImage—java.awt.Toolkit

```
public abstract Image createImage(ImageProducer producer)
```

Creates an image with an ImageProducer argument. See the ImageProducer class for more information.

createLabel—java.awt.Toolkit

```
protected abstract LabelPeer createLabel(Label target)
```

Returns a Peer interface to a newly created new Label.

createList—java.awt.Toolkit

```
protected abstract ListPeer createList(List target)
```

Returns a Peer interface to a newly created new List.

createMenu—java.awt.Toolkit

```
protected abstract MenuPeer createMenu(Menu target)
```

Returns a Peer interface to a newly created new Menu.

createMenuBar—java.awt.Toolkit

```
protected abstract MenuBarPeer createMenuBar(MenuBar target)
```

Returns a Peer interface to a newly created new MenuBar.

createMenuItem—java.awt.Toolkit

```
protected abstract MenuItemPeer createMenuItem(
    MenuItem target)
```

Returns a Peer interface to a newly created new MenuItem.

createPanel—java.awt.Toolkit

```
protected abstract PanelPeer createPanel(Panel target)
```

Returns a Peer interface to a newly created new Panel.

createScrollbar—java.awt.Toolkit

```
protected abstract ScrollbarPeer createScrollbar(
    Scrollbar target)
```

Returns a Peer interface to a newly created new Scrollbar.

createSocketImpl—java.net.SocketImplFactory

```
public abstract SocketImpl createSocketImpl()
```

Creates a new SocketImpl object.

createTextArea—java.awt.Toolkit

```
protected abstract TextAreaPeer createTextArea(
    TextArea target)
```

Returns a Peer interface to a newly created new TextArea.

createTextField—java.awt.Toolkit

```
protected abstract TextFieldPeer createTextField(
    TextField target)
```

Returns a Peer interface to a newly created new TextField.

createURLStreamHandler— java.net.URLStreamHandlerFactory

```
public abstract URLStreamHandler
    createURLStreamHandler(String protocol)
```

Creates a new URLStreamHandler object with the specified protocol. Protocal can be FTP, HTTP, and so on.

createWindow—java.awt.Toolkit

```
protected abstract WindowPeer createWindow(Window target)
```

Returns a Peer interface to a newly created new Window.

CropImageFilter— java.awt.image.CropImageFilter

```
public  CropImageFilter(int x, int y, int width, int height)
```

Constructs a CropImageFilter that extracts the pixels from the rectangle defined by x, y, width, and height.

currentClassLoader— java.lang.SecurityManager

```
protected ClassLoader currentClassLoader()
```

Returns the current ClassLoader object on the execution stack.

currentThread—java.lang.Thread

```
public static Thread currentThread()
```

Returns a reference to the Thread that is currently running.

currentTimeMillis—java.lang.System

```
public static long currentTimeMillis()
```

Returns the current time in milliseconds GMT since January 1, 1970. Also see the Date class.

> **NOTE:**
> For those of you who don't know, GMT stands for Greenwich Mean Time. Because everyone is in a different time zone, especially on the Internet, sometimes specifying an hour or date can be tricky. Greenwich Mean Time is the current time in Greenwich, England. Greenwich is where the time zones start, and where the date line crosses into a new date first.

darker—java.awt.Color

```
public Color darker()
```

Returns a darker version of a color.

DatagramPacket—java.net.DatagramPacket

```
public  DatagramPacket(byte ibuf[],
       int ilength{, InetAddress iaddr, int iport})
```

Constructs a DatagramPacket for receiving datagrams. The ibuf argument is where packet data is to be received, and the ilength argument is the number of bytes to be received. The iaddr and iport arguments, if given, contain the destination ip address and port number.

DataInputStream—java.io.DataInputStream

```
public  DataInputStream(InputStream in)
```

Constructs a new DataInputStream from an InputStream object.

DataOutputStream— java.io.DataOutputStream

```
public  DataOutputStream(OutputStream out)
```

Constructs a new DataOutputStream object from an OutputStream object.

Date—java.util.Date

```
public  Date({[String s / long date
    / int year, int month, int day{,int hrs, int min{,second}}]})
```

Creates a date from a String argument, a long date argument, or a year, month, day, and optional hour, minute, and second arguments (assumed zero if omitted). If there are no aguments passed to the Date constructor, today's date and time are created.

defineClass—java.lang.ClassLoader

```
protected final Class defineClass(byte data[],
    int offset, int length)
```

Returns a Class created by converting an array of bytes. Before the Class can be used it must be resolved. A ClassFormatError is thrown if the data does not contain a valid Class. Also see the loadClass and resolveClass methods.

delete—java.io.File

```
public boolean delete()
```

Deletes the file in a File object. Returns true if the file could be deleted, and false otherwise.

deleteObserver—java.util.Observable

```
public synchronized void deleteObserver(Observer o)
```

Deletes an observer from the observer list.

deleteObservers—java.util.Observable

```
public synchronized void deleteObservers()
```

Deletes all Observers from the observer list.

delItem—java.awt.List

```
public synchronized void delItem(int position)
```

Delete an item from a List. Also see the `clear` and `delItems` methods.

delItem—java.awt.peer.MenuPeer

```
public abstract void delItem(int index)
```

Deletes an item from a Menu.

delItems—java.awt.List

```
public synchronized void delItems(int start, int end)
```

Delete multiple items from the list beginning with `start` and ending with `end`.

delItems—java.awt.peer.ListPeer

```
public abstract void delItems(int start, int end)
```

Delete multiple items from the list beginning with `start` and ending with `end`.

deliverEvent—java.awt.Component

```
public void deliverEvent(Event e)
```

Triggers a Component's events. For related information, see the `handleEvent` and `postEvent` methods.

deliverEvent—java.awt.Container

```
public void deliverEvent(Event e)
```

Triggers an event. The appropriate component inside a container is located and the event inside that component is triggered. The `deliverEvent` method in the Container class overrides the deliverEvent method in the Component class. For more information, check out the handleEvent and postEvent methods.

delMenu—java.awt.peer.MenuBarPeer

```
public abstract void delMenu(int index)
```

Removes a menu identified by a specified index from a MenuBar.

deselect—java.awt.List

```
public synchronized void deselect(int index)
```

Deselects the List item at an index. Also see the select, isSelected, getSelectedIndex, getSelectedIndexes, getSelectedItem, and getSelectedItems methods.

deselect—java.awt.peer.ListPeer

```
public abstract void deselect(int index)
```

Deselects the List item at an index. Also see the select, isSelected, getSelectedIndex, getSelectedIndexes, getSelectedItem, and getSelectedItems methods.

destroy—java.applet.Applet

```
public void destroy()
```

Cleans up whatever resources are being held. If the applet is active it is stopped stopped. For more information, see the start, init, and stop methods.

destroy—java.lang.Process

```
public abstract void destroy()
```

Kills the subprocess in a Process object.

destroy—java.lang.Thread

```
public void destroy()
```

Destroys the current thread without any cleanup. This should only be used as a last resort.

destroy—java.lang.ThreadGroup

```
public final synchronous void destroy()
```

Destroys a Thread group. However, the destroy method doesn't stop the Threads in the Thread group. An IllegalThreadStateException is thrown if the ThreadGroup is not empty or if the Thread group was already destroyed.

Dialog—java.awt.Dialog

```
public  Dialog(Frame parent, {String title,} boolean modal)
```

Constructs a Dialog box inside a specified parent Frame. The Dialog has a title if one is specifed. If modal is true, the Dialog grabs all the input from the user and blocks input to other windows when shown. Also see the resize and show methods and the Frame class.

> **TIP:**
> **Initially, all Dialogs are invisible when they are constructed. Use the show method to make a Dialog visible.**

Dictionary—java.util.Dictionary

```
public  Dictionary()
```

Constructs a Dictionary object.

digit—java.lang.Character

```
public static int digit(char ch, int radix)
```

Returns the numeric value of the character digit using the specified radix. A radix is the base used, and will probably be 10 (for based–10 number systems). 16 (hexidecimal) and 8 (octal) may also prove useful. If the character is not a valid digit, a –1 is returned.

Dimension—java.awt.Dimension

```
public  Dimension({[Dimension d / int width, int height]})
```

Constructs a Dimension. If d is specified, the new dimension will be a copy of Dimension d. If width and height are specified, the new

dimension will set width and height to the appropriate values. If
`Dimension d` and `width` and `height` are omitted, a new Dimension is
created with zero height and zero width.

DirectColorModel—
java.awt.image.DirectColorModel

```
public  DirectColorModel(int bits, int redMask,
     int greenMask, int blueMask{,int alphaMask})
```

Constructs a `DirectColorModel` from the given masks specifying
which bits in the pixel contain the red, green, blue, and alpha
transparancy (if given) color components. If the `alphaMask` is omitted, pixels in this color model will all have alpha components of 255,
which is not transparaent.

disable—java.awt.Component

```
public synchronized void disable()
```

Disables a Component. For related methods, see the `isEnabled` and
`enable` methods.

disable—java.lang.Compiler

```
public static void disable()
```

Disables the Compiler object.

disable—java.awt.peer.ComponentPeer

```
public abstract void disable()
```

Disables a Component. For related methods, see the `isEnabled` and
`enable` methods.

disable—java.awt.MenuItem

```
public void disable()
```

Makes this menu item unselectable by the user. Also see the `enable`
method.

disable—java.awt.peer.MenuItemPeer

```
public abstract void disable()
```

Makes this menu item unselectable by the user. Also see the `enable` method.

dispose—java.awt.peer.ComponentPeer

```
public abstract void dispose()
```

Removes and deallocates (garbage collects) a Component. This method is used to release a Component's resources.

dispose—java.awt.Frame

```
public synchronized void dispose()
```

Removes and deallocates (garbage collects) a Frame. This method is used to release a Frame's resources. The `dispose` method in the Frame class overrides the `dispose` method in the Window class.

dispose—java.awt.Graphics

```
public abstract void dispose()
```

Disposes of a Graphics context immediately. Also see the `finalize` method.

> **TIP:**
> **A Graphics context cannot be used after being disposed of.**

dispose—java.awt.peer.MenuComponentPeer

```
public abstract void dispose()
```

Removes and deallocates (garbage collects) a `MenuComponent`. This method is used to release a `MenuComponent`'s resources.

dispose—java.awt.Window

```
public synchronized void dispose()
```

Releases all resources used by a Window object, thereby destroying the window.

Double—java.lang.Double

```
public  Double([double value / String s])
```

Constructs a Double wrapper for a double floating point number or from a String. A NumberFormatException exception is thrown if a String is used in the constructor and the String does not contain a valid number.

doubleToLongBits—java.lang.Double

```
public static long doubleToLongBits(double value)
```

Returns the bit representation of a double value.

doubleValue—java.lang.Double

```
public double doubleValue()
```

Returns the double floating point value of a Double. The doubleValue method in the Double class overrides the doubleValue method in the Number class.

doubleValue—java.lang.Float

```
public double doubleValue()
```

Returns the double floating point value of a Float. The doubleValue method in the Float class overrides the doubleValue method in the Number class.

doubleValue—java.lang.Integer

```
public double doubleValue()
```

Returns the value of an Integer as an double precision floating point decimal. The doubleValue method in the Integer class overrides the doubleValue method in the Number class.

doubleValue—java.lang.Long

```
public double doubleValue()
```

Returns the value of a Long as an double precision floating point decimal. The doubleValue method in the Long class overrides the doubleValue method in the Number class.

doubleValue—java.lang.Number

```
public abstract double doubleValue()
```

Returns the value of a number as a double data type.

draw3DRect—java.awt.Graphics

```
public void draw3DRect(int x, int y, int width,
    int height, boolean raised)
```

Draws a 3D rectangle defined by x, y, width, and height. Raised is a boolean value indicating whether the rectangle is raised. Also see the fill3DRect method.

drawArc—java.awt.Graphics

```
public abstract void drawArc(int x, int y, int width,
    int height, int startAngle, int angleSize)
```

Draws an arc bounded by a rectangle defined by x, y, width, and height using the current color. The arc is drawn from startAngle to startAngle + angleSize. 0 degrees is at the 3-o'clock position, and you can use positive or negative degrees. Also see the fillArc method.

drawBytes—java.awt.Graphics

```
public void drawBytes(byte data[], int offset,
    int length, int x, int y)
```

Draws ASCII bytes in the current font and color. The data argument is an array of bytes. The offset is the starting point in the array and the length is the ending point in an array. The x,y position is the starting point of the baseline of the bytes. Also see the drawString and drawChars methods.

drawChars—java.awt.Graphics

```
public void drawChars(char data[], int offset,
    int length, int x, int y)
```

Draws Unicode characters in the current font and color. The data argument is an array of characters. The offset is the starting point in the array and the length is the ending point in an array. The x,y position is the starting point of the baseline of the characters. Also see the drawString and drawBytes methods.

drawImage—java.awt.Graphics

```
public abstract boolean drawImage(Image img, int x, int y,
    {int width, int height,} {Color bgColor,}
    ImageObserver observer)
```

Draws an image at the specified coordinate (x, y). If width and height are specified, the image will be drawn inside the defined rectangle. If a background color is specified, the image will be drawn on top of a solid background color. If the image is incomplete, the image observer will be notified later. For more information, see the Image and ImageObserver classes.

drawLine—java.awt.Graphics

```
public abstract void drawLine(int x1, int y1,
    int x2, int y2)
```

Draws a line between the coordinates (x1,y1)and (x2,y2).

drawOval—java.awt.Graphics

```
public abstract void drawOval(int x, int y,
    int width, int height)
```

Draws an oval inside a rectangle defined by x, y, width, and height using the current color. Also check out the fillOval method.

drawPolygon—java.awt.Graphics

```
public abstract void drawPolygon([Polygon p/int xPoints[],
    int yPoints[], int nPoints])
```

Draws a polygon defined a `Polygon` class or `nPoints`, `xPoints`, and `yPoints`. `xPoints` and `yPoints` are arrays that contain coordinates. The `nPoints` argument defines the number of points in the polygon. Also see the `fillPolygon` method and the `Polygon` class.

drawRect—java.awt.Graphics

```
public void drawRect(int x, int y, int width, int height)
```

Draws the outline of a rectangle identified by x, y, `width`, and `height` using the current color. Also check out the `fillRect` and `clearRect` methods.

drawRoundRect—java.awt.Graphics

```
public abstract void drawRoundRect(int x, int y,
    int width, int height, int arcWidth, int arcHeight)
```

Draws an outlined rounded corner rectangle using the current color x, y, `width`, and `height` identify the rectangle. `arcWidth` is the arc horizontal diameter of the four corners and `arcHeight` is the arc vertical diameter of the four corners. Also check out the `fillRoundRect` method.

drawString—java.awt.Graphics

```
public abstract void drawString(String str, int x, int y)
```

Draws graphical text using the current font and color. The x,y position is the starting point of the baseline of the String. Also see the `drawChars` and `drawBytes` methods.

dumpStack—java.lang.Thread

```
public static void dumpStack()
```

Prints a stack trace for the current Thread.

echoCharIsSet—java.awt.TextField

```
public boolean echoCharIsSet()
```

Returns true if a TextField has a character set for echoing; otherwise, false is returned. Echo characters are useful when what the user is typing shouldn't be echoed back to the window (such as passwords). Also see the setEchoCharacter and getEchoChar methods.

elementAt—java.util.Vector

```
public final synchronous Object elementAt(int index)
```

Returns the object at a given index in a Vector. An ArrayIndexOutOfBoundsException is thrown if an invalid index was given.

elements—java.util.Dictionary

```
public abstract Enumeration elements()
```

Returns an Enumeration of a Dictionary's elements.

elements—java.util.Hashtable

```
public synchronized Enumeration elements()
```

Returns an Enumeration of the hashtable's elements. The elements method in the Hashtable class overrides the elements method in the Dictionary class.

elements—java.util.Vector

```
public final synchronous Enumeration elements()
```

Returns an Enumeration of Vector elements.

empty—java.util.Stack

```
public boolean empty()
```

Returns true if the stack is empty; otherwise, false is returned.

EmptyStackException— java.util.EmptyStackException

```
public EmptyStackException({String detailMessage})
```

The stack is empty and has no data. If `detailMessage` is specified, the `detailMessage` will be displayed when this throwable is thrown.

*enable—*java.awt.Component

```
public synchronized void enable({boolean cond})
```

Enables a `Component` if `cond` is true or omitted, and disables a `Component` if `cond` is false. For related methods, see the `enable` and `disable` methods.

*enable—*java.lang.Compiler

```
public static void enable()
```

Enables the Compiler object.

*enable—*java.awt.peer.ComponentPeer

```
public abstract void enable()
```

Enables a Component if `cond` is true, and disables a Component of `cond` is false. For related methods, see the `enable` and `disable` methods.

*enable—*java.awt.MenuItem

```
public void enable({boolean torf})
```

Makes a MenuItem selectable by the user if `torf` is true or omitted. If `torf` is false, this method disables the MenuItem. Also see the `disable` method.

*enable—*java.awt.peer.MenuItemPeer

```
public abstract void enable({boolean torf})
```

Makes a MenuItem selectable by the user if `torf` is true or omitted. If `torf` is false, this method disables the MenuItem. Also see the `disable` method.

encode—java.net.URLEncoder

```
public static String encode(String s)
```

Translates a String object into x-www-form-URLencoded format and returns the encoded String.

endsWith—java.lang.String

```
public boolean endsWith(String suffix)
```

Determines whether this string ends with a suffix.

ensureCapacity—java.lang.StringBuffer

```
public synchronized void ensureCapacity(int minimumCapacity)
```

Ensures that the `StringBuffer` capacity is at least equal to the number of `minimumCapacity` characters.

ensureCapacity—java.util.Vector

```
public final synchronous void ensureCapacity(int capacity)
```

Ensures that a Vector will always have at least a given capacity.

enumerate—java.lang.Thread

```
public static int enumerate(Thread threads[])
```

Copies all active threads into a threads array. The number of threads found is returned.

enumerate—java.lang.ThreadGroup

```
public int enumerate([Thread /ThreadGroup] list[]
    {, boolean recurse})
```

Copies references to every active Thread (if specified) or Thead Group (if specified) in this Thread group into the specified array.

EOFException—java.io.EOFException

```
public  EOFException({String detailMessage)
```

Constructs an exception indicating that the end of a file or stream has been reached during an input command. You can specify a detail message to appear if you want.

eolIsSignificant— java.io.StreamTokenizer

```
public void eolIsSignificant(boolean torf)
```

If the `torf` is true, end-of-lines characters are significant and will set the TT_EOL token. If false, EOL characters will be treated as white-space.

equals—java.util.BitSet

```
public boolean equals(Object obj)
```

Compares a BitSet with another object. A true value is returned if the two objects are equal, and a false is returned if the two objects aren't equal. The `equals` method in the `BitSet` class overrides the `equals` method in the `Object` class.

equals—java.lang.Boolean

```
public boolean equals(Object obj)
```

Compares a `Boolean` object with another object and returns true if the objects are equal and false if they are not equal. The `equals` method in the `Boolean` class overrides the `equals` method in the `Object` class.

equals—java.lang.Character

```
public boolean equals(Object obj)
```

Compares this Character with another object. A true value is returned if the methods are true, and a false value is returned if they are false. The `equals` method in the `Character` class overrides the `equals` method in the `Object` class.

equals—java.awt.Color

```
public boolean equals(Object obj)
```

Compares this object against the specified object and returns true if the objects are the same; false if the objects are different. The equals method in the Color class overrides the equals method in the Object class.

equals—java.util.Date

```
public boolean equals(Object obj)
```

Compares a Date with another object and returns true if the values are equal; otherwise, false is returned. The equals method in the Date class overrides the equals method in the Object class.

equals—java.lang.Double

```
public boolean equals(Object obj)
```

Compares a Double object with another object. The equals method in the Double class overrides the equals method in the Object class.

> **NOTE:**
> Although NaN values are not equal to each other, the equals method will compare two NaN values as the same. This is for use in hashtables.

equals—java.io.File

```
public boolean equals(Object obj)
```

Compares this File with another object. A true value is returned if the two objects are equal, and a false is returned if they are not. The equals method in the File class overrides the equals method in the Object class.

equals—java.lang.Float

```
public boolean equals(Object obj)
```

Compares a Float object with another object. The equals method in the Float class overrides the equals method in the Object class.

equals—java.awt.Font

```
public boolean equals(Object obj)
```

Compares a Font to another object. The equals method returns true if the Font and the object are the same and false if they're not. The equals method in the Font class overrides the equals method in the Object class.

equals—java.net.InetAddress

```
public boolean equals(Object obj)
```

Compares an InetAddress object with another object and returns true if they are equal. The equals method in the InetAddress object overrides the equals method in the Object class.

equals—java.lang.Integer

```
public boolean equals(Object obj)
```

Compares an Integer with an Object and returns true if they are equal. The equals method in the Integer class overrides the equals method in the Object class.

equals—java.lang.Long

```
public boolean equals(Object obj)
```

Compares an Long with an Object and returns true if they are equal. The equals method in the Long class overrides the equals method in the Object class.

equals—java.lang.Object

```
public boolean equals(Object obj)
```

Compares two Objects for equality. Returns true if the Objects are equal and false if they are not.

equals—java.awt.Point

```
public boolean equals(Object obj)
```

Checks whether a point is equal to another Object. The `equals` method in the `Point` class overrides the `equals` method in the `Object` class.

equals—java.awt.Rectangle

```
public boolean equals(Object obj)
```

Checks whether a rectangle is equal to another passed Object. The `equals` method in the `Rectangle` class overrides the `equals` method int the `Object` class.

equals—java.lang.String

```
public boolean equals(Object anObject)
```

Compares a String to another Object and returns true if the objects are equal. The `equals` method in the `String` class overrides the `equals` method in the `Object` class.

equals—java.net.URL

```
public boolean equals(Object obj)
```

Compares an URL with another Object. A true value is returned if the objects are equal, and a false is returned otherwise. The `equals` method in the `URL` class overrides the `equals` method in the `Object` class.

equalsIgnoreCase—java.lang.String

```
public boolean equalsIgnoreCase(String anotherString)
```

Compares a String to another Object and returns true if the objects are equal while ignoring case. The `equals` method in the `String` class overrides the `equals` method in the `Object` class.

Error—java.lang.Error

```
public Error({String detailMessage})
```

Error is the parent class for all other error objects. If `detailMessage` is specified, the `detailMessage` will be displayed when this throwable is thrown.

Event (large)—java.awt.Event

```
public  Event(Object target, long when, int id,
        int x, int y, int key, int modifiers {, Object arg})
```

Constructs an event with the specified target component, time stamp, event type, x and y coordinates, keyboard key, state of the modifier keys, and argument. If arg is omited, arg in the Event class is set to null.

Event (small)—java.awt.Event

```
public  Event(Object target, int id, Object arg)
```

Constructs an event with the specified target component, event type, and argument.

Exception—java.lang.Exception

```
public Exception({String detailMessage})
```

Exception is the parent (or grandparent) class that all Throwable exceptions descend from. If detailMessage is specified, the detailMessage will be displayed when this throwable is thrown.

exec—java.lang.Runtime

```
public Process exec(String [command / commandArray[] ]
      {, String environment[]})
```

Executes a system command passed by a string or the first element in a command array. If a command array is passed, the rest of the array is arguments to the system command. An array of string environment parameters can be passed (in the form of param=value). Returns a Process which has methods for optaining the stdin, stdout, and stderr of the subprocess. This method fails if executed by untrusted code. An IOException is thrown if an I/O error occurs during the command.

exists—java.io.File

```
public boolean exists()
```

Returns true if the file in a File object exists. Otherwise, false is returned.

exit—java.lang.Runtime

```
public void exit(int status)
```

Exits the virtual machine with a status exit code. This method does not return and kills the virtual Java machine, so use with caution.

exit—java.lang.System

```
public static void exit(int status)
```

Exits the virtual machine with an exit code. This method does not return, so use it with caution.

exitValue—java.lang.Process

```
public abstract int exitValue()
```

Returns the exit value for the subprocess in Process object. An `IllegalThreadStateException` is thrown if the subprocess has not yet terminated.

exp—java.lang.Math

```
public static double exp(double a)
```

Returns the exponential number e(2.718...) raised to the power of a. The value returned is also the antilog of the natural log. See the `log` function for more information.

File—java.io.File

```
public  File([File directory, String fileName /
     String pathName{, String fileName}])
```

Constructs a File object from the specified directory (string or File directory object) and the file name (if given). The `NullPointerException` is thrown if the path name is null.

FileDescriptor—java.io.FileDescriptor

```
public   FileDescriptor()
```

Constructs a `FileDescriptor` object. See the `getFD` method for more information.

FileDialog—java.awt.FileDialog

```
public   FileDialog(Frame parent, String title {, mode})
```

Creates a `FileDialog` for loading a file. parent is the owner of the `FileDialog` and title is the title of the `FileDialog`. If mode is specified, the the file mode (LOAD or SAVE) is recorded. If omitted, LOAD is assmumed. See the `LOAD` and `SAVE` attributes.

FileInputStream— java.io.FileInputStream

```
public   FileInputStream([String fileName / File fileObject
     / FileDescriptor fd)
```

Constructs a `FileInputStream` object using the file name, a file descriptor, or a File object. A `FileNotFoundException` exception is thrown if the file is not found.

FileNotFoundException— java.io.FileNotFoundException

```
public   FileNotFoundException({String detailMessage)
```

Constructs an exception indicating that a file was not found during an open command. You can specify a detail message to appear if you want.

FileOutputStream— java.io.FileOutputStream

```
public   FileOutputStream([String fileName / File fileObject
     / FileDescriptor fd)
```

Creates an output file by constructing a `FileOutputStream` object using the file name, a file descriptor, or a File object. A `IOException` exception is thrown if an I/O error occurs.

fill3DRect—**java.awt.Graphics**

```
public void fill3DRect(int x, int y, int width, int height,
    boolean raised)
```

Paints a highlighted 3D rectangle defined by x, y, width, and height using the current color. Raised is a boolean value indicating whether the rectangle is raised. Also see the draw3DRect method.

fillArc—**java.awt.Graphics**

```
public abstract void fillArc(int x, int y, int width,
    int height, int startAngle, int angleSize)
```

Fills an arc identified by x, y, width, height, startAngle, and angleSize using the current color. This draws a pie shape. See the drawArc method for more information.

fillInStackTrace—**java.lang.Throwable**

```
public Throwable fillInStackTrace()
```

Fills in the excecution stack trace for use when rethrowing a Throwable. The throwable itself is thrown. Also see the printStackTrace method.

fillOval—**java.awt.Graphics**

```
public abstract void fillOval(int x, int y, int width,
    int height)
```

Fills an oval inside a rectangle defined by x, y, width, and height using the current color. Also check out the drawOval method.

fillPolygon—**java.awt.Graphics**

```
public abstract void fillPolygon(
    [Polygon p/int xPoints[], int yPoints[], int nPoints])
```

Fills a polygon defined a Polygon class or nPoints, xPoints, and yPoints. xPoints and yPoints are arrays that contain coordinates. The nPoints argument defines the number of points in the polygon. Also see the drawPolygon method and the Polygon class.

fillRect—java.awt.Graphics

```
public abstract void fillRect(int x, int y,
    int width, int height)
```

Fills a rectangle (identified by x, y, width, and height) with the current color. Also check out the drawRect and clearRect methods.

fillRoundRect—java.awt.Graphics

```
public abstract void fillRoundRect(int x, int y,
    int width, int height, int arcWidth, int arcHeight)
```

Fills a round rectagle identified by x, y, width, height, arcWidth, and acrHeight with the current color. Also check out the drawRoundRect method.

FilteredImageSource—java.awt.image.FilteredImageSource

```
public  FilteredImageSource(ImageProducer ip,
    ImageFilter if)
```

Constructs an ImageProducer object from ImageProducer and ImageFilter objects. Also see the ImageFilter class, the ImageProducer class, and the createImage object.

filterIndexColorModel—java.awt.image.RGBImageFilter

```
public IndexColorModel filterIndexColorModel(
    IndexColorModel icm)
```

Returns a new IndexColorModel object that represents filtered colors by using the filterRGB function that RGBImageFilter child classes must provide.

TIP:
Use a –1 for coordinates in your icm argument of the filterIndexColorModel **method to filter a color table entry rather than a pixel value.**

FilterInputStream— java.io.FilterInputStream

```
protected   FilterInputStream(InputStream in)
```

Constructs an input stream filter from an `InputStream` object.

FilterOutputStream— java.io.FilterOutputStream

```
protected   FilterOutputStream(OutputStream out)
```

Constructs an output stream filter from an `OutputStream` object.

filterRGB— java.awt.image.RGBImageFilter

```
public abstract int filterRGB(int x, int y, int rgb)
```

This is an empty method. Subclasses must specify a method to convert a pixels using the default RGB ColorModel. Also see the `getRGBdefault` and `filterRGBPixels` methods.

filterRGBPixels— java.awt.image.RGBImageFilter

```
public void filterRGBPixels(int x, int y, int w,
     int h, int pixels[], int off, int scansize)
```

Filters pixels in the default RGB ColorModel by passing them through the `filterRGB` method. Also see the `getRGBdefault` and `filterRGB` methods.

finalize—java.io.FileInputStream

```
protected void finalize()
```

Executes the `close` method when garbage is collected. An `IOException` is thrown if an I/O error occurs. The `finalize` method in the `FileInputStream` class overrides the `finalize` method in the `Object` class.

finalize—java.io.FileOutputStream

```
protected void finalize()
```

Executes the `close` method when garbage is collected. An
`IOException` is thrown if an I/O error occurs. The `finalize`
method in the `FileOutputStream` class overrides the `finalize`
method in the `Object` class.

finalize—java.awt.Graphics

```
public void finalize()
```

Disposes of a Graphics context once it is no longer referenced. The
`finalize` method in the `Graphics` class overrides the `finalize`
method in the `Object` class. Also see the `dispose` method.

finalize—java.lang.Object

```
protected void finalize()
```

Code to perform when this object is garbage collected. The default is
that nothing needs to be performed, so you need to override the
`finalize` class for specific garbage collection. The `finalize`
method throws the Throwable object, which means that any exception or error thrown by a `finalize` method causes the finalization
to halt.

findSystemClass—
java.lang.ClassLoader

```
protected final Class findSystemClass(String name)
```

Loads a system `Class` by name. A `NoClassDefFoundError` error is
thrown if the `Class` is not found and a `ClassNotFoundException` is
thrown if a definition for the class can't be found.

first—java.awt.CardLayout

```
public void first(Container parent)
```

Goes to the first card of a container. `parent` is the name of the parent container.

firstElement—java.util.Vector

```
public final synchronous Object firstElement()
```

Returns the first element in a Vector. A NoSuchElementException is thrown if the Vector is empty.

Float—java.lang.Float

```
public  Float([float value / double value / String s])
```

Constructs a Float wrapper for a floating point number, a double floating point number, or from a String. A NumberFormatException exception is thrown if a String is used in the constructor and the String does not contain a valid number.

FloatToIntBits—java.lang.Float

```
public static long FloatToIntBits(Float value)
```

Returns the bit representation of a Float value.

floatValue—java.lang.Double

```
public float floatValue()
```

Returns the floating point value of a Double. The floatValue method in the Double class overrides the floatValue method in the Number class.

floatValue—java.lang.Float

```
public float floatValue()
```

Returns the floating point value of a Float. The floatValue method in the Float class overrides the floatValue method in the Number class.

floatValue—java.lang.Integer

```
public float floatValue()
```

Returns the value of an Integer as an floating point decimal. The floatValue method in the Integer class overrides the floatValue method in the Number class.

floatValue—java.lang.Long

```
public float floatValue()
```

Returns the value of an Long as an floating point decimal. The `floatValue` method in the `Long` class overrides the `floatValue` method in the `Number` class.

floatValue—java.lang.Number

```
public abstract float floatValue()
```

Returns the value of a number as a float data type. This may involve rounding if the Number is a Double object.

floor—java.lang.Math

```
public static double floor(double a)
```

Returns the largest whole number less than or equal to a.

FlowLayout—java.awt.FlowLayout

```
public  FlowLayout({int align {, int hgap, int vgap}})
```

Constructs a new Flow Layout with the specified alignment (if given) and specified horizontal and vertical gap values (if given).

flush—java.io.BufferedOutputStream

```
public synchronized void flush()
```

Flushes the buffered output stream. This will write any buffered output to the output stream. The `IOException` is thrown if any I/O error occurs. The flush method in the `BufferedOutputStream` overrides the `flush` method in the `FilterOutputStream` class.

flush—java.io.DataOutputStream

```
public void flush()
```

Flushes the buffered output stream. This will write any buffered output to the output stream. The `IOException` is thrown if any I/O error occurs. The `flush` method in the `DataOutputStream` overrides the `flush` method in the `FilterOutputStream` class.

flush—**java.io.FilterOutputStream**

```
public void flush()
```

Flushes the output stream. This will write any buffered output to the output stream. The IOException is thrown if any I/O error occurs. The flush method in the FilterOutputStream overrides the flush method in the OutputStream class.

flush—**java.awt.Image**

```
public abstract void flush()
```

Flushes all resources being used by this Image object. This is useful to force garbage collection on an Image which is no longer used.

flush—**java.io.OutputStream**

```
public void flush()
```

Flushes the buffered output stream. This will write any buffered output to the output stream. The IOException is thrown if any I/O error occurs.

flush—**java.io.PrintStream**

```
public void flush()
```

Flushes the buffered output stream. This will write any buffered output to the output stream. The IOException is thrown if any I/O error occurs. The flush method in the PrintStream overrides the flush method in the FilterOutputStream class.

Font—**java.awt.Font**

```
public  Font(String name, int style, int size)
```

Creates a new font with the specified name, style, and point size. See the name, style, and size attributes and the getFontList method for more information.

FontMetrics—**java.awt.FontMetrics**

```
protected  FontMetrics(Font font)
```

Constructs a new FontMetrics object with the specified font. Also see the Font class for more information.

forDigit—java.lang.Character

```
public static char forDigit(int digit, int radix)
```

Returns the character value for the specified digit in the specified radix. A radix is the base used, and will probably be 10 (for based-10 number systems). 16 (hexidecimal) and 8 (octal) may also prove useful. If the digit is not valid in the radix, a 0 character is returned.

forName—java.lang.Class

```
public static Class forName(String className)
```

Returns the Class object identified by the className. A ClassNotFoundException is thrown if the Class could not be found.

Frame—java.awt.Frame

```
public  Frame({String title})
```

Constructs a new Frame with a given title, or no title if a title argument is not passed.

> **NOTE:**
> All new frames are initially invisible. Use the show method to show an invisible frame.

freeMemory—java.lang.Runtime

```
public long freeMemory()
```

Returns the estimated number of free bytes in system memory. This number is not always accurate because it is just an estimation of the available memory. See the gc method in the System class to find the actual number of free bytes in system memory.

gc—java.lang.Runtime

```
public void gc()
```

Runs the garbage collector.

gc—**java.lang.System**

```
public static void gc()
```

Runs the garbage collector.

get—**java.util.BitSet**

```
public boolean get(int bit)
```

Returns a bit from a `BitSet` object.

get—**java.util.Dictionary**

```
public abstract Object get(Object key)
```

Returns an object associated with a Dictionary key in the hashtable. If the key can't be found, a null is returned.

get—**java.util.Hashtable**

```
public synchronized Object get(Object key)
```

Returns the object associated with a key in a hashtable. The `get` method in the `Hashtable` class overrides the `get` method in the `Dictionary` class.

getAbsolutePath—**java.io.File**

```
public String getAbsolutePath()
```

Returns the absolute file path name of a `File` object.

getAddress—**java.net.DatagramPacket**

```
public InetAddress getAddress()
```

Returns the ip address of a `DatagramPacket`.

getAddress—**java.net.InetAddress**

```
public byte[] getAddress()
```

Returns the raw IP address in network byte order. The highest order byte position is in `addr[0]`. To be prepared for 64-bit IP addresses, an array of up to 8 bytes is returned.

getAlignment—java.awt.Label

```
public int getAlignment()
```

Returns the alignment of a label. Also check out the setAlignment method and the LEFT, CENTER, and RIGHT attributes.

getAllByName—java.net.InetAddress

```
public static synchronized InetAddress[] getAllByName(
    String host)
```

Returns all the Internet address for a host name. An UnknownHostException is thrown if the host name could not be resolved.

getAllowUserInteraction— java.net.URLConnection

```
public boolean getAllowUserInteraction()
```

Returns the AllowUserInteraction attribute.

getAlpha—java.awt.image.ColorModel

```
public abstract int getAlpha(int pixel)
```

Returns the red component (from 0 to 255) of a pixel inside a ColorModel. Also see the getGreen and getBlue methods.

getAlpha— java.awt.image.DirectColorModel

```
public final int getAlpha(int pixel)
```

Returns the transparant (alpha) color compoment of a pixel. The getAlpha method in the DirectColorModel class overrides the getAlpha method in the ColorModel class. Also see the getBlue, getGreen, and getRed methods.

getAlpha— java.awt.image.IndexColorModel

```
public final int getAlpha(int pixel)
```

Returns the alpha color compoment for a pixel. The `getAlpha` method in the `IndexColorModel` class overrides the `getAlpha` method in the `ColorModel` class. Also see the `getGreen`, `getBlue`, and `getRed` methods.

getAlphaMask— java.awt.image.DirectColorModel

```
public final int getAlphaMask()
```

Returns a value that indicates where the transparent (alpha) color component bits are stored in a pixel. Also see `getBlueMask`, `getGreenMask`, and `getRedMask`.

getAlphas— java.awt.image.IndexColorModel

```
public final void getAlphas(byte a[])
```

Copies the array of alpha (transparent) color components of an `IndexColorModel` into the given array. Also see the `getGreens`, `getBlues`, and `getReds` methods.

getApplet—java.applet.AppletContext

```
public abstract Applet getApplet(String)
```

Gets an applet by name. Returns a null if the applet does not exist.

getAppletContext—java.applet.Applet

```
public AppletContext getAppletContext()
```

Gets a handle to the applet context. The applet context lets an applet control the applet's environment which is usually the browser or the applet viewer.

getAppletInfo—java.applet.Applet

```
public String getAppletInfo()
```

Returns a string containing information about the author, version, and copyright of the applet.

getApplets—java.applet.AppletContext

```
public abstract Enumeration getApplets()
```

Enumerates the applets in this context. Only applets that are accessible will be returned. This list always includes the applet itself.

getAppletStub—java.applet.AppletStub

```
public abstract AppletStub getAppletStub()
```

Gets a handler to the applet's context.

getAscent—java.awt.FontMetrics

```
public int getAscent()
```

Returns the font ascent. The font ascent is the distance from the base line to the top of the characters. Also see the `getMaxAscent` method.

getAudioClip—java.applet.Applet

```
public AudioClip getAudioClip(URL url {, String name})
```

Gets an audio clip given to or relative to an URL.

getAudioClip— java.applet.AppletContext

```
public abstract AudioClip getAudioClip(URL)
```

Gets an audio clip.

getBackground—java.awt.Component

```
public Color getBackground()
```

Returns the background color of a `Component` (or the parent's background color if a Component's background color is not found). For related methods, check out the `setForeground`, `getForeground`, and `setBackground` methods, or the `Color` class.

getBlue—java.awt.Color

```
public int getBlue()
```

Returns the blue component of a Color. Also see the `getRGB` method.

getBlue—java.awt.image.ColorModel

```
public abstract int getBlue(int pixel)
```

Returns the red component (from 0 to 255) of a pixel inside a `ColorModel`. Also see the `getGreen` and `getBlue` methods.

getBlue— java.awt.image.DirectColorModel

```
public final int getBlue(int pixel)
```

Returns the blue color compoment of a pixel. The `getBlue` method in the `DirectColorModel` class overrides the `getBlue` method in the `ColorModel` class. Also see the `getRed`, `getGreen`, and `getAlpha` methods.

getBlue— java.awt.image.IndexColorModel

```
public final int getBlue(int pixel)
```

Returns the blue color compoment for a pixel. The `getBlue` method in the `IndexColorModel` class overrides the `getBlue` method in the `ColorModel` class. Also see the `getGreen`, `getRed`, and `getAlpha` methods.

getBlueMask— java.awt.image.DirectColorModel

```
public final int getBlueMask()
```

Returns a value that indicates where the blue color component bits are stored in a pixel. Also see `getRedMask`, `getGreenMask`, and `getAlphaMask`.

getBlues— java.awt.image.IndexColorModel

```
public final void getBlues(byte b[])
```

Copies the array of blue color components of an IndexColorModel into the given array. Also see the getGreens, getReds, and getAlphas methods.

getBoolean—java.lang.Boolean

```
public static boolean getBoolean(String propertyName)
```

Returns a Boolean value from a property specified by propertyName.

getBoundingBox—java.awt.Polygon

```
public Rectangle getBoundingBox()
```

Returns a Rectangle object that defines the area spanned by this Polygon.

getByName—java.net.InetAddress

```
public static synchronized InetAddress getByName(
    String host)
```

Returns a network address for the host identified by a String argument. A null value for host returns the default address for the local machine. UnknownHostException is thrown if the address is not known.

getBytes—java.lang.String

```
public void getBytes(int srcBegin, int srcEnd,
    byte dst[], int dstBegin)
```

Copies characters in a String from beginning to end to a destination byte array. You can specify an offset to copy the characters from a given index in the destination array.

getChars—java.lang.String

```
public void getChars(int begin, int end, char dst[],
    int offset)
```

Copies characters in a String from beginning to end to a destination character array. You can specify an offset to copy the characters from a given index in the destination array.

getChars—java.lang.StringBuffer

```
public synchronized void getChars(int begin, int end,
    char dst[], int offset)
```

Returns characters into a destination array with a given offset. The characters returned are from the begin to the end arguments in the StringBuffer. An StringIndexOutOfBoundsException exception is thrown if begin, end, or offset are invalid.

getCheckboxGroup— java.awt.Checkbox

```
public CheckboxGroup getCheckboxGroup()
```

Returns the checkbox group of a Checkbox. Also see the setCheckboxGroup method and the CheckboxGroup class.

getClass—java.lang.Object

```
public final Class getClass()
```

Returns the Class of an Object.

getClassContext— java.lang.SecurityManager

```
protected Class[] getClassContext()
```

Returns a Class array containing the context of a class.

getClassLoader—java.lang.Class

```
public ClassLoader getClassLoader()
```

Returns the ClassLoader object of a Class, or null if the Class doesn't have a ClassLoader object. For more information, see the ClassLoader class.

getClipRect—java.awt.Graphics

```
public abstract Rectangle getClipRect()
```

Returns the bounding rectangle of the current clipping area. For more information, see the clipRect method.

getCodeBase—java.applet.Applet

```
public URL getCodeBase()
```

Gets the base URL. This is the URL of the applet itself. See getDocumentBase for more details.

getCodeBase—java.applet.AppletStub

```
public abstract URL getCodeBase()
```

Gets the base URL.

getColor—java.awt.Color

```
public static Color getColor(
    String nm {, [Color v / int rgb]})
```

Returns a color class of this Color or the color specified in Color v or by an RGB integer that corresponds to the color name.

getColor—java.awt.Graphics

```
public abstract Color getColor()
```

Returns the current color. For more information, see the Color class and the setColor method.

getColorModel—java.awt.Component

```
public synchronized ColorModel getColorModel()
```

Returns the ColorModel used to display a Component. For more information, see the ColorModel class.

getColorModel— java.awt.peer.ComponentPeer

```
public abstract ColorModel getColorModel()
```

Returns the ColorModel used to display a Component. For more information, see the ColorModel class.

getColorModel—java.awt.Toolkit

```
public abstract ColorModel getColorModel()
```

Returns the ColorModel of a screen.

getColumns—java.awt.TextArea

```
public int getColumns()
```

Returns the number of columns in a TextArea. Also see the getRows method.

getColumns—java.awt.TextField

```
public int getColumns()
```

Returns the number of columns in a TextField.

getComponent—java.awt.Container

```
public synchronized Component getComponent(
    int containerNumber)
```

Returns the nth component in a container. getComponent throws ArrayIndexOutOfBoundsException if containerNumber is less than 1 or greater than the number of components in this container.

getComponents—java.awt.Container

```
public synchronized Component[] getComponents()
```

Returns all the components in a container into a `Component` array.

getContent—java.net.ContentHandler

```
public abstract Object getContent(URLConnection urlc)
```

Recreates an object form an `URLConnection`. An `IOException` is thrown if an I/O error occurs while reading the object.

getContent—java.net.URL

```
public final Object getContent()
```

Returns the contents of an open connection. An `IOException` is thrown if an I/O exception has occurred.

getContent—java.net.URLConnection

```
public Object getContent()
```

Gets the object referred to by an `URLConnection`'s URL. `UnknownServiceException` is thrown if the protocol does not support content and an `IOException` is thrown if an I/O error occurs.

getContentEncoding— java.net.URLConnection

```
public String getContentEncoding()
```

Returns a String containing the content encoding of an `URLConnection` object, or a null if the content is not known.

getContentLength— java.net.URLConnection

```
public int getContentLength()
```

Returns the content length or –1 if the content length is not known.

getContentType— java.net.URLConnection

```
public String getContentType()
```

Returns the content type, or null if the content type is not known.

getCurrent—java.awt.CheckboxGroup

```
public Checkbox getCurrent()
```

Returns the current choice in a radio button.

getCursorType—java.awt.Frame

```
public int getCursorType()
```

Returns the cursor pointer type. Also see the setCursor method and the CROSSHAIR_CURSOR, DEFAULT_CURSOR, E_RESIZE_CURSOR, HAND_CURSOR, MOVE_CURSOR, NE_RESIZE_CURSOR, NW_RESIZE_CURSOR, N_RESIZE_CURSOR, SE_RESIZE_CURSOR, SW_RESIZE_CURSOR, S_RESIZE_CURSOR, TEXT_CURSOR, WAIT_CURSOR, and W_RESIZE_CURSOR attributes.

getData—java.net.DatagramPacket

```
public byte[] getData()
```

Returns the data contained in the DatagramPacket's buffer.

getDate—java.util.Date

```
public int getDate()
```

Returns the day of the month. Values are from 1 to 31.

getDate—java.net.URLConnection

```
public long getDate()
```

Returns the sending date of an URLConnection, or zero if the date is not known.

getDay—java.util.Date

```
public int getDay()
```

Returns the day of the week of a Date object. Valid values are 0 through 6 with 0 being Sunday.

getDefaultAllowUserInteraction—java.net.URLConnection

```
public static boolean getDefaultAllowUserInteraction()
```

Returns the static defaultAllowUserInteraction attribute.

getDefaultRequestProperty—java.net.URLConnection

```
public static String getDefaultRequestProperty(String key)
```

Returns the default value of a general request property identified by a key.

getDefaultToolkit—java.awt.Toolkit

```
public static synchronized Toolkit getDefaultToolkit()
```

Returns the default toolkit controlled by the awt.toolkit property. The AWTError is thrown if the toolkit was not found or could not be instantiated.

getDefaultUseCaches—java.net.URLConnection

```
public boolean getDefaultUseCaches()
```

Sets the static defaultUseCaches attribute to true if you want all following URLConnections use caching, and false if not. Also see the getDefaultUseCaches method.

getDescent—java.awt.FontMetrics

```
public int getDescent()
```

Returns the font descent. The font descent is the distance from the base line to the top of the characters. Also see the getMaxDescent method.

getDirectory—java.awt.FileDialog

```
public String getDirectory()
```

Returns the directory of the FileDialog.

getDocumentBase—java.applet.Applet

```
public URL getDocumentBase()
```

Gets the document URL. This is the URL of the document in which the applet is embedded. See getCodeBase for more details.

getDocumentBase— java.applet.AppletStub

```
public abstract URL getDocumentBase()
```

Gets the document URL.

getDoInput—java.net.URLConnection

```
public boolean getDoInput()
```

Returns the doInput attribute.

getDoOutput—java.net.URLConnection

```
public boolean getDoOutput()
```

Returns the doOutput attribute.

getEchoChar—java.awt.TextField

```
public char getEchoChar()
```

Returns the character to be used for echoing in a TextField object. Echo characters are useful when what the user is typing shouldn't be echoed back to the window (such as passwords). Also see the setEchoCharacter and echoCharIsSet methods.

getenv—java.lang.System

```
public static String getenv(String name)
```

Gets an environment variable or null if the name passed to the method is undefined. This method is obsolete and should not be used.

getErrorsAny—java.awt.MediaTracker

```
public synchronized Object[] getErrorsAny()
```

Returns an array of all media objects that have encountered an error. If no errors were encountered, a null is returned. For related information, see the isErrorAny and getErrorsID methods.

getErrorsID—java.awt.MediaTracker

```
public synchronized Object[] getErrorsID(int identification)
```

Returns an array MediaTracker objects with the specified identification that have encountered an error, or null if no errors were found. Also see the isErrorID and getErrorsAny methods.

getErrorStream—java.lang.Process

```
public abstract InputStream getErrorStream()
```

Returns the an InputStream connected to the error stream of the Process object.

getExpiration—java.net.URLConnection

```
public long getExpiration()
```

Returns the expiration date of an URLConnection, or zero if the date is not known.

getFamily—java.awt.Font

```
public String getFamily()
```

Returns the platform specific family name of a Font. Also see the getName method.

getFD—java.io.FileInputStream

```
public final FileDescriptor getFD()
```

Returns the file descriptor object associated with a FileInputStream object. An IOException is thrown if an I/O error occurs.

getFD—java.io.FileOutputStream

```
public final FileDescriptor getFD()
```

Returns the file descriptor object associated with a FileOutputStream object. An IOException is thrown if an I/O error occurs.

getFD—java.io.RandomAccessFile

```
public final FileDescriptor getFD()
```

Returns the file descriptor object of a RandomAccessFile object.

getFile—java.awt.FileDialog

```
public String getFile()
```

Returns the file of the FileDialog.

getFile—java.net.URL

```
public String getFile()
```

Returns the file name of an URL.

getFilenameFilter—java.awt.FileDialog

```
public FilenameFilter getFilenameFilter()
```

Returns the filter (such as *.TXT, MYFILE.*) used in a FileDialog. See the FilenameFilter class for more details.

getFilePointer—java.io.RandomAccessFile

```
public long getFilePointer()
```

Returns the current location of the file pointer. Also see the seek method.

getFilterInstance— java.awt.image.ImageFilter

```
public ImageFilter getFilterInstance(ImageConsumer ic)
```

Returns an ImageFilter object which will perform the filtering for an ImageConsumer. This method initializes the consumer attribute of the ImageFilter class. For more information, see the consumer attribute.

getFont—java.awt.Component

```
public Font getFont()
```

Returns the font of a Component (or the parent's font if a Component's font is not found). See setFont for a related method.

getFont—java.awt.Font

```
public static Font getFont(
    String propertyName {,Font default})
```

Returns a font identified by a given property name from the system properties list. If the font name is not found and a default Font is specified, then a default Font is returned.

getFont—java.awt.FontMetrics

```
public Font getFont()
```

Returns the font.

getFont—java.awt.Graphics

```
public abstract Font getFont()
```

Returns the current font. Also see the setFont method.

getFont—java.awt.MenuComponent

```
public Font getFont()
```

Returns the Font used in a MenuComponent, or a null if a Font is not used. Also see the setFont method.

getFont—java.awt.MenuContainer

```
public abstract Font getFont()
```

Returns the current font.

getFontMetrics—java.awt.Component

```
public FontMetrics getFontMetrics(Font font)
```

Returns the font metrics for a Component's font, or null if a Component is currently not on the screen. For related information, see the getFont method.

getFontMetrics— java.awt.peer.ComponentPeer

```
public abstract FontMetrics getFontMetrics(Font font)
```

Returns the font metrics for a Component's font, or null if a Component is currently not on the screen. For related information, see the getFont method.

getFontMetrics—java.awt.Graphics

```
public FontMetrics getFontMetrics({Font f})
```

Returns the font metrics of a specified Font or the current font if no Font is specified.

getFontMetrics—java.awt.Toolkit

```
public abstract FontMetrics getFontMetrics(Font font)
```

Returns the font metrics of a font.

getForeground—java.awt.Component

```
public Color getForeground()
```

Returns the foreground color of a Component (or the parent's foreground color if a Component's foreground color is not found). For related methods, check out the setForeground, getBackground, and setBackground methods, or the Color class.

getFotList—java.awt.Toolkit

```
public abstract String[] getFotList()
```

Returns the names of the fonts available in your system.

getGraphics—java.awt.Component

```
public Graphics getGraphics()
```

Returns the Graphics context for a Component, or null if a Component is currently not on the screen. For related information, see the `paint` method.

getGraphics— java.awt.peer.ComponentPeer

```
public abstract Graphics getGraphics()
```

Returns the Graphics context for a Component, or null if a Component is currently not on the screen. For related information, see the `paint` method.

getGraphics—java.awt.Image

```
public abstract Graphics getGraphics()
```

Returns a graphics object to draw into this image. This will only work for off-screen images. See the `Graphics` class for more information.

getGreen—java.awt.Color

```
public int getGreen()
```

Returns the green component of a Color. Also see the `getRGB` method.

getGreen—java.awt.image.ColorModel

```
public abstract int getGreen(int pixel)
```

Returns the red component (from 0 to 255) of a pixel inside a `ColorModel`. Also see the `getGreen` and `getBlue` methods.

getGreen—
java.awt.image.DirectColorModel

```
public final int getGreen(int pixel)
```

Returns the green color compoment of a pixel. The `getGreen` method in the `DirectColorModel` class overrides the `getGreen` method in the `ColorModel` class. Also see the `getBlue`, `getRed`, and `getAlpha` methods.

getGreen—
java.awt.image.IndexColorModel

```
public final int getGreen(int pixel)
```

Returns the green color compoment for a pixel. The `getGreen` method in the `IndexColorModel` class overrides the `getGreen` method in the `ColorModel` class. Also see the `getRed`, `getBlue`, and `getAlpha` methods.

getGreenMask—
java.awt.image.DirectColorModel

```
public final int getGreenMask()
```

Returns a value that indicates where the green color component bits are stored in a pixel. Also see `getBlueMask`, `getRedMask`, and `getAlphaMask`.

getGreens—
java.awt.image.IndexColorModel

```
public final void getGreens(byte g[])
```

Copies the array of green color components of an `IndexColorModel` into the given array. Also see the `getReds`, `getBlues`, and `getAlphas` methods.

getHeaderField—
java.net.URLConnection

```
public String getHeaderField([int n / String name])
```

Returns a String containing a header field name, or the value of the nth header field. A null if the header field is not known or an n was passed as an argument that was greater than the number of header fields.

getHeaderFieldDate— java.net.URLConnection

```
public long getHeaderFieldDate(String name, long Default)
```

Returns the header field date, or a default if the header field is not known.

getHeaderFieldInt— java.net.URLConnection

```
public int getHeaderFieldInt(String name, int Default)
```

Returns the header field integer, or a default if the header field is not known.

getHeaderFieldKey— java.net.URLConnection

```
public String getHeaderFieldKey(int n)
```

Returns the key for the nth header field, or null if there are fewer than n header fields.

getHeight—java.awt.FontMetrics

```
public int getHeight()
```

Returns the total height of the font. This is the distance between the baseline of adjacent lines of text. It is the sum of the leading + ascent + descent.

getHeight—java.awt.Image

```
public abstract int getHeight(ImageObserver observer)
```

Gets the height of the image. If the height is not known yet, the ImageObserver will be notified when it is known and a –1 will be returned immediately. Also check out the getWidth method and the ImageObserver class.

getHelpMenu—java.awt.MenuBar

```
public Menu getHelpMenu()
```

Returns the help menu from a MenuBar. Also see the setHelpMenu method.

getHost—java.net.URL

```
public String getHost()
```

Returns the host name.

getHostName—java.net.InetAddress

```
public String getHostName()
```

Returns the host name for this address.

getHours—java.util.Date

```
public int getHours()
```

Returns the hour (0 through 23) of a Date object.

getHSBColor—java.awt.Color

```
public static Color getHSBColor(float hue,
     float saturation, float brightness)
```

Returns a Color object from HSB (Hue, Saturation, Brightness) values. For related methods, see the getHSBColor, HSBtoRGB, RGBtoHSB, getRGBdefault, and getRGB methods.

getIconImage—java.awt.Frame

```
public Image getIconImage()
```

Returns the image that is displayed when a Frame is minimized. Also check out the setIconImage method.

getIfModifiedSince— java.net.URLConnection

```
public long getIfModifiedSince()
```

Returns the last modified date of a `URLConnections` object.

getImage—java.applet.Applet

```
public Image getImage(URL url {, String name})
```

Gets an image given to or relative to an URL. Note that this method always returns an image object immediatly, even if the image does not exist. The actual image data is loaded when it is first needed.

getImage—java.applet.AppletContext

```
public abstract Image getImage(URL)
```

Gets an image. This usually involves downloading it over the Internet. However, the environment may decide to cache images. This method takes an array of URLs, each of which will be tried until the image is found.

getImage—java.awt.Toolkit

```
public abstract Image getImage([String filename / URL url])
```

Returns an image from an URL or a picture file in a recognizable format.

getInCheck—java.lang.SecurityManager

```
public boolean getInCheck()
```

Returns true if a security check is in progress, and false if one isn't.

getInetAddress—java.net.ServerSocket

```
public InetAddress getInetAddress()
```

Returns the Internet address where the `ServerSocket` object is connected.

getInetAddress—java.net.Socket

```
public InetAddress getInetAddress()
```

Returns the address where the socket is connected.

getInputStream—java.lang.Process

```
public abstract InputStream getInputStream()
```

Returns the input stream connected to a `Process` object.

getInputStream—java.net.Socket

```
public InputStream getInputStream()
```

Returns the `InputStream` for a socket. An `IOException` is thrown if an I/O error occurs while retrieving the `InputStream` of the socket.

getInputStream— java.net.URLConnection

```
public InputStream getInputStream()
```

Returns an input stream that reads from the `URLConnection`. An `IOException` is thrown if an I/O error occurs and an `UnknownServiceException` is thrown if the protocol does not support input.

getInteger—java.lang.Integer

```
public static Integer getInteger(
    String nm{,[int / Integer] val})
```

Gets an Integer property. If the property does not exist, it will return 0 or the `val` argument if specified.

getInterfaces—java.lang.Class

```
public Class[] getInterfaces()
```

Returns the interfaces of a Class. An array of length 0 is returned if no interfaces are implemented in a Class.

getItem—java.awt.Choice

```
public String getItem(int index)
```

Returns the item at a index in a Choice. For related functions, see the countItems method.

getItem—java.awt.List

```
public String getItem(int index)
```

Returns the item associated with the specified index in a List. Also see the countItems method.

getItem—java.awt.Menu

```
public MenuItem getItem(int index)
```

Returns the menu item located at an index.

getLabel—java.awt.Button

```
public String getLabel()
```

Returns the label of the button. For more information, see setLabel.

getLabel—java.awt.Checkbox

```
public String getLabel()
```

Returns the label of a Checkbox. Also see the setLabel method.

getLabel—java.awt.MenuItem

```
public String getLabel()
```

Returns the label for a MenuItem. Also see the setLabel method.

getLastModified—java.net.URLConnection

```
public long getLastModified()
```

Returns the last modified date of an URLConnection, or zero if the date is not known.

getLayout—java.awt.Container

```
public LayoutManager getLayout()
```

Returns the layout manager for a container. See the `layout` and `setLayout` methods and the `LayoutManager` class for related information.

getLeading—java.awt.FontMetrics

```
public int getLeading()
```

Returns the standard leading, or line spacing, for the font. This is the logical amount of space to be reserved between the descent of one line of text and the ascent of the next line. The height metric is calculated to include this extra space.

getLength—java.net.DatagramPacket

```
public int getLength()
```

Returns the number of characters in a `DatagramPacket`'s buffer.

getLineIncrement—java.awt.Scrollbar

```
public int getLineIncrement()
```

Returns the line increment for a Scrollbar. A Scrollbar's line increment is the value that will be added or subtracted when the user scrolls up or down on the Scrollbar.

getLineNumber—java.io.LineNumberInputStream

```
public int getLineNumber()
```

Returns line number in a `LineNumberInputStream` object. Also see the `setLineNumber` method.

getLocalHost—java.net.InetAddress

```
public static InetAddress getLocalHost()
```

Returns the local host. An `UnknownHostException` is thrown if the local host could not be found or resolved.

getLocalizedInputStream—
java.lang.Runtime

```
public InputStream getLocalizedInputStream(InputStream in)
```

Localize an input stream. A localized input stream will automatically translate the input from the local format (ASCII) to Unicode.

getLocalizedOutputStream—
java.lang.Runtime

```
public OutputStream getLocalizedOutputStream(
    OutputStream out)
```

Localize an output stream. A localized output stream will automatically translate the output from Unicode to the local format (ASCII).

getLocalPort—java.net.ServerSocket

```
public int getLocalPort()
```

Returns the port of the ServerSocket.

getLocalPort—java.net.Socket

```
public int getLocalPort()
```

Returns the local port of the Socket.

getLong—java.lang.Long

```
public static Long getLong(String nm, [long / Long] val)
```

Gets a Long property. If the property does not exist, it will return 0 or the val argument if specified.

getMapSize—
java.awt.image.IndexColorModel

```
public final int getMapSize()
```

Returns the size of the color component arrays set in the IndexColorModel constructor.

getMaxAdvance—java.awt.FontMetrics

```
public int getMaxAdvance()
```

Returns the maximum advance width of any character in a FontMetrics Font, or –1 if the maximum advance width is not known.

getMaxAscent—java.awt.FontMetrics

```
public int getMaxAscent()
```

Returns the maximum ascent of all characters in a FontMetrics Font. No character will extend further above the baseline than this metric. Also see the getAscent method.

getMaxDecent—java.awt.FontMetrics

```
public int getMaxDecent()
```

The getMaxDecent() method is the same as getMaxDescent method. The getMaxDecent method is included for backward compatibility only, and should not be used as it may be obsolete in future releases.

getMaxDescent—java.awt.FontMetrics

```
public int getMaxDescent()
```

Returns the maximum descent of all characters. No character will descend futher below the baseline than this metric. Also see the getDescent method.

getMaximum—java.awt.Scrollbar

```
public int getMaximum()
```

Returns the maximum value of a Scrollbar. Also see the setValue, getValue, and getMinimum methods.

getMaxPriority—java.lang.ThreadGroup

```
public final int getMaxPriority()
```

Returns the maximum priority of a ThreadGroup.

getMenu—java.awt.MenuBar

```
public Menu getMenu(int index)
```

Returns the specified menu identified by the given index.

getMenuBar—java.awt.Frame

```
public MenuBar getMenuBar()
```

Returns a Frame's menu bar. Also check out the `setMenuBar` method.

getMessage—java.lang.Throwable

```
public String getMessage()
```

Returns the throwable's message.

getMinimum—java.awt.Scrollbar

```
public int getMinimum()
```

Returns the minimum value of a Scrollbar. Also see the `setValue`, `getValue`, and `getMaximum` methods.

getMinutes—java.util.Date

```
public int getMinutes()
```

Returns the minute (0 through 59) of a `Date` object.

getMode—java.awt.FileDialog

```
public int getMode()
```

Returns the mode of the `FileDialog`. See the `LOAD` and `SAVE` attributes for more details.

getMonth—java.util.Date

```
public int getMonth()
```

Returns a month from a date. The month value is from zero to 11 with zero being January, instead of from 1 to 12.

getName—java.lang.Class

```
public String getName()
```

Returns the name of a Class.

getName—java.io.File

```
public String getName()
```

Returns the file name of a File object.

> **TIP:**
> Only the file name, and not the directory path name, are returned with the getName function.

getName—java.awt.Font

```
public String getName()
```

Returns the name of a Font. Also see the getFamily method.

getName—java.lang.Thread

```
public final String getName()
```

Returns the Thread's name. Also see the setName method.

getName—java.lang.ThreadGroup

```
public final String getName()
```

Returns the name of a ThreadGroup object.

getOrientation—java.awt.Scrollbar

```
public int getOrientation()
```

Returns the orientation (HORIZONTAL or VERTICAL) for a Scrollbar. See the Scrollbar constructor for more information.

getOutputStream—java.lang.Process

```
public abstract OutputStream getOutputStream()
```

Returns the output stream connected to a Process object.

getOutputStream—java.net.Socket

```
public OutputStream getOutputStream()
```

Returns the OutputStream for a socket. An IOException is thrown if an I/O error occurs while retrieving the OutputStream of the socket.

getOutputStream—java.net.URLConnection

```
public OutputStream getOutputStream()
```

Returns an output stream that writes to the URLConnection. An IOException is thrown if an I/O error occurs and an UnknownServiceException is thrown if the protocol does not support output.

getPageIncrement—java.awt.Scrollbar

```
public int getPageIncrement()
```

Gets the page increment for a Scrollbar. A Scrollbar's page increment is the value that will be added or subtracted when the user pages up or down on the Scrollbar.

getParameter—java.applet.Applet

```
public String getParameter(String name)
```

Gets a parameter of the applet.

getParameter—java.applet.AppletStub

```
public abstract String getParameter(String name)
```

Gets a parameter of the applet.

getParameterInfo—java.applet.Applet

```
public String[][] getParameterInfo()
```

Returns an array of strings describing the parameters that are understood by this applet. The array consists of sets of three strings: name, type, and description.

getParent—java.awt.Component

```
public Container getParent()
```

Returns the parent of a Component.

getParent—java.io.File

```
public String getParent()
```

Returns the name of the parent directory. A null value is returned if there is no parent directory.

getParent—java.awt.MenuComponent

```
public MenuContainer getParent()
```

Returns the parent container of a MenuComponent.

getParent—java.lang.ThreadGroup

```
public final ThreadGroup getParent()
```

Returns the parent ThreadGroup of the current ThreadGroup.

getPath—java.io.File

```
public String getPath()
```

Returns the directory path name of a File object.

getPeer—java.awt.Component

```
public ComponentPeer getPeer()
```

Returns the peer of a Component.

getPeer—java.awt.MenuComponent

```
public MenuComponentPeer getPeer()
```

Returns a MenuComponent's peer. A peer lets you change the appearance of the menu component without changing the functionality of the menu component.

getPixelSize— java.awt.image.ColorModel

```
public int getPixelSize()
```

Returns the size of a pixel inside a ColorModel. See the pixel_bits attribute for more information.

getPort—java.net.DatagramPacket

```
public int getPort()
```

Returns the port number of a DatagramPacket.

getPort—java.net.Socket

```
public int getPort()
```

Returns the remote port of the Socket.

getPort—java.net.URL

```
public int getPort()
```

Returns the port number or a –1 if the port is not set.

getPriority—java.lang.Thread

```
public final int getPriority()
```

Returns a Thread's priority. Also see the setPriority method.

getProperties—java.lang.System

```
public static Properties getProperties()
```

Returns the system properties. Also see the setProperties method.

getProperty—java.awt.Image

```
public abstract Object getProperty(String name,
    ImageObserver observer)
```

Returns a property of a image. The `name` argument identifies the property to be fetched. If a property is not defined for an image, the `UndefinedProperty` object will be returned. If the properties for this image are not yet known, then this method will return null and the `ImageObserver` object will be notified when the properties are known. For more information, see the `ImageObserver` class and the `UndefinedProperty` attribute.

> **NOTE:**
> The Image property name "comment" should be used to store comments. Comments are a great way to describe the description of the Image, an Image's source file, an Image's author, or other pertinant information about the Image.

getProperty—java.util.Properties

```
public String getProperty(String key{, String defaultValue})
```

Returns a property with a specified hashtable key. If the key does not exist, the `defaultValue` is returned, or a null if the default value was not specified.

getProperty—java.lang.System

```
public static String getProperty(
    String key{, String default})
```

Returns a stirng containing a property identified by a key. A default is returned if the property is not defined and a default is specified.

getProtocol—java.net.URL

```
public String getProtocol()
```

Returns the protocol name.

getRed—java.awt.Color

```
public int getRed()
```

Returns the red component of a Color. Also see the `getRGB` method.

getRed—java.awt.image.ColorModel

```
public abstract int getRed(int pixel)
```

Returns the red component (from 0 to 255) of a pixel inside a ColorModel. Also see the `getGreen` and `getBlue` methods.

getRed— java.awt.image.DirectColorModel

```
public final int getRed(int pixel)
```

Returns the red color compoment of a pixel. The `getRed` method in the `DirectColorModel` class overrides the `getRed` method in the `ColorModel` class. Also see the `getBlue`, `getGreen`, and `getAlpha` methods.

getRed— java.awt.image.IndexColorModel

```
public final int getRed(int pixel)
```

Returns the red color compoment for a pixel. The `getRed` method in the `IndexColorModel` class overrides the `getRed` method in the `ColorModel` class. Also see the `getGreen`, `getBlue`, and `getAlpha` methods.

getRedMask— java.awt.image.DirectColorModel

```
public final int getRedMask()
```

Returns a value that indicates where the red color component bits are stored in a pixel. Also see `getBlueMask`, `getGreenMask`, and `getAlphaMask`.

getReds— java.awt.image.IndexColorModel

```
public final void getReds(byte r[])
```

Copies the array of red color components of an IndexColorModel into the given array. Also see the getGreens, getBlues, and getAlphas methods.

*getRef—*java.net.URL

```
public String getRef()
```

Returns the reference of an URL.

getRequestProperty— java.net.URLConnection

```
public String getRequestProperty(String key)
```

Returns a general request property identified by the key attribute.

*getRGB—*java.awt.Color

```
public int getRGB()
```

Returns the RGB value representing the color in the default RGB ColorModel. (Bits 24–31 are set to zero, 16–23 are the red component, 8–15 are the green component, and 0–7 are the blue component.) Also see the getRGBdefault, getRed, getGreen, and getBlue method.

*getRGB—*java.awt.image.ColorModel

```
public int getRGB(int pixel)
```

Returns the color of a pixel in the default RGB ColorModel. Also see the getRGBdefault method.

getRGB— java.awt.image.DirectColorModel

```
public final int getRGB(int pixel)
```

Returns the color of a pixel in the default RGB ColorModel. The getRGB method in the DirectColorModel class overrides the getRGB method in the ColorModel class. Also see the getBlue, getGreen, getAlpha, and the getRGBdefault methods.

getRGB— java.awt.image.IndexColorModel

```
public final int getRGB(int pixel)
```

Returns the color of a pixel in the default RGB color model. The getRGB method in the IndexColorModel class overrides the getRGB method in the ColorModel class. Also see the getRGBdefault method.

getRGBdefault— java.awt.image.ColorModel

```
public static ColorModel getRGBdefault()
```

Return a ColorModel which describes the default format for integer RGB values used throughout the AWT image interfaces (0–255 values of Alpha, Red, Green, and Blue).

getRows—java.awt.List

```
public int getRows()
```

Returns the number of items in a List.

getRows—java.awt.TextArea

```
public int getRows()
```

Returns the number of rows in a TextArea. Also see the getColumns method.

getRuntime—java.lang.Runtime

```
public static Runtime getRuntime()
```

Returns the Runtime object for the current platform.

getScreenResolution—java.awt.Toolkit

```
public abstract int getScreenResolution()
```

Returns the screen resolution in dots-per-inch.

getScreenSize—java.awt.Toolkit

```
public abstract Dimension getScreenSize()
```

Returns the size of the screen.

getSeconds—java.util.Date

```
public int getSeconds()
```

Returns the second (0 through 59) of a Date object.

getSecurityContext—java.lang.SecurityManager

```
public Object getSecurityContext()
```

Returns an Object which contains information to perform some of the security checks at a later time.

getSecurityManager—java.lang.System

```
public static SecurityManager getSecurityManager()
```

Returns the SecurityManager system security interface. Also see the setSecurityManager method.

getSelectedIndex—java.awt.Choice

```
public int getSelectedIndex()
```

Returns the index of the currently selected item.

getSelectedIndex—java.awt.List

```
public synchronized int getSelectedIndex()
```

Returns the selected item on a list. If no item is selected, a –1 is returned. Also see the `getSelectedIndexes, getSelectedItem, getSelectedItems, select, deselect,` and `isSelected` methods.

getSelectedIndexes—java.awt.List

```
public synchronized int[] getSelectedIndexes()
```

Returns an array of selected items from a list. Also see the `getSelectedIndex, getSelectedItem, getSelectedItems, select, deselect,` and `isSelected` methods.

getSelectedIndexes— java.awt.peer.ListPeer

```
public abstract int[] getSelectedIndexes()
```

Returns an array of selected items from a list. Also see the `getSelectedIndex, getSelectedItem, getSelectedItems, select, deselect,` and `isSelected` methods.

getSelectedItem—java.awt.Choice

```
public String getSelectedItem()
```

Returns the current item in a Choice. Also see the `getSelectedIndex` method.

getSelectedItem—java.awt.List

```
public synchronized String getSelectedItem()
```

Returns a List's selected item or null if no item is selected. Also see the `select, deselect, isSelected, getSelectedIndex, getSelectedIndex,` and `getSelectedItems` methods.

getSelectedItems—java.awt.List

`public synchronized String[] getSelectedItems()`

Returns a List's selected items into a String array. Also see the `select`, `deselect`, `isSelected`, `getSelectedIndex`, `getSelectedIndexes`, and `getSelectedItem` methods

getSelectedText— java.awt.TextComponent

`public String getSelectedText()`

Returns selected text contained in a `TextComponent`. Also see the `getText` and `setText` methods.

getSelectionEnd— java.awt.TextComponent

`public int getSelectionEnd()`

Returns the ending position of the selected text, or zero if no text is selected. Also see the `select`, `selectAll`, and `getSelectionStart` methods.

getSelectionEnd— java.awt.peer.TextComponentPeer

`public abstract int getSelectionEnd()`

Returns the ending position of the selected text, or zero if no text is selected. Also see the `select`, `selectAll`, and `getSelectionStart` methods.

getSelectionStart— java.awt.TextComponent

`public int getSelectionStart()`

Returns the starting position of the selected text, or zero if no text is selected. Also see the `select`, `selectAll`, and `getSelectionEnd` methods.

*getSelectionStart—*java.awt.peer.TextComponentPeer

```
public abstract int getSelectionStart()
```

Returns the starting position of the selected text, or zero if no text is selected. Also see the `select`, `selectAll`, and `getSelectionEnd` methods.

*getSize—*java.awt.Font

```
public int getSize()
```

Returns the point size of a Font. See the `size attribute` for more information.

*getSource—*java.awt.Image

```
public abstract ImageProducer getSource()
```

Returns the ImageProducer object that produces the pixels for the image. For more information, see the `ImageProducer` class.

*getState—*java.awt.Checkbox

```
public boolean getState()
```

Returns the boolean state of the `Checkbox`. Also see the `setState` method.

*getState—*java.awt.CheckboxMenuItem

```
public boolean getState()
```

Returns the state of a `CheckboxMenuItem`. Also see the `setState` method.

*getStyle—*java.awt.Font

```
public int getStyle()
```

Returns the style of a Font. See the `style` attribute and the `isPlain`, `isBold`, and `isItalic` methods for more information.

getSuperclass—java.lang.Class

```
public Class getSuperclass()
```

Returns the superclass (parent) of a Class.

getText—java.awt.Label

```
public String getText()
```

Returns the text of a label. See the setText method.

getText—java.awt.TextComponent

```
public String getText()
```

Returns the text contained in a TextComponent. Also check out the setText method.

getText—java.awt.peer.TextComponentPeer

```
public abstract String getText()
```

Returns the text contained in a TextComponent. Also check out the setText method.

getThreadGroup—java.lang.Thread

```
public final ThreadGroup getThreadGroup()
```

Returns the ThreadGroup of a Thread.

getTime—java.util.Date

```
public long getTime()
```

Returns a long which represents the number of milliseconds since 1/1/1970.

getTimezoneOffset—java.util.Date

```
public int getTimezoneOffset()
```

Returns the hours offset for the TimeZone that is appropriate for the local time.

getTitle—java.awt.Dialog

```
public String getTitle()
```

Returns the title of a Dialog. Also check out the setTitle method.

getTitle—java.awt.Frame

```
public String getTitle()
```

Returns the title of a Frame. Also check out the setTitle method.

getToolkit—java.awt.Component

```
public Toolkit getToolkit()
```

Returns the toolkit used to create the peer for a Component.

> **NOTE:**
> The Frame controls the toolkit that is used for a member component. If the Component is added to a Frame or moved to another Frame, the toolkit the Component uses may change.

getToolkit—java.awt.peer.ComponentPeer

```
public abstract Toolkit getToolkit()
```

Returns the toolkit used to create the peer for a Component.

getToolkit—java.awt.Window

```
public Toolkit getToolkit()
```

Returns the toolkit of a frame. The getToolkit method in the Window class overrides the getToolkit method in the Component class. For more information, check out the Toolkit class.

getTransparentPixel— java.awt.image.IndexColorModel

```
public final int getTransparentPixel()
```

Returns the index of the transparent pixel set in the IndexColorModel constructor. If no transparent pixel was set, a –1 is returned.

*getURL—*java.net.URLConnection

```
public URL getURL()
```

Returns the URL of an URLConnection object.

getUseCaches— java.net.URLConnection

```
public boolean getUseCaches()
```

Rturns the UseCaches attribute.

*getValue—*java.awt.Scrollbar

```
public int getValue()
```

Returns the value of a Scrollbar. Also see the setValue, getMinimum, and getMaximum methods.

*getVisible—*java.awt.Scrollbar

```
public int getVisible()
```

Returns the visible page area of a Scrollbar.

getVisibleIndex—java.awt.List

```
public int getVisibleIndex()
```

Returns the index of the item that was last made visible. See the makeVisible method for more details.

getWarningString—java.awt.Window

```
public final String getWarningString()
```

Returns the warning string for a window.

getWidth—java.awt.Image

```
public abstract int getWidth(ImageObserver observer)
```

Gets the width of the image. If the width is not known yet, then the ImageObserver will be notified when it is known, and a –1 will be returned immediately. Also check out the getHeight method and the ImageObserver class.

getWidths—java.awt.FontMetrics

```
public int[] getWidths()
```

Returns the widths of the first 256 characters in a Font. Also check out the charWidth, charsWidth, stringWidth, and bytesWidth methods.

getYear—java.util.Date

```
public int getYear()
```

Returns a year from a Date.

gotFocus—java.awt.Component

```
public boolean gotFocus(Event evt, Object what)
```

Triggered when a Component has received focus. For more information, check out the requestFocus and lostFocus methods.

grabPixels—java.awt.image.PixelGrabber

```
public boolean grabPixels({long ms})
```

Request the Image or ImageProducer to start delivering all of the pixels in the rectangle defined by the PixelGrabber constructor. You can specify a timeout value in milliseconds if you want. True is returned if the grabPixels method was successful. A false value is returned if an abort, error, or timeout occurs. If the transfer is interrupted by another thread, an InterruptedException exception is thrown.

Graphics—java.awt.Graphics

```
protected   Graphics()
```

Constructs a new Graphics object. Graphic contexts cannot be created directly and can only be inherited, passed as an argument, or created by a Component using the getGraphics method. For more information, see the getGraphics and create methods.

GridBagConstraints— java.awt.GridBagConstraints

```
public   GridBagConstraints()
```

Constructs a GridBagConstraints object.

GridLayout—java.awt.GridLayout

```
public   GridLayout(int rows, int cols {, hGap, vGap})
```

Constructs a grid layout with the specified rows and columns. The horizontal and vertical gaps may also be specified. GridLayout throws an IllegalArgumentException if the rows or columns are invalid.

grow—java.awt.Rectangle

```
public void grow(int horizontal, int vertical)
```

Enlarges the rectangle by horizontal or vertical measurements.

guessContentTypeFromName— java.net.URLConnection

```
protected static String guessContentTypeFromName(
    String fname)
```

A utility that tries to guess the content-type of an object based on its file name extension.

guessContentTypeFromStream—
java.net.URLConnection

```
protected static String guessContentTypeFromStream(
    InputStream is)
```

A utility that tries to guess the content-type of an object based on the content of its input stream. An IOException is thrown if there is an I/O error during execution.

handleEvent—java.awt.Component

```
public boolean handleEvent(Event evt)
```

Handles the event. Returns true if the event is handled and should not be passed to the parent of a Component. This event automatically calls other event methods if needed, such as the mouseEnter, mouseExit, mouseMove, mouseDown, mouseDrag, mouseUp, keyDown, and action methods. This should not be overridden unless you really see a need for overriding this method.

handleEvent—
java.awt.peer.ComponentPeer

```
public abstract boolean handleEvent(Event evt)
```

Handles the event. Returns true if the event is handled and should not be passed to the parent of a Component. This event automatically calls other event methods if needed, such as the mouseEnter, mouseExit, mouseMove, mouseDown, mouseDrag, mouseUp, keyDown, and action methods. This should not be overridden unless you really see a need for overriding this method.

hasChanged—java.util.Observable

```
public synchronized boolean hasChanged()
```

Returns true if an observable change has occurred.

hashCode—java.util.BitSet

```
public int hashCode()
```

Returns a hashcode for a BitSet. The hashCode method in the BitSet class overrides the hashCode method in the Object class.

hashCode—java.lang.Boolean

```
public int hashCode()
```

Returns a hashcode for a Boolean. The `hashCode` method in the Boolean class overrides the `hashCode` method in the Object class.

hashCode—java.lang.Character

```
public int hashCode()
```

Returns a hashcode for a Character. The `hashCode` method in the Character class overrides the `hashCode` method in the Object class.

hashCode—java.awt.Color

```
public int hashCode()
```

Computes a hashcode. `hashCode` in the Color class overrides `hashCode` in the Object class.

hashCode—java.util.Date

```
public int hashCode()
```

Returns a hashcode for a Date object. The `hashCode` method in the Date class overrides the `hashCode` method in the Object class.

hashCode—java.lang.Double

```
public int hashCode()
```

Returns the hashcode for a Double. The `hashCode` method in the Double class overrides the `hashCode` method in the Object class.

hashCode—java.io.File

```
public int hashCode()
```

Computes a hashcode for the file in a File object. The `hashCode` method in the File class overrides the `hashCode` method in the Object class.

hashCode—java.lang.Float

```
public int hashCode()
```

Returns the hashcode for a Float. The hashCode method in the Float class overrides the hashCode method in the Object class.

hashCode—java.awt.Font

```
public int hashCode()
```

Returns a hashcode for a Font. The hashCode method in the Font class overrides the hashCode method in the Object class.

hashCode—java.net.InetAddress

```
public int hashCode()
```

Returns the hashcode for an InetAddress object. The hashCode method in the InetAddress object overrides the hashCode method in the Object class.

hashCode—java.lang.Integer

```
public int hashCode()
```

Returns a hashcode for an Integer object. The hashCode method in the Integer class overrides the hashCode method in the Object class.

hashCode—java.lang.Long

```
public int hashCode()
```

Returns a hashcode for an Long object. The hashCode method in the Long class overrides the hashCode method in the Object class.

ihashCode—java.lang.Object

```
public int hashCode()
```

Returns a hashcode for this Object. Hashcodes are useful for storing Objects in hashtables.

hashCode—java.awt.Point

```
public int hashCode()
```

Returns the hashcode for a Point. The hashCode method in the Point class overrides the hashCode method in the Object class.

hashCode—java.awt.Rectangle

```
public int hashCode()
```

Returns the hashcode for this Rectangle. The hashCode method in the Rectangle class overrides the hashCode method int the Object class.

hashCode—java.lang.String

```
public int hashCode()
```

Returns a hashcode for this String. The hashCode method in the String class overrides the hashCode method in the Object class.

hashCode—java.net.URL

```
public int hashCode()
```

Returns a hashCode from a URL. The hashCode method in the URL class overrrides the hashCode method in the Object class.

Hashtable—java.util.Hashtable

```
public  Hashtable({int capacity{, float loadFactor}})
```

Constructs an empty Hashtable object with the specified capacity (or default if none is provided) and specified load factor (or default if none is provided). An IllegalArgumentException is thrown if the capacity or loadFactor are less than 1.

hasMoreElements—java.util.Enumeration

```
public abstract boolean hasMoreElements()
```

Returns true if the enumeration contains more elements; false if it's empty.

hasMoreElements—
java.util.StringTokenizer

```
public boolean hasMoreElements()
```

Returns true if the StringTokenizer has more elements.

hasMoreTokens—
java.util.StringTokenizer

```
public boolean hasMoreTokens()
```

Returns true if more tokens exist on a StringToken's String.

hide—java.awt.Component

```
public synchronized void hide()
```

Hides a Component. For related methods, see the isVisible and show methods.

hide—java.awt.peer.ComponentPeer

```
public abstract void hide()
```

Hides a Component. For related methods, see the isVisible and show methods.

HSBtoRGB—java.awt.Color

```
public static int HSBtoRGB(float hue, float saturation,
    float brightness)
```

Converts a HSB (Hue, Saturation, Brightness) format to an RGB value. For related methods, see the getHSBColor, RGBtoHSB, getRGBdefault, and getRGB methods.

IEEEremainder—java.lang.Math

```
public static double IEEEremainder(double f1, double f2)
```

Returns the remainder of f1 divided by f2. This is different than the modulus operator (%) in that modulus returns the floating point remainder of an integer divisor [f1 - ((int)(f1 / f2) * f2)] whereas the IEEEremainder returns the IEEE 754 defined remainder, which takes into account the significant numbers of both f1 and f2.

IllegalAccessError—
java.lang.IllegalAccessError

```
public IllegalAccessError({String detailMessage})
```

An attempt was made to use a class, variable, or method which is not available to the calling class. If detailMessage is specified, the detailMessage will be displayed when this throwable is thrown.

IllegalAccessException—
java.lang.IllegalAccessException

```
public IllegalAccessException({String detailMessage})
```

A particular method could not be found inside a class. If detailMessage is specified, the detailMessage will be displayed when this throwable is thrown.

IllegalArgumentException—
java.lang.IllegalArgumentException

```
public IllegalArgumentException({String detailMessage})
```

Arguments from a calling method do not match the called method. If detailMessage is specified, the detailMessage will be displayed when this throwable is thrown.

IllegalMonitorStateException—
java.lang.IllegalMonitorStateException

```
public IllegalMonitorStateException({String detailMessage})
```

An illegal monitor state has been detected. If detailMessage is specified, the detailMessage will be displayed when this throwable is thrown.

IllegalThreadStateException— java.lang.IllegalThreadStateException

```
public IllegalThreadStateException({String detailMessage})
```

A thread is not in the proper state for the requested operation. If `detailMessage` is specified, the `detailMessage` will be displayed when this throwable is thrown.

*Image—*java.awt.Image

```
public   Image()
```

Constructs an Image object

imageComplete— java.awt.image.PixelGrabber

```
public synchronized void imageComplete(int status)
```

The imageComplete method is called by the ImageProducer class when an image is done loading all of the pixels that an image contains or an error occurs.   For more information, see the `removeConsumer` method and the IMAGEABORTED, IMAGEERROR, SINGLEFRAMEDONE, and STATICIMAGEDONE attributes.

imageComplete— java.awt.image.ImageConsumer

```
public abstract void imageComplete(int status)
```

The `imageComplete` method is called when the `ImageProducer` is done delivering all of the pixels that the source image contains. For more information, see the `removeConsumer` method and the IMAGE-ABORTED, IMAGEERROR, SINGLEFRAMEDONE, and STATICIMAGEDONE attributes.

imageComplete— java.awt.image.ImageFilter

```
public void imageComplete(int status)
```

Filters the status in the `imageComplete` method of the `ImageConsumer` interface.

ImageFilter—java.awt.image.ImageFilter

```
public  ImageFilter()
```

Constructs a new ImageFilter object.

imageUpdate—java.awt.Component

```
public boolean imageUpdate(Image img, int flags,
    int x, int y, int width, int height)
```

Repaints a Component when the component's image has changed. `imageUpdate` returns true if image has changed or false if it hasn't changed. `img` is the image in the component. `x` and `y` specify the position within the parent container that you want to update. `width` and `height` control how much of the control you want to update. Using the same flags as the `ImageObserver` interface, flags can be `ABORT`, `ALLBITS`, `ERROR`, `FRAMEBITS`, `HEIGHT`, `PROPERTIES`, `SOMEBITS`, and `WIDTH`.

imageUpdate— java.awt.image.ImageObserver

```
public abstract boolean imageUpdate(Image img,
    int infoflags, int x, int y, int width, int height)
```

This method is called when information is available about an image which was previously requested using an asynchronous interface method call, such as `getHeight`, `getWidth`, or `drawImage`. This method returns true if further image updates are required, and false if all image information has been delivered. Constants are combined to form the `infoflags` argument which indicates what information about the image is now available. The `x`, `y`, `width`, and `height` arguments define the rectangle of the image. For more informaiton, see the `getWidth`, `getHeight`, and `drawImage` methods.

inClass—java.lang.SecurityManager

```
protected boolean inClass(String name)
```

Returns true if the given string is in a class.

inClassLoader— java.lang.SecurityManager

```
protected boolean inClassLoader()
```

Returns true if the current ClassLoader is set to null. Otherwise, false is returned.

IncompatibleClassChangeError— java.lang.IncompatibleClassChangeError

```
public IncompatibleClassChangeError(
    {String detailMessage})
```

IncompatibleClassChangeError is the parent class for all inter-class operational errors. If detailMessage is specified, the detailMessage will be displayed when this throwable is thrown.

IndexColorModel— java.awt.image.IndexColorModel

```
public   IndexColorModel(argument_list)
```

Constructs an IndexColorModel. The argument list can take two basic formats. You can use an argument list of (int bits, int size, byte red[], byte green[], byte blue[], {[int trans / byte alpha[]]}). In this list, bits describes the number of bits per pixel. Size is the size of each red, green, blue, and alpha (if given) array. Each array entry describes pixels in this color model. If the alpha array is omitted, each pixel will have alpha components of 255 except for an optional transparent pixel unless an alpha array is specified. A transparent pixel indicates a pixel is always transparent no matter what the alpha value is.

You can also have an argument list of (int bits, int size, byte packedMap[], int start, boolean hasAlpha {, int trans}). This describes a packed map of red, green, and blue values (with optional alpha values if the hasAlpha argument is set to true). The trans integer here, again, allows for an optional transparent pixel.

indexOf—java.lang.String

```
public int indexOf([int ch / String s]{, offset})
```

Returns the position within a String of the first occurrence of the specified character or String. A –1 is returned if the index is not found. An offset can be specified as a starting point, and the beginning of the string is assumed.

indexOf—java.util.Vector

```
public final synchronous int indexOf(
    Object elem{, int index})
```

Searches the vector for an Object and returns how far it is from the first position if it's found; otherwise, –1 is returned. An index can be specified to start searching at a point other than the beginning of the Vector.

IndexOutOfBoundsException— java.lang.IndexOutOfBoundsException

```
public IndexOutOfBoundsException({String detailMessage})
```

Parent class for `ArrayIndexOutOfBoundsException` and `StringIndexOutOfBoundsException`. Indicates that an array or string has exceeded its maximum length. If `detailMessage` is specified, then `detailMessage` will be displayed when this throwable is thrown.

init—java.applet.Applet

```
public void init()
```

Initializes the applet. You never need to call this directly; it is called automatically by the system once the applet is created. For more information, see the `start`, `stop`, and `destroy` methods.

InputStream—java.io.InputStream

```
public  InputStream()
```

Constructs an `InputStream` class.

insert—java.lang.StringBuffer

```
public synchronized StringBuffer insert(int offset,
    datatype argument)
```

Inserts an argument at the given offset in a StringBuffer. This argument can be an Object or a String object, or a character array, boolean, character, int, long, float, or double data type. The StringBuffer itself is returned. An `StringIndexOutOfBoundsException` exception is thrown if the offset is invalid.

insertElementAt—java.util.Vector

```
public final synchronous void insertElementAt(
    Object obj, int index)
```

Inserts the Vector element at an index. All subsequent indexes are moved up by one. An `ArrayIndexOutOfBoundsException` is thrown if the index was invalid.

insertText—java.awt.TextArea

```
public void insertText(String str, int position)
```

Inserts text into a TextArea at the specified position. Also see the `appendText`, `getText`, `setText`, and `replaceText` methods.

insertText—java.awt.peer.TextAreaPeer

```
public abstract void insertText(String str, int position)
```

Inserts text into a TextArea at the specified position. Also see the `appendText`, `getText`, `setText`, and `replaceText` methods.

insets—java.awt.Container

```
public Insets insets()
```

Returns the insets of the container. The insets indicate the size of the border of the container. Insets are often used to determine the usable window area in a Frame or Window. For more information, see the `Insets` class and the `LayoutManager` class.

insets—java.awt.peer.ContainerPeer

```
public abstract Insets insets()
```

Returns the insets of the container. The insets indicate the size of the border of the container. Insets are often used to determine the usable window area in a Frame or Window. For more information, see the `Insets` class and the `LayoutManager` class.

Insets—java.awt.Insets

```
public  Insets(int top, int left, int bottom, int right)
```

Constructs a new Inset with the specified top, left, bottom, and right insets.

inside—java.awt.Component

```
public synchronized boolean inside(int x, int y)
```

Checks whether a specified x,y location is inside the bounding box of a Component. For related information, see the `locate` method.

inside—java.awt.Polygon

```
public boolean inside(int x, int y)
```

Returns true if the point (x,y) is inside the Polygon. Otherwise, false is returned.

inside—java.awt.Rectangle

```
public boolean inside(int x, int y)
```

Checks if a x, y point lies inside a rectangle.

InstantiationError— java.lang.InstantiationError

```
public InstantiationError({String detailMessage})
```

You tried to instantiate an abstract class or an interface. You can only instantiate classes that are inherited from abstract classes. If `detailMessage` is specified, the `detailMessage` will be displayed when this throwable is thrown.

InstantiationException— java.lang.InstantiationException

```
public InstantiationException({String detailMessage})
```

An attempt was made to instantiate either an abstract class or an interface. If detailMessage is specified, the detailMessage will be displayed when this throwable is thrown.

intBitsToFloat—java.lang.Float

```
public static Float intBitsToFloat(long bits)
```

Returns a floating point number that corresponds to a given bit represention.

Integer—java.lang.Integer

```
public  Integer([int value / String s])
```

Constructs an Integer object and initializes it to a given integer or the value contained in a String. The radix of the string is assumed to be 10, and a NumberFormatException if a string contains an invalid number.

intern—java.lang.String

```
public String intern()
```

Returns a String that is equal to the String object but which is guaranteed to be from the unique String pool.

InternalError—java.lang.InternalError

```
public InternalError({String detailMessage})
```

An internal error has occurred in the Java virtual machine. If detailMessage is specified, the detailMessage will be displayed when this throwable is thrown.

interrupt—java.lang.Thread

```
public void interrupt()
```

Sends an interrupt to a Thread.

interrupted—java.lang.Thread

```
public static boolean interrupted()
```

Returns true if the current Thread has been interrupted. Otherwise, false is returned. See the `interrupt` and `isInterrupted` method for related information.

InterruptedException— java.lang.InterruptedException

```
public InterruptedException({String detailMessage})
```

Indicates that some other thread has interrupted this thread. If `detailMessage` is specified, the `detailMessage` will be displayed when this throwable is thrown.

InterruptedIOException— java.io.InterruptedIOException

```
public  InterruptedIOException({String detailMessage)
```

Constructs an exception indicating that an I/O operation has been interrupted. `bytesTransferred` is a class variable used to indicate how many bytes were transferred. You can specify a detail message to appear if you want.

intersection—java.awt.Rectangle

```
public Rectangle intersection(Rectangle r)
```

Returns the Rectangle that is the intersection of the current Rectangle and a passed Rectangle. If there is no intersection, a null is returned.

intersects—java.awt.Rectangle

```
public boolean intersects(Rectangle r)
```

Checks if two rectangles intersect.

intValue—java.lang.Double

```
public int intValue()
```

Returns the integer value of a Double. The `intValue` method in the Double class overrides the `intValue` method in the Number class.

intValue—java.lang.Float

```
public int intValue()
```

Returns the integer value of a Float. The `intValue` method in the Float class overrides the `intValue` method in the Number class.

intValue—java.lang.Integer

```
public int intValue()
```

Returns the value of an Integer as an int data type. The `intValue` method in the Integer class overrides the `intvalue` method in the Number class.

intValue—java.lang.Long

```
public int intValue()
```

Returns the value of an Long as an int data type. The `intValue` method in the Long class overrides the `intvalue` method in the Number class.

intValue—java.lang.Number

```
public abstract int intValue()
```

Returns the value of a number as an int data type. This may involve rounding.

invalidate—java.awt.Component

```
public void invalidate()
```

Invalidates a Component. For related information, see the `validate` and `layout` methods or the `LayoutManager` class.

IOException—java.io.IOException

```
public  IOException({String detailMessage)
```

Parent class to all java.io exceptions. Constructs an exception indicating that an I/O error has occurred. You can specify a detail message to appear if you want.

isAbsolute—java.io.File

```
public boolean isAbsolute()
```

Returns true if the file path in a File object is absolute. If the path is relative (and uses relative path information such as ..and .), a false is returned.

isActive—java.applet.Applet

```
public boolean isActive()
```

Returns true if the applet is active. An applet is marked active just before the start method is called. See start for more details.

isActive—java.applet.AppletStub

```
public abstract boolean isActive()
```

Returns true if the applet is active.

isAlive—java.lang.Thread

```
public final boolean isAlive()
```

Returns true if a Thread is active, meaning that the Thread has started and has not yet been stopped.

isBold—java.awt.Font

```
public boolean isBold()
```

Returns true if a Font is bold. Also see the getStyle method and the style attribute.

isConsumer—
java.awt.image.FilteredImageSource

```
public synchronized boolean isConsumer(ImageConsumer ic)
```

This method determines if an `ImageConsumer` object is currently registered with a `FilteredImageSource`. Also see the `startProduction`, `removeConsumer`, and `addConsumer` methods.

isConsumer—
java.awt.image.ImageProducer

```
public abstract boolean isConsumer(ImageConsumer ic)
```

This method determines if an `ImageConsumer` object is currently registered with an `ImageProducer`. Also see the `startProduction`, `removeConsumer`, and `addConsumer` methods.

isConsumer—
java.awt.image.MemoryImageSource

```
public synchronized boolean isConsumer(ImageConsumer ic)
```

This method determines if an `ImageConsumer` object is currently registered with a `MemoryImageSource`. Also see the `startProduction`, `removeConsumer`, and `addConsumer` methods.

isDaemon—java.lang.Thread

```
public final boolean isDaemon()
```

Returns true if the thread is a daemon, and false if it's not. See the `setDaemon` method for more information.

isDaemon—java.lang.ThreadGroup

```
public final boolean isDaemon()
```

Returns true if the ThreadGroup is a daemon and false if it is not. See the `setDaemon` method for more information.

isDigit—java.lang.Character

```
public static boolean isDigit(char ch)
```

Returns true if the specified character is an ASCII (ISO-LATIN-1) digit. Otherwise, false is returned.

isDirectory—java.io.File

```
public boolean isDirectory()
```

Returns true if the file in a File object is a directory. Otherwise, false is returned.

isEditable—java.awt.TextComponent

```
public boolean isEditable()
```

Returns true if a TextComponent is editable. Otherwise, false is returned. Also see the setEditable method.

isEmpty—java.util.Dictionary

```
public abstract boolean isEmpty()
```

Returns true if a Dictionary has no elements. Otherwise, false is returned.

isEmpty—java.util.Hashtable

```
public boolean isEmpty()
```

Returns true if the hashtable is empty. The isEmpty method in the Hashtable class overrides the isEmpty method in the Dictionary class.

isEmpty—java.awt.Rectangle

```
public boolean isEmpty()
```

Returns true if a rectangle is empty.

isEmpty—java.util.Vector

```
public final boolean isEmpty()
```

Returns true if the Vector has no values.

isEnabled—java.awt.Component

```
public boolean isEnabled()
```

Checks if a Component is enabled. Enabled is the default for components. For more information, see the `enable` and `disable` methods.

isEnabled—java.awt.MenuItem

```
public boolean isEnabled()
```

Returns true if a MenuItem is enabled. Otherwise, false is returned. See the `enable` and `disable` methods for more information.

isErrorAny—java.awt.MediaTracker

```
public synchronized boolean isErrorAny()
```

Checks the error status of all of the images and returns a true if any image downloads encountered an error. Otherwise, false is returned. For related information, see the `isErrorID` and `getErrorsAny` methods.

isErrorID—java.awt.MediaTracker

```
public synchronized boolean isErrorID(int identification)
```

Checks the error status of all of the images with the specified identification. A true value is returned if any images with the given identificaiton had an error during loading. For related information, see the `isErrorAny` and `getErrorsID` methods and the `ERRORED` attribute.

isFile—java.io.File

```
public boolean isFile()
```

Returns true if the file in a File object is a normal file. Otherwise, false is returned.

isInfinite (static)—*java.lang.Double*

```
public static boolean isInfinite(double v)
```

Checks to see if a double contains a value whose absolute value is greater than the double can hold. See the `NEGATIVE_INFINITY` and `POSITIVE_INFINITY` attributes for more information.

isInfinite (static)—java.lang.Float

```
public static boolean isInfinite(Float v)
```

Checks to see if a Float contains a value whose absolute value is greater than the Float can hold. See the NEGATIVE_INFINITY and POS-ITIVE_INFINITY attributes for more information.

isInfinite—java.lang.Double

```
public boolean isInfinite()
```

Returns true if a Double object contains a value whose absolute value is infinitely large. See the NEGATIVE_INFINITY and POSITIVE_INFINI-TY attributes for more information.

isInfinite—java.lang.Float

```
public boolean isInfinite()
```

Returns true if a Float object contains a value whose absolute value is infinitely large. See the NEGATIVE_INFINITY and POSITIVE_INFINITY attributes for more information.

isInterface—java.lang.Class

```
public boolean isInterface()
```

Returns true if a Class is an interface, and false if it is not.

isInterrupted—java.lang.Thread

```
public boolean isInterrupted()
```

Returns true if a Thread other than the current thread has been interrupted. Otherwise, false is returned. See the interrupt and inter-rupted methods for more details.

isItalic—java.awt.Font

```
public boolean isItalic()
```

Returns true if a Font is italic. Also see the getStyle method and the style attribute.

isLowerCase—java.lang.Character

```
public static boolean isLowerCase(char ch)
```

Returns true if the specified character is ASCII (ISO-LATIN–1) lower case. Otherwise, false is returned.

isModal—java.awt.Dialog

```
public boolean isModal()
```

Returns true if a Dialog is modal or false if it isn't. If a Dialog is modal, the Dialog grabs all the input from the user and blocks input to other windows when shown.

isNaN (static)—java.lang.Double

```
public static boolean isNaN(double v)
```

Checks to see if a double contains a value that is not a number. See the NaN attribute for more information.

isNaN (static)—java.lang.Float

```
public static boolean isNaN(Float v)
```

Checks to see if a Float contains a value that is not a number. See the NaN attribute for more information.

isNaN—java.lang.Double

```
public boolean isNaN()
```

Returns true if a Double object contains the special NaN value. Otherwise, false is returned.

isNaN—java.lang.Float

```
public boolean isNaN()
```

Returns true if a Float object contains the special NaN value. Otherwise, false is returned.

isPlain—java.awt.Font

```
public boolean isPlain()
```

Returns true if a Font is plain. Also see the `getStyle` method and the `style` attribute.

isResizable—java.awt.Dialog

```
public boolean isResizable()
```

Returns true if the user can resize the Dialog and false if he or she can't.

isResizable—java.awt.Frame

```
public boolean isResizable()
```

Returns true if a frame is resizable and false if it isn't resizable. Also check out the `setResizable` method.

isSelected—java.awt.List

```
public synchronized boolean isSelected(int index)
```

Returns true if the List item at an index has been selected. Otherwise, false is returned. Also see the `select`, `deselect`, `getSelectedIndex`, `getSelectedIndexes`, `getSelectedItem`, and `getSelectedItems` methods.

isShowing—java.awt.Component

```
public boolean isShowing()
```

Checks if a Component and the Component container is visible and showing on screen. For more information, see the `show` and `hide` methods.

isSpace—java.lang.Character

```
public static boolean isSpace(char ch)
```

Returns true if the specified character is an ASCII (ISO-LATIN–1) white space. Otherwise, false is returned.

isTearOff—java.awt.Menu

```
public boolean isTearOff()
```

Returns true if a menu is a tear-off menu. Otherwise, false is returned.

isUpperCase—java.lang.Character

```
public static boolean isUpperCase(char ch)
```

Returns true if the specified character is ASCII (ISO-LATIN–1) uppercase. Otherwise, false is returned.

isValid—java.awt.Component

```
public boolean isValid()
```

Checks if a Component is valid. Components are not valid when they are first shown on-screen. For more information, see the validate and invalidate methods.

isVisible—java.awt.Component

```
public boolean isVisible()
```

Checks if a Component is visible. Components are initially visible, except for top-level components, such as Frame. For more information, see the show and hide methods.

join—java.lang.Thread

```
public final synchronous void join(
    {long millis{, int nanos}})
```

Waits for a thread to die for a number of milliseconds and nanoseconds (if given). If zero milliseconds is provided or millis is omitted, this method waits forever for a Thread to die. An InterruptedException is thrown if another thread has interrupted this thread.

keyDown—java.awt.Component

```
public boolean keyDown(Event evt, int key)
```

Called when a key on the keyboard is pressed. The evt Event identifies the event that caused this method to execute. For more information, see the handleEvent method.

keys—java.util.Dictionary

```
public abstract Enumeration keys()
```

Returns an Enumeration of a Dictionary's keys.

keys—java.util.Hashtable

```
public synchronized Enumeration keys()
```

Returns an Enumeration of the hashtable's keys. The keys method in the Hashtable class overrides the keys method in the Dictionary class.

keyUp—java.awt.Component

```
public boolean keyUp(Event evt, int key)
```

Called when a key on the keyboard is released. The evt Event identifies the event that caused this method to execute. For more information, see the handleEvent method.

Label—java.awt.Label

```
public  Label({String label, {int allignment}})
```

Constructs a new label with the specified String of text (or an empty string if a label is not specified) and the specified alignment, if given.

last—java.awt.CardLayout

```
public void last(Container parent)
```

Goes to the last card of a container. parent is the name of the parent container.

lastElement—java.util.Vector

```
public final synchronous Object lastElement()
```

Returns the last element in a Vector. A NoSuchElementException is thrown if the Vector is empty.

lastIndexOf—**java.lang.String**

```
public int lastIndexOf([int ch / String s]{, offset})
```

Returns the position within a String of the last occurrence of the specified character or String. A –1 is returned if the index is not found. An `offset` can be specified as an ending point. It is assumed that the search begins from the end of the string.

lastIndexOf—**java.util.Vector**

```
public final synchronous int lastIndexOf(Object elem,
    int index)
```

Searches the vector backwards for an Object and returns how far it is from the first position if it's found. Otherwise, –1 is returned. An `index` can be specified as an ending point int the vector to start searching at a point other than the end of the Vector.

lastModified—**java.io.File**

```
public long lastModified()
```

Returns the last modification date and time. The return value should only be used to compare modification dates. It is meaningless as an absolute time.

layout—**java.awt.Component**

```
public void layout()
```

Lays out a Component. For related information, see the `validate` method or the `LayoutManager` class.

> **TIP:**
> The `layout` method is often called when a Component is validated.

layout—java.awt.Container

```
public synchronized void layout()
```

Performs a layout on a Container. The `layout` method in the Container class overrides the `layout` method in the Component class. See the `setLayout` and `getLayout` methods and the `LayoutManager` class for related information.

layoutContainer— java.awt.BorderLayout

```
public void layoutContainer(Container target)
```

Lays out the specified container. This method will actually reshape the components in the specified target container in order to satisfy the constraints of the `BorderLayout` object. `target` is the component being laid out. For more information, see the `Container` class documented in the InfoViewer.

layoutContainer—java.awt.CardLayout

```
public void layoutContainer(Container parent)
```

Performs a layout in a panel. `parent` is the name of the parent container.

layoutContainer—java.awt.FlowLayout

```
public void layoutContainer(Container target)
```

Lays out a container. This method reshapes the Components in a Container to satisfy the constraints of the BorderLayout object. See the `BorderLayout`, `Component`, and `Container` classes for more information.

layoutContainer—java.awt.GridLayout

```
public void layoutContainer(Container parent)
```

Lays out a grid with the components in the parent Container.

layoutContainer— java.awt.LayoutManager

```
public abstract void layoutContainer(Container parent)
```

Lays out the container in the specified panel. `parent` is the component which needs to be laid out.

*length—*java.io.File

```
public long length()
```

Returns the length of the file in a File object.

*length—*java.io.RandomAccessFile

```
public long length()
```

Returns the length of a file.

*length—*java.lang.String

```
public int length()
```

Returns the number of of characters in a String.

*length—*java.lang.StringBuffer

```
public int length()
```

Returns the number of characters in the `StringBuffer`.

*lineno—*java.io.StreamTokenizer

```
public int  lineno()
```

Returns the current line number.

LineNumberInputStream— java.io.LineNumberInputStream

```
public  LineNumberInputStream(InputStream in)
```

Constructs a new `LineNumberInputStream` using another `InputStream` object.

LinkageError—**java.lang.LinkageError**

```
public LinkageError({String detailMessage})
```

LinkageError is the parent for several other errors that involve multi-class operations. Linkage errors occur when a one class (Class1) has a dependency on another class (Class2), but Class2 was changed after Class1 was compiled. If detailMessage is specified, the detailMessage will be displayed when this throwable is thrown.

list—**java.awt.Component**

```
public void list({PrintStream out {, int indent}})
```

Prints out a list, starting at an indention (if specified), to a print stream or a printout stream (if specified).

list—**java.awt.Container**

```
public void list(PrintStream out, int indent)
```

Prints out a list of all Components in a Container to an out stream starting at a given indention. The list method in the Container class overrides the list method in the Component class.

list—**java.io.File**

```
public String[] list({FilenameFilter filter})
```

Lists the files in a directory. If a filter is provided, only those files that match the filter are listed. A String array of file and directory names is returned. Relative directories, like "." and "..", are not returned.

List—**java.awt.List**

```
public  List({int rows, boolean multipleSelections})
```

Creates a new scrolling list. The rows argument is the number of visible rows in the List when the List is constructed. The multipleSelections boolean argument is set to true or false indicating whether or not multiple rows are allowed to be selected at one time in a List.

list—java.util.Properties

```
public void list(PrintStream out)
```

Lists all the properties to a print stream.

list—java.lang.ThreadGroup

```
public synchronized void list()
```

Lists this ThreadGroup.

load—java.util.Properties

```
public synchronized void load(InputStream in)
```

Loads properties from an input stream. An IOException is thrown if there was an I/O error when reading from input stream.

load—java.lang.Runtime

```
public synchronized void load(String filename)
```

Loads a dynamic library from a path name. An UnsatisfiedLinkError is thrown if the file specified by the filename parameter does not exist. Also see the getRuntime method.

load—java.lang.System

```
public static void load(String filename)
```

Loads a dynamic library, given a complete path and file name. An UnsatisfiedLinkError error is thrown if the file name does not exist.

loadClass—java.lang.ClassLoader

```
protected abstract Class loadClass(String name,
    boolean resolve)
```

Returns a loaded class, or null if the class was not found. The loadClass method is used by the virtual Java machine to load a class. It resolves the specified name to a Class if resolve is set to true. A ClassNotFoundException is thrown if a class definition can't be found.

loadLibrary—java.lang.Runtime

```
public synchronized void loadLibrary(String libname)
```

Loads a dynamic library with the specified library name. An `UnsatisfiedLinkError` is thrown if the library specified by the libname parameter does not exist.

loadLibrary—java.lang.System

```
public static void loadLibrary(String libname)
```

Loads a dynamic library with a specified library name. An `UnsatisfiedLinkError` error is thrown if the libname library does not exist.

locate—java.awt.Component

```
public Component locate(int x, int y)
```

Returns a Component or subcomponent at x,y location. For related information, see the `inside` method.

locate—java.awt.Container

```
public Component locate(int x, int y)
```

Returns the component that contains the x,y position. The `locate` method returns a null if the component is not within the x and y coordinates. The `locate` method in the Container class overrides the `locate` method in the Component class. Also check out the `inside` method.

location—java.awt.Component

```
public Point location()
```

Returns a Component's current location in the parent's coordinate space. For more information, see the `move` method.

log—java.lang.Math

```
public static double log(double a)
```

Returns the natural logarithm (base e) of a. See the exp method for more information. The log method throws the ArithmeticException exception if a is less than zero.

> **NOTE:**
> The log method *does not* take the log to the base 10 as most calculators do. Instead, it takes the natural log of a number, which has a base of e. (See the E attribute for more informaiton.) In fact, there is no method for doing base 10 logs in Java or Visual J++. To take the base 10 log a number, try writing a log10 method:
>
> ```
> public static double log10(double a) throws
> ➡ArithmeticException {
>     try {
>         double logbase10 = Math.log(a) / Math.log(10);
>         return logbase10;
>     }
>     catch (ArithmeticException e){
>         customErrorMethod("An error has occured.")
>     }
> }
> ```
>
> This method will take the base 10 log of a number. You may find it useful in some numeric calculations.

Long—java.lang.Long

```
public  Long([long value / String s])
```

Constructs a Long object and initializes it to a given long integer or the value contained in a String. The radix of the string is assumed to be 10, and a NumberFormatException if a string contains an invalid number.

longBitsToDouble—java.lang.Double

```
public static double longBitsToDouble(long bits)
```

Returns a double floating point number that corresponds to a given bit representation.

longValue—java.lang.Double

```
public long longValue()
```

Returns the long integer value of a Double. The longValue method in the Double class overrides the longValue method in the Number class.

longValue—java.lang.Float

```
public long longValue()
```

Returns the long integer value of a Float. The longValue method in the Float class overrides the longValue method in the Number class.

longValue—java.lang.Integer

```
public long longValue()
```

Returns the value of an Integer as an long data type. The longValue method in the Integer class overrides the longValue method in the Number class.

longValue—java.lang.Long

```
public long longValue()
```

Returns the value of an Long as an long data type. The longValue method in the Long class overrides the longValue method in the Number class.

longValue—java.lang.Number

```
public abstract long longValue()
```

Returns the value of a number as a long data type. This may involve rounding.

loop—java.applet.AudioClip

```
public abstract void loop()
```

Starts playing the clip in a loop.

lostFocus—java.awt.Component

```
public boolean lostFocus(Event evt, Object what)
```

Triggered when a Component has lost focus. For related methods, see `requestFocus` and `gotFocus`.

lowerCaseMode— java.io.StreamTokenizer

```
public void lowerCaseMode(boolean torf)
```

If torf is true, `TT_WORD` tokens are forced to be lowercase.

makeVisible—java.awt.List

```
public void makeVisible(int index)
```

Forces an item at a specified index to be visible. Also see the `getVisibleIndex` method.

makeVisible—java.awt.peer.ListPeer

```
public abstract void makeVisible(int index)
```

Forces an item at a specified index to be visible. Also see the `getVisibleIndex` method.

MalformedURLException— java.net.MalformedURLException

```
public MalformedURLException({String detailMessage})
```

An URL that has been passed to a method is corrupt or unintelligible. If `detailMessage` is specified, the `detailMessage` will be displayed when this throwable is thrown.

mark—java.io.BufferedInputStream

```
public synchronized void mark(int readlimit)
```

Marks the current position in the input stream. The `reset` method will reposition the stream at the last marked position so that subsequent reads will re-read the same bytes. The `readlimit` argument is the maximum limit of bytes allowed to be read before the mark position becomes invalid. See the `markpos` and `marklimit` attributes for more information. The `mark` method in the `BufferedInputStream` class overrides the `mark` method in the `FilterInputStream` class.

mark—java.io.FilterInputStream

```
public synchronized void mark(int readlimit)
```

Marks the current position in the input stream. The `reset` method will reposition the stream at the last marked position so that subsequent reads will re-read the same bytes. The `readlimit` argument is the maximum limit of bytes allowed to be read before the mark position becomes invalid. See the `markpos` and `marklimit` attributes for more information. The `mark` method in the `FilterInputStream` class overrides the `mark` method in the `InputStream` class.

mark—java.io.InputStream

```
public synchronized void mark(int readlimit)
```

Marks the current position in the input stream. The `reset` method will reposition the stream at the last marked position so that subsequent reads will re-read the same bytes. The `readlimit` argument is the maximum limit of bytes allowed to be read before the mark position becomes invalid. See the `markpos` and `marklimit` attributes for more information.

mark—java.io.LineNumberInputStream

```
public void mark(int readlimit)
```

Marks the current position in the input stream. The `reset` method will reposition the stream at the last marked position so that subsequent reads will re-read the same bytes. The `readlimit` argument is the maximum limit of bytes allowed to be read before the mark position becomes invalid. See the `markpos` and `marklimit` attributes for more information. The `mark` method in the `LineNumberInputStream` class overrides the `mark` method in the `FilterInputStream` class.

markSupported— java.io.BufferedInputStream

```
public boolean markSupported()
```

Returns a boolean indicating if this stream type supports the mark and reset methods. The markSupported method in the BufferedInputStream class overrides the markSupported method in the FilterInputStream class.

markSupported— java.io.FilterInputStream

```
public boolean markSupported()
```

Returns a boolean indicating if this stream type supports the mark and reset methods. The markSupported method in the FilterInputStream class overrides the markSupported method in the InputStream class.

markSupported—java.io.InputStream

```
public boolean markSupported()
```

Returns a boolean indicating if this stream type supports the mark and reset methods.

markSupported— java.io.PushbackInputStream

```
public boolean markSupported()
```

Returns a boolean indicating if this stream type supports the mark and reset methods. The markSupported method in the PushbackInputStream class overrides the markSupported method in the FilterInputStream class.

max—java.lang.Math

```
public static int max(datatype a, datatype b)
```

Returns the greater of two values. The datatype can be integer, long, float, or double.

MediaTracker—java.awt.MediaTracker

```
public   MediaTracker(Component comp)
```

Constructs a `MediaTracker` object to track images for a Component.

MemoryImageSource— java.awt.image.MemoryImageSource

```
public   MemoryImageSource(int w, int h,
    {ColorModel cm,} [byte / int] pix[],
    int off, int scan{, Hashtable props})
```

Constructs an `ImageProducer` object which uses an array of bytes or integers to produce data for an `Image` object. If the `ColorModel` is omitted, the default RGB ColorModel is assumed. Also see the `createImage` method.

Menu—java.awt.Menu

```
public   Menu(String label {, boolean tearOff})
```

Constructs a Menu with a label. If `tearOff` is true, the menu can be torn off. (This means that the menu will still appear on-screen after the the mouse button has been released.) If `tearOff` is false or omitted, the menu can't be torn off.

MenuBar—java.awt.MenuBar

```
public   MenuBar()
```

Constructs a new menu bar.

MenuComponent— java.awt.MenuComponent

```
public   MenuComponent()
```

Construct a new `MenuComponent`.

MenuItem—java.awt.MenuItem

```
public   MenuItem(String label)
```

Constructs a new `MenuItem` and assigns a label to it.

> **CAUTION:**
> "-" is reserved to mean a separator between menu items. Therefore, it can't be used as a label in a `MenuItem`.

metaDown—java.awt.Event

```
public boolean metaDown()
```

Checks if the meta key is down. Also check out the `modifiers` attribute and the `shiftDown` and `controlDown` methods.

min—java.lang.Math

```
public static int min(datatype a, datatype b)
```

Returns the lesser of two values. The datatype can be integer, long, float, or double.

minimumLayoutSize— java.awt.BorderLayout

```
public Dimension minimumLayoutSize(Container target)
```

Returns the minimum dimensions needed to layout the components contained in the specified target container. `target` is the Container on which to do the layout. For more information, see the `Container` class documented in the InfoViewer or `preferredLayoutSize`.

minimumLayoutSize— java.awt.CardLayout

```
public Dimension minimumLayoutSize(Container parent)
```

Calculates the minimum size for the specified panel. `parent` is the name of the parent container. For more information, see the `maximumLayoutSize` method or the `preferredLayoutSize` method.

minimumLayoutSize—
java.awt.FlowLayout

```
public Dimension minimumLayoutSize(Container target)
```

Returns the minimum dimensions needed to layout the components contained in the specified target container. Also check out the `preferredLayoutSize` method and the `Component`, `Dimension`, and `Container` classes.

minimumLayoutSize—
java.awt.GridLayout

```
public Dimension minimumLayoutSize(Container parent)
```

Returns the minimum dimensions needed to layout components in a Container. Also check out the `preferredLayoutSize` method.

minimumLayoutSize—
java.awt.LayoutManager

```
public abstract Dimension minimumLayoutSize(
    Container parent)
```

Calculates the minimum size dimensions for the specified panel given the components in the specified parent container. `parent` is the component to be laid out. For more information, see `preferredLayoutSize`.

minimumSize—java.awt.Component

```
public Dimension minimumSize()
```

Returns a Component's minimum size. For related information, see the `preferredSize` method, or the `LayoutManager` or `Dimension` classes.

minimumSize—
java.awt.peer.ComponentPeer

```
public abstract Dimension minimumSize()
```

Returns a Component's minimum size. For related information, see the `preferredSize` method, or the `LayoutManager` or `Dimension` classes.

minimumSize—java.awt.Container

```
public synchronized Dimension minimumSize()
```

Returns the minimum size of a Container. The `minimumSize` method in the Container class overrides the `minimumSize` method in the Component class. Also, see the `preferredSize` method and the `Dimension` class.

minimumSize—java.awt.List

```
public Dimension minimumSize({int rows})
```

Returns the minimum dimensions needed for a List. If the number of rows is given, then `minimumSize` returns the preferred dimensions for a List with a given number of rows. The `minimumSize` method with no arguments in the List class overrides the `minimumSize` method in the Component class. Also see the `preferredSize` method.

minimumSize—java.awt.peer.ListPeer

```
public abstract Dimension minimumSize({int rows})
```

Returns the minimum dimensions needed for a List. If the number of rows is given, then `minimumSize` returns the preferred dimensions for a List with a given number of rows. Also see the `preferredSize` method.

minimumSize—java.awt.TextArea

```
public Dimension minimumSize({int rows, int cols})
```

Returns the minimum size Dimensions of a TextArea, or of a TextArea's specified rows and columns if given. The `minimumSize` method with no arguments in the `TextArea` class overrides the `minimumSize` method in the `Component` class.

minimumSize—java.awt.peer.TextAreaPeer

```
public abstract Dimension minimumSize({int rows, int cols})
```

Returns the minimum size Dimensions of a TextArea, or of a TextArea's specified rows and columns if given. The `minimumSize` method with no arguments in the `TextArea` class overrides the `minimumSize` method in the `Component` class.

minimumSize—java.awt.TextField

```
public Dimension minimumSize({int columns})
```

Returns the minimum size Dimensions needed for a TextField. If columns is specified, the minimum size Dimensions needed for a TextField with the specified amount of columns is returned. The minimumSize method in the TextField class overrides the minimumSize method in the Component class. Also see the preferredSize method.

minimumSize— java.awt.peer.TextFieldPeer

```
public abstract Dimension minimumSize({int columns})
```

Returns the minimum size Dimensions needed for a TextField. If columns is specified, the minimum size Dimensions needed for a TextField with the specified amount of columns is returned. The minimumSize method in the TextField class overrides the minimumSize method in the Component class. Also see the preferredSize method.

mkdir—java.io.File

```
public boolean mkdir()
```

Creates a directory. A true value is returned if the directory was successfully created. A false is returned if there was an error during the directory creation.

mkdirs—java.io.File

```
public boolean mkdirs()
```

Creates all directories in this path. This method returns true if all directories in this path are successfully created, and false otherwise.

mouseDown—java.awt.Component

```
public boolean mouseDown(Event evt, int x, int y)
```

An event that's called if the left mouse button is clicked. You override this event when you want to code for a mouse click. The evt Event identifies the event that caused this method to execute. x and y identify the coordinates where the mouse click took place. For more information, see the handleEvent method.

mouseDrag—java.awt.Component

```
public boolean mouseDrag(Event evt, int x, int y)
```

Called if the mouse is dragged. You drag the mouse when you move the mouse while holding the left mouse button down. The evt Event identifies the event that caused this method to execute. x and y identify the coordinates where the mouse click took place. For more information, see the handleEvent method.

mouseEnter—java.awt.Component

```
public boolean mouseEnter(Event evt, int x, int y)
```

Called when the mouse cursor enters a Component. The evt Event identifies the event that caused this method to execute. x and y identify the coordinates where the mouse click took place. For more information, see the handleEvent method.

mouseExit—java.awt.Component

```
public boolean mouseExit(Event evt, int x, int y)
```

Called when the mouse cursor leaves a Component. The evt Event identifies the event that caused this method to execute. x and y identify the coordinates where the mouse click took place. For more information, see the handleEvent method.

mouseMove—java.awt.Component

```
public boolean mouseMove(Event evt, int x, int y)
```

Called if the mouse moves while no buttons are being pressed. The evt Event identifies the event that caused this method to execute. x and y identify the coordinates where the mouse click took place. For more information, see the handleEvent method.

mouseUp—java.awt.Component

```
public boolean mouseUp(Event evt, int x, inty)
```

Called when the left mouse button is released. The evt Event identifies the event that caused this method to execute. x and y identify the coordinates where the mouse click took place. For more information, see the handleEvent method.

move—java.awt.Component

```
public void move(int x, int y)
```

Moves the Component to a new location in the parent's coordinate space. x and y denote the new position of the Component. For related methods, see the bounds, location, and reshape methods.

move—java.awt.Rectangle

```
public void move(int x, int y)
```

Moves the rectangle to new x,y coordinates.

move—java.awt.Point

```
public void move(int x, int y)
```

Moves a Point to a new x,y coordinate.

NegativeArraySizeException— java.lang.NegativeArraySizeException

```
public NegativeArraySizeException({String detailMessage})
```

An attempt was made to create an array with a negative size. If detailMessage is specified, the detailMessage will be displayed when this throwable is thrown.

newInstance—java.lang.Class

```
public Object newInstance()
```

Creates and returns a new instance of a Class. An InstantiationException exception is thrown if the instantiation fails (for example, if you run out of memory, try to instantiate an abstract class or an interface, and so on). An IllegalAccessException exception is thrown if the class or initializer is not available or accessible.

next—java.awt.CardLayout

```
public void next(Container parent)
```

Goes to the next card of a container. parent is the name of the parent container.

nextDouble—java.util.Random

```
public double nextDouble()
```

Returns the next random double between zero and one.

nextElement—java.util.Enumeration

```
public abstract Object nextElement()
```

Returns the next element of the enumeration. Calls to this method will enumerate successive elements. A NoSuchElementException is thrown if there are no more elements in an Enumeration.

nextElement—java.util.StringTokenizer

```
public Object nextElement()
```

Returns the next token of a StringTokenizer as an Object. A NoSuchElementException is thrown if there are no more tokens in the String.

nextFloat—java.util.Random

```
public float nextFloat()
```

Returns the next random float between zero and one.

nextFocus—java.awt.Component

```
public void nextFocus()
```

Moves the focus from a Component to the next Component. For related information, see requestFocus and gotFocus.

nextFocus—java.awt.peer.ComponentPeer

```
public abstract void nextFocus()
```

Moves the focus from a Component to the next Component. For related information, see requestFocus and gotFocus.

nextGaussian—java.util.Random

`public synchronized double nextGaussian()`

Returns the next random double between zero and one using the Gaussian distribution.

nextInt—java.util.Random

`public int nextInt()`

Returns the next random integer.

nextLong—java.util.Random

`public long nextLong()`

Returns the next random long.

nextToken—java.io.StreamTokenizer

`public int nextToken()`

Parses the next token from an input stream, and the `ttype` attribute is returned. If an error occurs, an `IOExceptions` is thrown.

nextToken—java.util.StringTokenizer

`public String nextToken({String delim})`

Returns the next token of StringToken's String. A `NoSuchElementException` is thrown if there are no more tokens in the String. You can specify a new delimiter set if you wish.

NoClassDefFoundError— java.lang.NoClassDefFoundError

`public NoClassDefFoundError({String detailMessage})`

A class definition could not be found. If `detailMessage` is specified, the `detailMessage` will be displayed when this throwable is thrown.

NoSuchElementException— java.util.NoSuchElementException

```
public NoSuchElementException({String detailMessage})
```

Signals that an enumeration is empty. If `detailMessage` is specified, the `detailMessage` will be displayed when this throwable is thrown.

NoSuchFieldError— java.lang.NoSuchFieldError

```
public NoSuchFieldError({String detailMessage})
```

A specified field could not be found. If `detailMessage` is specified, the `detailMessage` will be displayed when this throwable is thrown.

NoSuchMethodError— java.lang.NoSuchMethodError

```
public NoSuchMethodError({String detailMessage})
```

A specified method could not be found. If `detailMessage` is specified, the `detailMessage` will be displayed when this throwable is thrown.

NoSuchMethodException— java.lang.NoSuchMethodException

```
public NoSuchMethodException({String detailMessage})
```

A specified method could not be found. If `detailMessage` is specified, the `detailMessage` will be displayed when this throwable is thrown.

*notify—*java.lang.Object

```
public final void notify()
```

Notifies a waiting thread on a change in condition of another thread. The `notify` method can only be called from within a `syncrhonized` method. Also see the `wait` and `notifyAll` methods. An `IllegalMonitorStateException` is thrown if the current thread is not the owner of the Object's monitor.

notifyAll—**java.lang.Object**

```
public final void notifyAll()
```

Notifies all of the threads waiting for a condition to change. See the wait and notify methods for related information. An IllegalMonitorStateException is thrown if the current thread is not the owner of the Object's monitor.

notifyObservers (synchronized)— **java.util.Observable**

```
public synchronized void notifyObservers(Object arg)
```

Notifies all observers of the arg of an occuring change.

notifyObservers—**java.util.Observable**

```
public void notifyObservers()
```

Notifies all observers if an observable change occurs.

NullPointerException— **java.lang.NullPointerException**

```
public NullPointerException({String detailMessage})
```

An attempt was made to access a Class (for example, call a class method or access a class attribute) that has not been instantiated (and therefore is equal to null). If detailMessage is specified, the detailMessage will be displayed when this throwable is thrown.

Number—**java.lang.Number**

```
public  Number()
```

Constructs a Number object.

NumberFormatException— java.lang.NumberFormatException

```
public NumberFormatException({String detailMessage})
```

An invalid number format has occurred. This often happens when using the `tostring( )` method. If `detailMessage` is specified, the `detailMessage` will be displayed when this throwable is thrown.

Object—java.lang.Object

```
public  Object()
```

Constructs an Object.

Observable—java.util.Observable

```
public  Observable()
```

Constructs a new Observable object.

openConnection—java.net.URL

```
public URLConnection openConnection()
```

An `URLConnection` object is returned that contains a connection to the URL's remote object. An `IOException` is thrown if an the connection fails.

openConnection— java.net.URLStreamHandler

```
protected abstract URLConnection openConnection(URL u)
```

Opens an `URLConnection` to an URL. This method should be overridden by a subclass. An `IOException` is thrown if an I/O error occurs.

openStream—java.net.URL

```
public final InputStream openStream()
```

Opens and returns an input stream. An `IOException` is thrown if an I/O error occurs.

or—java.util.BitSet

```
public void or(BitSet set)
```

Logically ORs the current BitSet object with another BitSet object.

ordinaryChars—java.io.StreamTokenizer

```
public void ordinaryChars([int low, int high / int ch])
```

Specifies that characters between low and high or the specified character are treated as ordinary characters. These characters are stored in the ttype attribute when encountered.

OutOfMemoryError—java.lang.OutOfMemoryError

```
public OutOfMemoryError({String detailMessage})
```

The Java Virtual Machine that you're running has run out of memory. If detailMessage is specified, the detailMessage will be displayed when this throwable is thrown.

OutputStream—java.io.OutputStream

```
public  OutputStream()
```

Constructs an OutputStream object.

pack—java.awt.Window

```
public synchronized void pack()
```

Packs the components of the Window.

paint—java.awt.Canvas

```
public void paint(Graphics g)
```

Paints the canvas in the default background color. g is the specified Graphics window. paint in the Canvas class overrides paint in the Component class.

paint—java.awt.Component

```
public void paint(Graphics g)
```

Paints a Component. g is the specified Graphics window. For more information, see the update and repaint methods or the Graphics class.

paint—java.awt.peer.ComponentPeer

```
public abstract void paint(Graphics g)
```

Paints a Component. g is the specified Graphics window. For more information, see the update and repaint methods or the Graphics class.

paintAll—java.awt.Component

```
public void paintAll(Graphics g)
```

Paints a Component and its subcomponents. g is the specified Graphics window. For related information, see the update, paint, and repaint methods or the Graphics class.

paintComponents—java.awt.Container

```
public void paintComponents(Graphics g)
```

Paints the components in a Graphics window (specified by g) in a Container. Also check out the paint and paintAll methods and the Graphics class.

Panel—java.awt.Panel

```
public  Panel()
```

Constructs a new panel.

> **TIP:**
> **The default layout for all panels is** FlowLayout.

paramString—java.awt.Button

```
protected String paramString()
```

Returns the parameter String of this button. paramString in the Button class overrides paramString in the Component class.

paramString—java.awt.Component

```
protected String paramString()
```

Returns the parameter String of a Component.

paramString—java.awt.Checkbox

```
protected String paramString()
```

Returns the parameter String of a Checkbox. paramString in the Checkbox class overrides paramString in the Component class.

paramString—java.awt.CheckboxMenuItem

```
public String paramString()
```

Returns the parameter String of a CheckboxMenuItem. paramString in the CheckboxMenuItem class overrides paramstring in the MenuItem class.

paramString—java.awt.Choice

```
protected String paramString()
```

Returns the parameter String of a Choice. paramString in the Choice class overrides paramString in the Component class.

paramString—java.awt.Container

```
protected String paramString()
```

Returns the parameter String of a Container. The paramString method in the Container class overrides the paramString method in the Component class.

paramString—java.awt.Dialog

```
protected String paramString()
```

Returns the parameter String of this Dialog. The paramString method in the Dialog class overrides the paramString method in the Container class.

paramString—java.awt.Event

```
protected String paramString()
```

Returns the parameter String of an Event.

paramString—java.awt.FileDialog

```
protected String paramString()
```

Returns the parameter String of a FileDialog. The paramString method in the FileDialog class overrides the paramString method in the FileDialog class.

paramString—java.awt.Frame

```
protected String paramString()
```

Returns the parameter String of a Frame. The paramString method in the Frame class overrides the paramString method in the Container class.

paramString—java.awt.Label

```
protected String paramString()
```

Returns the parameter String of a label. The paramString method in the Label class overrides the paramString method in the Component class.

paramString—java.awt.List

```
protected String paramString()
```

Returns the parameter String of a list. The paramString method with no arguments in the List class overrides the paramString method in the Component class.

paramString— java.awt.MenuComponent

```
protected String paramString()
```

Returns the String parameter of a MenuComponent.

paramString—java.awt.MenuItem

```
public String paramString()
```

Returns the String parameter of a MenuItem. The `paramString` method in the MenuItem class overrides the `paramString` method in the MenuComponent class.

paramString—java.awt.Scrollbar

```
protected String paramString()
```

Returns the String parameters for a Scrollbar. The `paramString` method in the Scrollbar class overrides the `paramString` method in the Component class.

paramString—java.awt.TextArea

```
protected String paramString()
```

Returns the String of parameters used to construct a TextArea. The `paramString` method in the TextArea class overrides the `paramString` method in the TextComponent class.

paramString—java.awt.TextComponent

```
protected String paramString()
```

Returns the String of parameters used to construct a TextComponent. The `paramString` method in the TextComponent class overrides the `paramString` method in the Component class.

paramString—java.awt.TextField

```
protected String paramString()
```

Returns the String containing the parameters used in constructing a TextField. The `paramString` method in the TextField class overrides the `paramString` method in the Component class.

parentOf—java.lang.ThreadGroup

```
public final boolean parentOf(ThreadGroup g)
```

Returns true if this ThreadGroup is the parent of or equal to a passed ThreadGroup. Otherwise, false is returned.

parse—java.util.Date

```
public static long parse(String s)
```

Converts a String to a long date value.

parseInt—java.lang.Integer

```
public static int parseInt(String s{,int radix})
```

Returns an integer contained in a string. A radix is the base used, and defaults to 10 (for based-10 number systems). 16 (hexidecimal) and 8 (octal) may also prove useful. A NumberFormatException exception is thrown if the String passed to the parseInt method is not a valid integer.

parseLong—java.lang.Long

```
public static long parseLong(String s{,int radix})
```

Returns an integer contained in a string. A radix is the base used, and defaults to 10 (for based-10 number systems). 16 (hexidecimal) and 8 (octal) may also prove useful. A NumberFormatException exception is thrown if the String passed to the parseLong method is not a valid long integer.

parseNumbers— java.io.StreamTokenizer

```
public void parseNumbers()
```

Specifies that numbers should be parsed. This method accepts double precision floating point numbers and returns a ttype of TT_NUMBER with the value in nval.

*parseURL—*java.net.URLStreamHandler

```
protected void parseURL(URL u, String spec,
    int start, int limit)
```

Parses a String spec (defined by spec, start, and limit) into an URL.

*peek—*java.util.Stack

```
public Object peek()
```

Returns the object at the top of the Stack, but does not pop the object off the stack. An EmptyStackException is thrown if there are no elements on the stack.

*PipedInputStream—*java.io.PipedInputStream

```
public  PipedInputStream({PipedOutputStream pos})
```

Creates an input file. If a PipedOutputStream is specified, then the input stream is connected to the PipedOutputStream. If the PipedOutputStream is not yet specified, it must be specified before a PipedInputStream can be used. See the connect method for more details. An IOException is thrown if any I/O error occurs.

*PipedOutputStream—*java.io.PipedOutputStream

```
public  PipedOutputStream({PipedInputStream pis})
```

Creates an output file. If a PipedInputStream is specified, then the output stream is connected to the PipedInputStream. If the PipedInputStream is not yet specified, it must be specified before a PipedOutputStream can be used. See the connect method for more details. An IOException is thrown if any I/O error occurs.

PixelGrabber— java.awt.image.PixelGrabber

```
public  PixelGrabber([ImageProducer ip / Image img], int x,
     int y, int w, int h, int pix[], int off, int scansize)
```

Constructs a PixelGrabber object to grab pixels from an Image or ImageProducer found in the rectangle defined by x, y, w (width), and h (height). The pixels are stored in the `pix array` argument. `Offset` is where to store the first pixel, and `scansize` is the distance between rows of pixels in the array. Also see the `getRGBdefault` method.

*play—*java.applet.Applet

```
public void play(URL url {, String name})
```

Plays an audio clip given to or relative to an URL. Nothing happens if the audio clip could not be found.

*play—*java.applet.AudioClip

```
public abstract void play()
```

Starts playing the clip. Each time this method is called, the clip is restarted from the beginning.

*Point—*java.awt.Point

```
public  Point(int x, int y)
```

Constructs a Point object and sets the x and y coordinates.

*Polygon—*java.awt.Polygon

```
public  Polygon({int xcoords[], int ycoords[], int npoints})
```

Constructs and initializes a Polygon from arrays of x and y coordinates. The npoints argument describes how many points are in the polygon. If xcoords, ycoords, and npoints are omitted, an empty polygon is created.

pop—**java.util.Stack**

`public Object pop()`

Pops an object off the stack. An `EmptyStackException` is thrown if there are no elements on the stack.

postEvent—**java.awt.Component**

`public boolean postEvent(Event e)`

Posts an event to a Component to be delivered after the current method. A call is made to `handleEvent` with the `postEvent` method. If `handleEvent` returns false, then the event is passed on to the parent of the Component for execution. Otherwise, this Component executes the event. For more information, see the `handleEvent` and `deliverEvent` methods.

postEvent—**java.awt.MenuComponent**

`public boolean postEvent(Event evt)`

Posts the specified event to the menu to be triggered after the current method is finished executing.

postEvent—**java.awt.MenuContainer**

`public abstract boolean postEvent(Event evt)`

Posts an event to be executed.

pow—**java.lang.Math**

`public static double pow(double a, double b)`

Returns a raised to the b power. An `ArithmeticException` is possibly thrown if a and b are both less than zero.

preferredLayoutSize— **java.awt.BorderLayout**

`public Dimension preferredLayoutSize(Container target)`

Returns the preferred dimensions for this layout given the components in the specified target container. `target` is the component which needs to be laid out. For more information, see the `minimumLayoutSize` method and the `Container` class documented in the InfoViewer.

preferredLayoutSize—
java.awt.CardLayout

```
public Dimension preferredLayoutSize(Container parent)
```

Calculates the preferred size for the specified panel and returns the panel's dimensions. `parent` is the name of the parent container. For more information, see the `minimumLayoutSize` method.

preferredLayoutSize—
java.awt.FlowLayout

```
public Dimension preferredLayoutSize(Container target)
```

Returns the preferred dimensions for a layout given the components in the `Container` argument. See the Component, Dimension, and Container classes and the `minimumLayoutSize` method for related informaiton.

preferredLayoutSize—
java.awt.GridLayout

```
public Dimension preferredLayoutSize(Container parent)
```

Returns the preferred dimensions needed to layout components in a Container. Also check out the `minimumLayoutSize` method.

preferredLayoutSize—
java.awt.LayoutManager

```
public abstract Dimension preferredLayoutSize(
    Container parent)
```

Calculates the preferred size dimensions for the specified panel given the components in the specified parent container. `parent` is the component to be laid out. For more information, see `minimumLayoutSize`.

preferredSize—java.awt.Component

```
public Dimension preferredSize()
```

Returns a Component's preferred size. For related information, see the `minimumSize` method, or the LayoutManager or Dimension classes.

preferredSize— java.awt.peer.ComponentPeer

```
public abstract Dimension preferredSize()
```

Returns a Component's preferred size. For related information, see the `minimumSize` method, or the LayoutManager or Dimension classes.

preferredSize—java.awt.Container

```
public synchronized Dimension preferredSize()
```

Returns the preferred size of a Container. The `preferredSize` method in the Container class overrides the `preferredSize` method in the Component class. Also, see the `minimumSize` method and the Dimension class.

preferredSize—java.awt.List

```
public Dimension preferredSize({int rows})
```

Returns the preferred dimensions needed for a List. If the number of rows is given, then `preferredSize` returns the preferred dimensions for a List with a given number of rows. The `preferredSize` method with no arguments in the List class overrides the `preferredSize` method in the Component class. Also see the `minimumSize` method.

preferredSize—java.awt.peer.ListPeer

```
public abstract Dimension preferredSize({int rows})
```

Returns the preferred dimensions needed for a List. If the number of rows is given, then `preferredSize` returns the preferred dimensions for a List with a given number of rows. Also see the `minimumSize` method.

preferredSize—java.awt.TextArea

```
public Dimension preferredSize({int rows, int cols})
```

Returns the preferred size Dimensions of a TextArea, or of a TextArea's specified rows and columns if given. The `preferredSize` method with no arguments in the TextArea class overrides the `preferredSize` method in the Component class.

preferredSize— java.awt.peer.TextAreaPeer

```
public abstract Dimension preferredSize(
    {int rows, int cols})
```

Returns the preferred size Dimensions of a TextArea, or of a TextArea's specified rows and columns if given. The `preferredSize` method with no arguments in the TextArea class overrides the `preferredSize` method in the Component class.

preferredSize—java.awt.TextField

```
public Dimension preferredSize({int columns})
```

Returns the preferred size Dimensions needed for a TextField. If `columns` is specified, the preferred size Dimensions needed for a TextField with the specified amount of columns is returned. The `preferredSize` method in the TextField class overrides the `preferredSize` method in the Component class. Also see the `minimumSize` method.

preferredSize— java.awt.peer.TextFieldPeer

```
public abstract Dimension preferredSize({int columns})
```

Returns the preferred size Dimensions needed for a TextField. If `columns` is specified, the preferred size Dimensions needed for a TextField with the specified amount of columns is returned. The `preferredSize` method in the TextField class overrides the `preferredSize` method in the Component class. Also see the `minimumSize` method.

prepareImage—*java.awt.***Component**

```
public boolean prepareImage(Image image,
    {int width, int height,}ImageObserver observer)
```

Prepares an image for rendering on a Component. Image data is downloaded in another thread. Then the screen image is generated. An ImageObserver object will be notified as the image is being prepared. True is returned if the image has already been prepared. Otherwise, false is returned. For more information, see the Image and ImageObserver classes. You may specify the width and height of the new image. Otherwise, the default width and height is the width and height of the control.

prepareImage— *java.awt.peer.***ComponentPeer**

```
public abstract boolean prepareImage(Image image,
    {int width, int height,}ImageObserver observer)
```

Prepares an image for rendering on a Component. Image data is downloaded in another thread. Then, the screen image is generated. An ImageObserver object will be notified as the image is being prepared. True is returned if the image has already been prepared. Otherwise, false is returned. For more information, see the Image and ImageObserver classes. You may specify the width and height of the new image. Otherwise, the default width and height is the width and height of the control.

prepareImage—*java.awt.***Toolkit**

```
public abstract boolean prepareImage(Image image,
    int width, int height, ImageObserver observer)
```

Prepares an image for rendering at a specified width and height.

previous—*java.awt.***CardLayout**

```
public void previous(Container parent)
```

Goes to the previous card of a container. parent is the name of the parent container.

print (non-string)—java.io.PrintStream

```
public void print(element)
```

Prints an element. The element can be an Object, character, integer, long integer, floating point number, double precision floating point number, or boolean. The `print` method is overloaded to handle each datatype.

print (string)—java.io.PrintStream

```
public synchronized void print([String s / char[] s])
```

Prints a string or a character array.

print—java.awt.Component

```
public void print(Graphics g)
```

Prints a Component. The `print` method usually calls the `paint` method, depending on your Web browser. g is the Graphics window. For related information, see the `paint` method or the Graphics class.

print—java.awt.peer.ComponentPeer

```
public abstract void print(Graphics g)
```

Prints a Component. The `print` method usually calls the `paint` method, depending on your Web browser. g is the Graphics window. For related information, see the `paint` method or the Graphics class.

printAll—java.awt.Component

```
public void printAll(Graphics g)
```

Prints a Component and its subcomponents. g is the Graphics window. For related information, see the `print` method or the Graphics class.

printComponents—java.awt.Container

```
public void printComponents(Graphics g)
```

Prints the components in a Graphics window (specified by g) in a Container. Also see the `print` and `printAll` methods and the Graphics class.

println—java.io.PrintStream

```
public void println({element})
```

Prints a newline character. If an element is specified, the element is printed before the newline character. The element can be an Object, String, character array, character, integer, long integer, floating point number, double precision floating point number, or boolean. The println method is overloaded to handle each datatype.

printStackTrace—java.lang.Throwable

```
public void printStackTrace({PrintStream s})
```

Prints the Throwable and the Throwable's stack trace into a specified PrintStream, or into the standard print stream if no other print stream is specified.

PrintStream—java.io.PrintStream

```
public  PrintStream(OutputStream out{,boolean autoflush})
```

Constructs a new PrintStream from an OutputStream. If autoflush is omitted or set to false, no auto flushing occurs. If autoflush is set to true, flushing automatically occurs every time a newline character is written to the PrintStream buffer.

Process—java.lang.Process

```
public  Process()
```

Constructs a Process object.

Properties—java.util.Properties

```
public  Properties({Properties defaults})
```

Constructs an empty Properties object. If defaults are specifed, the defaults are set for the Properties object.

propertyNames—java.util.Properties

```
public Enumeration propertyNames()
```

Returns an enumeration of all the property keys.

ProtocolException— java.net.ProtocolException

```
public ProtocolException({String detailMessage})
```

A connect gets an EPROTO return. This exception is specifically caught in the Sock class. If detailMessage is specified, the detailMessage will be displayed when this throwable is thrown.

*push—*java.util.Stack

```
public Object push(Object item)
```

Pushes an object onto the stack.

*pushBack—*java.io.StreamTokenizer

```
public void pushBack()
```

Pushes back a stream token onto the StreamTokenizer buffer. This is handy for parsing.

PushbackInputStream— java.io.PushbackInputStream

```
public  PushbackInputStream(InputStream in)
```

Constructs a PushbackInputStream from an InputStream object.

*put—*java.util.Dictionary

```
public abstract Object put(Object key, Object value)
```

Puts an object into a Dictionary. The key is the hashtable key and the value is the value associated with that hashtable key. A NullPointerException is thrown if the key or the value are null.

*put—*java.util.Hashtable

```
public synchronized Object put(Object key, Object value)
```

Places the specified element into the hashtable, using the specified key. The element may be retrieved by calling the get method with the same key. The key and the element cannot be null, or a

`NullPointerException` is thrown. The put method in the Hashtable class overrides the put method in the Dictionary class.

quoteChar—java.io.StreamTokenizer

```
public void quoteChar(int ch)
```

Identifies the character that starts and ends a quote.

random—java.lang.Math

```
public static synchronized double random()
```

Generates a random number between 0.0 and 1.0.

Random—java.util.Random

```
public  Random({long seed})
```

Constructs a new random number generator. If a seed is provided, the random number is generated with the specific seed.

RandomAccessFile— java.io.RandomAccessFile

```
public  RandomAccessFile(
    [File fileObject / String fileName], String mode)
```

Constructs a `RandomAccessFile` with the specified file name or specified File object and the specified mode. Valid modes are "r" for read-only access and "rw" for read and write access. An `IOException` is thrown if an I/O error occurs.

read (byte)— java.io.BufferedInputStream

```
public synchronized int read()
```

Reads a byte of data. This method will block output to a file until input is available. The byte read is returned, or a –1 if the end of the stream is reached. `IOException` is thrown if an I/O error has occured. The read method in the `BufferedInputStream` class overrides the read method in the `FilterInputStream` class.

read (byte)—
java.io.ByteArrayInputStream

```
public synchronized int read()
```

Reads a byte of data. This method will block output to a file until input is available. The byte read is returned, or a –1 if the end of the stream is reached. `IOException` is thrown if an I/O error has occured. The `read` method in the `ByteArrayInputStream` class overrides the `read` method in the `InputStream` class.

read (byte)—java.io.FileInputStream

```
public int read()
```

Reads a byte of data. This method will block output to a file until input is available. The byte read is returned, or a –1 if the end of the stream is reached. `IOException` is thrown if an I/O error has occured. The `read` method in the `FileInputStream` class overrides the `read` method in the `InputStream` class.

read (byte)—java.io.FilterInputStream

```
public int read()
```

Reads a byte of data. This method will block output to a file until input is available. The byte read is returned, or a –1 if the end of the stream is reached. `IOException` is thrown if an I/O error has occured. The `read` method in the `FilterInputStream` class overrides the `read` method in the `InputStream` class.

read (byte)—java.io.InputStream

```
public abstract int read()
```

Reads a byte of data. This method will block output to a file until input is available. The byte read is returned, or a –1 if the end of the stream is reached. `IOException` is thrown if an I/O error has occured.

read (byte)—
java.io.LineNumberInputStream

```
public int read()
```

Reads a byte of data. This method will block output to a file until input is available. The byte read is returned, or a –1 if the end of the stream is reached. `IOException` is thrown if an I/O error has occured. The `read` method in the `LineNumberInputStream` class overrides the `read` method in the `FilterInputStream` class.

read (byte)—java.io.PipedInputStream

```
public synchronized int read()
```

Reads a byte of data. This method will block output to a file until input is available. The byte read is returned, or a –1 if the end of the stream is reached. `IOException` is thrown if an I/O error has occured. The `read` method in the `PipedInputStream` class overrides the `read` method in the `InputStream` class.

read (byte)— java.io.PushbackInputStream

```
public int read()
```

Reads a byte of data. This method will block output to a file until input is available. The byte read is returned, or a –1 if the end of the stream is reached. `IOException` is thrown if an I/O error has occured. The `read` method in the `PushbackInputStream` overrides the `read` method in the `FilterInputStream` class.

read (byte)—java.io.RandomAccessFile

```
public int read()
```

Reads a byte of data. This method will block output to a file until input is available. The byte read is returned, or a –1 if the end of the stream is reached. `IOException` is thrown if an I/O error has occured.

read (byte)— java.io.SequenceInputStream

```
public int read()
```

Reads a byte of data. This method will block output to a file until input is available. The byte read is returned, or a –1 if the end of the stream is reached. `IOException` is thrown if an I/O error has occured. The `read` method in the `SequenceInputStream` class overrides the `read` method in the `InputStream` class.

read (byte)— java.io.StringBufferInputStream

```
public synchronized int read()
```

Reads a byte of data. This method will block output to a file until input is available. The byte read is returned, or a –1 if the end of the stream is reached. The read method in the StringBufferInputStream class overrides the read method in the InputStream class.

read (byte array)— java.io.BufferedInputStream

```
public synchronized int read(
    byte buffer[], int offset, int maximumBytes)
```

Reads bytes starting from an offset into a buffer. The read method blocks output until all bytes are read, or until maximumBytes are read. The number of bytes read is returned, or a –1 if the end of the stream is reached. IOException is thrown if an I/O error has occured. The read method in the BufferedInputStream class overrides the read method in the FilterInputStream class.

read (byte array)— java.io.ByteArrayInputStream

```
public synchronized int read(
    byte buffer[], int offset, int maximumBytes)
```

Reads bytes starting from an offset into a buffer. The read method blocks output until all bytes are read, or until maximumBytes are read. The number of bytes read is returned, or a –1 if the end of the stream is reached. The read method in the ByteArrayInputStream overrides the read method in the InputStream class.

read (byte array)— java.io.DataInputStream

```
public final int read(
    byte buffer[]{, int offset, int maximumBytes})
```

Reads bytes starting from an offset (if specified) into a buffer. The read method blocks output until all bytes are read, or until maximumBytes (if specified) are read. The number of bytes read is returned, or a –1 if the end of the stream is reached. `IOException` is thrown if an I/O error has occured. The `read` method in the `DataInputStream` class overrides the `read` method in the `FilterInputStream` class.

read (byte array)— java.io.FileInputStream

```
public int read(
    byte buffer[]{, int offset, int maximumBytes})
```

Reads bytes starting from the current stream pointer (or from an offset if given) into a buffer. The read method blocks output until all bytes are read (or until `maximumBytes` are read if `maximumBytes` is provided). The number of bytes read is returned, or a –1 if the end of the stream is reached. `IOException` is thrown if an I/O error has occured. The `read` method in the `FileInputStream` class overrides the `read` method in the `InputStream` class.

read (byte array)— java.io.FilterInputStream

```
public int read(byte buffer[], int offset, int maximumBytes)
```

Reads bytes starting from an offset into a buffer. The `read` method blocks output until all bytes are read, or until `maximumBytes` are read. The number of bytes read is returned, or a –1 if the end of the stream is reached. `IOException` is thrown if an I/O error has occured. The `read` method in the `FilterInputStream` class overrides the `read` method in the `InputStream` class.

read (byte array)—java.io.InputStream

```
public int read(byte buffer[], int offset, int maximumBytes)
```

Reads bytes starting from an offset into a buffer. The `read` method blocks output until all bytes are read, or until `maximumBytes` are read. The number of bytes read is returned, or a –1 if the end of the stream is reached. `IOException` is thrown if an I/O error has occured.

read (byte array)— java.io.LineNumberInputStream

```
public int read(byte buffer[], int offset, int maximumBytes)
```

Reads bytes starting from an offset if given into a buffer. The read method blocks output until all bytes are read or until maximumBytes are read. The number of bytes read is returned, or a –1 if the end of the stream is reached. IOException is thrown if an I/O error has occured. The read method in the LineNumberInputStream class overrides the read method in the FilterInputStream class.

read (byte array)— java.io.PipedInputStream

```
public synchronized int read(
    byte buffer[], int offset, int maximumBytes)
```

Reads bytes starting from an offset into a buffer. The read method blocks output until all bytes are read, or until maximumBytes are read. The number of bytes read is returned, or a –1 if the end of the stream is reached. IOException is thrown if an I/O error has occured. The read method in the PipedInputStream class overrides the read method in the InputStream class.

read (byte array)— java.io.PushbackInputStream

```
public int read(byte buffer[], int offset, int maximumBytes)
```

Reads bytes starting from an offset into a buffer. The read method blocks output until all bytes are read, or until maximumBytes are read. The number of bytes read is returned, or a –1 if the end of the stream is reached. IOException is thrown if an I/O error has occured. The read method in the PushbackInputStream overrides the read method in the FilterInputStream class.

read (byte array)— java.io.RandomAccessFile

```
public int read(
    byte buffer[]{, int offset, int maximumBytes})
```

Reads bytes starting from an offset (if given) into a byte array . The read method blocks output until all bytes are read, or until maximumBytes (if given) are read. The number of bytes read is returned, or a –1 if the end of the stream is reached. IOException is thrown if an I/O error has occured.

read (byte array)— java.io.SequenceInputStream

```
public int read(byte buffer[], int offset, int maximumBytes)
```

Reads bytes starting from an offset into a buffer. The read method blocks output until all bytes are read, or until maximumBytes are read. The number of bytes read is returned, or a –1 if the end of the stream is reached. IOException is thrown if an I/O error has occured. The read method in the SequenceInputStream class overrides the read method in the InputStream class.

read (byte array)— java.io.StringBufferInputStream

```
public synchronized int read(
    byte buffer[], int offset, int maximumBytes)
```

Reads bytes starting from an offset into a buffer. The read method blocks output until all bytes are read, or until maximumBytes are read. The number of bytes read is returned, or a –1 if the end of the stream is reached. The read method in the StringBufferInputStream overrides the read method in the InputStream class.

readBoolean—java.io.DataInput

```
public abstract boolean readBoolean()
```

Reads a boolean and returns it. This method throws EOFException if the end of file is reached and IOException for all other I/O errors.

readBoolean—java.io.DataInputStream

```
public final boolean readBoolean()
```

Reads and returns a boolean.

readBoolean—java.io.RandomAccessFile

```
public final boolean readBoolean()
```

Reads a boolean and returns it.

readByte—java.io.DataInput

```
public abstract byte readByte()
```

Reads a byte and returns it. This method throws EOFException if the end of file is reached and IOException for all other I/O errors.

readByte—java.io.DataInputStream

```
public final byte readByte()
```

Reads and returns an 8-bit (ASCII) byte.

readByte—java.io.RandomAccessFile

```
public final byte readByte()
```

Reads an 8-bit (ASCII) byte and returns it.

readChar—java.io.DataInput

```
public abstract char readChar()
```

Reads a 16-bit (unicode) character and returns it. This method throws EOFException if the end of file is reached and IOException for all other I/O errors.

readChar—java.io.DataInputStream

```
public final char readChar()
```

Reads and returns a 16-bit (Unicode) character.

readChar—java.io.RandomAccessFile

```
public final char readChar()
```

Reads a 16-bit (Unicode) character and returns it.

readDouble—java.io.DataInput

```
public abstract double readDouble()
```

Reads a 64-bit double precision floating point number and returns it. This method throws EOFException if the end of file is reached and IOException for all other I/O errors.

readDouble—java.io.DataInputStream

```
public final double readDouble()
```

Reads and returns a 64-bit double precision floating point number.

readDouble—java.io.RandomAccessFile

```
public final double readDouble()
```

Reads a 64-bit double precision floating point number and returns it.

readFloat—java.io.DataInput

```
public abstract float readFloat()
```

Reads a 32-bit floating point number and returns it. This method throws EOFException if the end of file is reached and IOException for all other I/O errors.

readFloat—java.io.DataInputStream

```
public final float readFloat()
```

Reads and returns a 32-bit floating point number.

readFloat—java.io.RandomAccessFile

```
public final float readFloat()
```

Reads a 32-bit floating point number and returns it.

readFully—java.io.DataInput

```
public abstract void readFully(
    byte buffer[]{, int offset, int maximumBytes})
```

Reads bytes starting from an offset (if given) into a buffer. The readFully method blocks output until all bytes are read, or until maximumBytes (if given) is read. This method throws EOFException if the end of file is reached and IOException for all other I/O errors.

readFully—java.io.DataInputStream

```
public final void readFully(byte buffer[]{, int offset,
    int maximumBytes})
```

Reads bytes starting from an offset (if given) into a buffer. The readFully method blocks output until all bytes are read, or until maximumBytes (if given) is read. This method throws EOFException if the end of file is reached and IOException for all other I/O errors.

readFully—java.io.RandomAccessFile

```
public final void readFully(
    byte buffer[]{, int offset, int maximumBytes})
```

Reads bytes starting from an offset (if given) into a buffer. The readFully method blocks output until all bytes are read, or until maximumBytes (if given) is read. Returns the number of bytes read or –1 if the end of the stream is reached. This method throws IOException for all other I/O errors.

readInt—java.io.DataInput

```
public abstract int readInt()
```

Reads a 32-bit integer and returns it. This method throws EOFException if the end of file is reached and IOException for all other I/O errors.

readInt—java.io.DataInputStream

```
public final int readInt()
```

Reads and returns a 32-bit integer.

readInt—**java.io.RandomAccessFile**

```
public final int readInt()
```

Reads a 32-bit integer and returns it.

readLine—**java.io.DataInput**

```
public abstract String readLine()
```

Reads a string up to an end of line character and returns the string. (The end of line character is not returned with the string.) This method throws EOFException if the end of file is reached and IOException for all other I/O errors.

readLine—**java.io.DataInputStream**

```
public final String readLine()
```

Reads in a line into a returned String that has been terminated by \\n, \\r, \\r\\n, or EOF.

readLine—**java.io.RandomAccessFile**

```
public final String readLine()
```

Reads a String line terminated by \\n or EOF and returns it.

readLong—**java.io.DataInput**

```
public abstract long readLong()
```

Reads a 64-bit long and returns it. This method throws EOFException if the end of file is reached and IOException for all other I/O errors.

readLong—**java.io.DataInputStream**

```
public final long readLong()
```

Reads and returns a 64-bit long integer.

readLong—**java.io.RandomAccessFile**

```
public final long readLong()
```

Reads a 64-bit long and returns it.

readShort—java.io.DataInput

```
public abstract short readShort()
```

Reads a 16-bit short integer and returns it. This method throws EOFException if the end of file is reached and IOException for all other I/O errors.

readShort—java.io.DataInputStream

```
public final short readShort()
```

Reads and returns a 16-bit short integer.

readShort—java.io.RandomAccessFile

```
public final short readShort()
```

Reads a 16-bit short integer and returns it.

readUnsignedByte—java.io.DataInput

```
public abstract int readUnsignedByte()
```

Reads an unsigned byte and returns it. This method throws EOFException if the end of file is reached and IOException for all other I/O errors.

readUnsignedByte—java.io.DataInputStream

```
public final int readUnsignedByte()
```

Reads and returns an unsigned 8-bit byte.

readUnsignedByte—java.io.RandomAccessFile

```
public final int readUnsignedByte()
```

Reads an 8-bit unsigned byte and returns it.

readUnsignedShort—java.io.DataInput

```
public abstract int readUnsignedShort()
```

Reads a 16-bit unsigned short integer and returns it. This method throws EOFException if the end of file is reached and IOException for all other I/O errors.

readUnsignedShort— java.io.DataInputStream

```
public final int readUnsignedShort()
```

Reads and returns a 16-bit unsigned short integer.

readUnsignedShort— java.io.RandomAccessFile

```
public final int readUnsignedShort()
```

Reads 16-bit short integer and returns it.

readUTF (non-static)— java.io.DataInputStream

```
public final String readUTF()
```

Reads and returns a UTF (ASCII) format String.

readUTF (static)— java.io.DataInputStream

```
public final static String readUTF(DataInput in)
```

Reads and returns a UTF format String from an input stream.

readUTF—java.io.DataInput

```
public abstract String readUTF()
```

Reads bytes into a String until all bytes are read from an 8-bit UTF file. (ASCII files are stored in this manner.) This method throws EOFException if the end of file is reached and IOException for all other I/O errors.

readUTF—java.io.RandomAccessFile

```
public final String readUTF()
```

Reads a UTF (ASCII) formatted String and returns it.

Rectangle—java.awt.Rectangle

```
public   Rectangle({argument list})
```

Constructs a new rectangle. The `argument list`, if provided, can define the rectangle width and height as well as x,y coordinates. Valid argument lists are: `(int x, int y, int width, int height)`, `(int width, int height)`, `(Point p, Dimension d)`, `(Point p)`, and `(Dimension d)`.

regionMatches—java.lang.String

```
public boolean regionMatches({boolean ignoreCase,}
     int otherOffset, String otherString, int offset, int len)
```

Returns true if a region of this String matches the specified region in an `otherString`. The `offset` and length define the compare substring. The `otherOffset` defines the substring to compare in the `otherString`. If you want to, you can specify true in the `ignoreCase` argument to make the compare case insensitive.

rehash—java.util.Hashtable

```
protected void rehash()
```

Rehashes a hashtable into a bigger table.

remove—java.awt.Container

```
public synchronized void remove(Component comp)
```

Removes a component from a container. Also see the `add` (layout and non-layout) method.

remove—java.util.Dictionary

```
public abstract Object remove(Object key)
```

Removes a value associated with a key from a Dictionary. The value of the key is returned, or null if the key was not found.

*remove—*java.awt.Frame

```
public synchronized void remove(MenuComponent menu)
```

Removes a menu bar from a Frame.

*remove—*java.util.Hashtable

```
public synchronized Object remove(Object key)
```

Removes a value associated with a key from a hashtable. The Object removed is returned, or a null if the Object can't be found. The `remove` method in the Hashtable class overrides the `remove` method in the Dictionary class.

*remove—*java.awt.Menu

```
public synchronized void remove(
    [int index/MenuComponent item)
```

Deletes an item identified by an `index` or a `MenuComponent` from a menu.

*remove—*java.awt.MenuBar

```
public synchronized void remove(
    [int index / MenuComponent m])
```

Removes a menu identified by a specified `index` or by a `MenuComponent` from a MenuBar.

*remove—*java.awt.MenuContainer

```
public abstract void remove(MenuComponent comp)
```

Removies a menu item.

*removeAll—*java.awt.Container

```
public synchronized void removeAll()
```

Removes all components from a container. Also see the `add` (layout and non-layout) and `remove` methods.

removeAllElements—java.util.Vector

```
public final synchronous void removeAllElements()
```

Removes all elements from a Vector.

removeConsumer(ImageConsumer ic— java.awt.image.FilteredImageSource

```
public synchronized void removeConsumer(ImageConsumer ic)
```

This method removes an `ImageConsumer` object from the list of consumers currently registered to an `FilteredImageSource`. Also see the `startProduction`, `isConsumer`, and `addConsumer` methods.

removeConsumer(ImageConsumer ic— java.awt.image.MemoryImageSource

```
public synchronized void removeConsumer(ImageConsumer ic)
```

This method removes an `ImageConsumer` object from the list of consumers currently registered to an `MemoryImageSource`. Also see the `startProduction`, `isConsumer`, and `addConsumer` methods.

removeConsumer— java.awt.image.ImageProducer

```
public abstract void removeConsumer(ImageConsumer ic)
```

This method removes an `ImageConsumer` object from the list of consumers currently registered to an `ImageProducer`. Also see the `startProduction`, `isConsumer`, and `addConsumer` methods.

removeElement—java.util.Vector

```
public final synchronous boolean removeElement(Object obj)
```

Removes the first occurance of an object from a Vector. A true is returned if the object was found and removed successfully. Otherwise, a false is returned.

removeElementAt—java.util.Vector

```
public final synchronous void removeElementAt(int index)
```

Removes the Vector element at an index. All subsequent indexes are moved down by one. An `ArrayIndexOutOfBoundsException` is thrown if the index was invalid.

removeLayoutComponent— java.awt.BorderLayout

```
public void removeLayoutComponent(Component comp)
```

Removes the specified component from the layout. `comp` is the component to be removed.

removeLayoutComponent— java.awt.CardLayout

```
public void removeLayoutComponent(Component comp)
```

Removes the specified component from the layout.

removeLayoutComponent— java.awt.FlowLayout

```
public void removeLayoutComponent(Component comp)
```

Removes a component from a layout.

removeLayoutComponent— java.awt.GridLayout

```
public void removeLayoutComponent(Component comp)
```

Removes a component a layout.

removeLayoutComponent— java.awt.LayoutManager

```
public abstract void removeLayoutComponent(Component comp)
```

Removes the specified component from the layout. `comp` is the component to be removed.

removeNotify—java.awt.Component

```
public synchronized void removeNotify()
```

Notifies a Component to destroy a peer. For more information, see `getPeer` and `addNotify`.

removeNotify—java.awt.Container

```
public synchronized void removeNotify()
```

Notifies a Container and all Components contained in a Container to remove their peers. The `removeNotify` method in the Container class overrides the `removeNotify` method in the Component class. Also check out the `removeNotify` method.

removeNotify—java.awt.List

```
public synchronized void removeNotify()
```

Removes the peer for this list. A peer lets lets you change the list's appearance without changing its functionality. The `removeNotify` method in the List class overrides the `removeNotify` method in the Component class. Also check out the `addNotify` method.

removeNotify—java.awt.Menu

```
public synchronized void removeNotify()
```

Removes the peer from a menu. A peer lets you change the appearance of the menu without changing its functionality. The `removeNotify` method in the Menu class overrides the `removeNotify` method in the MenuComponent class.

removeNotify—java.awt.MenuBar

```
public void removeNotify()
```

Removes the peer from a MenuBar. A peer lets you change the appearance of the menu without changing its functionality. The `removeNotify` method in the MenuBar class overrides the `removeNotify` method in the MenuComponent class.

removeNotify— java.awt.MenuComponent

```
public void removeNotify()
```

Removes a menu component's peer. A peer lets you change the appearance of the menu component without changing the functionality of the menu component.

removeNotify— java.awt.TextComponent

```
public synchronized void removeNotify()
```

Removes a TextComponent's peer. A peer lets you change the appearance of a TextComponent without changing its functionality. The removeNotify method in the TextComponent class overrides the removeNotify method in the Component class.

renameTo—java.io.File

```
public boolean renameTo(File dest)
```

Renames the file in a File object. A true is returned if the rename was successful; otherwise, a false is returned.

repaint—java.awt.Component

```
public void repaint({long tm}
    {, int x, int y, int width, int height})
```

Repaints a Component. The repaint method calls the update method within tm milliseconds or as soon as possible if tm is omitted. Repaints the part of a Component specified by x, y (coordinates within the parent container), and width and height. If x, y, width, and height are omitted, the entire component is repainted. For related information, see the update, paint, and paintall methods.

repaint— java.awt.peer.ComponentPeer

```
public abstract void repaint({long tm}
    {, int x, int y, int width, int height})
```

Repaints a Component. The `repaint` method calls the `update` method within `tm` milliseconds or as soon as possible if `tm` is omitted. Repaints the part of a Component specified by x, y (coordinates within the parent container), and `width` and `height`. If x, y, `width`, and `height` are omitted, the entire component is repainted. For related information, see the `update`, `paint`, and `paintall` methods.

replace—java.lang.String

```
public String replace(char o, char n)
```

Replaces all the occurance of the o (old) character with the n (new) character.

replaceItem—java.awt.List

```
public synchronized void replaceItem(
    String newValue, int index)
```

Replaces an item in a List at the given index.

replaceText—java.awt.TextArea

```
public void replaceText(String str, int start, int end)
```

Searches for and replaces text in a TextArea from the start position to the end position. Also see the `appendText`, `insertText`, `getText`, and `setText` methods.

replaceText—java.awt.peer.TextAreaPeer

```
public abstract void replaceText(
    String str, int start, int end)
```

Searches for and replaces text in a TextArea from the start position to the end position. Also see the `appendText`, `insertText`, `getText`, and `setText` methods.

requestFocus—java.awt.Component

```
public void requestFocus()
```

Requests that focus be given to a Component. The `gotFocus()` method will be called if this method is successful. See the `gotFocus` method for related information.

requestFocus— java.awt.peer.ComponentPeer

```
public abstract void requestFocus()
```

Requests that focus be given to a Component. The `gotFocus()` method will be called if this method is successful. See the `gotFocus` method for related information.

requestTopDownLeftRightResend— java.awt.image.FilteredImageSource

```
public void requestTopDownLeftRightResend(ImageConsumer ic)
```

This method is used by an `ImageConsumer` to request that an `FilteredImageSource` attempt to resend the image data one more time in `TOPDOWNLEFTRIGHT` order. See the `setHint` method for more information.

requestTopDownLeftRightResend— java.awt.image.ImageProducer

```
public abstract void requestTopDownLeftRightResend(
       ImageConsumer ic)
```

This method is used by an `ImageConsumer` to request that an `ImageProducer` attempt to resend the image data one more time in `TOPDOWNLEFTRIGHT` order. See the `setHint` method for more information.

requestTopDownLeftRightResend— java.awt.image.MemoryImageSource

```
public void requestTopDownLeftRightResend(ImageConsumer ic)
```

This method is used by an `ImageConsumer` to request that an `ImageProducer` attempt to resend the image data one more time in `TOPDOWNLEFTRIGHT` order. See the `setHint` method for more information.

resendTopDownLeftRight— java.awt.image.ImageFilter

```
public void resendTopDownLeftRight(ImageProducer ip)
```

Responds to a request for a TOPDOWNLEFTRIGHT ordered resend of the pixel data from an ImageConsumer. The ip argument is the ImageProducer that is feeding this instance of an ImageFilter and is the ImageProducer that the request should be forwarded to.

> **NOTE:**
> An ImageFilter **can respond to a** resendTopDownLeftRight **(TDLR) request in one of three ways:**
>
> - If an ImageFilter processes pixels in TDLR order, then the request is automatically forwarded by default to the indicated ImageProducer using the consumer attribute as the requesting ImageConsumer. No override is necessary.
>
> - If an ImageFilter can resend the pixels in the right order on its own, then it can override the TDLR request and simply resend the pixels in TDLR order as specified in the ImageProducer class.
>
> - If an ImageFilter cannot send pixels in the right order, the TDLR request returns from this method without resending and the request will be ignored.

reset—java.io.BufferedInputStream

```
public synchronized void reset()
```

Repositions the stream to the last marked position. An IOException is thrown if the stream has not been marked or if the mark has been invalidated. See the mark method for more information. The reset method in the BufferedInputStream class overrides the reset method in the FilterInputStream class.

reset—java.io.ByteArrayInputStream

```
public synchronized void reset()
```

Resets the buffer to the beginning. The reset method in the ByteArrayInputStream class overrides the reset method in the InputStream class.

reset—java.io.ByteArrayOutputStream

```
public synchronized void reset()
```

Resets the buffer so that it can be used again.

reset—java.io.FilterInputStream

```
public synchronized void reset()
```

Repositions the stream to the last marked position. An IOException is thrown if the stream has not been marked or if the mark has been invalidated. See the mark method for more information. The reset method in the FilterInputStream class overrides the reset method in the InputStream class.

reset—java.io.InputStream

```
public synchronized void reset()
```

Repositions the stream to the last marked position. An IOException is thrown if the stream has not been marked or if the mark has been invalidated. See the mark method for more information.

reset—java.io.LineNumberInputStream

```
public void reset()
```

Repositions the stream to the last marked position. An IOException is thrown if the stream has not been marked or if the mark has been invalidated. See the mark method for more information. The reset method in the LineNumberInputStream class overrides the reset method in the FilterInputStream class.

reset—java.io.StringBufferInputStream

```
public synchronized void reset()
```

Repositions the StringBufferInputStream to the beginning of the buffer. The reset method in the StringBufferInputStream class overrides the reset method in the InputStream class.

resetSyntax—java.io.StreamTokenizer

```
public void resetSyntax()
```

Resets the syntax table so that all characters are treated as special.

reshape—java.awt.Component

```
public synchronized void reshape(int x, int y,
    int width, int height)
```

Reshapes the Component to a new size (denoted by width and height) and location on the parent's coordinate space (denoted by x and y). For related methods, see the bounds, move, and resize methods.

reshape— java.awt.peer.ComponentPeer

```
public abstract void reshape(int x, int y,
    int width, int height)
```

Reshapes the Component to a new size (denoted by width and height) and location on the parent's coordinate space (denoted by x and y). For related methods, see the bounds, move, and resize methods

reshape—java.awt.Rectangle

```
public void reshape(int x, int y, int width, int height)
```

Reshapes a rectangle to correspond to a new width, height, and x, y coordinates.

resize—java.applet.Applet

```
public void resize([int width, int height]/[Dimension d])
```

Requests that the applet be resized. This method overrides the resize method in the Componenet class.

resize—java.awt.Component

```
public void resize([int width, int height] / [Dimension d])
```

Resizes the Component to a new width and height or a new Component Dimension. For related information, see the Dimension class or the bounds, size, and reshape methods.

resize—java.awt.Rectangle

```
public void resize(int width, int height)
```

Resizes the rectangle to a new width and height.

resolveClass—java.lang.ClassLoader

```
protected final void resolveClass(Class c)
```

Resolves classes referenced by this Class. This must be done before the Class can be used. Class names referenced by the resulting Class are resolved by calling `loadClass()`. Also see the `defineClass` method.

resume—java.lang.Thread

```
public final void resume()
```

Resumes a Thread after a the Thread's suspend method has been called. See the `suspend` method for more information.

resume—java.lang.ThreadGroup

```
public final synchronous void resume()
```

Resumes all the Threads and subgroups in this ThreadGroup.

RGBImageFilter— java.awt.image.RGBImageFilter

```
public   RGBImageFilter()
```

Constructs an RGBImageFilter object.

RGBtoHSB—java.awt.Color

```
public static float[] RGBtoHSB(int red, int green,
     int blue, float hsbvals[])
```

Converts an RGB format defined by red, green, and blue variables to an HSB (Hue, Saturation, Brightness) format. The HSB values are stored in the `hsbvals` array and are also returned from the `RGBtoHSB` method. For related methods, see the `getHSBColor`, `HSBtoRGB`, `getRGBdefault`, and `getRGB` methods.

rint—java.lang.Math

```
public static double rint(double a)
```

Converts a double value into a double format integral value.

round—java.lang.Math

```
public static int round([float / double] a)
```

Rounds off a floating point or double precision floating point value to the nearest whole number.

run—java.lang.Runnable

```
public abstract void run()
```

The run method is executed when a runnable object is activated. The run method and the Runable class should be used in place of an inherited Thread object whenever feasible due to overhead.

run—java.lang.Thread

```
public void run()
```

The run method is the actual body of a Thread. The run method is called after the Thread has started. To use a thread, you must override this method or create a Thread with a Runnable target.

runFinalization—java.lang.Runtime

```
public void runFinalization()
```

Runs the finalization methods of any objects pending finalization.

> **NOTE:**
> Usually, you will call the runFinalization method because finalization methods will be called asynchronously by the finalization thread. However, if you're running low on system resource, you may want to finalize synchronously.

runFinalization—java.lang.System

```
public static void runFinalization()
```

Runs the `finalization` methods of any classes pending finalization.

RuntimeException— java.lang.RuntimeException

```
public RuntimeException({String detailMessage})
```

Parent class to many exceptions. This error occurs during the run-time of a program inside a Java virtual machine. If `detailMessage` is specified, the `detailMessage` will be displayed when this throwable is thrown.

sameFile—java.net.URL

```
public boolean sameFile(URL other)
```

Compares two URLs excluding "ref" fields. A true value is returned if the URLs reference the same remote object. However, the two URLs will still test equal if they point to different subpieces of the remote object.

save—java.util.Properties

```
public synchronized void save(OutputStream out,
    String header)
```

Saves the properties in an output stream.

Scrollbar—java.awt.Scrollbar

```
public  Scrollbar({int orientation
    {, int value, int pageSize, int minimum, int maximum}})
```

Constructs a new Scrollbar. The `orientation` argument can be `HORI-ZONTAL` or `VERTICAL`. If omitted, `VERTICAL` is assumed. The `value` argument where the Scrollbar is set to, or zero if omitted. The `pageSize` argument is the size of the viewing area controlled by the Scrollbar. The `minumum` and `maximum` values of a Scrollbar determine what the value of the Scrollbar will be at the two ends of the Scrollbar.

search—java.util.Stack

```
public int search(Object o)
```

Sees if an object is on the stack and returns the number of the objects above the object on the stack.

SecurityException—java.lang.SecurityException

```
public SecurityException({String detailMessage})
```

An operation attempted by a Visual J++ program is not allowed due to security reasons. If detailMessage is specified, the detailMessage will be displayed when this throwable is thrown.

SecurityManager—java.lang.SecurityManager

```
protected   SecurityManager()
```

Constructs a new SecurityManager object. A SecurityException is thrown if the SecurityManager object can't be constructed.

seek—java.io.RandomAccessFile

```
public void seek(long pos)
```

Sets the file pointer to the specified absolute position. Also see the getFIlePointer method. The pos argument is the absolute position to set the file pointer.

select—java.awt.Choice

```
public synchronized void select([int index/String str])
```

Selects (chooses) the item at an index or with a specified String in a Choice. select throws an IllegalArgumentException if the item position is less than one or greater than the number of items in a Choice. For related items, see getItem, getSelectedItem, and getSelectedIndex.

select—java.awt.List

```
public synchronized void select(int index)
```

Selects the item at the specified index. Also see the `deselect`, `isSelected`, `getSelectedIndex`, `getSelectedIndexes`, `getSelectedItem`, and `getSelectedItems` methods.

select—java.awt.peer.ListPeer

```
public abstract void select(int index)
```

Selects the item at the specified index. Also see the `deselect`, `isSelected`, `getSelectedIndex`, `getSelectedIndexes`, `getSelectedItem`, and `getSelectedItems` methods.

select—java.awt.TextComponent

```
public void select(int selStart, int selEnd)
```

Selects the text between the `selStart` positions and the `selEnd` positions.

select— java.awt.peer.TextComponentPeer

```
public abstract void select(int selStart, int selEnd)
```

Selects the text between the `selStart` positions and the `selEnd` positions.

selectAll—java.awt.TextComponent

```
public void selectAll()
```

Selects all the text in a `TextComponent`.

SequenceInputStream— java.io.SequenceInputStream

```
public  SequenceInputStream(
    [Enumeration e / InputStream s1, InputStream s2])
```

Constructs a new SequenceInputStream object and initializes it to a list of InputStream objects defined in an Enumeration object, or a combination of two InputStream objects.

ServerSocket—java.net.ServerSocket

```
public  ServerSocket(int port[, int count])
```

Constructs a server socket and binds it to the specified local port. You can connect to an anonymous port by specifying the port number to be 0. If you specify a count, the ServerSocket will listen to the port for a given number of milliseconds.

set—java.util.BitSet

```
public void set(int bit)
```

Sets a bit in a BitSet Object.

set—java.net.URL

```
protected void set(String protocol, String host,
    int port, String file, String ref)
```

Sets the fields of the URL. This method is never called because it is protected and the class is final, but URLStreamHandlers also have a set function that can modify URL fields.

setAlignment—java.awt.Label

```
public void setAlignment(int alignment)
```

Sets the alignment for a label. If an improper alignment is sent, setAlignment throws the IllegalArgumentException. See the getAlignment method and the LEFT, CENTER, and RIGHT attributes.

setAlignment—java.awt.peer.LabelPeer

```
public abstract void setAlignment(int alignment)
```

Sets the alignment for a label. If an improper alignment is sent, setAlignment throws the IllegalArgumentException. See the getAlignment method and the LEFT, CENTER, and RIGHT attributes.

setAllowUserInteraction—java.net.URLConnection

```
public void setAllowUserInteraction(
    boolean allowUserInteraction)
```

Sets the AllowUserInteraction attribute to true if you want the URLConnection allows user interaction, and false if not. Also see the getAllowUserInteraction method.

setBackground—java.awt.Component

```
public synchronized void setBackground(Color c)
```

Sets the background color of a Component. c is the color the container will use. For related information, check out the getForeground, setForeground, and setBackground methods, and the Color class.

setBackground—java.awt.peer.ComponentPeer

```
public abstract void setBackground(Color c)
```

Sets the background color of a Component. c is the color the container will use. For related information, check out the getForeground, setForeground, and setBackground methods, and the Color class.

setChanged—java.util.Observable

```
protected synchronous void setChanged()
```

Sets an observable change.

setCharAt—java.lang.StringBuffer

```
public synchronized void setCharAt(int position, char ch)
```

Sets the character at a given position in a StringBuffer to a new character. An StringIndexOutOfBoundsException exception is thrown if the position is invalid.

setCheckboxGroup—java.awt.Checkbox

```
public void setCheckboxGroup(CheckboxGroup g)
```

Sets the CheckboxGroup to the specified group. g is the new CheckboxGroup. Also see the getCheckboxGroup method and the CheckboxGroup class.

setCheckboxGroup—java.awt.peer.CheckboxPeer

```
public abstract void setCheckboxGroup(CheckboxGroup g)
```

Sets the CheckboxGroup to the specified group. g is the new CheckboxGroup. Also see the getCheckboxGroup method and the CheckboxGroup class.

setColor—java.awt.Graphics

```
public abstract void setColor(Color newColor)
```

Sets the current color to a new color. This is often used to change the paint color in a Graphics object. For more information, see the Color class and the getColor method.

setColorModel—java.awt.image.ImageConsumer

```
public abstract void setColorModel(ColorModel model)
```

Sets the ColorModel object used for the majority of the pixels reported using the setPixels method calls. See the ColorModel class for more information.

> **NOTE:**
> Each set of pixels delivered using setPixels contains its own ColorModel object, so it's not quite right to assume that the setColorModel method will set pixels for *all* setPixels method calls.

setColorModel—
java.awt.image.ImageFilter

```
public void setColorModel(ColorModel model)
```

Filters the `ColorModel` defined in the `setColorModel` method of the `ImageConsumer` interface.

setColorModel—
java.awt.image.PixelGrabber

```
public void setColorModel(ColorModel model)
```

Sets the `ColorModel` associated with an image.

setColorModel—
java.awt.image.RGBImageFilter

```
public void setColorModel(ColorModel model)
```

Substitues a new `ColorModel` for the orginal `ColorModel` whenever the original `ColorModel` appears in the `setPixels` method. Also see the `substituteColorModel` and `RGBdefault` methods and the ImageConsumer class.

> **NOTE:**
> When using the `setColorModel` method in the `RGBImageFilter` class, if the new `ColorModel` is an `IndexColorModel` and the `canFilterIndexColorModel` attribute is true, then a filtered version of the original `ColorModel` (rather than a straight replacement `ColorModel`) is used.

setContentHandlerFactory—
java.net.URLConnection

```
public static synchronized void setContentHandlerFactory(
    ContentHandlerFactory fac)
```

Sets the ContentHandler factory for an URLConnection. This method can only be called once, and an Error object is thrown if it's called more than once.

setCurrent—java.awt.CheckboxGroup

```
public synchronized void setCurrent(Checkbox box)
```

Sets the current choice to the specified Checkbox. If the Checkbox belongs to a different group, no action is taken.

setCursor—java.awt.Frame

```
public void setCursor(int cursorType)
```

Set the cursor pointer to a predefined cursor. Also see the getCursor method and the CROSSHAIR_CURSOR, DEFAULT_CURSOR, E_RESIZE_CURSOR, HAND_CURSOR, MOVE_CURSOR, NE_RESIZE_CURSOR, NW_RESIZE_CURSOR, N_RESIZE_CURSOR, SE_RESIZE_CURSOR, SW_RESIZE_CURSOR, S_RESIZE_CURSOR, TEXT_CURSOR, WAIT_CURSOR, and W_RESIZE_CURSOR attributes.

setCursor—java.awt.peer.FramePeer

```
public abstract void setCursor(int cursorType)
```

Set the cursor pointer to a predefined cursor. Also see the getCursor method and the CROSSHAIR_CURSOR, DEFAULT_CURSOR, E_RESIZE_CURSOR, HAND_CURSOR, MOVE_CURSOR, NE_RESIZE_CURSOR, NW_RESIZE_CURSOR, N_RESIZE_CURSOR, SE_RESIZE_CURSOR, SW_RESIZE_CURSOR, S_RESIZE_CURSOR, TEXT_CURSOR, WAIT_CURSOR, and W_RESIZE_CURSOR attributes.

setDaemon—java.lang.Thread

```
public final void setDaemon(boolean on)
```

Marks the Thread as a daemon. When there are only daemon threads running on a system, a Java class will exit. An IllegalThreadStateException is the Thread is active. Also see the isDaemon method.

setDaemon—java.lang.ThreadGroup

```
public final void setDaemon(boolean daemon)
```

Sets the daemon status of a ThreadGroup.

setDate—java.util.Date

```
public void setDate(int day)
```

Sets that day of a Date object. Values for day range from 1 to 31.

setDefaultAllowUserInteraction— java.net.URLConnection

```
public static void setDefaultAllowUserInteraction(
    boolean defaultallowuserinteraction)
```

Sets the static defaultAllowUserInteraction attribute to true if you want all following URLConnections to allows user interaction, and false if not. Also see the getDefaultAllowUserInteraction method.

setDefaultRequestProperty— java.net.URLConnection

```
public static void setDefaultRequestProperty(
    String key, String value)
```

Sets the default value of a general request property identified by a key. All subsequent URLConnections are initialized with these properties when constructed.

setDefaultUseCaches— java.net.URLConnection

```
public void setDefaultUseCaches(boolean defaultusecaches)
```

Returns the defaultUseCaches attribute of an URLConnection object.

setDimensions— java.awt.image.CropImageFilter

```
public void setDimensions(int width, int height)
```

Sets the dimensions of a cropped image and passes the new dimensions to the ImageConsumer. The setDimensions method in the CropImageFilter class overrides the setDimensions method in the ImageFilter class. See the ImageConsumer class for more information.

setDimensions— java.awt.image.ImageConsumer

```
public abstract void setDimensions(int width, int height)
```

Sets the dimensions of an image.

setDimensions— java.awt.image.ImageFilter

```
public void setDimensions(int width, int height)
```

Filters the image defined by the setDimensions method of the ImageConsumer interface. See the ImageConsumer class for more information.

setDimensions— java.awt.image.PixelGrabber

```
public void setDimensions(int width, int height)
```

Sets dimensions so a PixelGrabber can retrieve pixels.

*setDirectory—*java.awt.FileDialog

```
public void setDirectory(String dir)
```

Set the directory of the FileDialog.

setDirectory— java.awt.peer.FileDialogPeer

```
public abstract void setDirectory(String dir)
```

Set the directory of the FileDialog.

*setDoInput—*java.net.URLConnection

```
public void setDoInput(boolean doinput)
```

Sets the DoInput attribute to true if you want the URLConnection is used for input, and false if not. Also see the getDoInput method.

setDoOutput—java.net.URLConnection

```
public void setDoOutput(boolean dooutput)
```

Sets the `DoOutput` attribute to true if you want the `URLConnection` is used for output, and false if not. Also see the `getDoOutput` method.

setEchoCharacter—java.awt.TextField

```
public void setEchoCharacter(char c)
```

Sets the echo character for a TextField. Echo characters are useful when what the user is typing shouldn't be echoed back to the window (such as passwords). Also see the `echoCharIsSet` and `getEchoChar` methods.

setEchoCharacter— java.awt.peer.TextFieldPeer

```
public abstract void setEchoCharacter(char c)
```

Sets the echo character for a TextField. Echo characters are useful when what the user is typing shouldn't be echoed back to the window (such as passwords). Also see the `echoCharIsSet` and `getEchoChar` methods.

setEditable—java.awt.TextComponent

```
public void setEditable(boolean torf)
```

Sets a TextComponent to editable if the value of `torf` is true. If the value of `torf` is false, the TextComponent is set to not editable. Also see the `isEditable` method.

setEditable— java.awt.peer.TextComponentPeer

```
public abstract void setEditable(boolean torf)
```

Sets a TextComponent to editable if the value of `torf` is true. If the value of `torf` is false, the TextComponent is set to not editable. Also see the `isEditable` method.

setElementAt—java.util.Vector

```
public final synchronous void setElementAt(Object obj,
    int index)
```

Sets the Vector element at an index to a given Object.
The previous element at that index is overridden. An
ArrayIndexOutOfBoundsException is thrown if the index was invalid.

setFile—java.awt.FileDialog

```
public void setFile(String file)
```

Sets the file for this FileDialog to the specified file. This will become
the default file if set before the FileDialog is shown.

setFile—java.awt.peer.FileDialogPeer

```
public abstract void setFile(String file)
```

Sets the file for this FileDialog to the specified file. This will become
the default file if set before the FileDialog is shown.

setFilenameFilter—java.awt.FileDialog

```
public void setFilenameFilter(FilenameFilter filter)
```

Sets the filter (such as *.txt, myfile.*) used in a FileDialog. See
the FilenameFilter class for more details.

setFilenameFilter—java.awt.peer.FileDialogPeer

```
public abstract void setFilenameFilter(
    FilenameFilter filter)
```

Sets the filter (such as *.txt, myfile.*) used in a FileDialog. See
the FilenameFilter class for more details.

setFont—java.awt.Component

```
public synchronized void setFont(Font f)
```

Sets the font of a Component. f is the font class of the new font. For
more information, see the Font class and the getFont method.

setFont—java.awt.peer.ComponentPeer

```
public abstract void setFont(Font f)
```

Sets the font of a Component. f is the font class of the new font. For more information, see the Font class and the getFont method.

setFont—java.awt.Graphics

```
public abstract void setFont(Font font)
```

Sets the font for any text operations in the graphics object. Also check out the Font class and the getFont, drawString, drawBytes, and drawChars methods.

setFont—java.awt.MenuComponent

```
public void setFont(Font font)
```

Sets the font for a MenuComponent. Also see the getFont method.

setForeground—java.awt.Component

```
public synchronized void setForeground(Color c)
```

Sets the foreground color of a Component. c is the color the container will use. For related information, check out the getForeground, getBackground, and setBackground methods, and the Color class.

setForeground— java.awt.peer.ComponentPeer

```
public abstract void setForeground(Color c)
```

Sets the foreground color of a Component. c is the color the container will use. For related information, check out the getForeground, getBackground, and setBackground methods, and the Color class.

setHelpMenu—java.awt.MenuBar

```
public synchronized void setHelpMenu(Menu helpmenu)
```

Sets the help menu on a MenuBar to the specified menu.

setHints— java.awt.image.ImageConsumer

```
public abstract void setHints(int hintflags)
```

The setHints method should be called before any calls to the setPixels method. The hints argument is a bit mask that determines the manner in which the pixels will be delivered. See the COMPLETESCANLINES, RANDOMPIXELORDER, SINGLEFRAME, SINGLEPASS, and TOPDOWNLEFTRIGHT attributes for more information.

> **NOTE:**
> The ImageProducer **can deliver the pixels in any order. The** ImageConsumer **may be able to scale or convert the pixels to the destination** ColorModel **more efficiently or with higher quality if it knows some information about how the pixels will be delivered up front.**
>
> **If, on the other hand, the** ImageProducer **does deliver pixels as it "hinted" in the** setHint **method, graphical performance can actually degrade.**

setHints—java.awt.image.ImageFilter

```
public void setHints(int hints)
```

Filters the hints set in the ImageConsumer interface.

setHints—java.awt.image.PixelGrabber

```
public void setHints(int hints)
```

The setHints method should be called before any calls to the setPixels method. The hints argument is a bit mask that determines the manner in which the pixels will be delivered. See the COMPLETESCANLINES, RANDOMPIXELORDER, SINGLEFRAME, SINGLEPASS, and TOPDOWNLEFTRIGHT attributes and the setProperties method for more information.

setHours—java.util.Date

```
public void setHours(int hours)
```

Sets the hour (0 through 23) of a Date object.

setIconImage—java.awt.Frame

```
public void setIconImage(Image image)
```

Sets the image to display when a Frame is minimized. Also check out the getIconImage method.

> **TIP:**
> Not all operating systems support the minimized windows.

setIconImage—java.awt.peer.FramePeer

```
public abstract void setIconImage(Image image)
```

Sets the image to display when a Frame is minimized. Also check out the getIconImage method.

setIfModifiedSince—java.net.URLConnection

```
public void setIfModifiedSince(long ifmodifiedsince)
```

Allows you to set the modified date of an URLConnection.

setLabel—java.awt.Button

```
public void setLabel(String label)
```

Sets the button with the specified label. For more information, see getLabel.

setLabel—java.awt.peer.ButtonPeer

```
public abstract void setLabel(String label)
```

Sets the button with the specified label. For more information, see getLabel.

setLabel—java.awt.Checkbox

```
public void setLabel(String label)
```

Sets the checkbox with the specified label. Also see the getLabel method.

setLabel—java.awt.peer.CheckboxPeer

```
public abstract void setLabel(String label)
```

Sets the checkbox with the specified label. Also see the getLabel method.

setLabel—java.awt.MenuItem

```
public void setLabel(String label)
```

Changes the label of a MenuItem. Also see the getLabel method.

setLabel—java.awt.peer.MenuItemPeer

```
public abstract void setLabel(String label)
```

Changes the label of a MenuItem. Also see the getLabel method.

setLayout—java.awt.Container

```
public void setLayout(LayoutManager mgr)
```

Sets the layout manager for a container. See the layout and getLayout methods and the LayoutManager class for related information.

setLength—java.lang.StringBuffer

```
public synchronized void setLength(int newLength)
```

Sets the StringBuffer to a new length. This can cause lost characters if the length is reduced, and new characters will be set to ASCII 0. A StringIndexOutOfBoundsException exception is thrown if the newLength is invalid.

setLineIncrement—java.awt.Scrollbar

```
public void setLineIncrement(int increment)
```

Sets the line increment for a Scrollbar. A Scrollbar's line increment is the value that will be added or subtracted when the user scrolls up or down on the Scrollbar.

setLineIncrement—java.awt.peer.ScrollbarPeer

```
public abstract void setLineIncrement(int increment)
```

Sets the line increment for a Scrollbar. A Scrollbar's line increment is the value that will be added or subtracted when the user scrolls up or down on the Scrollbar.

setLineNumber—java.io.LineNumberInputStream

```
public void setLineNumber(int lineNumber)
```

Sets the line number in a `LineNumberInputStream` object. Also see the `getLineNumber` method.

setMaxPriority—java.lang.ThreadGroup

```
public final synchronous void setMaxPriority(int pri)
```

Sets the maximium priority of Threads in a ThreadGroup.

setMenuBar—java.awt.Frame

```
public synchronized void setMenuBar(MenuBar menu)
```

Sets a Frame's menu bar. Also check out the `getMenuBar` method.

setMenuBar—java.awt.peer.FramePeer

```
public abstract void setMenuBar(MenuBar menu)
```

Sets a Frame's menu bar. Also check out the `getMenuBar` method.

setMinutes—java.util.Date

```
public void setMinutes(int minutes)
```

Sets the minute (0 through 59) of a Date object.

setMonth—java.util.Date

```
public void setMonth(int month)
```

Sets the month. Use 0 through 11 for the month, with 0 being January.

setMultipleSelections—java.awt.List

```
public void setMultipleSelections(boolean torf)
```

Sets whether this list should allow multiple selections depending on whether `torf` is true or false. Also see the `allowsMultipleSelections` method.

setMultipleSelections—java.awt.peer.ListPeer

```
public abstract void setMultipleSelections(boolean torf)
```

Sets whether this list should allow multiple selections depending on whether `torf` is true or false. Also see the `allowsMultipleSelections` method.

setName—java.lang.Thread

```
public final void setName(String name)
```

Sets the Thread's name. Also see the `getName` method.

setPageIncrement—java.awt.Scrollbar

```
public void setPageIncrement(int l)
```

Sets the page increment for a Scrollbar. A Scrollbar's page increment is the value that will be added or subtracted when the user pages up or down on the Scrollbar.

setPageIncrement— java.awt.peer.ScrollbarPeer

```
public abstract void setPageIncrement(int 1)
```

Sets the page increment for a Scrollbar. A Scrollbar's page increment is the value that will be added or subtracted when the user pages up or down on the Scrollbar.

setPaintMode—java.awt.Graphics

```
public abstract void setPaintMode()
```

Sets the paint mode to overwrite any painted colors with the current color. This is the default mode, but the mode can also be changed to XOR mode using the setXORMode method.

setPixels— java.awt.image.CropImageFilter

```
public void setPixels(int x, int y, int w, int h,
    ColorModel model, [int / byte] pixels[],
    int offset, int scansize)
```

Sets the pixels in a rectangular region to a specific pixel arrangement and ColorModel. The pixel array can be integer or byte. The pixel at position (a,b) is stored in the pixels array at index (b * scansize + a + offset). For more information, see the ColorModel class and the setColorModel method. The setPixels method in the CropImageFilter class overrides the setPixels method in the ImageFilter class.

setPixels— java.awt.image.ImageConsumer

```
public abstract void setPixels(int x, int y, int w, int h,
    ColorModel model, [byte / int] pixels[], int offset,
    int scansize)
```

Delivers the pixels of an image. The x, uy, w (width) and h (height) define the rectangle where the image will be rendered. The model argument is a ColorModel object used to convert the pixels into their corresponding color and alpha components. The pixels array is either bytes or integers which contain the pixels to be displayed. The

pixel at position (a,b) is stored in the pixels array at index (b *
scansize + a + offset). For more information, see the
ColorModel class and the setColorModel method.

setPixels—java.awt.image.ImageFilter

```
public void setPixels(int x, int y, int w, int h,
    ColorModel model, [byte / int] pixels[],
    int off, int scansize)
```

Filters the information provided in the setPixels method of the
ImageConsumer interface.

setPixels—java.awt.image.PixelGrabber

```
public void setPixels(int x, int y, int width, int height,
    ColorModel model, [byte / int] pixels[],
    int offset, int scan)
```

Sets the ColorModel object used for the majority of the pixels reported using the setPixels method calls. See the ColorModel class for
more information.

setPixels—java.awt.image.RGBImageFilter

```
public void setPixels(int x, int y, int w, int h,
    ColorModel model, [byte / int] pixels[],
    int off, int scansize)
```

If an alternate ColorModel has been defined, this method converts
the buffer of byte pixels to the new ColorModel by calling the
filterRGBPixels method. The setPixels method in the
RGBImageFilter class overrides the setPixels method in the
ImageFilter class. Also check out the getRGBdefault and
filterRGBPixels methods.

setPriority—java.lang.Thread

```
public final void setPriority(int newPriority)
```

Sets the priority of a Thread. An IllegalArgumentException exception is thrown if the newPriority is less than MIN_PRIORITY attribute
or more than MAX_PRIORITY attribute. Also see getPriority.

setProperties—java.awt.image.CropImageFilter

```
public void setProperties(Hashtable props)
```

Sets properties inside a cropped reagion. The setProperties method in the CropImageFilter class overrides the setProperties method in the ImageFilter class.

setProperties—java.awt.image.ImageConsumer

```
public abstract void setProperties(Hashtable props)
```

Sets properties associated with an image.

setProperties—java.awt.image.ImageFilter

```
public void setProperties(Hashtable props)
```

Adds properties to the source object. The setProperties method also adds properties to the source object indicating which filters have been used.

setProperties—java.awt.image.PixelGrabber

```
public void setProperties(Hashtable props)
```

Sets properties associated with an image.

setProperties—java.lang.System

```
public static void setProperties(Properties props)
```

Sets the system properties. Also see the getProperties method.

setRequestProperty— java.net.URLConnection

```
public void setRequestProperty(String key, String value)
```

Sets a general request property. The key attribute is the keyword by which the request is known (such as "accept"), and the value attribute is the value associated with the key.

setResizable—java.awt.Dialog

```
public void setResizable(boolean resizable)
```

Sets the resizable flag in a Dialog to true if you want the Dialog resizable or false if you don't.

setResizable—java.awt.peer.DialogPeer

```
public abstract void setResizable(boolean resizable)
```

Sets the resizable flag in a Dialog to true if you want the Dialog resizable or false if you don't.

setResizable—java.awt.Frame

```
public void setResizable(boolean resizable)
```

Sets a Frame's resizability. If true is the argument, the Frame becomes resizable. If false is the argument, then the Frame becomes static. Also check out the getResizable method.

setResizable—java.awt.peer.FramePeer

```
public abstract void setResizable(boolean resizable)
```

Sets a Frame's resizability. If true is the argument, the Frame becomes resizable. If false is the argument, then the Frame becomes static. Also check out the getResizable method.

setSeconds—java.util.Date

```
public void setSeconds(int second)
```

Sets the second (0 through 59) of a Date object.

setSecurityManager—java.lang.System

```
public static void setSecurityManager(SecurityManager s)
```

Sets the SecurityManager object for a System. This method can only be called once, or a SecurityException will be thrown. Also see the getSecurityManager method.

setSeed—java.util.Random

```
public synchronized void setSeed(long seed)
```

Reseeds the random number generator of a Random object.

setSize—java.util.Vector

```
public final synchronous void setSize(int newSize)
```

Sets the size of a vector. If the size decreases, elements could be lost. New elements are added if the size increases are set to null.

setSocketFactory— java.net.ServerSocket

```
public static synchronized void setSocketFactory(
    SocketImplFactory fac)
```

Sets the socket factory for the ServerSocket object. This method can only be called once, or a SocketException is thrown.

setSocketImplFactory—java.net.Socket

```
public static synchronized void setSocketImplFactory(
    SocketImplFactory fac)
```

Sets the SocketImplFactory. This method can only be called once, or a SocketException is thrown. Also, an IOException is thrown if an I/O error occurs during the setting of the SocketImplFactory.

setState—java.awt.Checkbox

```
public void setState(boolean state)
```

Sets the Checkbox to the specifed boolean state. Also see the getState method.

setState—java.awt.CheckboxMenuItem

```
public void setState(boolean t)
```

Sets the state of a CheckboxMenuItem. The state can be true or false.

setState—java.awt.peer.CheckboxMenuItemPeer

```
public abstract void setState(boolean t)
```

Sets the state of a CheckboxMenuItem. The state can be true or false. Also see the getState method.

setState—java.awt.peer.CheckboxPeer

```
public abstract void setState(boolean state)
```

Sets the Checkbox to the specifed boolean state. Also see the getState method.

setStub—java.applet.Applet

```
public final void setStub(AppletStub stub)
```

Sets the applet stub. This is done by automatically by the system.

setText—java.awt.Label

```
public void setText(String label)
```

Sets the text of a label. Also see the getText method.

setText—java.awt.peer.LabelPeer

```
public abstract void setText(String label)
```

Sets the text of a label. Also see the getText method.

setText—java.awt.TextComponent

```
public void setText(String t)
```

Sets the text of a TextComponent to the specified text. Also check out the getText method.

setText—java.awt.peer.TextComponentPeer

```
public abstract void setText(String t)
```

Sets the text of a TextComponent to the specified text. Also check out the getText method.

setTime—java.util.Date

```
public void setTime(long time)
```

Sets the time. The time argument is the number of milliseconds since 1/1/1970.

setTitle—java.awt.Dialog

```
public void setTitle(String title)
```

Sets the title of a Dialog. Also check out the getTitle method.

setTitle—java.awt.peer.DialogPeer

```
public abstract void setTitle(String title)
```

Sets the title of a Dialog. Also check out the getTitle method.

setTitle—java.awt.Frame

```
public void setTitle(String title)
```

Sets the title for a Frame. Also check out the getTitle method.

setTitle—java.awt.peer.FramePeer

```
public abstract void setTitle(String title)
```

Sets the title for a Frame. Also check out the getTitle method.

setURL—java.net.URLStreamHandler

```
protected void setURL(URL u, String protocol, String host,
    int port, String file, String ref)
```

Sets URL attributes. Only classes extended from `URLStreamHandler` can modify URL attributes; even URL objects can't modify their own attributes.

setURLStreamHandlerFactory—java.net.URL

```
public static synchronized void setURLStreamHandlerFactory(
    URLStreamHandlerFactory fac)
```

Sets the `URLStreamHandler` factory. This method can only be called once, or an Error object is thrown.

setUseCaches—java.net.URLConnection

```
public void setUseCaches(boolean usecaches)
```

Allows you to set an `URLConneciton` to use caches if true is passed, or to not use caches if false is passed. Caches can improve performance, but sometimes it's necessary to avoid them.

setValue—java.awt.Scrollbar

```
public void setValue(int value)
```

Sets the value of a Scrollbar to the specified value. Also see the `getValue`, `getMinimum`, and `getMaximum` methods.

> **NOTE:**
> If the `value` argument sent to the `setValue` method is greater than the minimum or maximum value, the argument becomes the minimum or maximum value.

setValue—java.awt.peer.ScrollbarPeer

```
public abstract void setValue(int value)
```

Sets the value of a Scrollbar to the specified value. Also see the `getValue`, `getMinimum`, and `getMaximum` methods.

setValues—java.awt.Scrollbar

```
public void setValues(int value, int pageSize,
     int minimum, int maximum)
```

Sets the values for a Scrollbar. The `value` argument where the Scrollbar is set to. The `pageSize` argument is the size of the viewing area controlled by the Scrollbar. The `minumum` and `maximum` values of a Scrollbar determine what the value of the Scrollbar will be at the two ends of the Scrollbar.

setValues—java.awt.peer.ScrollbarPeer

```
public abstract void setValues(int value, int pageSize,
     int minimum, int maximum)
```

Sets the values for a Scrollbar. The `value` argument where the Scrollbar is set to. The `pageSize` argument is the size of the viewing area controlled by the Scrollbar. The `minumum` and `maximum` values of a Scrollbar determine what the value of the Scrollbar will be at the two ends of the Scrollbar.

setXORMode—java.awt.Graphics

```
public abstract void setXORMode(Color alternate)
```

Sets the paint mode to alternate between the current color and an alternate color. When drawing operations are performed, pixels that are the current color will be changed to the alternate and vice versa, while pixels of colors other than the current or alternated colors will be changed in an unpredictable manner.

> **NOTE:**
> If a Graphics Object is in XOR mode and you draw a picture twice, the Graphics object will be restored to it's original settings. In other words, if you want to undo an XOR drawing, simply draw it again in XOR mode.

setYear—java.util.Date

```
public void setYear(int year)
```

Sets the year in a Date object.

shiftDown—java.awt.Event

```
public boolean shiftDown()
```

Checks if the shift key is down. Also check out the `modifiers` attribute and the `controlDown` and `metaDown` methods.

show—java.awt.Component

```
public void show({boolean cond})
```

Shows a Component if `cond` is true or omitted, and hides a Component of `cond` is false. Also check out the `isVisible` and `hide` methods.

show—java.awt.CardLayout

```
public void show(Container parent, String name)
```

Goes to a Component name in a container. `parent` is the name of the parent container and `name` is the component name.

show—java.awt.peer.ComponentPeer

```
public abstract void show({boolean cond})
```

Shows a Component if `cond` is true or omitted, and hides a Component of `cond` is false. Also check out the `isVisible` and `hide` methods.

show—java.awt.Window

```
public synchronized void show()
```

Makes a window visible and brings the window to the front. The `show` method in the Window class overrides the `show` method in the Container class. Also see the `hide` method.

showDocument— java.applet.AppletContext

```
public abstract void showDocument(URL, {string})
```

Shows a new document. If a String is passed containing the target window or frame, `showDocument` shows a new document in a target window or frame. `showDocument` could be ignored by the applet context. `showDocument` method accepts the following target strings: `_self` (shows in current frame); `_parent` (shows in parent frame); `_top` (shows in top-most frame); `_blank` (shows in new unnamed top-level window).

showStatus—java.applet.Applet

```
public void showStatus(String msg)
```

Shows a status message in the applet's context.

showStatus— java.applet.AppletContext

```
public abstract void showStatus(String)
```

Shows a status string.

sin—java.lang.Math

```
public static double sin(double a)
```

Returns the trigonomectric sine of an angle measured in radians.

size—java.util.BitSet

```
public int size()
```

Returns the BitSet's size.

size—java.io.ByteArrayOutputStream

```
public int size()
```

Returns the size of the buffer in a `ByteArrayOutputStream`.

size—java.awt.Component

```
public Dimension size()
```

Returns the current size of a Component. For more information, see the `resize` method.

size—java.io.DataOutputStream

```
public final int size()
```

Returns the number of bytes written so far to the `DataOutputStream`.

size—java.util.Dictionary

```
public abstract int size()
```

Returns the number of elements in a Dictionary.

size—java.util.Hashtable

```
public int size()
```

Returns the number of elements in a Hashtable object. The `size` method in the Hashtable class overrides the `size` method in the Dictionary class.

size—java.util.Vector

```
public final int size()
```

Returns the number of elements in a Vector.

skip—java.io.BufferedInputStream

```
public synchronized long skip(long maximumBytes)
```

Repositions the stream input pointer by skipping bytes. The `skip` method blocks output until all bytes are skipped, or until `maximumBytes` are skipped. The `skip` method returns the actual number of bytes skipped, or a –1 at the end of the stream. This method throws IOException for all other I/O errors. The skip method in the BufferedInputStream class overrides the skip method in the FilterInputStream class.

skip—java.io.ByteArrayInputStream

```
public synchronized long skip(long maximumBytes)
```

Repositions the stream input pointer by skipping bytes. The skip method blocks output until all bytes are skipped, or until maximumBytes are skipped. The skip method returns the actual number of bytes skipped, or a –1 at the end of the stream. The skip method in the ByteArrayInputStream class overrides the skip method in the InputStream class.

skip—java.io.FileInputStream

```
public long skip(long maximumBytes)
```

Repositions the stream input pointer by skipping bytes. The skip method blocks output until all bytes are skipped, or until maximumBytes are skipped. The skip method returns the actual number of bytes skipped, or a –1 at the end of the stream. This method throws IOException for all other I/O errors. The skip method in the FileInputStream class overrides the skip method in the InputStream class.

skip—java.io.FilterInputStream

```
public long skip(long maximumBytes)
```

Repositions the stream input pointer by skipping bytes. The skip method blocks output until all bytes are skipped, or until maximumBytes are skipped. The skip method returns the actual number of bytes skipped, or a –1 at the end of the stream. This method throws IOException for all other I/O errors. The skip method in the FilterInputStream class overrides the skip method in the InputStream class.

skip—java.io.InputStream

```
public long skip(long maximumBytes)
```

Repositions the stream input pointer by skipping bytes. The skip method blocks output until all bytes are skipped, or until maximumBytes are skipped. The skip method returns the actual number of bytes skipped, or a –1 at the end of the stream. This method throws IOException for all other I/O errors.

skip—java.io.LineNumberInputStream

```
public long skip(long maximumBytes)
```

Repositions the stream input pointer by skipping bytes. The skip method blocks output until all bytes are skipped, or until maximumBytes are skipped. The skip method returns the actual number of bytes skipped, or a –1 at the end of the stream. This method throws IOException for all other I/O errors. The skip method in the LineNumberInputStream class overrides the skip method in the FilterInputStream class.

skip—java.io.StringBufferInputStream

```
public synchronized long skip(long maximumBytes)
```

Repositions the stream input pointer by skipping bytes. The skip method blocks output until all bytes are skipped, or until maximumBytes are skipped. The skip method returns the actual number of bytes skipped, or a –1 at the end of the stream. The skip method in the FileInputStream class overrides the skip method in the InputStream class.

skipBytes—java.io.DataInput

```
public abstract int skipBytes(int maximumBytes)
```

Repositions the stream input pointer by skipping bytes. The skipBytes method blocks output until all bytes are skipped, or until maximumBytes are skipped. The skipBytes method returns the actual number of bytes skipped. This method throws EOFException if the end of file is reached and IOException for all other I/O errors.

skipBytes—java.io.DataInputStream

```
public final int skipBytes(int maximumBytes)
```

Repositions the stream input pointer by skipping bytes. The skipBytes method blocks output until all bytes are skipped, or until maximumBytes are skipped. The skipBytes method returns the actual number of bytes skipped. This method throws EOFException if the end of file is reached and IOException for all other I/O errors.

skipBytes—java.io.RandomAccessFile

```
public int skipBytes(int maximumBytes)
```

Repositions the stream input pointer by skipping bytes. The skipBytes method blocks output until all bytes are skipped, or until maximumBytes are skipped. The skipBytes method returns the actual number of bytes skipped or –1 if the end of stream is reached. This method throws IOException for all other I/O errors.

slashSlashComments— java.io.StreamTokenizer

```
public void slashSlashComments(boolean torf)
```

If the torf is true, this StreamTokenizer object will recognize C++ style(//) comments.

slashStarComments— java.io.StreamTokenizer

```
public void slashStarComments(boolean torf)
```

If the torf is true, this StreamTokenizer object will recognize C style(/*) comments.

sleep—java.lang.Thread

```
public static void sleep(long millis{, int nanos})
```

Causes a thread to sleep for a given number of milliseconds and nanoseconds (if given). An InterruptedException exception is thrown if another thread has interrupted this thread.

Socket—java.net.Socket

```
public  Socket([String host / InetAddress address],
    int port{, boolean stream})
```

Constructs a socket and connects it to the specified address or host on the specified port. The stream argument lets you specify whether you want a stream (true) or datagram socket (false). The default is a stream. An `UnknownHostException` is thrown if the host name can not be resolved, and an `IOException` occurs if any I/O error occurs during the construction of the socket.

SocketException— java.net.SocketException

```
public SocketException({String detailMessage})
```

An error has occurred while attempting to use a socket (like winsock). If `detailMessage` is specified, the `detailMessage` will be displayed when this throwable is thrown.

sqrt—java.lang.Math

```
public static double sqrt(double a)
```

Takes the square root of `a`. An `ArithmeticException` is thrown if the value of `a` is less than zero.

Stack—java.util.Stack

```
public  Stack()
```

Constructs a `LIFO` stack to store objects.

StackOverflowError— java.lang.StackOverflowError

```
public StackOverflowError({String detailMessage})
```

The memory stack is full. You are calling programs too deep, or using too large (or too many) variables in your path of execution. If `detailMessage` is specified, the `detailMessage` will be displayed when this throwable is thrown.

start—java.applet.Applet

```
public void start()
```

Called to start the applet. You never need to call this method directly, it is called when the applet's document is visited. For more information, see the `init`, `stop`, and `destroy` methods.

start—java.lang.Thread

```
public synchronized void start()
```

Starts this thread. This will cause the run method to be called. An IllegalThreadStateException exception is thrown if this thread was already started.

startProduction— java.awt.image.FilteredImageSource

```
public void startProduction(ImageConsumer ic)
```

This method both registers an ImageConsumer object as a consumer and starts an immediate reconstruction of the image data in an FilteredImageSource for delivery to the consumer. Also see the removeConsumer, isConsumer, and addConsumer methods.

startProduction— java.awt.image.ImageProducer

```
public abstract void startProduction(ImageConsumer ic)
```

This method both registers an ImageConsumer object as a consumer and starts an immediate reconstruction of the image data in an ImageProducer for delivery to the consumer. Also see the removeConsumer, isConsumer, and addConsumer methods.

startProduction— java.awt.image.MemoryImageSource

```
public void startProduction(ImageConsumer ic)
```

This method both registers an ImageConsumer object as a consumer and starts an immediate reconstruction of the image data in an MemoryImageSource for delivery to the consumer. Also see the removeConsumer, isConsumer, and addConsumer methods.

startsWith—java.lang.String

```
public boolean startsWith(String prefix{, int toffset})
```

Determines whether this String starts with some prefix. An offset can be used to see if the string is occurs in a specific position.

status—java.awt.image.PixelGrabber

```
public synchronized int status()
```

Return the status of the pixels. The status returned is a bitwise OR of all relevant ImageObserver constants (ABORT, ALLBITS, ERROR, FRAMEBITS, HEIGHT, PROPERTIES, SOMEBITS, and WIDTH). See the ImageObserver class for more information.

statusAll—java.awt.MediaTracker

```
public int statusAll(boolean loadall)
```

Returns the boolean OR of the status of all of the media being tracked. If the loadall argument is true, starts loading any images that are not yet being loaded. If loadall is false, no images start loading that haven't yet loaded. For more information, see the statusID method and the LOADING, ABORTED, ERRORED, and COMPLETE attributes.

statusID—java.awt.MediaTracker

```
public int statusID(int identification, boolean loadall)
```

Returns the boolean OR of the status of all of the media being tracked with a given identificaiton. If the loadall argument is true, starts loading any images with the given identification that are not yet being loaded. If loadall is false, no images start loading that haven't yet loaded. For more information, see the statusAll method and the LOADING, ABORTED, ERRORED, and COMPLETE attributes.

stop—java.applet.Applet

```
public void stop()
```

Called to stop the applet. It is called when the applet's document is no longer on the screen. It is guaranteed to be called before destroy() is called. You never need to call this method directly. For more information, see the init, start, and destroy methods.

stop—java.applet.AudioClip

```
public abstract void stop()
```

Stops playing the clip.

stop—java.lang.Thread

```
public final void stop({Throwable o})
```

Stops a Thread by tossing an instance of an throwable Object. If a throwable object is not specified, an instance of `ThreadDeath` is thrown.

stop—java.lang.ThreadGroup

```
public final synchronous void stop()
```

Stops all the Threads and subgroups in this ThreadGroup.

StreamTokenizer— java.io.StreamTokenizer

```
public  StreamTokenizer(InputStream I)
```

Constructs a stream tokenizer that parses an input stream. Numbers, Strings quoted with single and double quotes, and alphabetics are recognized.

String—java.lang.String

```
public  String({arguments})
```

Constructs a new String. If there are no arguments specified, the String is empty. You can specify the following arguments to initialize your string: `(String value)` copies a string; `(StringBuffer value)` copies a StringBuffer object to the String; `(char value[]{,int offset, int count})` copies a character array or subarray into the string; `(byte value[], int hibyte{,int offset, int count})` copies a byte array or subarray into a string, but because characters are Unicode and therefore 16 bits, and bytes are 8 bits, the `hibyte` value can be set to initialize (usually to zero) the first 8 bits of the Unicode characters in the String.

StringBuffer—java.lang.StringBuffer

```
public  StringBuffer({[int length / String s]})
```

Constructs a StringBuffer object. If no arguments are provided, an empty StringBuffer is constructed. If a length is passed, then the

StringBuffer is initialized to that length. If a String is passed, then the StringBuffer is initialized to that String.

StringBufferInputStream— java.io.StringBufferInputStream

```
public   StringBufferInputStream(String s)
```

Constructs a `StringBufferInputStream` from a String.

StringIndexOutOfBoundsException— java.lang.StringIndexOutOfBounds Exception

```
public StringIndexOutOfBoundsException(
     {String detailMessage})
```

An attempt was made to access a string that is greater than its length. If `detailMessage` is specified, the `detailMessage` will be displayed when this throwable is thrown.

StringTokenizer— java.util.StringTokenizer

```
public   StringTokenizer(
     String str{ String delim{, boolean returnDelims}})
```

Constructs a StringTokenizer on a String. If a delimiter is specifed, then that delimiter is used to separate tokens. Otherwise, \\t\\r\\n (with a space at the beginning) is used. You can specify that you want to return the delimeters as tokens or skip them. The default is to not return delimiters as tokens.

stringWidth—java.awt.FontMetrics

```
public int stringWidth(String str)
```

Returns the width of a String in a FontMetrics Font. Also check out the `charWidth`, `charsWidth`, and `bytesWidth` methods.

substituteColorModel— java.awt.image.RGBImageFilter

```
public void substituteColorModel(
    ColorModel oldcm, ColorModel newcm)
```

Substitues a new ColorModel for the orginal ColorModel whenever the original ColorModel appears in the `setPixels` method.

substring—java.lang.String

```
public String substring(int begin[, int end)
```

Returns a substring of this string. A `StringIndexOutOfBoundsException` is thrown if you try to retrieve a value that is greater than the length of the string or less than zero.

suspend—java.lang.Thread

```
public final void suspend()
```

Suspends a Thread's execution. See the `resume` method for more information.

suspend—java.lang.ThreadGroup

```
public final synchronous void suspend()
```

Suspends all the Threads and subgroups in this ThreadGroup. See the `resume` method for more details.

sync—java.awt.Toolkit

```
public abstract void sync()
```

Syncs the graphics state. This is often used with animation.

tan—java.lang.Math

```
public static double tan(double a)
```

Returns the trigonomectric tangent of an angle measured in radians.

TextArea—java.awt.TextArea

```
public  TextArea({String text}{{,}int rows, int cols})
```

Constructs a new TextArea object and loads the TextArea with the specified text, if given. This constructor can also specify the number of rows and columns in the text area.

TextField—java.awt.TextField

```
public  TextField({String text}{{,} int columns})
```

Constructs a new TextField. If text is passed, the new TextField is initialized with the specified text. If columns are passed, the new TextField is initialized with the number of columns.

Thread—java.lang.Thread

```
public  Thread(
    {ThreadGroup group}{{,}Runnable target}{{,}String name})
```

Constructs a new Thread in the specified Thread group (if given) with the given name (if given) or that applies the run method of a specified Runable target (if given).

ThreadDeath—java.lang.ThreadDeath

```
public ThreadDeath({String detailMessage})
```

An instance of ThreadDeath is thrown in the victim thread when thread.stop() is called. This is not a subclass of Exception but rather a subclass of Error because too many people already catch Exception. Instances of this class should be caught explicitly. If detailMessage is specified, the detailMessage will be displayed when this throwable is thrown.

ThreadGroup—java.lang.ThreadGroup

```
public  ThreadGroup({ThreadGroup parent,} String name)
```

Creates a new ThreadGroup with a specified name in the specified parent ThreadGroup (if given). If the parent ThreadGroup is provided but is null, a NullPointerException is thrown.

Throwable—java.lang.Throwable

```
public   Throwable({String message})
```

Constructs a new Throwable with the specified detail message (if given).

toBack—java.awt.Window

```
public void toBack()
```

Sends the Window to the back. Also see the toFront and show methods.

toBack—java.awt.peer.WindowPeer

```
public abstract void toBack()
```

Sends the Window to the back. Also see the toFront and show methods.

toByteArray— java.io.ByteArrayOutputStream

```
public synchronized byte[] toByteArray()
```

Returns a copy of the output data.

toCharArray—java.lang.String

```
public char[] toCharArray()
```

Creates a character array and returns a character array representation of the String.

toExternalForm—java.net.URL

```
public String toExternalForm()
```

Reverses the parsing of an URL and returns a String containing a fully qualified absolute URL.

toExternalForm—java.net.URLStreamHandler

```
protected String toExternalForm(URL u)
```

Reverses the parsing of the URL and returns the unparsed String.

toFront—java.awt.Window

```
public void toFront()
```

Brings the window to the front. Also see the toBack and show methods.

toFront—java.awt.peer.WindowPeer

```
public abstract void toFront()
```

Brings the window to the front. Also see the toBack and show methods.

toGMTString—java.util.Date

```
public String toGMTString()
```

Converts a Date to a String using the Internet GMT conventions.

toLocaleString—java.util.Date

```
public String toLocaleString()
```

Converts a Date to a String using local date formats.

toLowerCase—java.lang.Character

```
public static char toLowerCase(char ch)
```

Returns the lowercase character value of the specified ASCII (ISO-LATIN-1) character. Characters that are not uppercase letters are returned without modification. See the toUpperCase method.

toLowerCase—java.lang.String

```
public String toLowerCase()
```

Converts all of the characters in a String to lowercase and returns the String.

Toolkit—**java.awt.Toolkit**

```
public  Toolkit()
```

Constructs a Toolkit object.

toString (static)—**java.lang.Double**

```
public static String toString(double d)
```

Returns a String containing the value of a passed double floating point number.

toString (static)—**java.lang.Float**

```
public static String toString(Float d)
```

Returns a String containing the value of a passed floating point number.

toString (static)—**java.lang.Integer**

```
public static String toString(int i{, int radix})
```

Returns a String object containing a character representation of an integer with a given radix. A radix is the base used, and defaults to 10 (for based–10 number systems). 16 (hexidecimal) and 8 (octal) may also prove useful.

toString (static)—**java.lang.Long**

```
public static String toString(long i{, int radix})
```

Returns a String object containing a character representation of an integer with a given radix. A radix is the base used, and defaults to 10 (for based–10 number systems). 16 (hexidecimal) and 8 (octal) may also prove useful.

toString—**java.util.BitSet**

```
public String toString()
```

Converts a BitSet to a String. The `toString` method in the BitSet class overrides the `toString` method in the Object class.

toString—**java.lang.Boolean**

```
public String toString()
```

Converts a Boolean to a String. The toString method in the Boolean class overrides the toString method in the Object class.

toString—**java.awt.BorderLayout**

```
public String toString()
```

Returns the String representation of this BorderLayout's values. This method overrides the toString method in the Object class.

toString— **java.io.ByteArrayOutputStream**

```
public String toString({int hibyte})
```

Converts output data to a string. If a hibyte is specified, the top 8 bits of each 16-bit Unicode character are set to the hibyte character. The toString method in the ByteArrayOutputStream class overrides the toString method in the Object class.

toString—**java.awt.Component**

```
public String toString()
```

Returns a String containing a Component's values. toString in the Component class overrides tostring in the Object class.

toString—**java.awt.CardLayout**

```
public String toString()
```

Returns the String representation of this CardLayout's values. The toString method in the CardLayout class overrides the toString method in the Object class.

toString—**java.lang.Character**

```
public String toString()
```

Returns a String object containing a character's value. The toString method in the Character class overrides the toString method in the Object class.

toString—java.awt.CheckboxGroup

```
public String toString()
```

Convert's a CheckboxGroup's value to a string. toString in the CheckboxGroup class overrides toString in the Object class.

toString—java.lang.Class

```
public String toString()
```

Returns a String containing the name of this class or interface. A "class" or "interface" precedes the class name depending on whether the Class object contains a class or an interface. The tostring method in the Class class overrides the toString method in the Object class.

toString—java.awt.Color

```
public String toString()
```

Returns the name of the color in the Color class. The toString method in the Color class overrides the toString method in the Object class.

toString—java.util.Date

```
public String toString()
```

Converts a date to a String. The toString method in the Date class overrides the toString method in the Object class.

toString—java.awt.Dimension

```
public String toString()
```

Returns a String containing a Dimension's values.The toString method in the Dimension class overrides the toString method in the Object class.

toString—java.lang.Double

```
public String toString()
```

Returns a String containing the value of a the Double object. The toString method in the Double class overrides the toString method in the Object class.

toString—java.awt.Event

```
public String toString()
```

Returns a string containing an Event's values. The `toString` method in the Event class overrides the `toString` method in the Object class.

toString—java.io.File

```
public String toString()
```

Returns a String object containing the file path in a File object. The `toString` method in the File class overrides the `toString` method in the Object class.

toString—java.lang.Float

```
public String toString()
```

Returns a String containing the value of a the Float object. The `toString` method in the Float class overrides the `toString` method in the Object class.

toString—java.awt.FlowLayout

```
public String toString()
```

Returns a String containing a FlowLayout's values. The `toString` method in the FlowLayout class overrides the `toString` method in the Object class.

toString—java.awt.Font

```
public String toString()
```

Stores the Font into a string. The `toString` method in the Font class overrides the `toString` method in the Object class.

toString—java.awt.FontMetrics

```
public String toString()
```

Returns the String containing a FontMetric's values. The `toString` method in the FontMetric class overrides the `toString` method in the Object class.

toString—java.awt.Graphics

```
public String toString()
```

Returns a String containing a Graphic's value. The `toString` method in the Graphics class overrides the `toString` method in the Object class.

toString—java.awt.GridLayout

```
public String toString()
```

Returns a String containing a GridLayout's values. The `toString` method in the GridLayout class overrides the `toString` method in the Object class.

toString—java.util.Hashtable

```
public synchronized String toString()
```

Creates a large string containing the hashtable contents. The `toString` method in the Hashtable class overrides the `toString` method in the Object class.

toString—java.net.InetAddress

```
public String toString()
```

Converts the InetAddress to a String. The `toString` method in the InetAddress class overrides the `toString` method in the Object class.

toString—java.awt.Insets

```
public String toString()
```

Returns a String object containing an Inset's values. The `toString` method in the Insets class overrides the `toString` method in the Object class.

toString—java.lang.Integer

```
public String toString()
```

Returns a String object containing an a character representation of an integer with a base–10 radix. The `toString` method in the Integer class overrides the `toString` method in the Object class.

toString—java.lang.Long

```
public String toString()
```

Returns a String object containing an a character representation of an integer with a base–10 radix. The `toString` method in the Long class overrides the `toString` method in the Object class.

toString—java.awt.MenuComponent

```
public String toString()
```

Returns the String containing a MenuComponent's values. The `toString` method in the MenuComponent class overrides the `toString` method in the Object class.

toString—java.lang.Object

```
public String toString()
```

Returns a String that represents the value of this Object. It is recommended that all subclasses override this method.

toString—java.awt.Point

```
public String toString()
```

Returns a String containing a Point's coordinates. The `toString` method in the Point class overrides the `toString` method in the Object class.

toString—java.awt.Rectangle

```
public String toString()
```

Returns a String containing a Rectangle's values. The `toString` method in the Rectangle class overrides the `toString` method in the Object class.

toString—java.net.ServerSocket

```
public String toString()
```

Returns a String containing the implementation address and implementation port of a ServerSocket. The `toString` method in the ServerSocket overrides the `toString` method in the Object class.

toString—java.net.Socket

```
public String toString()
```

Returns the String value of a Socket. The toString method in the Socket class overrides the toString method in the Object class.

toString—java.io.StreamTokenizer

```
public String toString()
```

Returns the String containing the stream token. The toString method in the StreamTokenizer class overrides the toString method in the Object class.

toString—java.lang.String

```
public String toString()
```

Returns the String. The toString method in the String class overrides the toString method in the Object class.

toString—java.lang.StringBuffer

```
public String toString()
```

Converts a StringBuffer to a String. The toString method in the StringBuffer class overrides the toString method in the Object class.

toString—java.lang.Thread

```
public String toString()
```

Returns a String representation of the Thread. This is the thread's name, priority, and thread group. The toString method in the Thread class overrides the toString method in the Object class.

toString—java.lang.ThreadGroup

```
public String toString()
```

Returns a String containing information about a ThreadGroup object. The toString method in the ThreadGroup class overrides the toString method in the Object class.

toString—java.lang.Throwable

```
public String toString()
```

Returns a description of the Throwable. The toString method in the Throwable class overrides the toString method in the Object class.

toString—java.net.URL

```
public String toString()
```

Returns a String containing URL information. The toString method in the URL class overrides the toString method in the Object class.

toString—java.net.URLConnection

```
public String toString()
```

Returns the String containing URLConnection information. The toString method in the URLConnection class overrides the toString method in the Object class.

toString—java.util.Vector

```
public final synchronous String toString()
```

Returns a String containing Vector elements. The toString method inside the Vector class overrides the toString method inside the Object class.

totalMemory—java.lang.Runtime

```
public long totalMemory()
```

Returns the total number of bytes in system memory.

toUpperCase—java.lang.Character

```
public static char toUpperCase(char ch)
```

Returns the uppercase character value of the specified ASCII (ISO-LATIN-1) character. Characters that are uppercase letters or have no uppercase counterpart are returned without modification. See the toLowerCase method.

toUpperCase—java.lang.String

```
public String toUpperCase()
```

Converts all of the characters in a String to uppercase and returns the String.

traceInstructions—java.lang.Runtime

```
public void traceInstructions(boolean torf)
```

Enables the tracing of instructions if `torf` is true. Otherwise, disables the tracing of instructions.

traceMethodCalls—java.lang.Runtime

```
public void traceMethodCalls(boolean on)
```

Enables the tracing of method calls if `torf` is true. Otherwise, disables the tracing of method calls.

translate—java.awt.Event

```
public void translate(int x, int y)
```

Translates an event to trigger the same event at the x, y coordinates within the same component.

translate—java.awt.Graphics

```
public abstract void translate(int x, int y)
```

Assigns a new x, y origin to a Graphics object.

translate—java.awt.Point

```
public void translate(int x, int y)
```

Translates a Point to a new x,y coordinate.

translate—java.awt.Rectangle

```
public void translate(int x, int y)
```

Translates the rectangle to new x, y coordinates.

trim—java.lang.String

```
public String trim()
```

Removes all leading and trailing spaces from a String and returns the String.

trimToSize—java.util.Vector

```
public final synchronous void trimToSize()
```

Removes any anused capacity of a Vector. Subsequent insertions will cause a reallocation.

uncaughtException— java.lang.ThreadGroup

```
public void uncaughtException(Thread t, Throwable e)
```

This method is called when a Thread is this group exists because of an uncaught exception.

union—java.awt.Rectangle

```
public Rectangle union(Rectangle r)
```

Computes the union of two rectangles. The largest Rectangle that contains both of the other rectangles is returned.

UnknownError— java.lang.UnknownError

```
public UnknownError({String detailMessage})
```

An unknown (but *serious!*) error has occured in the execution of your program. If detailMessage is specified, the detailMessage will be displayed when this throwable is thrown.

UnknownHostException—
java.net.UnknownHostException

```
public UnknownHostException({String detailMessage})
```

The address of the host specified by a network client could not be resolved. If `detailMessage` is specified, the `detailMessage` will be displayed when this throwable is thrown.

UnknownServiceException—
java.net.UnknownServiceException

```
public UnknownServiceException(
     {String detailMessage})
```

An attempt was made to use a service that is not supported by the network. If `detailMessage` is specified, the `detailMessage` will be displayed when this throwable is thrown.

unread—java.io.PushbackInputStream

```
public void unread(int ch)
```

Pushes back a character onto a `PushbackInputStream`. An `IOException` is thrown if more than one character is pushed back onto the `PushbackInputStream` between reads. See the `read` method.

UnsatisfiedLinkError—
java.lang.UnsatisfiedLinkError

```
public UnsatisfiedLinkError({String detailMessage})
```

Visual J++ has loaded another class, but cannot reconcile all the links to that other class. If `detailMessage` is specified, the `detailMessage` will be displayed when this throwable is thrown.

update—java.awt.Component

```
public void update(Graphics g)
```

Updates a Component in response to a call to the `repaint` method. `g` is the specified Graphics window. For more information, see the `paint` and `repaint` methods or the Graphics class.

update—java.util.Observer

```
public abstract void update(Observable o, Object arg)
```

Called when observers in the observable list need to be updated. See the Observable class for more information.

URL (protocol)—java.net.URL

```
public  URL(
    String protocol, String host, {int port,} String file)
```

Constructs an absolute URL from the specified protocol, host, port (if given), and file. If the port is omitted, the port number used will be the default for the protocol. A MalformedURLException is thrown if an unknown protocol is passed as an argument.

URL (spec)—java.net.URL

```
public  URL({URL context, }String spec)
```

Constructs an URL from the unparsed URL. If context is omitted or is null, the absolute spec is used. Otherwise, the spec is used relative the the URL context. A MalformedURLException is thrown if the protocol is unknown.

URLConnection— java.net.URLConnection

```
protected  URLConnection(URL url)
```

Constructs an URL connection to a given URL.

URLStreamHandler— java.net.URLStreamHandler

```
public  URLStreamHandler()
```

Constructs an URLStreamHandler object.

UTC—java.util.Date

```
public static long UTC(int year, int month, int day,
        int hrs, int min, int sec)
```

Returns a UTC value from the passed arguments. Interpretes the parameters in UTC, not in the local time zone.

UTFDataFormatException— java.io.UTFDataFormatException

```
public   UTFDataFormatException({String detailMessage)
```

Constructs an exception indicating that a malformed UTF–8 string has been read in a input stream. You can specify a detail message to appear if you wish.

valid—java.io.FileDescriptor

```
public boolean valid()
```

Returns true if the FileDescriptor is valid. Otherwise, false is returned. See the getFD method for more information.

validate—java.awt.Component

```
public void validate()
```

Validates a Component. For related information, see the invalidate and layout methods or the LayoutManager class.

validate—java.awt.Container

```
public synchronized void validate()
```

Validates a Container and all the Container's components. The validate method in the Container class overrides the validate method in the Component class. Also, see the invalidate method.

valueOf—java.lang.Boolean

```
public static Boolean valueOf(String s)
```

Converts a string to a Boolean.

valueOf—java.lang.Double

```
public static double valueOf(String s)
```

Returns a double floating point number obtained by converting a String. A `NumberFormatException` exception is thrown if the String does not contain a valid number.

valueOf—java.lang.Float

```
public static Float valueOf(String s)
```

Returns a floating point number obtained by converting a String. A `NumberFormatException` exception is thrown if the String does not contain a valid number.

valueOf—java.lang.Integer

```
public static Integer valueOf(String s{, int radix})
```

Assuming the specified String represents an integer, returns a new Integer object initialized to that value. A radix is the base used, and defaults to 10 (for based–10 number systems). 16 (hexidecimal) and 8 (octal) may also prove useful. Throws an exception if the String cannot be parsed as an integer.

valueOf—java.lang.Long

```
public static Long valueOf(String s{, int radix})
```

Assuming the specified String represents an integer, returns a new Long object initialized to that value. A radix is the base used, and defaults to 10 (for based–10 number systems). 16 (hexidecimal) and 8 (octal) may also prove useful. Throws an exception if the String cannot be parsed as an int.

valueOf—java.lang.String

```
public static String valueOf(datatype argument)
```

Returns a string representation of an argument. The `datatype` of the argument can be Object, character array (`char data[]{,offset, count}`), boolean, character, integer, long, float, or double.

> **NOTE:**
> When using an Object for the argument in the `vauleOf`
> method in the String class, the Object's `toString` method
> can determine how the Object "wants" to be represented
> in a String.

Vector—java.util.Vector

```
public  Vector({int capacity{, int capacityIncrement})
```

Constructs a vector. If capacity is passed, then the Vector is initialized
to that size. Otherwise, a default capacity is used. The
`capacityIncrement` is passed to tell how much to grow when the current capacity is used up. If the `capacityIncrement` is omitted, the
Vector will double in size for each capacity increment.

VerifyError—java.lang.VerifyError

```
public VerifyError({String detailMessage})
```

A class has not passed the byte-code verification tests. If
`detailMessage` is specified, the `detailMessage` will be displayed
when this throwable is thrown.

VirtualMachineError— java.lang.VirtualMachineError

```
public VirtualMachineError({String detailMessage})
```

`VirtualMachineError` is the parent class to several serious environment errors. It indicates that some serious resource problem exists on
the host Java machine. If `detailMessage` is specified, the
`detailMessage` will be displayed when this throwable is thrown.

wait—java.lang.Object

```
public final void wait({long timeout{, int nanos}})
```

Causes a thread to wait until it is notified. If a `timeout` is given, the
thread only waits for a specified number of miliseconds. If the `nanos`
are specifed, the nanoseconds are added to the millisecond. The `wait`
method can only be called from within a `synchronized` method. See
the `notify` and `notifyAll` methods for related information. The

`wait` method throws the `InterruptedException` excpetion if another thread has interrupted this thread.

waitFor—java.lang.Process

```
public abstract int waitFor()
```

Waits for the Process to complete. If the Process has already terminated, the exit value is simply returned. If the Process has not yet terminated, the calling thread will be blocked until the Process is completed. An `InterruptedException` exception is thrown if another thread has interrupted this thread.

waitForAll—java.awt.MediaTracker

```
public synchronized boolean waitForAll({long timeout})
```

Starts loading any images that are not yet being loaded, and waits until all images are loaded or a timeout has elapsed. If an image load was aborted or encountered an error then that image is considered loaded. True is returned if all images are loaded. Otherwise, false is returned. The `InterruptedException` exception is thrown if another thread interrupted the load. See the `waitForID`, `isErrorAny`, and `isErrorID` methods for more information.

waitForID—java.awt.MediaTracker

```
public synchronized boolean waitForID(
    int identification {, long timeout})
```

Starts loading any images with a specified identificaiton that are not yet being loaded, and waits until all images with that identification are loaded or a timeout has elapsed (if a timeout was given). If an image load was aborted or encountered an error, then that image is considered loaded. True is returned if all images are loaded. Otherwise, false is returned. The `InterruptedException` exception is thrown if another thread interrupted the load. See the `waitForAll`, `isErrorAny`, and `isErrorID` methods for more information.

whitespaceChars— java.io.StreamTokenizer

```
public void whitespaceChars(int low, int high)
```

Specifies that characters between low and high are treated as whitespace characters.

Window—java.awt.Window

```
public  Window(Frame parent)
```

Constructs a new Window dialog box. The `parent` argument is the owner of the dialog box. Also see the `resize` and `show` methods.

> **NOTE:**
> All new Windows, like the Frame class they are inherited from, are initially invisible. Use the `show` method to show an invisible frame. Additionally, Window objects behave as dialog boxes and will block input to other windows when shown.

wordChars—java.io.StreamTokenizer

```
public void wordChars(int low, int high)
```

Specifies that characters between low and high are treated as word characters.

write (byte array)— java.io.BufferedOutputStream

```
public synchronized void write(
    byte buffer[], int offset, int len)
```

Writes bytes starting from an offset from a buffer into a stream. The `write` method blocks output until all bytes are wrtten. `IOException` is thrown if an I/O error has occured. The `write` method in the BufferedOutputStream overrides the `write` method in the FilterOutputStream class.

write (byte array)— java.io.ByteArrayOutputStream

```
public synchronized void write(
    byte buffer[], int offset, int length)
```

Writes bytes starting from an offset from a buffer into a stream. The `write` method blocks output until all bytes are wrtten. The `write` method in the ByteArrayOutputStream overrides the write method in the OutputStream class.

write (byte array)—java.io.DataOutput

```
public abstract void write(byte b[]{,int off, int len})
```

Writes an array, or subarray (if offset and length are specified), of bytes. This method throws IOException if an I/O error occurs during processing.

write (byte array)— java.io.DataOutputStream

```
public synchronized void write(byte b[]{,int off, int len})
```

Writes an array, or subarray (if offset and length are specified), of bytes. This method throws IOException if an I/O error occurs during processing. The write method in the DataOutputStream class overrides the write method in the FilterOutputStream class.

write (byte array)— java.io.FileOutputStream

```
public void write(byte b[]{,int off, int len})
```

Writes an array, or subarray (if offset and length are specified), of bytes. This method blocks all output until complete. This method throws IOException if an I/O error occurs during processing. The write method in the FileOutputStream class overrides the write method in the OutputStream class.

write (byte array)— java.io.FilterOutputStream

```
public void write(byte b[]{,int off, int len})
```

Writes an array, or subarray (if offset and length are specified), of bytes. This method throws IOException if an I/O error occurs during processing. The write method in the FilterOutputStream overrides the write method in the OutputStream class.

write (byte array)— java.io.OutputStream

```
public abstract void write(byte b[]{,int off, int len})
```

Writes an array, or subarray (if offset and length are specified), of bytes. This method throws IOException if an I/O error occurs during processing.

write (byte array)— java.io.PipedOutputStream

```
public void write(byte buffer[], int offset, int len)
```

Writes bytes starting from an offset from a buffer into a stream. The write method blocks output until all bytes are wrtten. IOException is thrown if an I/O error has occured. The write method in the PipedOutputStream overrides the write method in the OutputStream class.

write (byte array)—java.io.PrintStream

```
public void write(byte buffer[], int offset, int len)
```

Writes bytes to a PrintStream starting from an offset from a buffer into a stream. The write method blocks output until all bytes are wrtten. IOException is thrown if an I/O error has occured. The write method in the PrintStream overrides the write method in the FilterOutputStream class.

write (byte array)— java.io.RandomAccessFile

```
public void write(byte b[]{,int off, int len})
```

Writes an array, or subarray (if offset and length are specified), of bytes. This method throws IOException if an I/O error occurs during processing.

write (byte)— java.io.BufferedOutputStream

```
public synchronized void write(int b)
```

Writes a byte to a BufferedOutputStream. This method will block all other file I/O until the byte is actually written. The write method throws IOException if an I/O error occurs. The write method in the BufferedOutputStream class overrides the write method in the FilterOutputStream class.

write (byte)— java.io.ByteArrayOutputStream

```
public synchronized void write(int b)
```

Writes a byte to a buffer.

write (byte)—java.io.DataOutput

```
public abstract void write(int b)
```

Writes a byte. This method blocks all output until complete. This method throws IOException if an I/O error occurs during processing.

write (byte)—java.io.DataOutputStream

```
public synchronized void write(int b)
```

Writes a byte. This method blocks all output until complete. This method throws IOException if an I/O error occurs during processing. The write method in the DataOutputStream class overrides the write method in the FilterOutputStream class.

write (byte)—java.io.FileOutputStream

```
public void write(int b)
```

Writes a byte. This method blocks all output until complete. This method throws IOException if an I/O error occurs during processing. The write method in the FileOutputStream class overrides the write method in the OutputStream class.

write (byte)—java.io.FilterOutputStream

```
public void write(int b)
```

Writes a byte. This method blocks all output until complete. This method throws IOException if an I/O error occurs during processing. The write method in the FilterOutputStream overrides the write method in the OutputStream class.

write (byte)—java.io.OutputStream

```
public abstract void write(int b)
```

Writes a byte. This method blocks all output until complete. This method throws IOException if an I/O error occurs during processing.

write (byte)— java.io.PipedOutputStream

```
public void write(int b)
```

Writes a byte to a BufferedOutputStream. This method will block all other file I/O until the byte is actually written. The write method throws IOException if an I/O error occurs. The write method in the PipedOutputStream class overrides the write method in the OutputStream class.

write (byte)—java.io.PrintStream

```
public void write(int b)
```

Writes a byte to a PrintStream. This method will block all other file I/O until the byte is actually written. The write method throws IOException if an I/O error occurs. The write method in the PrintStream class overrides the write method in the FilterOutputStream class.

write (byte)—java.io.RandomAccessFile

```
public void write(int b)
```

Writes a byte. This method blocks all output until complete. This method throws IOException if an I/O error occurs during processing.

writeBoolean—java.io.DataOutput

```
public abstract void writeBoolean(boolean v)
```

Writes a boolean. This method throws IOException if an I/O error occurs during processing.

writeBoolean—java.io.DataOutputStream

```
public final void writeBoolean(boolean v)
```

Writes a boolean. This method throws IOException if an I/O error occurs during processing.

writeBoolean—java.io.RandomAccessFile

```
public final void writeBoolean(boolean v)
```

Writes a boolean.

writeByte—java.io.DataOutput

```
public abstract void writeByte(int v)
```

Writes an 8-bit byte. This method throws IOException if an I/O error occurs during processing.

writeByte—java.io.DataOutputStream

```
public final void writeByte(int v)
```

Writes an 8-bit byte. This method throws IOException if an I/O error occurs during processing.

writeByte—java.io.RandomAccessFile

```
public final void writeByte(int v)
```

Writes an 8-bit (ASCII) byte.

writeBytes—java.io.DataOutput

```
public abstract void writeBytes(String s)
```

Writes a String as a sequence of (ASCII) bytes. This method throws `IOException` if an I/O error occurs during processing.

writeBytes—java.io.DataOutputStream

```
public final void writeBytes(String s)
```

Writes a String as a sequence of (ASCII) bytes. This method throws `IOException` if an I/O error occurs during processing.

writeBytes—java.io.RandomAccessFile

```
public final void writeBytes(String s)
```

Writes a string of 8-bit (ASCII) bytes.

writeChar—java.io.DataOutput

```
public abstract void writeChar(int v)
```

Writes a 16-bit (Unicode) character. This method throws `IOException` if an I/O error occurs during processing.

writeChar—java.io.DataOutputStream

```
public final void writeChar(int v)
```

Writes a 16-bit (Unicode) character. This method throws `IOException` if an I/O error occurs during processing.

writeChar—java.io.RandomAccessFile

```
public final void writeChar(int v)
```

Writes a 16-bit (Unicode) character.

writeChars—java.io.DataOutput

```
public abstract void writeChars(String s)
```

Writes a String as a sequence of chars. This method throws `IOException` if an I/O error occurs during processing.

writeChars—java.io.DataOutputStream

```
public final void writeChars(String s)
```

Writes a String as a sequence of chars. This method throws `IOException` if an I/O error occurs during processing.

writeChars—java.io.RandomAccessFile

```
public final void writeChars(String s)
```

Writes a string of 16-bit (Unicode) bytes.

writeDouble—java.io.DataOutput

```
public abstract void writeDouble(double v)
```

Writes a 64-bit double precision floating point number. This method throws `IOException` if an I/O error occurs during processing.

writeDouble— java.io.DataOutputStream

```
public final void writeDouble(double v)
```

Writes a 64-bit double precision floating point number. This method throws `IOException` if an I/O error occurs during processing.

writeDouble— java.io.RandomAccessFile

```
public final void writeDouble(double v)
```

Writes a 64-bit double precision floating point number.

writeFloat—java.io.DataOutput

```
public abstract void writeFloat(float v)
```

Writes a 32-bit floating point number. This method throws `IOException` if an I/O error occurs during processing.

writeFloat—java.io.DataOutputStream

```
public final void writeFloat(float v)
```

Writes a 32-bit floating point number. This method throws `IOException` if an I/O error occurs during processing.

writeFloat—java.io.RandomAccessFile

```
public final void writeFloat(float v)
```

Writes a 32-bit floating point number.

writeInt—java.io.DataOutput

```
public abstract void writeInt(int v)
```

Writes a 32-bit integer. This method throws `IOException` if an I/O error occurs during processing.

writeInt—java.io.DataOutputStream

```
public final void writeInt(int v)
```

Writes a 32-bit integer. This method throws `IOException` if an I/O error occurs during processing.

writeInt—java.io.RandomAccessFile

```
public final void writeInt(int v)
```

Writes a 32-bit integer.

writeLong—java.io.DataOutput

```
public abstract void writeLong(long v)
```

Writes a 64-bit long integer. This method throws `IOException` if an I/O error occurs during processing.

writeLong—java.io.DataOutputStream

```
public final void writeLong(long v)
```

Writes a 64-bit long integer. This method throws `IOException` if an I/O error occurs during processing.

writeLong—java.io.RandomAccessFile

```
public final void writeLong(long v)
```

Writes a 64-bit long integer.

writeShort—java.io.DataOutput

```
public abstract void writeShort(int v)
```

Writes a 16-bit short integer. This method throws IOException if an I/O error occurs during processing.

writeShort—java.io.DataOutputStream

```
public final void writeShort(int v)
```

Writes a 16-bit short integer. This method throws IOException if an I/O error occurs during processing.

writeShort—java.io.RandomAccessFile

```
public final void writeShort(int v)
```

Writes a 16-bit short integer.

writeTo—java.io.ByteArrayOutputStream

```
public synchronized void writeTo(OutputStream out)
```

Writes the contents of the ByteArrayOutputStream to another stream. IOException is thrown if an I/O error occurs.

writeUTF—java.io.DataOutput

```
public abstract void writeUTF(String str)
```

Writes a String in UTF (ASCII) format. Also see the writeBytes method. This method throws IOException if an I/O error occurs during processing.

writeUTF—java.io.DataOutputStream

```
public final void writeUTF(String str)
```

Writes a String in UTF (ASCII) format. Also see the `writeBytes` method. This method throws `IOException` if an I/O error occurs during processing.

writeUTF—java.io.RandomAccessFile

```
public final void writeUTF(String str)
```

Writes a String in UTF (ASCII) format.

xor—java.util.BitSet

```
public void xor(BitSet set)
```

Logically XORs (exclusive ORs) the current BitSet object with another BitSet object.

yield—java.lang.Thread

```
public static void yield()
```

Causes the current Thread to yield control to any other Threads that may be running. If no other Threads are running, the `yield` method will have no effect.

Chapter 14

Java Class Hierarchy

Inheritance plays an important role in Java development. All classes included with Visual J++ are inherited from another class, or inherited from java.lang.Object if no parent class is specified.

Because classes are inherited, child classes have access to all protected and public attributes and methods contained in the parent classes. Therefore, you often have more functionality contained in a class than is listed by the class declaration.

Although it usually takes very little research to know the ancestor of a class, sometimes it's useful to know what classes have descendent classes, and what those descendants are. Knowing the descendents of a class will let you make decisions on which type of parent class is best suited for your development needs. Table 14.1 lists the descendents of all Java super classes.

Table 14.1
Java Superclasses and Subclasses

Superclass	Subclass
java.awt.image.ColorModel	java.awt.image.DirectColorModel
	java.awt.image.IndexColorModel
java.awt.peer.ComponentPeer	java.awt.peer.ButtonPeer
	java.awt.peer.CanvasPeer
	java.awt.peer.CheckboxPeer
	java.awt.peer.ChoicePeer
	java.awt.peer.ContainerPeer
	java.awt.peer.LabelPeer
	java.awt.peer.ListPeer
	java.awt.peer.ScrollbarPeer
	java.awt.peer.TextComponentPeer
java.awt.Container	java.awt.Panel
java.awt.Dialog	java.awt.FileDialog
java.util.Dictionary	java.util.Hashtable
java.lang.Error	java.awt.AWTError
	java.lang.LinkageError
	java.lang.ThreadDeath
	java.lang.VirtualMachineError
java.lang.Exception	java.awt.AWTException
	java.lang.classNotFoundException
	java.lang.CloneNotSupportedException
	java.lang.IllegalAccessException
	java.lang.InstantiationException
	java.lang.InterruptedException
	java.io.IOException
	java.lang.NoSuchMethodException
	java.lang.RuntimeException
java.io.FilterInputStream	java.io.BufferedInputStream
	java.io.DataInputStream
	java.io.LineNumberInputStream
	java.io.PushbackInputStream
java.io.FilterOutputStream	java.io.BufferedOutputStream

Superclass	Subclass
	java.io.DataOutputStream
	java.io.PrintStream
java.util.Hashtable	java.util.Properties
java.lang.IllegalArgumentException	java.lang.IllegalThreadStateException
	java.lang.NumberFormatException
java.lang.IncompatibleClassChangeError	java.lang.AbstractMethodError
	java.lang.IllegalAccessError
	java.lang.InstantiationError
	java.lang.NoSuchFieldError
	java.lang.NoSuchMethodError
java.lang.IndexOutOfBoundsException	java.lang.ArrayIndexOutOfBoundsException
	java.lang.StringIndexOutOfBoundsException
java.io.InputStream	java.io.ByteArrayInputStream
	java.io.FileInputStream
	java.io.FilterInputStream
	java.io.PipedInputStream
	java.io.SequenceInputStream
	java.io.StringBufferInputStream
java.io.IOException	java.io.EOFException
	java.io.FileNotFoundException
	java.io.InterruptedIOException
	java.net.MalformedURLException
	java.net.ProtocolException
	java.net.SocketException
	java.net.UnknownHostException
	java.net.UnknownServiceException
	java.io.UTFDataFormatException
java.lang.LinkageError	java.lang.classCircularityError
	java.lang.classFormatError
	java.lang.IncompatibleClassChangeError
	java.lang.NoClassDefFoundError
	java.lang.UnsatisfiedLinkError

Table 14.1
Continued

Superclass	Subclass
	java.lang.VerifyError
java.awt.MenuComponent	java.awt.MenuBar
	java.awt.MenuItem
java.awt.peer.MenuComponentPeer	java.awt.peer.MenuBarPeer
	java.awt.peer.MenuItemPeer
java.awt.MenuItem	java.awt.CheckboxMenuItem
	java.awt.Menu
java.lang.Number	java.lang.Double
	java.lang.Float
	java.lang.Integer
	java.lang.Long
java.lang.Object	java.util.BitSet
	java.lang.Boolean
	java.awt.BorderLayout
	java.awt.CardLayout
	java.lang.Character
	java.awt.CheckboxGroup
	java.lang.class
	java.lang.classLoader
	java.awt.Color
	java.awt.image.ColorModel
	java.lang.Compiler
	java.awt.Component
	java.net.ContentHandler
	java.net.DatagramPacket
	java.net.DatagramSocket
	java.util.Date
	java.util.Dictionary
	java.awt.Dimension
	java.awt.Event
	java.io.File
	java.io.FileDescriptor

Superclass	Subclass
	java.awt.image.FilteredImageSource
	java.awt.FlowLayout
	java.awt.Font
	java.awt.FontMetrics
	java.awt.Graphics
	java.awt.GridBagConstraints
	java.awt.GridBagLayout
	java.awt.GridLayout
	java.awt.Image
	java.awt.image.ImageFilter
	java.net.InetAddress
	java.io.InputStream
	java.awt.Insets
	java.lang.Math
	java.awt.MediaTracker
	java.awt.image.MemoryImageSource
	java.awt.MenuComponent
	java.lang.Number
	java.util.Observable
	java.io.OutputStream
	java.awt.image.PixelGrabber
	java.awt.Point
	java.awt.Polygon
	java.lang.Process
	java.util.Random
	java.io.RandomAccessFile
	java.awt.Rectangle
	java.lang.Runtime
	java.lang.SecurityManager
	java.net.ServerSocket
	java.net.Socket
	java.net.SocketImpl

Table 14.1
Continued

Superclass	Subclass
	java.io.StreamTokenizer
	java.lang.String
	java.lang.StringBuffer
	java.util.StringTokenizer
	java.lang.System
	java.lang.Thread
	java.lang.ThreadGroup
	java.lang.Throwable
	java.awt.Toolkit
	java.net.URL
	java.net.URLConnection
	java.net.URLEncoder
	java.net.URLStreamHandler
	java.util.Vector
java.io.OutputStream	java.io.ByteArrayOutputStream
	java.io.FileOutputStream
	java.io.FilterOutputStream
	java.io.PipedOutputStream
java.awt.Panel	java.applet.Applet
java.lang.RuntimeException	java.lang.ArithmeticException
	java.lang.ArrayStoreException
	java.lang.classCastException
	java.util.EmptyStackException
	java.lang.IllegalArgumentException
	java.lang.IllegalMonitorStateException
	java.lang.IndexOutOfBoundsException
	java.lang.NegativeArraySizeException
	java.util.NoSuchElementException
	java.lang.NullPointerException
	java.lang.SecurityException
java.awt.TextComponent	java.awt.TextArea
	java.awt.TextField

Superclass	Subclass
java.lang.Throwable	java.lang.Error
	java.lang.Exception
java.lang.VirtualMachineError	java.lang.InternalError
	java.lang.OutOfMemoryError
	java.lang.StackOverflowError
	java.lang.UnknownError
java.awt.Window	java.awt.Dialog
	java.awt.Frame

Appendix A

Reserved Words

Visual J++ has many reserved words that you are not allowed to use in your programs except to perform the function that Java and Visual J++ have intended. Table A.1 lists these reserved words.

Reserved Word	Description
abstract	The *abstract* keyword declares that a class cannot be instantiated; only its descendants can be. This keyword also is used to declare virtual methods in an ancestor class.
boolean	*boolean* is used to declare a boolean data type inside a class or method. A boolean data type has two values: *true* and *false*.
break	The break keyword is used to break out of a loop or switch block. When breaking out of a loop, it is usually contained within an *if* statement. It is usually the last line of each *case* in a *switch* block.
byte	*byte* is used to declare an 8-bit single character data type inside a class or method. A byte variable can be used to store ASCII characters
case	The *case* keyword is a keyword that is used in a *switch* statement. A *switch* statement is used to execute one of several sections of code depending on the value of a variable.
catch	The *catch* keyword is used to trap errors within a *try* block.
char	*char* is used to declare a 16-bit single character data type inside a class or method. A char variable can be used to store Unicode characters
class	The *class* keyword is used to declare a class inside a Visual J++ module.
const	The *const* keyword is not currently used in Visual J++, but may be implemented by Java and Visual J++ in future releases.
continue	The *continue* keyword is used to skip all following statements in a loop and continue with the next iteration of the loop. *continue* is usually embedded within an *if* or *switch* block.
default	The *default* keyword is used to execute statements in a *switch* block if all cases within the *switch* block are false. It is the functional equivalent to an *else* statement in an *if...else if...else if...else* block.
do	The *do* keyword (in conjunction with the *while* keyword) is used to form a post-test loop.
double	*double* is used to declare a double-precision floating point number inside a class or method.
else	The *else* keyword is used within an *if* statement structure to execute a block of statements if the condition tested in the *if* statement fails.

Reserved Word	Description
extends	The *extends* keyword is used for inheritance. When one class (Class1) *extends* another class (Class2), then Class1 is inherited from Class2.
false	The *false* keyword is a constant used to test for a false condition or to assign a false value to a boolean variable.
final	The *final* keyword is a modifier. When a class is declared *final*, then that class is not allowed to be inherited. When a method is declared *final*, then that method is never allowed to be overridden by subclasses. When an attribute or variable is declared *final*, then that variable is to be initialized immediately, used as a constant, and never modified.
finally	The *finally* keyword is used to catch all errors not previously caught in a *try...catch* block.
float	*float* is used to declare a single-precision floating point number inside a class or method.
for	The *for* keyword is used to set up a loop with initialization, condition testing, and a statement to be run during each iteration of the loop. It is very similar to the C/C++ *for* statement.
goto	The *goto* keyword is not currently used in Visual J++, but may be implemented by Java and Visual J++ in future releases.
if	The *if* statement is used to test a condition and then execute a set of code if that condition is true.
implements	The *implements* keyword is used to implement an interface inside a class.
import	The *import* keyword is used to automatically reference a package or class outside the current module.
instanceof	The *instanceof* operator tests whether a variable is an instance of a particular class. This is useful when you have a class array of inherited classes. *instanceof* can be used to test each class instance to see what subclass it belongs to.
int	*int* is used to declare an integer number inside a class or method.
interface	The *interface* keyword is used to set up Java interfaces. Interfaces are not classes, but contain methods that are grouped together. Interfaces are the key to OLE and COM support inside Java.

continues

Table A.1
Continued

Reserved Word	Description
long	*long* is used to declare a long integer number inside a class or method.
native	The *native* keyword is used to declare a function as external to Visual J++. This is often used with external C++ functions that a Visual J++ program can execute.
new	The *new* keyword is used to instantiate a class. *new* will set up memory, run any constructors, and return a pointer to the new class.
null	*null* is a constant. All instances of classes are initialized to null until set up with a *new* command or until assigned to an existing class.
package	The *package* keyword is used to group classes together. Although Visual J++ projects have made packages somewhat obsolete, packages are still used in older Java modules ported to Visual J++, and the Java class structure uses packages. Packages can also be used to share scope among different classes, but this violates encapsulation and is usually indicative of bad program design.
private	*private* is a scope modifier for attributes and methods. A private attribute or method is accessible (visible) only within the same class as the private attribute or method is declared.
private protected	*private protected* is a scope modifier for attributes and methods. Although actually two keywords, they keyword functionality changes when *private* and *protected* are combined. A private protected attribute or method is accessible (visible) only within the same class as the private attribute or method is declared descendants (subclasses) of the class. Unlike protected classes, private protected classes are not accessible to other classes in the same package.
protected	*protected* is a scope modifier for attributes and methods. A protected attribute or method is accessible (visible) only within the same class as the private attribute or method is declared, descendants (subclasses) of the class, and other classes in the same package, if applicable.
public	*public* is a scope modifier for classes, attributes and methods. A public class, attribute or method is accessible (visible) to any other method, even those methods in other classes.

Reserved Word	Description
return	The *return* keyword is used to send control back from a called method to the calling method or function. If there was no calling method, control is passed back to the operating system. The *return* keyword is also used to pass variables back from the called method to the calling method or function.
short	*short* is used to declare a small integer number inside a class or method.
static	*static* is a modifier for methods and attributes. When an attribute is declared static, memory is immediately set up for that attribute, and only one attribute exists for every instance of that attribute. A static attribute can also be accessed from any class that has access to the class, even without instantiating the class. Static methods can be called without instantiating a class.
super	The *super* keyword is used to call the ancestor constructor as the first line of your descendent constructor. It's also used to access ancestor attributes that have been overridden by descendent attributes.
switch	A *switch* statement is used to execute one of several sections of code depending on the value of a variable.
synchronized	The *synchronized* keyword is used as a method modifier and a statement. A synchronized static method modifier locks the class to make sure no other threads can modify the class concurrently. A synchronized non-static modifier locks the instance of the class to make sure that no other threads can modify the class instance concurrently. As a statement, *synchronized* is used to lock an object or array before executing a block of code.
this	The *this* keyword refers to the current instance of a class. *this* is often used for a class to pass itself to an outside method or to call a constructor from another constructor.
throw	The *throw* keyword is used to force an error signal to occur.
throws	The *throws* keyword is used when a method is declared to indicate that this method can cause the thrown exception or error.

continues

Reserved Word	Description
transient	The *transient* keyword is an attribute modifier that indicates a variable is used for a class "scratch" variable, and therefore does not need to be saved to disk when the class is saved or cloned to other instances of a class.
true	The *true* keyword is a constant used to test for a true condition or to assign a true value to a boolean variable.
try	*try* is used to set up an error catching block. Any errors caught are processed by *catch* and *finally* blocks.
void	The *void* keyword is used in method declarations. A *void* method indicates that the method does not return any value to the calling method.
volatile	The *volatile* keyword is used in attribute declarations. Specifying that an attribute is *volatile* indicates that the attribute may be changed asynchronously. This usually means that the variable is part of the hardware configuration and the value may change from time to time *without any action of any class method.* Therefore, no optimizations should be performed on a *volatile* attribute.
while	The *while* keyword is used to form a pre-test loop. *while* can also be used in conjunction with the *do* statement to form a post-test loop.

Appendix B

The HTML Language

Web pages are written in a language called *Hypertext Markup Language*, or *HTML*. HTML is a language that was developed for publishing documents on the Internet's World Wide Web. Java and Visual J++ classes can be embedded with HTML commands.

HTML is not exactly a programming language; rather, it's formatting codes and links similar to those found in old Word and WordPerfect documents or in old RunOff editors. As programming tools go, HTML is a really nice tool for quick development.

> **TIP:**
> Before you burden yourself with programming in a language like Visual J++, you should ask yourself whether the same task could be accomplished using HTML. You'll find that your programs are shorter and easier to maintain, and your development time will decrease.
>
> Remember, HTML and Visual J++ often work in conjunction with each other. It would be a mistake to avoid the ease of use in HTML simply because you have a powerful programming language like Visual J++.

HTML Structure

Take your typical Web page, like Prima's home page (www.primapublishing.com). Figure B.1 shows a scaled down version of the Prima home page.

Figure B.1
Prima's home page can be found at www.prima-publishing.com.

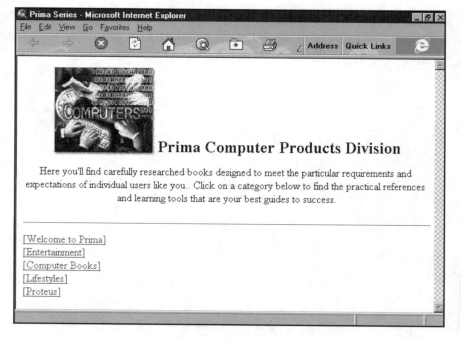

In traditional programming languages, the home page in figure B.1 would take a long time to program. If you use HTML, however, the process is quite simple. This is event by looking at the following HTML script (an explanation of the script follows this listing).

```
<html>
<head>
<title>
Prima Series
</title>
</head>

<body>
<h2>
<img src="../Drawings/prima.jpg" align=middle width=150
➥height=133>
<EM>
Prima
</EM>
<STRONG>
Computer Products Division
</STRONG>
</h2>

<p><CENTER>
Here you'll find carefully researched books designed to meet the
➥particular requirements and
expectations of individual users like you.. Click on a category
➥below to find the practical references
and learning tools that are your best guides to success.
</p>

<hr>

<a href="../info/info.html">[Welcome to Prima]</a><br>
<a href="../enter/enter.html">[Entertainment]</a><br>
<a href="../series/series.html">[Computer Books]</a><br>
<a href="../life/life.html">[Lifestyles]</a><br>
```

```
<a href="../proteus/proteus.html">[Proteus]</a>

</body>
</html>
```

As you can see, an HTML document is simply a text file containing text and codes. The preceding script uses the following codes:

- All HTML code is placed between <html> and </html> symbols at the top and the bottom of the HTML script.

- All beginning information (such as titles) is placed between <head> and </head> symbols.

- The title, enclosed by <title> and </title>, is used to display the title of the HTML document in the toolbar (refer to Figure B.1). The title must be placed in the <head> section.

- <body> and </body> are used to define the body of the HTML.

- <H1>, <H2>, and so on (up to <H6>) are used to emphasize text to a lesser and lesser degree for each heading level. Similarly, <EM> and <STRONG> are used for emphasis by usually italics and bold, respectively. <CENTER>, <LEFT>, and <RIGHT> can be used to position text on the window.

- <img... is used to define an image on your web page. The picture file (SRC), the alignment (top, middle, or bottom), and the width and height must all be defined.

- <p> and </p> are used to signify the start and end of a paragraph. There's usually a double space between paragraphs.
 is used for a line break to return to the next line.

- <hr> is used to draw a horizontal line across the Web page.

- <a> and </a> are used to establish links to other addresses.

There are other HTML commands, but as you can see, you can do most of what you want using the preceding commands.

NOTE:
You are not allowed to include a <, >, &, or " as text in your document because HTML looks at these as commands. To display a character, you must use *escape sequences*. Valid escape sequences are as follows:

&lt	Less than sign
&gt	Greater than sign
&amp	Ampersand
&quot	Quote
	En space
	Em space
	No break space
&endash	En Dash
&emdash	Em Dash
&reg	Register mark
&copy	Copyright mark

<Applet> and *<Param>*

When coding Visual J++, you need to use the <Applet> HTML tag to embed your Visual J++ class into your HTML document. Consider the following HTML script:

```
<html>
<head>
<title>Hello World</title>
</head>
<body>
```

```
<applet CODE="HelloWorldApplet.class" WIDTH=150
➥HEIGHT=25></applet>
</body>
</html>
```

This simple HTML code embeds the HelloWorldApplet class inside an HTML document. Now, browsers that are Java and Visual J++ aware will run the HelloWorldApplet class whenever the HTML is loaded.

In the following example:

```
<applet code=Sounds.class width=200 height=200>
<param name=sounds value="sounds.au">
```

the <applet> key is immediately followed by the <param> key. This allows your HTML to pass parameters to your applet. In this case, the Sounds class will run, and the SOUNDS.AU file name will be passed as a parameter.

> **WARNING:**
> There are a lot of alpha and beta versions of Java. This Java may not be supported with newer browsers. To run an older Java class on your Web page, you must use the <app> HTML tag instead of the <applet> HTML tag.

HTML Reference

Table B.1 shows a list of most available HTML tags usable in the HTML language.

> **TIP:**
> HTML documentation is available on the Internet. To find detailed lists of up-to-date HTML tags, search for "HTML and tags" using your Internet World Wide Web browser.

NOTE:
The HTML syntax supported by Microsoft Internet Explorer is marked with the Internet Explorer icon.

WARNING:
Because Internet Explorer and Netscape are constantly adding new tags to their products, some tags only work with one of the two browsers. Also, new tags are being added and/or replaced all the time. (For example, there's talk of an `<embed>` tag replacing or supplementing the `<applet>` tag and allowing multiple language support rather than just Java and Visual J++ support.)

Table B.1

HTML Tag	Tag Name	Description
`<!- >`	Comment	This tag is used to comment your code.
`<A>`	Anchor	This tag is used to anchor or link your site to another Web site in the `<BODY>` section of your HTML document.
`<ABBREV>`	Abbreviation	This displays normal text, but allows Web browsers to index your Web site.
`<ACRONYM>`	Acronym	This displays normal text, but allows Web browsers to index your Web site.
`<ADDRESS>`	Address	The address tag is used to display address or contact information, slightly indented and usually in italics.
`<APP>`	Applet (Java alpha)	This key allows you to embed Java `alpha` classes. Since Java 1.0 went into production, this tag is pretty much obsolete.
`<APPLET>`	Applet	This key allows you to embed Java and Visual J++ classes.
`<AREA>`	Area	Allows you to define hot spots within an image.

continues

Table B.1
Continued

HTML Tag	Tag Name	Description
`<AU>`	Author	Same as `<AUTHOR>`.
`<AUTHOR>`	Author	Displays the author of the text or Web page. This is picked up by browser indexers.
`<B>`	Bold	Defines text that should be displayed in a boldface font.
`<BANNER>`	Banner	Defines text that does not scroll with the rest of the document.
`<BASE>`	Base	Defines the URL address of the current Web site. This is typically used to allow you to change the location of the Web site without changing the links to figures, Visual J++ classes, and so on.
`<BASEFONT>`	BaseFont	Defines the font that relative font changes are based on.
`<BGSOUND>`	Background Sound	Defines a WAV, AU, or MID resource that will be played when the page is opened.
`<BIG>`	Big Text	Displays text in a larger font than usual.
`<BLOCKQUOTE>`	Block Quote	The block quote tag defines text that is quoted from somewhere else.
`<BODY>`	Body	Defines the body of the document.
` `	LineBreak	Starts any additional text on the next line.
`<BQ>`	Block Quote	Same as `<BLOCKQUOTE>`.
`<CAPTION>`	Caption	Defines the caption of a figure or table and is used within `FIG` or `TABLE` tags.
`<CENTER>`	Center	Centers text until the current paragraph ends or the next paragraph begins. Note: The HTML 3.0 construct, `<P ALIGN= CENTER>`*text*`</P>`, should be used instead of the `<CENTER>` tag because the `<CENTER>` tag is not really part of the HTML standard—it's part of Netscape's and Internet Explorer's valid tags.
`<CITE>`	Citation	Defines text that cites a book or other work.

HTML Tag	Tag Name	Description
`<CODE>`	Code	Defines text that is displayed in a proportional (fixed width) font.
`<CREDIT>`	Credit	Defines text that credits a figure or quote. `<CREDIT>` is used in `FIG` or `BQ` tags.
`<DD>`	Definition (in a list) (in a list)	Defines a definition that's part of a definition list.
`<DEL>`	Deleted Text	Marks text that has been deleted. This is useful in a group environment where the rest of the team needs to be aware of what is deleted out of a document.
`<DFN>`	Definition	Defines text that may define a term.
`<DIR>`	Directory List	Lists items (see `<LI>`) that do not have a bullet or number in front of them.
`<DIV>`	Division	Divides a document into sections.
`<DL>`	Definition List	Begins a definition list.
`<DT>`	Definition Term	Defines terms inside a definition list.
`<EM>`	Emphasized	Emphasizes text—most browsers display this as italics.
`<FIG>`	Figure	Defines a figure to be displayed in your HTML document.
`<FN>`	Footnote	Defines footnote text, which is often displayed in a pop-up window.
`<FONT>`	Font	Defines a font that differs from the base font in size or color.
`<FORM>`	Form	Defines a form that is made up of input elements like check boxes, radio buttons, and data entry fields.
`<H1>`	Heading 1	The first level heading in a body.
`<H2>`	Heading 2	The second level heading in a body.
`<H3>`	Heading 3	The third level heading in a body.
`<H4>`	Heading 4	The fourth level heading in a body.

continues

HTML Tag	Tag Name	Description
`<H5>`	Heading 5	The fifth level heading in a body.
`<H6>`	Heading 6	The sixth level heading in a body.
`<HEAD>`	Head	Head defines the heading part of your HTML document.
`<HR>`	Horizontal Rule	Draws a horizontal line across your Web page. This is often used to separate sections of your web pages.
`<HTML>`	HTML	`<HTML>` and `</HTML>` are used to enclose all your HTML statements in a Web page.
`<I>`	Italic	Displays text as italic.
`<IMG>`	Inline Image	Displays an image (JPG or GIF picture) in your HTML document. (The `<FIG>` tag is an improvement over the **<IMG>** tag.)
`<INPUT>`	Form Input	Using `<INPUT>`, you can define check boxes, files, images, passwords, radio buttons, ranges, resets, scribbles, or text.
`<INS>`	Inserted Text	Marks text that has been inserted. This is useful in a group environment where the rest of the team needs to be aware of what is inserted into a document.
`<ISINDEX>`	Is Index	Declares that the current HTML document is a searchable index. This tag is only valid in the `<HEAD>` section.
`<KBD>`	Keyboard	Defines text that should be shown in a proportional (fixed width) font.
`<LANG>`	Language	Used to alter the language used for a block of text.
`<LH>`	List Heading	Used to define a heading for an ordered (`<OL>`), unordered (`<UL>`), or directory (`<DIR>`) list.
`<LI>`	List Item	Used to define an entry for an ordered (`<OL>`), unordered (`<UL>`), menu (`<MENU>`), or directory (`<DIR>`) list.

HTML Tag	Tag Name	Description
`<LINK>`	Link	Establishes a link to another URL in the `<HEAD>` section.
`<LISTING>`	Listing	Defines a program listing. `<LISTING>` is somewhat obsolete—use `<PRE>` instead.
`<MAP>`	Map	Defines `<AREA>` tags over an inline image.
`<MARQUEE>`	Marquee	Defines a moving piece of text, like a marquee.
`<MATH>`	Math	Defines a formula or equation.
`<MENU>`	Menu List	Allows you to define a list (`<LI>`) to act as a menu.
`<META>`	Meta	Declares that HTTP meta name/value pairs are used for this Web page.
`<NOBR>`	No Break	Indicates that no lines will implement line breaks except those explicitly coded with a ` ` tag.
`<NOTE>`	Note	Displays text in note format.
`<OPTION>`	Form Select Option	Allows you to specify options for your HTML document.
`<OL>`	Ordered List	Displays a list with numbered items.
`<OVERLAY>`	Overlay	Speeds up image rendering by drawing small changes over a base figure. However, `<OVERLAY>` can cause a maintenance headache with your Web pages.
`<P>`	Paragraph	Defines a block of text to be displayed in paragraph form. Also, allows you to specify formatting characteristics (like `<CENTER>`) to a block of text.
`<PERSON>`	Person	Defines a person in your document. `<PERSON>` displays like normal text, but is used by indexers to make persons on your Web page accessible by Web browsers.

continues

Table B.1
Continued

HTML Tag	Tag Name	Description
`<PRE>`	Preformatted	Defines text that should be shown in a proportional (fixed width) font with the line breaks and other white space specified. There is no need to use ` `, `<TAB>`, and so on with `<PRE>` because the formatting is defined by the source.
`<Q>`	Quote	Displays text with quotes around it. You can also use the `&quot` escape character to display a quote.
`<RANGE>`	Range	Defines a range within a document.
`<S>`	Strike through	Displays text with strike through font.
`<SAMP>`	Sample	Defines text that should be shown as literal characters in a proportional (fixed width) font.
`<SELECT>`	Form Select	Defines a form in your HTML document.
`<SMALL>`	Small Text	Displays text in a smaller font than usual.
`<SPOT>`	Spot	Used to specify a location in a document where there is no tag.
`<STRONG>`	Strong	Used to emphasize text, usually displayed as bold.
`<SUB>`	Subscript	Displays text as a subscript, which is a little smaller and below the line of normal text.
`<SUP>`	Superscript	Displays text as a superscript, which is a little smaller and above the line of normal text.
`<TAB>`	Horizontal Tab	Used to place a horizontal tab inside your HTML document.
`<TABLE>`	Table	Initiates a table in your HTML document.
`<TD>`	Table Data	Defines table data for a table row in a table in your HTML document. `<TD>` can only be used within a `<TR>` description.
`<TEXTAREA>`	Form Text Area	Defines a text area in your HTML form.

HTML Tag	Tag Name	Description
`<TH>`	Table Header	Defines a header for a table in your HTML document.
`<TITLE>`	Title	Defines a title for your HTML Web page. This is usually displayed in the title bar of your browser.
`<TR>`	Table Row	Defines a row in a table in your HTML document.
`<TT>`	Teletype	Defines text in proportional (fixed width) font.
`<U>`	Underlined	Defines text to be underlined.
`<UL>`	Unordered List	Displays a list with bulleted items.
`<VAR>`	Variable	Displays text as a variable. Most browsers display `<VAR>`-defined text in italics.
`<WBR>`	Word Break	Identifies a place where a word can be broken, or where a line can be broken inside a `<NOBR>` block.
`<XMP>`	Example	Defines example text. `<XMP>` is somewhat obsolete. See `<PRE>` and `<SAMP>` for other alternatives.

Appendix C

Unicode

The ASCII standard has long fallen short in several areas, including international language support, mathematical and technical writings, and symbols. The Unicode Worldwide Character Standard (or just *Unicode*) is Java's answer to this dilemma. Unicode is a character coding system designed to support multiple languages, both modern and ancient, as well as technical writings.

The secret to Unicode's versatility is simply that Unicode uses two bytes for storage rather than ASCII's one byte. ASCII only allows 256 unique characters whereas Unicode allows 65,534 unique characters.

> **NOTE:**
> The Unicode Standard is copyrighted by the Unicode Consortium, and Unicode is a trademark of the Unicode Consortium. Because of the huge size of Unicode, listing the entire Unicode is impractical for this appendix. There are two books on the entire Unicode standards:
>
> ❂ *The Unicode Standard, Worldwide Character Encoding, Version 1.0, Volume 1*, Addison-Wesley, 1990 (ISBN 0-201-56788-1).
>
> ❂ *The Unicode Standard, Worldwide Character Encoding, Version 1.0, Volume 2*, Addison-Wesley, 1992 (ISBN 0-201-60845-6).

You can specify a Unicode symbol in a string by the formatting command "\u*xxxx*" where *xxxx* is a number that corresponds to the proper Unicode number.

Unicode is broken into several categories, which are listed in Table C.1

Table C.1
Unicode Categories

Hexadecimal Range	Unicode Category
0000 - 1FFF	Alphabets
2000 - 2FFF	Symbols and Punctuation
3000 - 4DFF	Chinese, Japanese, and Korean Auxiliary and Unified Ideographs
A000 - DFFF	Reserved for Future Assignment
E000 - FFFD	Restricted Use
FFFE - FFFF	Excluded from the Unicode Standard

> **NOTE:**
> Note that FFFE and FFFF are two characters that are excluded from Unicode. This is *probably* by design so you can flag invalid strings in your Unicode-based languages. (In other words, high values are not valid for Unicode characters.)

Alphabets

The Unicode alphabets are derived from 24 supported scripts. These characters cover the major written languages of the world. Table C.2 describes alphabets that are supported in Unicode.

Table C.2
Alphabets Supported in Unicode

Hexadecimal Range	Alphabet Supported in Unicode
0020 - 007E	Basic Latin (The graphic part of US-ASCII)
00A0 - 00FF	Latin Supplement (Extended ASCII)
0100 - 017F	Latin Extended-A
0180 - 024F	Latin Extended-B
0250 - 02AF	IPA Extensions
02B0 - 02FF	Spacing Modifier Letters
0300 - 036F	Combining Diacritical Marks
0370 - 03CF	Basic Greek
03D0 - 03FF	Greek Symbols and Coptic
0400 - 04FF	Cyrillic
0500 - 052F	Unassigned
0530 - 058F	Armenian
0590 - 05CF	Hebrew Extended-A
05D0 - 05EA	Basic Hebrew
05EB - 05FF	Hebrew Extended-B
0600 - 0652	Basic Arabic
0653 - 06FF	Arabic Extended
0700 - 08FF	Ethiopic (still under construction)
0900 - 097F	Devanagari
0980 - 09FF	Bengali
0A00 - 0A7F	Gurmukhi
0A80 - 0AFF	Gujarati
0B00 - 0B7F	Oriya
0B80 - 0BFF	Tamil
0C00 - 0C7F	Telugu
0C80 - 0CFF	Kannada
0D00 - 0D7F	Malayalam
0D80 - 0DFF	Sinhalese (still under construction)

continues

Table C.2
Continued

Hexadecimal Range	Alphabet Supported in Unicode
0E00 - 0E7F	Thai
0E80 - 0EFF	Lao
0F00 - 0F7F	Burmese (still under construction)
0F80 - 0FDF	Khmer (still under construction)
1000 - 105F	Tibetan (still under construction)
1060 - 109F	Mongolian (still under construction)
10A0 - 10CF	Georgian Extended
10D0 - 10FF	Basic Georgian
1100 - 11FF	Hangul Jamo
1200 - 125F	Ethiopian (still under construction)
1E00 - 1EFF	Latin Extended Additional
1F00 - 1FFF	Greek Extended

Unsupported Languages

Some modern written languages are not yet supported or are only partially supported in Unicode 1.1 due to the need for further research into how to encode certain scripts. The following languages have not yet been finalized in the Unicode standard (and are listed as still under construction in Table C.2):

- Burmese

- Ethiopian

- Ethiopic (Amharic, Geez)

- Sinhalese (Sri Lankan)

- Khmer (Cambodian)

- Tibetan

- Mongolian

The following languages have filed a petition for Unicode support:

- Cherokee

- Cree

- Maldivian (Dihevi)

- Moso (Naxi)

- Pahawh Hmong

- Rong (Lepcha)

- Tai Lu

- Tai Mau

- Tifinagh

- Yi (Lolo)

> **NOTE:**
> **Of these languages that have applied for Unicode support, Cherokee seems to be the furthest along by having their own graphical character font defined in the computer. They may soon get Unicode support in the next version of Unicode.**

The ASCII Codes

Regular ASCII (0-127) and Extended ASCII (128-255) codes make up the first 1-256 characters of Unicode. They're also used in HTML to help format screens. Table C.3 lists the first 127 characters. This table can be used for String sort order in your English-based programs.

Table C.3
ASCII Chart
(Character Codes
0 - 127)

000 blank (Null)	032 space	064 @	096 `
001 happy face	033 !	065 A	097 a
002 inv. happy face	034 "	066 B	098 b
003 ♥	035 #	067 C	099 c
004 ♦	036 $	068 D	100 d
005 ♣	037 %	069 E	101 e
006 ♠	038 &	070 F	102 f
007 •	039 '	071 G	103 g
008 ∘	040 (	072 H	104 h
009 ●	041)	073 I	105 i
010 ○	042 *	074 J	106 j
011 ♂	043 +	075 K	107 k
012 ♀	044 ,	076 L	108 l
013 single note	045 –	077 M	109 m
014 double note	046 .	078 N	110 n
015 sun	047 /	079 O	111 o
016 ▶	048 0	080 P	112 p
017 ◀	049 1	081 Q	113 q
018 ↕	050 2	082 R	114 r happy face
019 ‼	051 3	083 S	115 s
020 ¶	052 4	084 T	116 t
021 §	053 5	085 U	117 u
022 rectangle	054 6	086 V	118 v
023 up/down to line	055 7	087 W	119 w
024 ↑	056 8	088 X	120 x
025 ↓	057 9	089 Y	121 y
026 →	058 :	090 Z	122 z
027 ←	059 ;	091 [	123 {
028 ∟	060 <	092 \	124	
029 ↔	061 =	093]	125 }
030 ▲	062 >	094 »	126 »
031 ▼	063 ?	095 _	127 house

Symbols and Punctuation

Symbols and punctuation are often similar in several languages. Unicode codes 2000 - 27BF are used to specify punctuation, as shown in Table C.4.

Hexadecimal Range	Symbol or Punctuation Supported in Unicode
2000 - 206F	General Punctuation
2070 - 209F	Superscripts and Subscripts
20A0 - 20CF	Currency Symbols
20D0 - 20FF	Combining Diacritical Marks for Symbols
2100 - 214F	Letter-like Symbols
2150 - 218F	Number Forms
2190 - 21FF	Arrows
2200 - 22FF	Mathematical Operators
2300 - 23FF	Miscellaneous Technical
2400 - 243F	Control Pictures
2440 - 245F	Optical Character Recognition
2460 - 24FF	Enclosed Alphanumerics
2500 - 257F	Box Drawings
2580 - 259F	Block Elements
25A0 - 25FF	Geometric Shapes
2600 - 26FF	Miscellaneous Symbols
2700 - 27BF	Dingbats

CJK Auxiliary and Unified Ideographs

Some languages don't use an alphabet paradigm in their written work. Languages such as Chinese, Japanese, and Korean (CJK) use word-based alphabets. As these countries represent a large portion of the world's population and the world's technical base, they cannot be ignored by any multi-lingual support. Consequently, these languages require special consideration from Unicode. Table C.5 shows how Unicode categorizes the CJK languages.

Table C.5
CJK Auxiliary and
Unified Ideographs
Supported in Unicode

Hexadecimal Range	Alphabet Supported in Unicode
3000 - 303F	CJK Symbols and Punctuation
3040 - 309F	Hiragana
30A0 - 30FF	Katakana
3100 - 312F	Bopomofo
3130 - 318F	Hangul Compatibility Jamo
3190 - 319F	CJK Miscellaneous (Kaeriten)
3200 - 32FF	Enclosed CJK Letters and Months
3300 - 33FF	CJK Compatibility
3400 - 3D2D	Hangul
3D2E - 44B7	Hangul Supplementary-A
44B8 - 4DFF	Hangul Supplementary-B
4E00 - 9FFF	CJK Unified Ideographs

Restricted Use

Restricted use codes are codes that are used for compatibility, combination characters, and form variants. Table C. 6 lists the Unicode restricted use codes.

Table C.6
Unicode Restricted
Use Codes

Hexadecimal Range	Restricted Use Breakdown in Unicode
E000 - F8FF	Private Use Area
F900 - FAFF	CJK Compatibility Ideographs
FB00 - FB4F	Alphabetic Presentation Forms
FB50 - FDFF	Arabic Presentation Forms-A
FE20 - FE2F	Combinint Half Marks
FE30 - FE4F	CJK Compatibility Forms (verticals and overlines)
FE50 - FE6F	Small Form Variants
FE70 - FEFE	Arabic Presentation Forms-B
FF00 - FFEF	Half-width and Full-width Forms
FFF0 - FFFD	Specials

Converting Between Unicode and ASCII Using UTF

Often, the data you'll be reading into your English-based programs is in ASCII format. ASCII characters take one byte instead of two, so some conversion is necessary. Java and Visual J++ provide a Universal Translation Format (UTF-8) with the `java.io.DataInputStream.readUTF( )` and `java.io.DataOutputStream.writeUTF( )` methods. These methods automatically convert Unicode into ASCII based on the following table:

Unicode Start	Unicode End	UTF-8 size
'\u0000' (0)	'\u007F' (255)	8 bits (ASCII 0 - 255)
'\u0080' (256)	'\u07FF' (2047)	11 bits
'\u0800' (2048)	'\uFFFF' (65535)	16 bits

As you can see, UTF-8 encoding can be used to convert Unicode to ASCII, because ASCII is all contained in the 8 bit (1 byte) size of the UTF-8 standard.

Index

A

Other books from Prima Publishing, Computer Products Division

ISBN	Title	Release Date
0-7615-0064-2	Build a Web Site	Available Now
1-55958-744-X	The Windows 95 Book	Available Now
0-7615-0383-8	Web Advertising and Marketing	Available Now
1-55958-747-4	Introduction to Internet Security	Available Now
0-7615-0063-4	Researching on the Internet	Available Now
0-7615-0693-4	Internet Information Server	Summer 1996
0-7615-0678-0	Java Applet Powerpack, Vol. 1	Summer 1996
0-7615-0685-3	JavaScript	Summer 1996
0-7615-0684-5	VBScript	Summer 1996
0-7615-0726-4	The Webmaster's Handbook	Summer 1996
0-7615-0691-8	Netscape Fast Track Server	Summer 1996
0-7615-0733-7	Essential Netscape Navigator Gold	Summer 1996
0-7615-0759-0	Web Page Design Guide	Summer 1996